LEVEL CROSSING

New Edition • Volume 2

Cornelsen

LEVEL CROSSING · New Edition · Volume 2

Verfasser

David Christie, Banbury *(Sequence 1, 3, 4, 5, 6)*
Ekkehard Sprenger, Preetz *(Sequence 2)*
Thomas Wöhlke, Weinheim *(Exam Practice)*

Beratende Mitwirkung

Dr. Hannspeter Bauer, Köln
Rolf Meiseberg, Bottrop
Dr. Rupert Paetz, Dinslaken
Anette Schmücker, Dinslaken
Birgit Schreier, Wiesbaden

Redaktion

Dr. Marion Kiffe *sowie* Doreen Arnold, Dr. Ilka Soennecken, Ralph Williams,
Hannah Joy Winters (Assistenz)

Layoutkonzept

WERNERWERKE, Cordes + Werner GbR, Berlin

Design und technische Umsetzung

Yvonne Thron, Berlin

Umschlaggestaltung

Ulrike Kuhr

Weitere Bestandteile des Lehrwerkes

- Audio-CD (978-3-06-032491-0)
- Video-DVD (978-3-06-032490-3)
- Teacher's Manual (978-3-06-032488-0)

www.cornelsen.de

1. Auflage, 2. Druck 2013

Alle Drucke dieser Auflage sind inhaltlich unverändert und können im Unterricht nebeneinander verwendet werden.

Druck: Stürtz GmbH, Würzburg

ISBN 978-3-06-032318-0

Inhalt gedruckt auf säurefreiem Papier aus nachhaltiger Forstwirtschaft.

CONTENTS

SEQUENCE 01: BRITAIN: PAST, PRESENT AND FUTURE 10

In this sequence you will read about various factors that have shaped Britain: its ***Empire****, its* ***society*** *today and how individuals view and inhabit it. You will learn about* ***immigrants****,* ***new English literature****, and the role Britain plays in today's world and especially in* ***Europe****.*

TOPIC	TEXT TYPES	SKILLS	
Lead-in	Pictures	Describing pictures / Developing a mindmap	10
01 The days of Empire			**12**
1 Images of Empire	Pictures	Describing and analysing pictures	12
KEY FACTS: Building the British Empire			14
2 The British in India	A first hand account and an extract from a non-fiction book	Listening / Reading / Analysing a writer's aims / Writing a letter to the editor	16
3 The white man's burden	A poem	Describing pictures / Analysing a poem / Writing a speech	19
4 A disappearing world	Extracts from a novel	Reading / Comparing characters / Analysing point of view	21
SPOTLIGHT ON: Point of view			26
IMPROVE YOUR WRITING: Using the simple present for writing about texts			26
5 The British Empire: good or bad?	–	Writing / Comparing advantages and disadvantages	27
IMPROVE YOUR WRITING: Comparing advantages and disadvantages			27
02 British life and politics			**28**
1 How the United Kingdom is governed	An information booklet	Visualising information / Making a quiz	29
KEY FACTS: Britain's political parties			31
2 The Queen at work	Videos	Viewing / Analysing video	32
KEY FACTS: The constitutional monarchy of the UK			32
3 Who wants a monarchy?	Statistics	Interpreting statistics	33
SPOTLIGHT ON: Interpreting statistics			34
4 Britain's social classes	A video and an extract from a novel	Viewing / Writing a diary entry / Writing a review / Reading / Analysing a novel extract / Mediating	35
03 New voices			**39**
KEY FACTS: Immigration into Britain since World War II			40
1 In-a Brixtan Markit	A poem	Listening / Analysing a poem / Writing a report or dialogue	42
2 BBC Video Nation	Videos	Viewing / Analysing videos	44
3 Dancing to their tune?	Extracts from a novel	Reading / Analysing a narrative perspective / Characterising people / Writing a dialogue	45
IMPROVE YOUR WRITING: Expressing an opinion			50

04 Finding a role in today's world			**51**
1 The Commonwealth	Videos	Viewing / Analysing videos	**52**
KEY FACTS: The Commonwealth of Nations			**52**
2 London: a world city	A newspaper article	Reading / Analysing an argumentative text / Writing an argumentative text / Role play	**53**
SPOTLIGHT ON: Argumentative texts			**55**
3 Britain and Europe	An extract from an essay	Reading / Making a bar chart / True/false / Analysing the writer's intention /	**56**
KEY FACTS: Britain and Europe			**56**
IMPROVE YOUR WRITING: Using varied adjectives			**59**
4 Britain's future role in the world	A web article	Reading / Analysing text type / Writing and presenting an interview	**60**

SEQUENCE 02: NORTH AMERICAN DREAMS 62

This sequence explores the concept of a great dream often connected to the USA and Canada. You will learn about the ***ideals*** *of the USA's founders, their revolutionary* ***values*** *and their* ***belief*** *in a better world. You will see how many people have tried to realise their personal dreams in North America: from early settlers to former slaves, immigrants and Native Americans. You will learn how this American Dream is part of an American* ***national identity****. But you will also see that the* ***reality*** *for many people can be harsh. The final topic deals specifically with* ***Canada*** *as a* ***promised land*** *for immigrants. Here you will learn why more and more of them tend to prefer the* ***suburbs*** *to the* ***city****.*

TOPIC	TEXT TYPES	SKILLS	
Lead-in	Pictures	Describing pictures / Collecting ideas	**62**
01 The USA: The making of a nation			**64**
1 Free and independent states	An extract from a historical document	Explaining a timeline / Reconstructing a summary / Analysing a line of argumentation / Describing a painting	**64**
KEY FACTS: The Bill of Rights			**66**
2 Europeans and Americans	A public letter	Summarising / Analysing the intention of a text	**67**
3 Moving west	A first-hand account	Analysing point of view and tone / Comparing expectations / Designing a poster	**69**
KEY FACTS: Moving west			**69**
02 Creating dreams in the US			**73**
1 My dream realised	An autobiography	Analysing the structure of a plot / Writing a literary analysis / Doing research	**74**
KEY FACTS: Immigration to the USA			**77**
2 Zeitoun's story	An extract from a biography	Characterising a person / Writing an interior monologue	**78**
3 The new immigrants	A book extract	Structuring a text / Analysing purpose and style / Rewriting a text in another tone	**82**
SPOTLIGHT ON: Style			**85**

03 Dreams and doubts			**86**
1 Frederick Douglass	A poem	Reading / Analysing a poem / Analysing imagery	87
KEY FACTS: The fight against discrimination of African Americans			88
2 Hunger in New York City	A poem	Writing an acrostic / Analysing a poem's perspective / Writing a poem / Conducting an interview	89
KEY FACTS: Native Americans			90
SPOTLIGHT ON: Elements of poetry			91
3 More than a storm	An extract from a non-fiction book	Reading / Analysing a text / Analysing a cartoon / Writing a letter	92
4 America and the world	A radio interview	Listening	95
04 The Canadian mosaic			**96**
1 A promised land?	An extract from a novel	Reading / Characterising the narrator / Analysing the tone / Acting out a conversation	97
KEY FACTS: Black Loyalists			97
SPOTLIGHT ON: Analysing narrative texts			102
IMPROVE YOUR WRITING: Formulating a text analysis			102
2 A dream of multiculturalism	A book extract and a newspaper article	Reading / Structuring information / Summarising	104
KEY FACTS: Canada as a multicultural society			104
3 A better life in the suburbs	A newspaper article	Reading / Analysing a writer's intentions / Designing a poster	109
4 Volunteering in Canada	A newspaper article	Mediating	111

SEQUENCE 03: GOING GLOBAL 112

*This sequence focuses on the global world of today. You will concentrate on the global **world of work** and **business**, on English as a **global language** and on challenges for political organisations working globally, such as the United Nations Organisation and its **peacekeeping** missions.*

TOPIC	TEXT TYPES	SKILLS	
Lead-in	Pictures	Describing pictures / Collecting ideas	112
01 Living in a globalised world			**114**
1 Multinational companies	An extract from a careers website	Reading / Analysing the writer's intentions / Holding a silent discussion / Writing a letter of application	114
IMPROVE YOUR WRITING: 'by doing sth.' / '(in order) to do sth.'			115
2 Sharing knowledge	Listening text	Listening / Summarising	116
3 The changing world map	An online article	True/false / Examining the author's attitude / Writing a newspaper article	117
4 Globish around the world	A video	Viewing / Making a timeline / Analysing a video / Writing an email	119
KEY FACTS: The development of the English language			119

5 A globalised world	Key facts box	Collecting material / Completing a key facts box	121
KEY FACTS: Aspects of globalisation			121
02 Challenges of globalisation			122
1 Rich and poor	Maps and a video	Analysing and comparing maps / Viewing / Analysing a video / Rewriting the video voiceover	123
SPOTLIGHT ON: Irony			124
2 Rich multinationals, poor people	A video	Viewing / Doing research / Doing a presentation / Making a documentary radio programme	125
3 The economics of global warming	A newspaper article	Reading / Analysing the tone of a text / Writing a speech	126
4 Global culture	Two online articles	Reading / Examining the writer's attitudes / Holding a panel discussion	128
03 Keeping the world's peace			130
KEY FACTS: Conflicts around the world			131
1 The experience of war	An extract from a short story	Summarising / Characterising a person / Writing an email	133
SPOTLIGHT ON: Creative writing			134
2 The victims of war	A report and statistics	Summarising / Visualising statistics / Discussing issues to do with refugees	135
3 What is peacekeeping?	Extracts from a speech	Reading / Analysing a speaker's aims in a speech	138
KEY FACTS: The United Nations Organisation			138
4 Singing for peace	A rap song	Listening / Analysing a song / Writing a post	142
04 Into a global future			143
SPOTLIGHT ON: Cartoons			144
1 Globalisation: for or against?	Articles from newspapers, online magazines and brochures	Sharing information in 'Expert groups' / Mediation	145
2 This House believes ...	–	Preparing and carrying out a debate / Keeping minutes / Writing an article for an e-zine	151
SPOTLIGHT ON: A formal debate			151

SEQUENCE 04: INDIA RISING 152

*India's **post-colonial experience** is examined in this sequence. After a short historical overview you will look at India, both as a country full of **tradition** and one that is undergoing **change**. You will see how **society's** norms, e.g. castes, shape the lives of **individuals** and how society is arranged according to the concept of **'them and us'**. And you're going to have a look at the changing **norms** and **values** in the lives of **men and women**.*

TOPIC	TEXT TYPES	SKILLS	
Lead-in	Pictures	Describing pictures / Collecting ideas	152
01 Birth of a nation			154
1 Modern India's many roots	Informative texts from various sources	Reading / Writing a quiz	154

2 Partition	An online article	Reading / Making a timeline / Summarising / Creative writing	157
3 The birth of a nation	A speech	Reading / Analysing a speech	160
SPOTLIGHT ON: Speeches			161
02 The new India			**162**
1 A visit to Infosys	A video	Viewing / Analysing a video / Doing a role-play	163
2 India's new middle class	A newspaper feature article	Reading / Summarising / Analysing the writer's intention / Mediating	164
3 Poverty in India	An article and statistics	Reading / Understanding and explaining statistics	166
KEY FACTS: India's caste system			166
IMPROVE YOUR WRITING: Connecting sentences			168
4 Untouchable	Listening	Listening / Designing a poster	169
KEY FACTS: Dalits			169
5 A British Indian's view of the new India	A newspaper article	Reading / Answering true/false questions / Analysing a writer's intention / Mediating	170
03 Women and men in India today			**172**
1 Marriage in India	Marriage ads	Reading / Organising a talk show	173
2 Changing roles	A blog	Reading / Analysing a blog / Doing a role-play	175
3 The dark sides of being a woman in India	A documentary video	Viewing / Analysing a video / Writing a review	177
4 Good advice is rarer than rubies	A short story	Reading / Analysing a short story / Creative writing	178
04 India on screen			**183**
1 The boy from the slums who wins a quiz show	Extracts from a novel, a radio play and a film script	Reading / Listening / Comparing literary genres	184
SPOTLIGHT ON: Fictional genres			184
KEY FACTS: Vikas Swarup *Q&A* (2005)			185
2 Welcome to Bollywood	An informative text	Doing research / Giving a presentation	192

SEQUENCE 05: SHAKESPEARE AND HIS WORLD 194

*In this sequence you will get an overview of Shakespeare, his life, his times and his work. You will read **sonnets** as well as extracts from his famous plays **Macbeth**, **Hamlet** and **Romeo and Juliet** and study characters in **extreme situations**.*

TOPIC	TEXT TYPES	SKILLS	
Lead-in	Pictures	Describing pictures / Collecting ideas	194
01 Shakespeare and his times			**196**
1 Shakespeare's life	Text from a website	Collecting, structuring and presenting information in a suitable form / Doing further research	196
2 England's golden age	An informative text		197
3 Performing plays in Shakespeare's times	An extract from a non-fiction book		199

02 Speaking in verse			**201**
1 A sonnet	Sonnets 18 and 73	Listening / Reading / Analysing a sonnet / Analysing imagery	202
2 Thee's and thou's	An extract from *Hamlet*	Reading / Acting out a scene / Summarising / Analysing a scene	204
KEY FACTS: Shakespeare's English			206
3 Shakespeare's verse	–	Analysing Shakespeare's verse	207
03 Looking at a play			**208**
1 The prologue	The prologue of *Romeo and Juliet*	Reading / Analysing structure and rhyme scheme / Analysing the function of a prologue	209
2 Juliet's balcony	Extracts from Act II, Scene II	Reading / Acting out a scene / Analysing the scene / Writing a diary entryy	210
3 Friar Laurence's plan	Extracts from Act IV, Scene I	Reading / Rewriting a scene / Analysing the function of this scene / Writing a diary entry	213
4 No happy ending	Extracts from Act V, Scene III	Reading / Presenting freeze-frame tableaux / Analysing the structure of a drama / Defining tragedy	215
SPOTLIGHT ON: Rhetorical devices			217
04 Shakespeare today			**218**
1 Why bother with Shakespeare?	A web article	Mediating / Doing presentations	219
2 Problems with Shakespeare	A newspaper feature article	True/false / Analysing text type and the writer's intentions / Commenting	221
3 Helping to understand?	A modern translation and a comic book *(Macbeth)*	Completing sentences / Analysing the scenes / Comparing the versions / Analysing a comic strip / Writing an email	223

SEQUENCE 06: FUTURE WORLDS 228

The last sequence deals with aspects of future worlds and ***utopias****: you will experience how* ***ideals*** *can (or can't) become* ***reality****, and how* ***visions*** *may lead to* ***change****. You will read excerpts from a* ***Science Fiction*** *novel. And you will examine what influence the digital age has had on* ***media*** *use. You will then discuss the pros and cons of cloning, one example of the achievements of* ***science*** *and* ***technology****.*

TOPIC	TEXT TYPES	SKILLS	
Lead-in	Pictures	Describing pictures / Collecting ideas	228
01 Imagining a different world			**230**
1 100 years from now	An old magazine article	Reading / Analysing the writer's intention / Writing predictions	230
2 Life in *1984*	Extracts from *1984*	Reading / Describing a dystopian world / Analysing an exposition / Conducting an interview / Analysing points of view / Writing a review	233
3 Paradise on Earth?	A text from a website	Reading / Writing an email	238
4 Utopia	–	Imagining a utopian world	240
KEY FACTS: Utopias and dystopias			240

02 Living in the digital society			**241**
1 Living without your iPod …	Extracts from a book	Reading / Summarising / Analysing writing style and language / Performing a role-play	242
IMPROVE YOUR WRITING: Including examples and referencing			244
2 Virtual environments	Videos	Viewing	247
3 Is Big Brother here already?	A newspaper article	Completing sentences / Presenting arguments	248
03 New sciences, better world?			**250**
1 In the future there will be dinosaurs	Extracts from a novel	Reading / Analysing point of view / Rewriting text / Characterising / Analysing plot structure / Writing an article	251
SPOTLIGHT ON: 'Showing' and 'telling' as narrative techniques			252
KEY FACTS: The real Jurassic Park: cloning animals			258
2 Feeding the world	An article from an online encyclopaedia	Reading / Conducting a role-play / Mediating	260
KEY FACTS: Genetic modification			260
04 Sci-fi!			**265**
1 Choosing a memory keeper	Extracts from a short story	Reading / Defining Science Fiction	266

REFERENCE SECTION	**272**
Activity chest	272
Glossary	276
Skills	286
Exam Practice	311
Business English	324
Everyday English	328
Wordfields	334
Acknowledgements	340
Words for tasks	344

Abbreviations and symbols

adj.	adjective
adv.	adverb
n.	noun
v.	verb
AE	American English
BE	British English
fml.	formal
infml.	informal
sb.	somebody
sth.	something

🔊	CD 2	sound file on CD
👁	DVD 1	film or video on DVD
✕ Extra		additional tasks (optional)
For possible solutions: Webcode: LC323180-332-1		is a code that can be entered at www.cornelsen.de/webcode. This connects you directly to a specific website related to a section of the textbook.

SEQUENCE

01

BRITAIN: PAST, PRESENT AND FUTURE

Britain once ruled over the largest empire the world has ever seen and was victorious in World War II. However, much has changed since then. What is British society like today, and what is the nation's role in the modern world? In this sequence, we look at Britain – past, present and future.

At the London Stock Exchange

British soldiers on patrol

Collect ideas

1. Describe the pictures and point out what aspects of Britain they highlight.
2. Make notes about each picture, saying what you see in them, and adding as much information as you can about their theme. Then use 'Double circles' to compare ideas with other students.

▶ Activity chest 5

3. Develop a mindmap about Britain, using the words and ideas you have collected.

London street scene

Queen Elisabeth II visits Ottawa, Canada

Nelson's column in Trafalgar Square

Ascot Racecourse

Demonstration in central London

TOPIC

01 The days of Empire

The Royal Coat of Arms of the UK

1 Images of Empire (Pictures)

empire: Kaiserreich

In roughly a century between 1815 and 1921, Britain built up and ruled over the largest empire the world has ever seen. In 1921, it covered a quarter of the globe and contained a quarter of the world's population. First, you are going to look at some images from the 'days of Empire'.

A Before you begin

Note down what you already know about the British Empire – countries that belonged to it, for example, or how it has affected the modern world. Consider what you have learned in other subjects. Structure your ideas in a mindmap. State in 2–3 sentences which concepts you think are central to the British Empire.

B Describing and analysing the pictures

1. First, look at all the pictures in class. What are your first impressions? What themes or ideas etc. do they deal with? What historical period of time do they show?

▶ Skills 2.1

2. Work in small groups to look at one of the pictures in detail, then describe and explain it to the class.
   a Describe what the picture shows, where it is set, what is happening, etc.
   b Examine
      - who the artist made the picture for at the time;
      - what idea or impression the artist wants to express;
      - what techniques or devices are used in the picture.

The picture / It	shows / depicts / portrays …	
In the foreground / on the right	a man / some soldiers / is (are) …	
We can imagine that	X has just happened / Y is going to / is about to happen	
In order to understand the context, it is necessary to know that …		
In this picture	the artist	intends to / sets out to / attempts to …
The artist	wishes to convey the idea	that …
The message of the picture is …		
The artist	uses a number of techniques	to achieve his/her goal. For example, …
The overall mood	of the picture is … (dramatic / dreamlike / …)	
This	is achieved by	… showing / creating the impression that …
The picture	is full of / contains a number of important details such as …	
The artist includes these in order to ...		
To sum up: …		

C Reacting to the pictures

1. Choose one person from the pictures and imagine what he or she would tell you about the British Empire. Write 5–8 sentences.
2. Describe your reaction to these images.
3. List aspects of the British Empire that you would like to know more about.

Illustration from a magazine, 1881. The soldiers are British.

Cartoon from a magazine, 1892. The man is holding a telegraph cable in his hands – a new piece of technology at the time.

Poster produced by the Empire Marketing Board, 1927. This was the official organisation which arranged for the sale of products from around the Empire in Britain.

KEY FACTS Building the British Empire

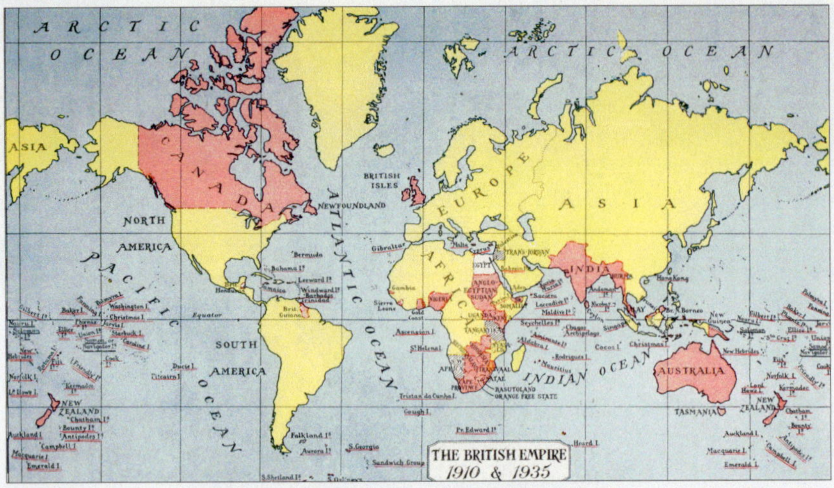

Principal countries of the British Empire

The Age of European Discovery and Britain's First Empire

From around 1400, European explorers began sailing around the world and mapping new countries in what is known as the Age of European Discovery. For example, Christopher Columbus, an explorer for the Spanish crown, landed in America in 1492. Britain's first successful overseas colony Virginia (on the east coast of America) was not founded until 1607. However, it was soon followed by what was to become known as the First British Empire. This began when the Pilgrim Fathers landed on the north-east coast of America in 1620 and led to the founding of the 13 colonies which form the basis of modern day USA. Virginia provided Britain with raw materials – the most important was tobacco. The Pilgrim Fathers, however, had come to escape religious persecution in Britain (they were Puritans, a religious sect that was illegal after the Protestant Reformation in England). But Britain's First Empire did not last very long. In 1775, the 13 colonies rebelled over the taxes they had to pay to Britain and in 1783, the Americans defeated the British in the American War of Independence. Apart from some colonies in the Caribbean and parts of Canada, Britain was without an empire.

Britain as the dominant world power

After the loss of its American colonies, Britain focused its attention on other parts of the world. Two developments made it possible for Britain not only to build a second empire but to make it the biggest ever in world history. The first of these was that by 1815, following the defeat of Napoleon, Britain had become the dominant power in the world. At that time, Britain also 'ruled the waves' – its ships could sail safely anywhere in the world without interference from other European navies. The second factor was that between around 1770 and 1840, Britain became the world's richest and most technologically advanced nation due to the Industrial Revolution, which had started there. British factories produced almost half the world's manufactured goods and its guns and ships were better than those of its rivals, mainly France and the Netherlands.

The Second British Empire

1 India and other countries in Asia

The country that became the heart of Britain's Second Empire lay not in the west but in the east. India, together with Burma, Hong Kong, Singapore, modern day Malaysia and a

1 *discovery:* act of finding sth. that was not known before
2 *explorer:* person who discovers new land
map sth.: make a map of sth.
3 *age:* Ära
9 *raw material:* Rohstoff
provide sb. with sth.: give sth. to sb.
10 *escape sth./sb.:* get away from sth./sb.
persecution: Verfolgung
12 *tax:* money that you pay to the government
14 *Caribbean* [ˌkærɪˈbiːən]: Karibik
22 *interference* [ˌ--ˈ--]: act of stopping sb./sth.
navy: Marine

number of islands in the Pacific, all offered a vast wealth of resources – cotton, tea, rice, wood, rubber and, above all, spices, which were a great luxury in Europe. Britain's first contact with Asia had, in fact, been made by a trading company, the British East India Company, in the early 1600s. By 1750, however, the company had become so large and powerful – it had its own army made up of Indian soldiers – that it basically ruled over India and its Indian Princes as if it were a small nation. Many Indians were unhappy with this situation and in 1857, the Indian soldiers rebelled (the Indian Mutiny). Britain sent its own army to end the rebellion, and in 1858, the British government dissolved the East India Company and took direct control of India.

In India, the period of rule from 1858 until India became independent in 1947 is known as the 'British Raj' [rɑːdʒ] (Hindi for *reign, kingdom*). India continued to provide Britain with its raw materials (and to be a market for the goods it produced) and thousands of British people went there as soldiers or administrators to rule over the country.

2 Australia and New Zealand

Broadly speaking, there were two different kinds of colonies in the British Empire: those where the British ruled over a native population (as in India) and those where British people went to live – for example, to farm. Australia and New Zealand fall into this second category. Both had been claimed for the British by the explorer Captain Cook in 1769–70. Since they were a long way from Britain, interest in them was at first small but then a reason suddenly emerged to make Australia useful. Until the 13 American colonies became independent, Britain had sent convicts there from its prisons. Starting in 1878, Australia became the new penal colony for around the next 50 years. Later, 'ordinary' British people moved there (and to New Zealand) to start new lives. One other fact must not be forgotten. The native inhabitants of Australia (the Aborigines) and of New Zealand (the Maoris), suffered badly from the arrival of Europeans. They were killed and their land was taken. In Australia, the Aborigine population fell by 90% and the Maori population in New Zealand by 40% between 1620 and 1920.

3 Africa

The British colonisation of Africa can be divided into two periods. The first was in South Africa. Britain needed a colony here so that its ships sailing to India could stop and take on food and water (it had 'strategic' importance). However, the Dutch already had a colony here and when Britain invaded in 1795 there were two bitter wars between the original Dutch settlers (the 'Boers') and the British. A treaty was eventually signed with the Dutch in 1910. From then on white British and white Dutch settlers shared the country but under British rule. The second period was marked by the colonisation of countries throughout the rest of Africa. Many of these parts of Africa were largely unkown to Europeans until the middle of the 19th century (they called it the 'Dark Continent') and when missionaries and explorers from various European countries (chiefly Britain, France, Germany and Belgium) began to open up this unknown land, everyone wanted to claim the new territory. It was simply a matter of imperialism – the wish to have a bigger empire than any other nation. This 'Scramble for Africa' as it was called led to the Berlin Conference in 1884 to divide up the continent. Britain got the largest share (around 40%) and – after World War I (1914–18) – also took Germany's colonies.

31 *vast wealth:* enormer Wohlstand
32 *rubber:* Gummi
spice: Gewürz
33 *trading company:* Handelsgesellschaft
37 *mutiny:* Aufstand
38 *dissolve sth.:* officially end sth.
43 *administrator:* person who manages a company or institution
48 *claim sth./sb.:* say that sth. belongs to you
50 *emerge:* start to exist
51 *convict* ['--]: prisoner
52 *penal colony* ['piːnl]: colony where prisoners are sent
54 *native inhabitant:* person who lived in a place before others came there
55 *suffer from sth.:* unter etwas leiden
61 *Dutch:* holländisch
71 *scramble for sth.:* fight with sb. in order to get sth.

Activities

▶ Skills 7.4, 8

1. Work in small groups. Each group studies one section of the text and makes a presentation to the class.
2. Develop a mindmap of the British Empire. Consider the following aspects: the different reasons for colonisation, different types of colonies, key dates, countries.

2 The British in India (A first hand account and an extract from a book)

CD 1

first hand account: Zeitzeugenbericht
judge: Richter

You are going to listen to an account of the lives of British people in India during the Empire. Then you are going to read a text about the effects of the British Empire on the lives of Indian people.

A Before you begin

British people who came to live in India during the Empire were usually soldiers in the British Army or they worked for British companies. The most important group, however, was made up of the 'officials' – judges, army officers, administrators – and their wives. These people came exclusively from the British upper class.

Imagine in what way life was different for British people from life at home. Think about the climate, contact with Indians, customs, food, etc. Make notes.

B Listen to the account

Nancy Vernede, a young woman who came to India in 1931 to join her parents, talks about a dinner party. She wrote the text, but here it has been read by an actor.
The words on the left may help you to understand the text.

khitmagar: servant who brings food and drink
ICS / Senior Service: Indian Civil Service
bride: woman who is about to marry
host/ hostess: man/woman who has invited guests
course (of a meal): part (of a meal)
pass sb. the hint: give sb. a sign

▶ Skills 6

1. Listen to the recording. Collect information under the following headings:
   - the situation described by the speaker;
   - the speaker's ideas and feelings;
   - the speaker's contact with Indian people.
2. Get together with a partner and compare notes, then present them to the class.
3. Look again at your notes about the speaker's situation and say which elements probably come from British culture and which from Indian. Fill in the table.

PROBABLY BRITISH CULTURE	PROBABLY INDIAN CULTURE	UNSURE

4. What does this tell you about colonial culture in India?

▶ Glossary 1.2

Extra Your teacher will give you a transcript of Nancy Vernede's account. Work together with a partner and compare how the account differs from a text in a history book. Think of its language, its mode of presentation, its intention, its general validity.

C Reading: India during the British Empire, 1902

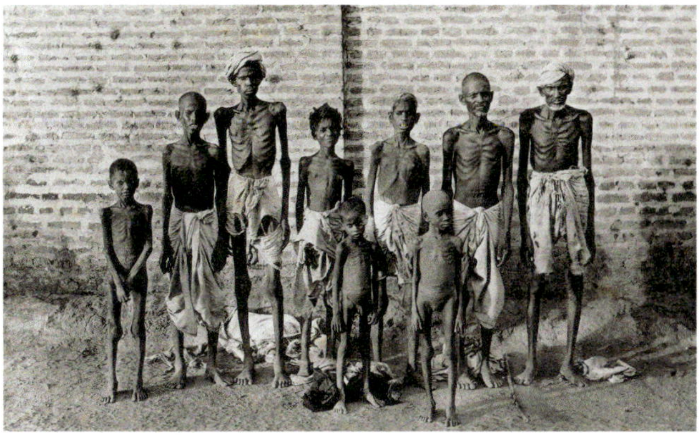

Famine victims in India, 1903

Romesh Dutt (1848–1909)

In 1902, Romesh Dutt published *The Economic History of India*, a book about the economic situation of India under the British Raj. Dutt was Indian and worked for the British in India as a senior civil servant, one of the few Indians who had top positions in the Empire. You are going to read an extract from his book.

1 *unalloyed satisfaction:* uneingeschränkte Zufriedenheit
2 *legitimate pride:* berechtigter Stolz
confer sth. on sb.: give sth. to sb.
3 *blessing:* sth. that is good and helpful
6 *require sth.:* need sth.
7 *efficacious* [ˌefɪ'keɪʃəs] (fml): having the intended effect
frame a law: write up a law
8 *purity:* excellent quality
10 *admiration:* feeling of respect for sth./sb.
11 *contemplate sth.* ['---]: think about sth.
14 *famine:* Hungersnot
desolate sb./sth.: leave sb./sth. without hope
15 *extent* [-'-]: Ausmaß
18 *faired-sized:* quite big
23 *narrow sth.:* make sth. smaller
24 *manufacturing:* producing goods in large quantities
agricultural: landwirtschaftlich
25 *loom:* Webstuhl
supply sb./sth.: (here) jdn./etwas beliefern

Englishmen can look back on their work in India, if not with unalloyed satisfaction, at least with some legitimate pride. They have conferred on the people of India what is the greatest human blessing – Peace. They have introduced Western Education, bringing an ancient and civilised nation in touch with modern thought, modern sciences, modern institutions and life. They have built up an administration which, though it requires reform with the progress of the times, is yet strong and efficacious. They have framed wise laws, and have established Courts of Justice, the purity of which is as absolute as in any country on the face of the earth. These are results which no honest critic of British work in India regards without high admiration.

On the other hand, no open-minded Englishman contemplates the material condition of the people of India under British rule with equal satisfaction. The poverty of the Indian population at the present day is unparalleled in any civilised country; the famines which have desolated India within the last quarter of the nineteenth century are unexampled in their extent and intensity in the history of ancient or modern times. By a moderate calculation, the famines of 1877 and 1878, of 1889 and 1892, of 1897 and 1900, have carried off fifteen millions of people. The population of a faired-sized European country has been swept away from India within twenty-five years. [...]

What are the causes of this intense poverty and these repeated famines in India? [...] It is, unfortunately, a fact which no well-informed Indian official will ignore, that, in many ways, the sources of national wealth in India have been narrowed under British rule. India in the eighteenth century was a great manufacturing as well as a great agricultural country, and the products of the Indian loom supplied the markets of Asia and of Europe. It is, unfortunately, true that the East Indian Company and the British Parliament, following the selfish commercial policy of a hundred years ago, discouraged Indian manufacturers in the early years of British rule in order to encourage the rising manufacturers of England. Their fixed policy, pursued during the last decades of the eighteenth century and the first decades of the nineteenth, was to make India subservient to the industries of Great Britain, and to make the Indian people grow raw produce only, in order to supply material for the looms and manufactories of Great Britain. [...]

Agriculture is now virtually the only remaining source of national wealth in India, and four-fifths of the Indian people depend on agriculture. But the Land Tax levied by the British Government is not only excessive, but, what is worse, it is fluctuating and uncertain in many provinces. In England, the Land Tax was between one shilling and four shillings in the pound, i.e., between 5 and 20 per cent of the rental, during a hundred years before 1798. [...] In Bengal the Land Tax was fixed at over 90 per cent of the rental, and in Northern India at over 80 per cent of the rental, between 1793 and 1822. It is true that the British Government only followed the precedent of the previous Mahomedan rulers, who also claimed an enormous Land Tax. But the difference was this, that what the Mahomedan rulers claimed they never fully realised; what the British rulers claimed they realised with rigour. The last Mahomedan ruler of Bengal, in the last year of his administration (1764), realised a land revenue of £817,553; within thirty years the British rulers realised a land revenue of £2,680,000 in the same Province. [...] 'No Native Prince demands the rent which we do,' wrote Bishop Heber in 1826, after travelling all through India, and visiting British and Native States. 'A Land Tax like that which now exists in India,' wrote Colonel Briggs in 1830, 'was never known under any Government in Europe or Asia.'

29 *pursue sth.:* follow sth., stick to sth.
30 *subservient:* less important
31 *raw produce:* Roherzeugnis
34 *wealth* [welθ]: Wohlstand
35 *levy a tax:* eine Steuer erheben
37 *fluctuate:* change in size
39 *rental:* Pacht
42 *precedent* ['---]: *(here)* Beispiel
Mahomedan: Muslim
44 *realise sth.: (here)* etwas tatsächlich fordern
45 *rigour:* strictness
49 *native state:* von Einheimischen regierter Staat

[From: *The Economic History of India under Early British Rule* by Romesh Dutt, 1902]

D Understanding the text

▶ Activity chest 12

Outline the situation of India and its people as described in this extract. Use a 'Placemat' to collect and compare ideas, then present your results to the class.

E Analysing the text

▶ Glossary 1.1

▶ Glossary 3.1

1. Analyse the intention of the text.
   a Who was the text written for and what was the writer's intention? Explain why you think so.
   b What type of text is this (informative, argumentative, ...)? Say why.
2. With a partner, look at how the writer tries to achieve the goals you identified above. Think about the structure of the text, the rhetorical devices he uses, the use of statistics and quotations, and the general tone of his writing. Report to the class.

F Reacting to the text

When Dutt's book appeared, many letters were written to the *Times* newspaper about it. Imagine that you are either (a) an educated Indian living in India or (b) someone living in Britain. Write a letter to the *Times*.

3 'The White Man's burden' (A poem)

Rudyard Kipling was one the most popular writers in Britain during the Empire. Born in India, he travelled widely around the empire and was a prolific writer of novels, poems and short stories. You are going to read two verses from a poem written by Kipling in 1899 called 'The white man's burden'.

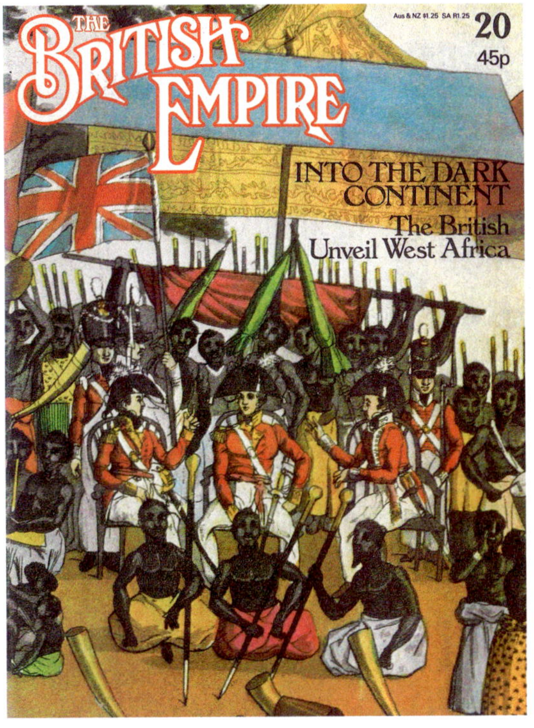

Rudyard Kipling: born in India 1865, died in England 1936

A Before you begin

1. The picture above is the front cover of a popular British magazine. It is from roughly the same time as Kipling's poem.
   a Describe the picture.
   b Examine the relationship between Blacks and Whites in the picture. Also consider the choice of vocabulary in the picture.
2. Now speculate what the poem 'The white man's burden' might be about.

B Understanding the verses

▶ Glossary 2.4.1, Skills 1.2.4

There are two verses from Kipling's poem on the next page. On the right there is a prose version of each verse. Work in groups.

1. Find in the text the missing words from each verse to complete the text.
2. Say in your own words:
   a What is the white man's task after he has colonised a country?
   b What are the people like who already live there?

burden: heavy weight
2 *ye (archaic):* you
breed sb.: give birth to sb.
4 *serve sb's need:* give sb. the things they need
captive: prisoner
5 *wait on sb.:* be a servant to sb.
harness: (Pferde)Geschirr
6 *fluttered:* blown around like a flag in the wind
7 *sullen:* angry and unfriendly
10 *tawdry:* looking beautiful, but worthless
11 *toil:* hard work

The White Man's burden

Take up the White Man's burden –
Send forth the best ye breed –
Go bind your sons to exile
To serve your captives' need;
To wait in heavy harness,
On fluttered folk and wild –
Your new-caught, sullen peoples,
Half-devil and half-child. […]

Take up the White Man's burden –
No tawdry rule of kings,
But toil of serf and sweeper –
The tale of common things.
The ports ye shall not enter,
The roads ye shall not tread,
Go mark them with your living,
And mark them with your dead.

Do the duty that every white person has to do. Send abroad your very best young people. Make them live far away from their homeland – in … (1). In these foreign countries, they must … (2) the people they have captured. Like horses, they must wear a heavy … (3) and serve strange and wild people. These moody people that you have caught recently, they are half … (4) and half child. […]

Do the duty that every white person has to do. Do not rule like other … (5) whose rule looked good but was worthless, like cheap jewellery. You must work hard like a servant or a sweep; live a life of … (6) things. Go to … (7) that you must not enter and walk along … (8) that you must not step on. Change these countries by living and dying in them.

[From: *McClure's Magazine*, 1899]

C Analysing the verses

▶ Glossary 3.1

Work together with a partner. Collect ideas about the questions below, then discuss in class.

1. Kipling uses a number of images, e.g. 'harness' (l. 5), 'serf', 'sweeper' (l. 11). Explain their meaning. How do these images characterise the relationship between colonisers and the native population?

The image of a … makes me think of / belongs to / comes from …
A … is a person who / thing used for …
… implies …
Contrary to … / Surprisingly …
… is / are characterised as …
superior/inferior/dominant / give sb. orders

▶ Glossary 2.4.1

2. In this poem the speaker directly addresses a listener. Describe the effect this has.

D Reacting to the verses

1. Talk in class. Give your personal reactions to this poem as someone living in today's world. Remember: it was a common idea in Kipling's time that white races were superior to other races – indeed, many believed this was a scientific fact.
2. Write a speech defending or criticising the attitude expressed in the poem.

4 A disappearing world (Extracts from a novel)

Achebe [ə'tʃeɪbi]

Written in 1958, *Things Fall Apart* has been described as the first African novel. Its author is the Nigerian writer Chinua Achebe (born 1930). You are going to read three extracts from the novel, which is set in Nigeria at the end of the 19th century.

Chinua Achebe in 1958 showing his newly published novel

A Before you read

Speculate on possible themes that Achebe deals with in his book. Consider what you have learned about the colonisation of Africa and take into account the title of the novel.

Extract 1

warrior: fighter
seed: small part of a plant from which another plant will grow
crop: plants that you grow for food

The protagonist (central character) in the novel is Okonkwo, a young man who is a respected warrior in battles with neighbouring clans. However, his parents are poor and so Okonkwo begins his manhood with little money: he needs help to begin a farm. In his society, a poor man must get seeds from a wealthier man and use them to grow plants. Until the young farmer becomes richer and has his own seeds, he gives back part of the crop to the wealthier man. The following extract is from near the beginning of the novel, when no English people have arrived in the area yet.

1 *barn:* building on a farm for keeping animals and food
3 *the highest but one title:* der zweithöchste Titel / das zweithöchste Amt
4 *yam:* type of vegetable
5 *cock:* male chicken
9 *harvest:* Ernte
15 *pave the way:* den Weg ebnen
18 *goatskin:* leather made from a goat *(= Ziege)*
19 *fasten sth.* ['fɑːsn]: fix sth. to sth. else
rafter: part of the roof of a house

There was a wealthy man in Okonkwo's village who had three huge barns, nine wives and thirty children. His name was Nwakibie and he had taken the highest but one title which a man could take in the clan. It was for this man that Okonkwo worked to earn his first seed yams.

He took a pot of palm-wine and a cock for Nwakibie. Two elderly neighbours were sent for, and Nwakibie's two grown-up sons were also present in his *obi*. He presented a kola nut and an alligator pepper, which was passed round for all to see and then returned to him. He broke it, saying: 'We shall all live. We pray for life, children, a good harvest and happiness. You will have what is good for you and I will have what is good for me.' […]

After the kola nut had been eaten Okonkwo brought his palm-wine from the corner of the hut where it had been placed and stood it in the centre of the group. He addressed Nwakibie, calling him 'Our father'.

'Nna ayi', he said. 'I have brought you this little kola. As our people say, a man who pays respect to the great paves the way for his own greatness. I have come to pay you my respects and also to ask a favour. But let us drink the wine first.'

Everybody thanked Okonkwo and the neighbours brought out their drinking horns from the goatskin bags they carried. Nwakibie brought down his own horn, which was fastened to the rafters. The younger of his sons, who was also the youngest man in the group, moved to the centre, raised the pot on his left knee and began to pour out the wine. The first cup went to Okonkwo, who must taste his wine before anyone else. Then the group drank, beginning with the eldest man.

[...] After the wine had been drunk Okonkwo laid his difficulties before Nwakibie.

'I have come to you for help,' he said. 'Perhaps you can already guess what it is. I have cleared a farm but have no yams to sow. I know what it is to ask a man to trust another with his yams, especially these days when young men are afraid of hard work. I am not afraid of work. The lizard that jumped from the high iroko tree to the ground said he would praise himself if no one else did. I began to fend for myself at an age when most people still suck at their mothers' breasts. If you give me some yam seeds I shall not fail you.'

A Nigerian village: photo taken in 1930

Nwakibie cleared his throat. 'It pleases me to see a young man like you these days when our youth have gone so soft. Many young men have come to me to ask for yams but I have refused because I knew they would just dump them in the earth and leave them to be choked by weeds. When I say no to them they think I am hard-hearted. But it is not so. Eneke the bird says that since men have learnt to shoot without missing, he has learnt to fly without perching. I have learnt to be stingy with my yams. But I can trust you. I know it as I look at you. As our fathers said, you can tell a ripe corn by its look. I shall give you twice four hundred yams. Go ahead and prepare your farm.'

29 *lizard:* Eidechse
31 *praise yourself:* say good things about yourself
32 *fend for yourself:* look after yourself, take care of yourself
35 *fail sb.:* disappoint sb.
41 *dump sth.:* put sth. down carelessly
42 *choke sb.:* kill sb. by stopping their breathing
weed: worthless plant
44 *perch:* land and stay in a place
stingy ['stɪndʒi]: geizig

B Understanding the text

1. When Okonkwo asks Nwakibie for yams, his actions and his statements seem to follow an order. List the different steps he has to take to convince Nwakibie. Compare your ideas with a partner's, then report to the class.
2. What picture does Achebe paint of Nigerian society at this time? Think about: the relationship between the two main characters in the extract, the language they use and the traditions and values we learn about. Give concrete examples from the text.

✕ **Extra** Explain the meaning of ll. 29–31 and ll. 43–44.

✕ **Extra** Draw a picture or write a description of Okonkwo as you imagine him and present it to the class.

Extract 2

Okonkwo accidentally kills someone. The strict rules of his clan state that he has to spend seven years away from his village Umuofia in a neighbouring region, Mbanta. In this extract he has just returned to Umuofia and is talking to his old friend Obierika.

Umuofia had indeed changed during the seven years Okonkwo had been in exile. The church had come and led many astray. Not only the low-born and the outcast but sometimes a worthy man had joined it. Such a man was Ogbuefi Ugonna. […]

But apart from the church, the white men had also brought a government. They had built a court where the District Commissioner judged cases in ignorance. He had court messengers who brought men to him for trial. Many of these messengers came from Umuru on the bank of the Great River, where the white men first came many years before and where they had built the centre of their religion and trade and government. These court messengers were greatly hated in Umuofia because they were foreigners and also arrogant and high-handed. They were called *kotma*, and because of their ash-coloured shorts they earned the additional name of Ashy-Buttocks. They guarded the prison, which was full of men who had offended against the white man's law. Some of these prisoners had thrown away their twins and some had molested the Christians. They were beaten in the prison by the *kotma* and made to work every morning clearing the government compound and fetching wood for the white Commissioner and the court messengers. Some of these prisoners were men of title who should be above such mean occupation. They were grieved by the indignity and mourned for their neglected farms. […]

A meeting of village elders – the men of title in the community

Okonkwo's head was bowed in sadness as Obierika told him these things.

'Perhaps I have been away too long,' Okonkwo said, almost to himself. 'But I cannot understand these things you tell me. What is it that has happened to our people? Why have they lost the power to fight?'

'Have you not heard how the white man wiped out Abame?' asked Obierika.

'I have heard,' said Okonkwo. 'But I have also heard that Abame people were weak and foolish. Why did they not fight back? Had they no guns and matchets? We would be cowards to compare ourselves with the men of Abame. Their fathers had never dared to stand before our ancestors. We must fight these men and drive them from the land.'

'It is already too late,' said Obierika sadly. 'Our own men and our sons have joined the ranks of the stranger. They have joined his religion and they help to uphold his government. If we should try to drive out the white men in Umuofia we should find it easy. There are only two of them. But what of our own people who are following their way and have been given power? They would go to Umuru and bring the soldiers, and we would be like Abame.' He paused for a long time and then said: 'I told you on my last visit to Mbanta how they hanged Aneto.'

'What has happened to that piece of land in dispute?' asked Okonkwo.

'The white man's court has decided that it should belong to Nnama's family, who had given much money to the white man's messengers and interpreter.'

2 *lead sb. astray:* make sb. do things that are wrong
3 *outcast:* person who does not belong to a society
6 *court:* Gericht
District Commissioner: person in charge of a district within the Empire
in ignorance: without knowing enough
7 *court messenger:* Gerichtsbote
trial: Gerichtsverhandlung
21 *throw away your twins:* Some Nigerian parents would leave their newborn twins in the wilderness as they were believed to bring bad luck.
23 *molest sb.:* jdn. belästigen
25 *compound:* area with buildings surrounded by a fence
27 *man of title:* person with a high office
mean occupation: low job
28 *grieve sb.:* make sb. sad
indignity: situation in which you are not treated with respect
mourn for sth.: be sad because sth. is no longer there
35 *matchet (= machete):* big and very sharp knife
46 *land in dispute:* land that people quarrel about

'Does the white man understand our custom about land?'

'How can he when he does not even speak our tongue? But he says that our customs are bad; and our own brothers who have taken up his religion also say that our customs are bad. How do you think we can fight when our own brothers have turned against us? The white man is very clever. He came quietly and peaceably with his religion. We were amused at his foolishness and allowed him to stay. Now he has won our brothers, and our clan can no longer act like one. He has put a knife on the things that held us together and we have fallen apart.'

49 *custom:* tradition, normal behaviour

C Understanding the text

1. The central theme of this extract is the changes that were brought about by the white people. In a copy of the table below, list the changes that the British have brought to Nigeria and then find information or speculate about the situation before their arrival.

CHANGES SINCE THE BRITISH CAME	SITUATION BEFORE THEIR ARRIVAL
– *many people in the village are now Christians (ll. 2–3)* – …	– *people maybe had their traditional religion*

2. Why, according to Obierika, are the whites so successful in bringing about these changes?
3. After reading this extract, try to explain the meaning of the novel's title. Go back to your results for task **A** and say which of your ideas were correct.
4. Compare the characters of Okonkwo and his friend Obierika as they are portrayed in this extract. Make sure you consider their attitudes to the changes that have taken place and what should be done about them. Find adjectives to describe each man.

✕ **Extra** After this meeting, Okonkwo goes back to his house and thinks about what Obierika has told him. Collect ideas, then write his interior monologue.

Extract 3

This extract is the end of the novel. Okonkwo has become angrier and angrier about the white people and has got into trouble with the British authorities. Finally, he kills one of the government's messengers. He urges the villagers to throw out the white men, but they refuse and walk away, leaving Okonkwo alone. The next day, the British District Commissioner arrives with some soldiers to arrest Okonkwo.

There was a small bush behind Okonkwo's compound. The only opening into this bush from the compound was a little round hole in the red-earth wall through which fowls went in and out in their endless search for food. The hole would not let a man through. It was to this bush that Obierika led the Commissioner and his men. They skirted round the compound, keeping close to the wall. The only sound they made was with their feet as they crushed dry leaves.

Then they came to the tree from which Okonkwo's body was dangling, and they stopped dead.

'Perhaps your men can help us bring him down and bury him,' said Obierika. 'We have sent for strangers from another village to do it for us, but they may be a long time coming.'

3 *fowl:* chicken and other birds
7 *dangle from sth.:* hang down from sth.
8 *stop dead:* abruptly stop walking
9 *bury sb.* ['beri]: put sb. in a hole and cover with earth

The District Commissioner changed instantaneously. The resolute administrator in him gave way to the student of primitive customs.

'Why can't you take him down yourselves?' he asked.

'It is against our custom,' said one of the men. 'It is an abomination for a man to take his own life. It is an offence against the Earth, and a man who commits it will not be buried by his clansmen. His body is evil, and only strangers may touch it. That is why we ask your people to bring him down, because you are strangers.'

'Will you bury him like any other man?' asked the Commissioner.

'We cannot bury him. Only strangers can. We shall pay your men to do it. When he has been buried we will then do our duty by him. We shall make sacrifices to cleanse the desecrated land.'

Obierika, who had been gazing steadily at his friend's dangling body, turned suddenly to the District Commissioner and said ferociously: 'That man was one of the greatest men in Umuofia. You drove him to kill himself; and now he will be buried like a dog ...' He could not say any more. His voice trembled and choked his words.

'Shut up!' shouted one of the messengers, quite unnecessarily.

'Take down the body,' the Commissioner ordered his chief messenger, 'and bring it and all these people to court.'

'Yes, sah,' the messenger said, saluting.

The Commissioner went away, taking three or four of the soldiers with him. In the many years in which he had toiled to bring civilization to different parts of Africa he had learnt a number of things. One of them was that a District Commissioner must never attend to such undignified details as cutting down a dead man from the tree. Such attention would give the natives a poor opinion of him. In the book which he planned to write he would stress that point. As he walked back to the court he thought about that book. Every day brought him some new material. The story of this man who had killed a messenger and hanged himself would make interesting reading. One could almost write a whole chapter on him. Perhaps not a whole chapter but a reasonable paragraph, at any rate. There was so much else to include, and one must be firm in cutting out details. He had already chosen the title of the book, after much thought: *The Pacification of the Primitive Tribes of the Lower Niger*.

[From: *Things Fall Apart* by Chinua Achebe, 1958]

15 *abomination:* repulsive, disgusting thing
21 *sacrifice (n.):* Opfer
22 *cleanse sth.* [klenz]: make sth. clean again
desecrate sth. ['---]: use sth. in an evil way
24 *ferocious:* wild, aggressive
33 *toil:* work hard
43 *pacification:* act of making sb. peaceful
44 *tribe:* (Volks-)Stamm

D Understanding the text

1. Outline in a few sentences where, when, how and why Okonkwo's death happens.
2. In the text, Achebe contrasts the District Commissioner's reaction to Okonkwo's death to that of the villagers. Juxtapose the two attitudes and comment on them.

✕ **Extra** Comment on the sentence 'Such attention would give the natives a poor opinion of him [the District Commissioner]' (l. 36). What does this tell you about the Commissioner's attitude towards Nigerians?

✕ **Extra** When the Commissioner goes home he talks to another British official about the day's events. Write and act out the conversation with a partner.

E Understanding and analysing all three extracts

► Activity chest 11

Collect ideas for the tasks below. Write your answer to the question, then use 'Peer review' groups to correct and improve your answer.

1. Outline the impact of the British on Nigeria as described in these extracts.
2. Examine how the text extracts convey a certain attitude to these changes. Discuss the use of the narrator, the plot and the language. The **SPOTLIGHT** box below will help you with one aspect of your answer. Give examples to support your view.

► Glossary 2.1, 2.2.1, 3.2; Skills 1.2.3

Narrator / Point of view

- what type of narrator?
- effect on reader?

Plot

- How does the plot illustrate 'change'?
- How does the plot make the impact of the British 'dramatic'?

Language

- general style (simple?)
- use of Nigerian words (how? effect on reader?)
- the characters' language

SPOTLIGHT ON Point of view *(Erzählperspektive)*

A very important aspect of a narrative text is the point of view from which the story is told – in other words, who tells us the story. The storyteller is called the narrator. There are three main types of narrator and each one influences the way the reader understands the events and the characters' thoughts and feelings in a different way.

Note: The narrator is never the writer himself or herself! The narrator is either a character in the story or someone outside the story who is observing what is happening – a 'voice'.

USEFUL PHRASES FOR WRITING ABOUT POINT OF VIEW		
In this story,	the writer/author/novelist uses a … narrator.	
This means that	the story is told from the point of view of … / through the eyes of …	the main character / one of the characters in the story / an observer
For example,	in line XX … / at the beginning of the story …	
One (important) reason why the writer chooses to tell the story in this way is …		
This kind of narrator (also) enables the author to …		
The effect on the reader	is (that) …	
Another consequence of this narrative viewpoint		is (that) …

IMPROVE YOUR WRITING Using the simple present for writing about texts

With only a few exceptions, the tense to use when you write about a text is the *simple present*. Below is a summary written by a student – but some of the tenses are wrong. Write the summary again correctly.

The story of Okonkwo is set in Nigeria before the British arrived there. In the story we see how the arrival of the British changes the country, and most importantly, how these changes had a tragic effect on Okonkwo himself. At the beginning of the story the author Chinua Achebe paints a picture of a country in which it is clear that there were strict rules about how to behave and where there are complex customs and laws which all Nigerians understood and obeyed. As the British start to colonise the country, first with missionaries and then with other settlers who formed a government, the traditional society of Nigeria began to disintegrate. In the words of the title: 'Things fall apart'. While many of the inhabitants of Okonkwo's village could accept these changes, Okonkwo can't. However, when he tries to get his people to rise up with him against the British, they refused. Okonkwo kills a government messenger in anger and then kills himself. At the end of the novel the British District Commissioner saw Okonkwo's body hanging from a tree. He didn't understand the tragedy of Okonkwo's death. For him, the most interesting thing was that he could write about it in his book.

5 The British Empire: good or bad?

Currently, there is much debate in Britain about whether the Empire was good or bad. You are now going to collect your ideas on that topic.

1. Go back to the mindmap you made for task 3 on p. 10. Revising once more what you have learned about the Empire, add to your mindmap.
2. Work in groups and think of all the aspects of the Empire that you have learned about. Copy and complete the table below. Compare your ideas in class.

ADVANTAGES OF THE BRITISH EMPIRE	DISADVANTAGES OF THE BRITISH EMPIRE
- made the world more global - …	- … - …

3. Write a text in which you discuss the advantages and disadvantages of the British Empire and come to your own conclusion. Before you do that, it may be helpful to work through the task below.

IMPROVE YOUR WRITING Comparing advantages and disadvantages

When discussing a topic, you have to point out the positive and negative aspects of something: the pros and cons or advantages and disadvantages. To make your writing more readable, more convincing and better structured, it would be helpful to use some of the phrases below.
In small groups, look through the phrases and make sure you understand them. Then write them under the following headings:

INTRODUCING THE TOPIC	COMPARING ADVANTAGES AND DISADVANTAGES	CONCLUDING THE TOPIC
…	…	…

- *X has both advantages and disadvantages.*
- *The final picture is very mixed.*
- *The other side of the coin is, however, (that) …*
- *To sum up, …*
- *Let us look at the pros and cons of …*
- *Broadly speaking, …*
- *On the one hand (NOT: ~~side~~!)*
- *In conclusion, …*
- *There are more … than … to Y.*
- *On the other hand (NOT: ~~side~~!), however, …*
- *On the plus side, there is / we can add …*
- *On balance, …*
- *X is an interesting example …*
- *Among the (dis)advantages we can point to …*
- *The advantages/disadvantages outweigh the diasadvantages/advantages.*
- *Taking everything into consideration, it is possible to say that …*
- *When looking at X, we can say that …*
- *There are both pros and cons to X.*
- *There are more pros/cons than cons/pros.*
- *The downside, however, is (that) …*

TOPIC 02

British life and politics

When we visit a foreign country, we feel that there are things about it which are special, which give it a national identity. Britain is no exception. In this topic you are going to look at three aspects of the country today: its monarchy, its political system, and its social classes.

Collect ideas

The words and phrases in the word cloud below relate to the three aspects of British life mentioned above. Make a table, put the words into the three categories and compare with a partner. Then use as many words and phrases as you can to describe the pictures and to make sentences about the three aspects.

The picture above on the right shows … This is where …
Britain has a monarchy. At the moment, I think the monarch is …

reign (v): regieren
constitutional monarchy: konstitutionelle Monarchie (Monarchie, bei der die Rechte des Monarchen durch eine Verfassung eingeschränkt sind)
govern sb./sth.: jdn./etwas regieren
elect sb.: choose sb. for a political job by voting for them

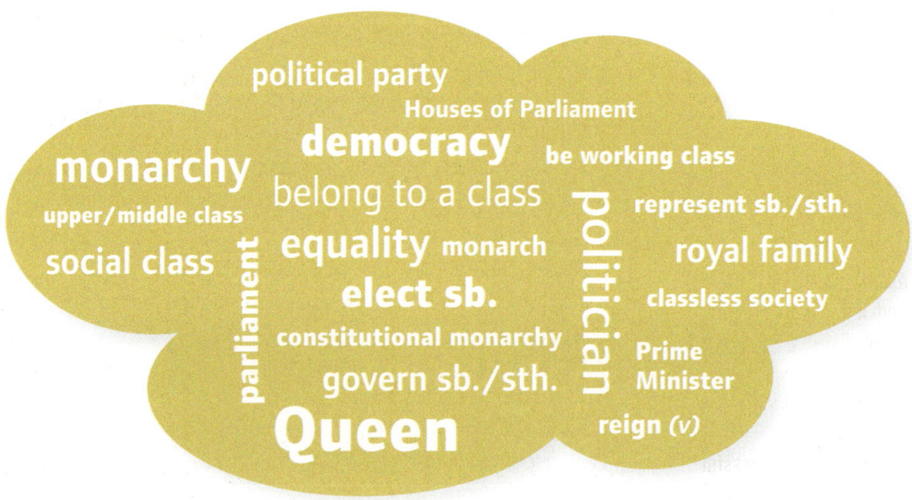

1 How the United Kingdom is governed (An information booklet)

Immigrants to the United Kingdom who wish to become British citizens have to take an exam. Below is an extract from the official booklet to prepare people for the exam. It deals with how the UK is governed.

A Understanding the text

Work in groups to draw a diagram which shows how the UK is governed.

Government

The system of government in the United Kingdom is a parliamentary democracy. The UK is divided into 646 parliamentary constituencies and at least every five years voters in each constituency elect their Member of Parliament (MP) in a general election. All of the elected MPs form the House of Commons. Most MPs belong to a political party and the party with the largest number of MPs forms the government. [...]

The House of Commons

The House of Commons is the more important of the two chambers in Parliament, and its members are democratically elected. Nowadays the Prime Minister and almost all the Cabinet members are members of the House of Commons. The members of the House of Commons are called 'Members of Parliament' or MPs for short. Each MP represents a parliamentary constituency, or area of the country: there are 646 of these. MPs have a number of different responsibilities. They represent everyone in their constituency, they help to create new laws, they scrutinize and comment on what the government is doing, and they debate important national issues. [...]

The House of Commons

The House of Lords

The House of Lords

Members of the House of Lords, known as peers, are not elected and do not represent a constituency. The role and membership of the House of Lords have recently undergone big changes. Until 1958 all peers were either 'hereditary', meaning that their titles were inherited, senior judges, or bishops of the Church of England. Since 1958 the Prime Minister has had the power to appoint peers just for their own lifetime. These peers, known as Life Peers, have usually had a distinguished career in politics, business, law or some other profession. This means

3 *constituency:* Wahlbezirk
4 *voter:* Wähler/in
9 *chamber:* Kammer (Verfassungsorgan in der parlamentarischen Demokratie)
11 *Cabinet:* cf. ll. 43–50
16 *scrutinize sth.:* check and control sth.
21 *undergo sth.:* experience sth.
22 *inherit sth.:* receive sth. from a person after their death
judge: Richter
23 *appoint sb.:* choose sb. for a position
25 *distinguished:* successful

that debates in the House of Lords often draw on more specialist knowledge than is available to members of the House of Commons. [...] While the House of Lords is usually the less important of the two chambers of Parliament, it is more independent of the government. It can suggest amendments or propose new laws, which are then discussed by the House of Commons. The House of Lords can become very important if the majority of its members will not agree to pass a law for which the House of Commons has voted. The House of Commons has powers to overrule the House of Lords, but these are very rarely used.

The Prime Minister

10 Downing Street

The Prime Minister (PM) is the leader of the political party in power. He or she appoints the members of the Cabinet and has control over many important public appointments. The official home of the Prime Minister is 10 Downing Street, in central London, near the Houses of Parliament; he or she also has a country house not far from London called Chequers. The Prime Minister can be changed if the MPs in the governing party decide to do so, or if he or she wishes to resign. More usually, the Prime Minister resigns when his or her party is defeated in a general election.

The Cabinet

The Prime Minister appoints about 20 senior MPs to become ministers in charge of departments. These include the Chancellor of the Exchequer, responsible for the economy, the Home Secretary, responsible for law, order and immigration, the Foreign Secretary, and ministers (called 'Secretaries of State') for education, health and defence. [...] These ministers form the Cabinet, a small committee which usually meets weekly and makes important decisions about government policy which often then have to be debated or approved by Parliament.

The Opposition

The second largest party in the House of Commons is called the Opposition. The Leader of the Opposition is the person who hopes to become Prime Minister if his or her party wins the next general election. The Leader of the Opposition leads his or her party in pointing out the government's failures and weaknesses; one important opportunity to do this is at Prime Minister's Questions which takes place every week while Parliament is sitting. The Leader of the Opposition also appoints senior Opposition MPs to lead the criticism of government ministers, and together they form the Shadow Cabinet.

[From: *Life in the United Kingdom*, 2009]

26 *draw on sth.:* use sth.
29 *amendment:* change or addition to a law
propose sth.: suggest sth.
33 *overrule sb./sth.:* jdn./etwas überstimmen
40 *resign:* zurücktreten
41 *defeat sb./sth.:* jdn. besiegen
44 *in charge of sth.:* responsible for sth.
45 *department:* Regierungsressort

✕ **Extra:** Write a quiz on the text above and test your fellow students. Below are two examples.

a	*The public democratically elect the members of both Houses of Parliament.* A True B False
b	*How many politicians are there in the Cabinet?* A About 30 B About 40 C About 20 D About 10

KEY FACTS Britain's political parties

The political spectrum

In order to understand British political parties it helps to look at the way in which political ideas are often organised on a left–right spectrum. In Britain, extreme policies (i.e. far right or far left) are not popular, so most parties are nearer to the centre. However, we can still say that they tend towards the left or the right.

- progressive
- liberal
- socialist
- (far left: communist, anarchist)

LEFT — CENTRE — RIGHT

- conservative
- capitalist
- monarchist
- (far right: nationalist, fascist)

The Conservative Party (party colour blue)

The Conservative Party (nicknamed the 'Tory Party' or the 'Tories') is Britain's main centre-right party. It is also its oldest party, dating back to the 17th century when it represented the aristocrats and the Church of England. Today, it is the party of business and free enterprise. Many of its members are also anti-Europe.

The Liberal Party / The Liberal Democratic Party (party colour yellow)

The original Liberal Party was founded in the 19th century and until around 1920 it was the main political party to oppose the Conservatives with centre-left ideas. From 1920 until the 1980s it almost disappeared from British politics, but then was re-born as the Liberal Democratic Party (nicknamed the 'Lib Dems'). Today, it is still the smallest of the three major parties. It is still committed to liberal ideas and the only major party to be fully pro-Europe.

The Labour Party (party colour red)

The Labour Party is Britain's leading centre-left party and during the 20th century did the most to transform Britain into its modern state. Founded in 1900, it worked with the newly-created trade unions to fight for the rights of working people. After World War II it was the Labour Party which created the Welfare State. Today, the party is closer to the centre and less radical, but still believes in protecting poorer people.

Three famous British politicians

8 *nickname sth./sb.:* jdm./etwas einen Spitznamen geben
9 *free enterprise:* freies Unternehmertum
12 *found sth.:* etwas gründen
21 *trade union:* Gewerkschaft
22 *welfare state:* Wohlfahrtsstaat

Winston Churchill *(1874–1965) Britain's Conservative PM during World War II*

Margaret Thatcher *(born 1925) Conservative PM 1979–90, was anti-Europe and anti-trade union*

Tony Blair *(born 1953) Labour PM 1997–2007, with 'New Labour' he moved the party towards the centre*

Activities

1. Draw a time-line to show the development of the three parties. Mark on key dates, events and people that you learn about in the text.

✕ **Extra:** Find out about the parties and politicians that are important in Britain at the moment and/or some of Britain's other parties (such as the Greens). Report to the class.

2 The Queen at work (Videos)

DVD 1–4

You will know that the UK today is a monarchy. But what duties and rights does the British monarch actually have? To find out about this, you are going to watch some videos from the monarchy's website.

A Before you watch

Read the KEY FACTS about the constitutional monarchy, then look at the four stills from the videos. Speculate about what may be happening in each picture and collect some ideas about the Queen's duties.

KEY FACTS The constitutional monarchy of the UK

The United Kingdom today has a constitutional monarchy: the monarch is the head of state, but he or she can act only within the regulations of the constitution; power lies completely with parliament. The monarch can only 'advise, warn and encourage' government.

A
State Opening of Parliament: ceremony in which the monarch begins ('opens') each parliamentary year, the session • *Black Rod:* official person in the Houses of Parliament • *speech:* Rede • *legislation:* laws • *carriage:* Kutsche

B
livestock: animals (sheep, cattle, pigs etc.) which are sold alive at a market • *Royal Welsh Show:* annual show in Wales to which farmers bring their animals to win prizes

C
Remembrance Day: 11 November each year when British people remember dead soldiers, sailors etc. • *Cenotaph:* tall stone monument which commemorates dead soldiers, sailors etc. It stands in a wide street in Central London called Whitehall • *wreath:* Kranz • *bomb disposal expert:* soldier who makes explosives (bombs etc.) safe • *veteran:* former soldier, sailor etc.

D
reception: ceremony in which sb. welcomes people to a place • *forthcoming:* bevorstehend

B Understanding the videos

1. Watch the videos and take notes on the basic information that you get: where? what is happening? why? what is the Queen's role in each video?
2. Outline the different aspects of the monarch's job that are illustrated. Discuss what they tell you about his or her relationship to the British and his or her role in public life. What do the British seem to think of their monarch?

Extra: Go on to the British Monarchy website (www.royal.gov.uk). Find out more about e.g. Black Rod, a day in the life of the Queen, another member of the Royal Family. Report to the class.

3 Who wants a monarchy? (Statistics)

survey: act of asking a number of people for their opinion
favour sth.: etwas bevorzugen

In 2007 people in Britain were asked their opinions about the monarchy. The table below contains the most important results of that survey.

A Before you look at the statistics

What do you think: are British people generally in favour of the monarchy?

B Understanding the statistics

Would you favour Britain becoming a republic or remaining a monarchy?

	Total	Male	Female	18–24	25–34	35–44	45-54	55–64	65+
Republic	16%	21%	12%	23%	22%	17%	13%	19%	8%
Monarchy	76%	73%	80%	68%	65%	77%	80%	74%	88%
Don't know	8%	6%	9% *	9%	13%	7% *	7%	7%	5% *

*As the percentages have been rounded up, the figures add up to just over 100.

[From: http://populuslimited.uk]

▶ Skills 3

1. What percentage …?
   - of people in general are in favour of a monarchy?
   - of people in general are against a monarchy?
   - of people in general could not decide if they wanted a monarchy or a republic?
2. Sum up the information you collected in 1 in a sentence.

The survey	shows / makes clear that …
According to the survey, …	

3. The two pie charts below show how men and women replied. Decide which pie chart is which, then copy and label the key. Finally sum up the results in your own words.

Fig. 1

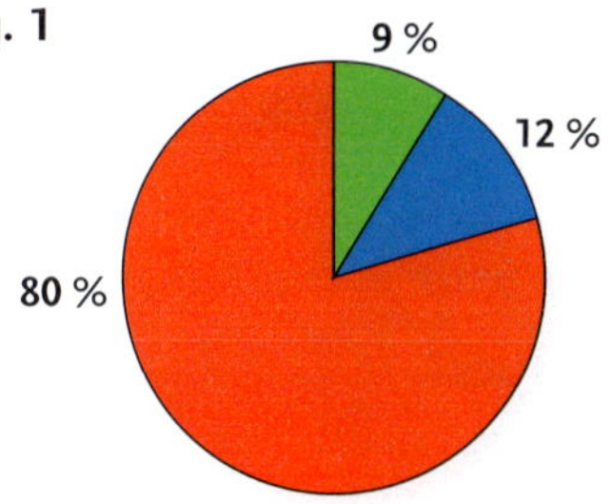

Fig. 2

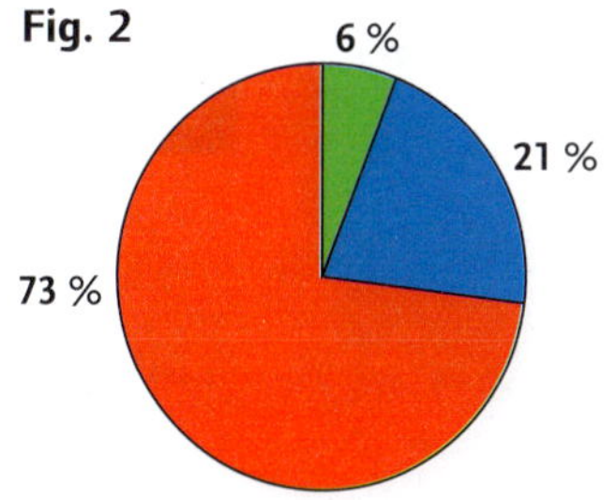

Key: [green]: … [blue]: … [red]: …

In the second and third column of the table In Figures 1 and 2	we learn about … gender attitudes / differences in opinions according to gender / how men and women feel about …	
Men and women	feel roughly the same / have slightly different ideas about …	
Figures 1 and 2	illustrate / highlight …	
From the pie charts	we can see that	men/women are more/less in favour of the monarchy than …
Around … per cent of …	say/claim/feel that the monarchy is … as opposed to … per cent of …	

4. Compare the bar chart and the line graph below with the table on page 33. What do the chart and the graph show?
5. Sum up the information contained in the bar chart and the line graph.

Fig. 3

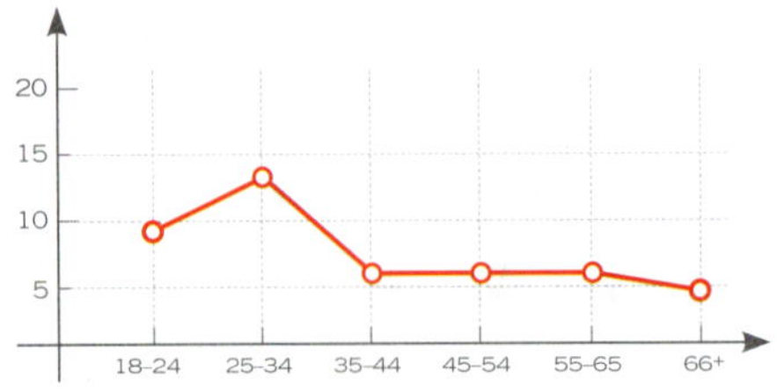

Fig. 4

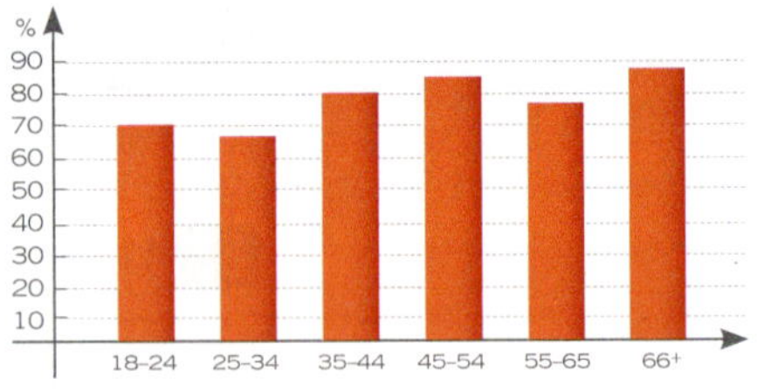

The bar chart / line graph	gives an insight into / provides information about the opinions of people in different age groups
The monarchy is	most/least popular in the … age groups
More/fewer people in the … age group	are in favour of the monarchy than …
The age group which is	most/least in favour of the monarchy is …

C Reacting to the statistics

1. Are the results what you expected about British attitudes to the monarchy? Why (not)? Does any particular result surprise you? Why?
2. When newspapers report surveys they often pick out one result and base their article on it. Choose one key result of the statistics, then write a headline and the first paragraph of a newspaper article about these results.
3. Guess how many Germans would prefer a monarchy in Germany. Justify your opinion.
4. Discuss who is the better head of state, a monarch or an elected president.

▶ Skills 3

SPOTLIGHT ON Interpreting statistics

When you do research on a topic, you will often come across statistics. It is therefore helpful to be able to interpret them and to explain them in your own words.

Different types of statistics

Statistics can be represented as 'raw data', i.e. just figures (see e.g. the table on p. 33). More often, however, bar charts or pie charts are used to make the data clearer to the reader. In texts, such diagrams are often referred to as 'Fig. 1', 'Fig. 2' etc. (Fig. = 'figure').

Percentages

Use a singular verb with a singular or uncountable noun: '60% of German wine is white wine.'
Use a plural verb with a plural noun: '53% of readers prefer fiction.'

Useful phrases

The table / bar/pie chart shows the number of / percentages of / relationship between …
… is more/less popular with older/younger people than with …
It is the most/least popular with …
More/fewer people … than …
The falling/growing percentages of … show that …

4 Britain's social classes (A video and an extract from a novel)

DVD 5, 6

Upstairs, Downstairs **was a very popular British TV series in the 1970s about a rich family in London in 1903. It contrasted the lives of the rich people 'upstairs' and their servants 'downstairs'. You are going to watch two excerpts from the first episode, in which a young woman arrives to apply for a position, i.e. a job, as a servant.**

A Before you watch

Make sure you know what the following words mean, then say whether they rather belonged 'upstairs', 'downstairs' or to both worlds.

> beautiful rooms • butler • cook • education • expensive clothes • gentleman • hierarchy • humility • illiteracy • jewels • kitchen • lady • manual work • marriage • refined manners • servant • small wages • uniform • wealth

B Understanding the video

Excerpt 1: *(Mrs Pratt's) Agency:* agency which found servants for rich families • *house parlour maid:* servant who cleaned the house and did general jobs indoors

Excerpt 2: *domestic service:* work as a servant • *servants' hall:* room downstairs where servants ate and spent free time • *on trial:* auf Probe • *(your) betters:* people better than you • *humility:* Demut

1. Watch the two excerpts and make a table for the main scenes. Fill in the most important information in columns 1–3.

1. Scene	2. Characters	3. Setting	4. What happens?	5. Techniques used

2. Watch excerpt 1 for a second time and fill in as many details as you can in columns 4–5. Point out what, in your opinion, is the most important thing you learn about life in such a house at this time.
3. Watch excerpt 2 again and fill in columns 4–5. Describe and explain
   - the impression you get of the young woman who wants to be a servant;
   - the impression you get of the lady of the household;
   - the impression you get of the butler.

   Make sure to give examples from the clips to support your ideas. Exchange your ideas with a partner.

C Analysing the video

Now you are going to analyse how various aspects of the social background of the story (e.g. the status and way of life of different characters, their relationship and social attitudes, etc.) are conveyed through visual film techniques and the use of sound.

▶ Skills 4

Get together in groups and choose the scenes where you find the most interesting visual and sound techniques. Divide the scenes between you so that each group watches a different scene. Analyse them and fill in columns 4–5 in the table from task B. You may want to consider the following aspects:

Aspects conveyed: ***e.g. the status of different characters / atmosphere in the household / social attitudes in Britain at this time / aspects of a servant's life / …***
Techniques used: ***camera angles / sound / ways of speaking / dress / behaviour / visual details / …***

D Reacting to the video

1. Imagine you are the young woman who applies for the job. At the end of the day, she writes about her experiences in her diary. Write her diary entry.
2. You have been asked to review the first episode of this new TV series for a magazine. Write your text, pointing out what the episode can tell viewers about British society in the early 1900s and how well you think it does so. Use 'Peer review' groups to correct and improve your text, then present the best text in your group to the class.

▶ Activity chest 11

E An extract from a novel: Before you read

You are now going to read an extract from the novel *Blue Collar*. It was written in 2009 by the British writer Danny King and is based on his life. Before you read the extract, look at this newspaper clipping. Speculate about his life and the possible theme of his novel.

Love across the class divide: He's from a council estate. She's a millionaire's daughter. So what happened when their worlds collided?

By Rachel Porter

Danny King, 40, grew up on a council estate and went into the building trade. His wife Jeannie, 37, is the daughter of a company CEO and went to private schools and university before starting a high-flying career in PR.

[From: *Daily Mail*, 3 June 2009]

council estate: area of a town with houses or flats with very low rents
collide with sth.: crash into sth.
CEO (= Chief Executive Officer): person with the highest rank in a company
PR (= public relations): business of creating a positive public image of sb./sth., e.g. a company

F Understanding the extract

builder: person who builds or repairs houses/buildings

The narrator and central character in *Blue Collar* is Terry, a builder. In this extract he is at a dinner party with his rich new girlfriend Charley. Her rich friend CT is the host and CT's friend Russell is helping with the dinner.

Find a suitable title for this extract. Take into account the central event, the people involved, and what you believe to be the author's intention. When you present it to the class, be ready to explain it.

'Here we are. Is everyone hungry?' Russell asked, [...].

He put my dinner down in front of me and I saw that it consisted of an extra-thin bit of bacon wrapped around a bit of salmon, sat on top of a load of really burnt peas (which I later found out were lentils. I'd heard of these before, but had never actually ever seen them) and all covered in cream.

OK, I'll admit it, I'm not the most sophisticated bloke in the world – no, seriously, I'm not – so I hadn't done that much posh grub in my time, but really, please, tell me, how was this nicer than a chicken dinner? Or a chicken curry? Or chicken and chips? Or chicken casserole? Or chicken nuggets? I mean, if I was having people around for dinner and I wanted to impress them (and the butcher's had run out of chicken) I'd get a steak in for everyone. A big dirty great slab of sirloin with onions, mushrooms, grilled tomatoes, a baked potato, a bit of salad and a scattering of mustard and pepper. I'd expect a good write-up if I served up six plate-loads of that to everyone, so what was the deal with the cat food challenge in front of us this evening?

Fish, as well? I'd specifically told Charley that I didn't like fish, and here in front of me was a fish. [...]
'Has it got bones in it?' I asked, digging open my fish with the funny-looking knife and fork I found by the side of my plate.

'No, it shouldn't have, I boned the fish myself this afternoon,' Russell told me, almost making me choke on my Stella again. Childish, I know, but he said it, not me.

Unfortunately 'shouldn't have' didn't carry the sorts of cast-iron guarantees I needed to commence Operation Wolf It Down again, so I had to rethink my options and selected a different strategy to beat this particular dish.

The 'eat a bit, drink a bit' option wasn't really a goer either, as I wasn't sure I'd be shown the same sympathy and understanding if I hurled a second mouthful across the table if it all got a bit too much for me, so this called for Strategy C.

'Here, CT, have you got any brown sauce?'

'Erm... er, yes... I think. I'm sure we must have,' he replied, looking at Russell in pity.

6 *salmon:* type of expensive fish
8 *lentils:* Linsen
12 *sophisticated:* having a lot of experience of the world; knowing about fashion, culture and other things
bloke (ifml): *man, guy*
13 *grub* (sl): Fraß
19 *write-up:* Bewertung
27 *Stella (= Stella Artois):* a brand of beer
29 *cast-iron guarantee:* guarantee which cannot be broken (*cast-iron* = aus Gusseisen)
30 *commence* (fml): begin
wolf sth. down (ifml): eat food very quickly, especially by putting a lot of it in your mouth at once
option: possibility
35 *brown sauce:* dark and very strong sauce

Russell himself chose not to say anything, he just stared at the dinner in front of me with a mixture of sadness and resignation in his eyes.

'You can't beat a bit of brown sauce,' I reassured everyone, and you certainly couldn't. Nothing completely annihilated something else's original taste quite like brown sauce. It was the napalm of all condiments.

'Here you go,' CT said, reluctantly handing me a plastic squeezy bottle as if it were a gun and I was his son. He looked like he desperately wanted to urge caution but wasn't quite sure how to go about it, so I quickly popped the lid and put him out of his pickle with a sweeping flourish all over my dinner.

'That got it,' I told him, and CT just agreed. It certainly had.

I mashed it all up together and stirred in half the lentils while I was at it, then helped myself to an enormous forkful before anyone could ask me if I wanted a bib, and I must say, it wasn't very nice. Even with half a bottle of brown sauce all over it.

'A sauce-on-everything man, huh?' Clive commented. I was going to tell him 'yeah, everything except pudding' but decided to hold fire until I saw what crème brûleé was. I struggled on with my lot, determined that I should finish every morsel for fear of looking like a big ignorant rude dummy, and within four minutes it was mission accomplished. Bring on the pudding and then we're out of here. What time is it?

'Attend a lot of dinner parties, do you?' Russell asked.

'This is my first one,' I corrected him.

[From: *Blue Collar* by Danny King, 2009]

42 *annihilate sth.:* destroy sth. completely
43 *napalm:* agent used in bombs that causes severe burns to the skin
condiment: Gewürz
44 *reluctant:* not really wanting to do sth.
48 *pickle* (ifml): *(here)* difficult or unpleasant situation (*pickle* = vegetable in vinegar)
with a sweeping flourish: mit einer ausladenden Geste
54 *bib:* piece of cloth you put around a child's neck so that they do not dirty their clothes when eating
57 *crème brûleé:* type of dessert
59 *morsel:* small amount / piece of sth., especially food

G Analysing the extract

King shows us the big difference between Terry and his hosts. Examine how he does this. Work in a small group to collect ideas about the following points, then report to the class:

▶ Glossary 2.2.1

- the kind of narrator (point of view);
- the way Terry describes aspects of the meal, especially the food;

▶ Glossary 3.1

- any rhetorical devices used and their effect.

H Reacting to the extract

1. As in *Upstairs, Downstairs*, this extract deals with a class divide. Point out if and how the class divide has changed according to the video and the text.
2. Discuss to what extent a class divide also exists in your society.
3. Imagine you are Terry's girlfriend Charley. You have just returned from the dinner party and write your personal feelings in your diary. Write Charley's diary entry.

TOPIC 03

New voices

Collect ideas

Work in groups and collect ideas about the questions below, then report to the class.

1. Look at the photo. Where and when might it have been taken? What is the 'mood' of the picture?
2. What content matter could the picture be related to (i.e. what themes, ideas etc. might it deal with)? Explain your answer.
3. Point out how the picture might be connected to historical aspects of the UK.
4. In this topic you are going to listen to the voices – in literature and in film – of members of ethnic minorities in Britain. From what you know generally about the situation of minorities – in Germany as well as in Britain – list some of the themes the speakers might want to deal with. Give specific examples if you can.

▶ Activity chest 13

✕ **Extra** Look back at the word cloud on p. 28. Using your dictionary, make a word cloud for this topic as you have discussed it above. Compare with a partner, then share with the class.

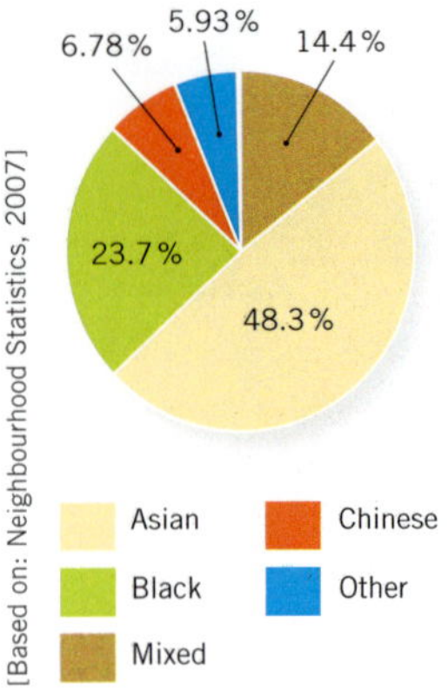

Ethnic minorities in Britain

KEY FACTS Immigration into Britain since World War II

In 2007, just under 12 per cent of British people belonged to an ethnic minority. The large majority lived in England – only small numbers were found in Wales or Scotland. In England they were concentrated in certain regions, most importantly London and a number of former industrial cities in the West Midlands (i.e. around Britain's second largest city, Birmingham) and the north-east and north-west of the country. British Asians (people from India, Pakistan and Bangladesh) were by far the largest group in England, making up almost half of the total. Black British people (from Africa or the Caribbean) came second, and those of Chinese origin third.

The first immigrants

At the end of World War II in 1945, Britain was bankrupt. It needed rapidly to rebuild its industries, but because so many lives had been lost, there was a lack of workers. During the war, thousands of people from Britain's old Empire had fought for the 'mother country' and in the late 1940s the British government invited the first of its non-white Empire citizens to come to Britain to work. They were from the West Indies (the Caribbean), principally from the island of Jamaica, and the first group of almost 500 men and women landed in London on a ship called Empire Windrush in 1948. Most settled in London and for many British people, the first black person they saw was one of the West Indian bus drivers that had been recruited by London transport. Others became nurses or moved to other parts of Britain to take up jobs in factories. Reaction to the West Indian immigrants was mixed: they were needed and had been invited to come, but many British people worried that their arrival would change British life and culture. This led, on occasions, to racial tensions.

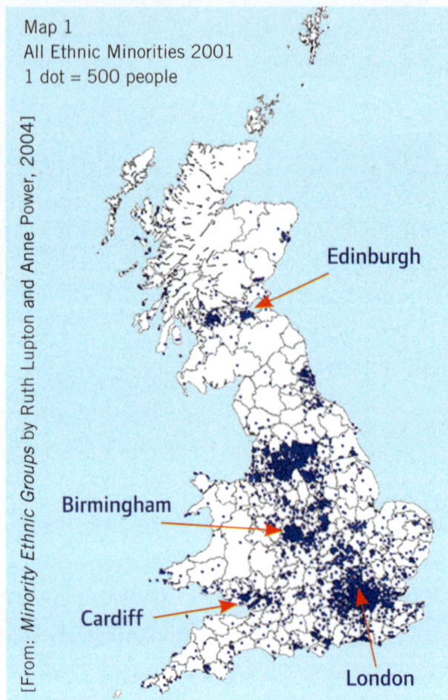

Largest concentrations of ethnic minority populations in England, Scotland and Wales

British Asians

From the mid-1950s onwards, a second wave of immigrants arrived in Britain: the 'British Asians'. They came from India, which had belonged to the British Empire (cf. p. 14), but became independent from Britain in 1947. At the same time it had been divided into two different countries – based largely on religious differences: mainly Hindu India and mainly Muslim Pakistan. This 'Partition of India' as it was called led to significant bloodshed and massive movements of population, so that many people looked to Britain for safety. The first to arrive in Britain were largely from Pakistan, followed by Indians from the Punjab, an area which had been divided between India and Pakistan. Most of them settled in the West Midlands, taking manual jobs on railways and in textile factories. Other Indians came in smaller numbers to work as doctors. In 1972, events in Africa also brought more Asians to Britain. Britain's former colonies in East Africa had large Asian populations, but when Idi Amin became the military dictator of the East African country of Uganda in 1972, one of his first acts was to expel all 80,000 of Uganda's Asians. Thousands headed for Britain where they began to rebuild their lives, often becoming successful businesspeople and

1 *ethnic minority:* ethnische Minderheit
10 *bankrupt:* without any money
11 *lack of sth:* shortage of sth.
43 *manual job:* job that requires working with your hands
47 *expel sb.:* send sb. out of the country against their will

shop owners (as they had been in Uganda). This new wave of immigrants also tended to make their homes in the British Midlands and the north of England, since a sizeable Asian community already existed there.

British reactions to immigration: the 1960s and 70s

When the first Black and Asian immigrants came to Britain, they were allowed to enter freely. As mass immigration continued throughout the 1950s and 60s, however, racial tensions began to grow in Britain. They reached perhaps their worst point in 1968, when a politician named Enoch Powell made a speech (often called 'The Rivers of Blood' speech) in which he warned that Britain faced disaster if it continued to allow uncontrolled numbers of non-white immigrants into the country. Under political pressure, the government brought in three new laws in the decade leading up to 1972, making it increasingly harder for non-white people to enter Britain. They continued to arrive, but in smaller numbers and only if they had a work permit or could prove they already had relatives in the country.

Chinese immigrants

A first wave of Chinese immigrants from Britain's former colony in Hong Kong to Britain occurred after World War II. A second wave was triggered in 1984 when Britain agreed to transfer Hong Kong's sovereignty to the Chinese government in 1997.

Recent immigration

Immigration to Britain has been increasing since the late 1990s. After the enlargement of the European Union in 2004 many Eastern Europeans came to Britain to find work. Many Africans, especially Nigerians, have sought refuge in Britain. Britain holds the world's second largest Nigerian community after Nigeria itself.

British society today

Much has happened in Britain since the 1970s. In 1976, the government set up the Commission for Racial Equality. Its task is to deal with discrimination and prejudice in all their forms. Black and Asian people themselves have also worked in many walks of life – as journalists, actors, or TV presenters, for example – to make Britain a more racially integrated place. In 2010, there were 27 Black or Asian MPs and the descendants of those first non-white immigrants now hold important jobs in universities, the medical profession and business. British life has been transformed by the music, culture and fashions of its immigrant communities, with an Indian curry, Chicken Tikka Massala, voted Britain's 'favourite dish' in 2008. Of course, as in all multi-ethnic societies, the process of living together is always developing. Britain is not without its problems in this respect from time to time. But there is no doubt that, since the second World War, it has become a completely different country – and that British culture has been enriched by its immigrants.

61 *work permit* [' – –]: permission to work

Activities

▶ Skills 3

1. Sum up the information provided by the pie chart and the map.
2. Make a timeline of the different waves of immigration into the UK. Note down who came from where, when, why and what their professions were.
3. Imagine you are a member of one of Britain's ethnic minorities living in Britain today. Collect ideas on when and why your family may have come to the UK, and where from. Speculate about some of their experiences upon arrival and your own impressions of modern Britain. Give a talk in front of your friends.

1 'In-A Brixtan Markit' (A poem)

You are going to listen to James Berry, a Black British poet, reading one of his poems. The poem describes an experience Berry had as a young man just after first arriving in Britain from Jamaica in the early 1950s. Brixton ('Brixtan') is an area of London in which many early West Indian immigrants settled.

James Berry (born 1924)

CD 2

A Before you listen

Look at the title and speculate on what the poem may be about.

B Listening to the poem

With your book closed, listen to James Berry reading his poem. Note down what you understand, then compare with a partner.

C Reading and understanding the poem

Activity chest 12

Look at the tasks below, then read the poem. Use a 'Placemat' to prepare your answers.

2 *believin I:* believing I am
7 *like them did a-wait fi me:* as if they were waiting for me
10 *deh:* there
11 *yam:* Jamswurzel
dasheen: Wasserbrotwurzel
12 *a han a banana:* a hand *(= bunch)* of bananas
a piece a: a piece of
13 *mi lates Bob Marley:* my latest Bob Marley record
14 *all a sudden:* all of a sudden *(= suddenly)*
15 *mi head nah fi mi:* my head was not for me *(= I was not in control of my thoughts)*
yah: here
somody: somebody
16 *nah!:* isn't it?
17 *hol on:* hold on *(= wait)*
18 *dohn:* don't
shove sb.: push sb.
19 *neidda:* neither
fis: face
21 *battn down:* batten down *(= die Schotten dicht machen)*

In-A Brixtan Markit

I walk in-a Brixtan Markit
believin I a respectable man,
you know. An wha happn?

Policeman come straight up
an search mi bag!
Man – straight to me.
Like them did a-wait fi me.
Come search mi bag, man.

Fi mi bag!
An wha them si in deh?
Two piece a yam, a dasheen,
a han a banana, a piece a pork
an mi lates Bob Marley.

Man all a suddn I feel
mi head nah fi mi. This yah now
is when man kill somody, nah!

'Tony', I sey, 'hol on. Hol on,
Tony. Dohn shove. Dohn shove.
Dohn move neidda fis, tongue
nor emotion. Battn down, Tony.
Battn down.' An, man, Tony win.

[From: *Hot Earth Cold Earth* by James Berry, 1995]

1. The poem describes an event. Sum up what happens.
2. Copy the chart below and complete it.

THE POLICEMAN'S BEHAVIOUR AND HIS ATTITUDE TOWARDS TONY	TONY'S FEELINGS BEFORE, DURING, AND AT THE END OF THE EVENT
- The policeman … - …	- At the beginning, he feels he … - …

3. Point out what the poem tells you about the situation of West Indians in Britain at this time.

D Analysing the poem

▶ Skills 1.2.4

Work on the following tasks on your own, then exchange ideas with a partner.

1. Perhaps the most striking aspect of the poem is the language in which it is written, an English dialect called Creole, which is used in the West Indies.
   a Collect examples from the poem and give their standard English equivalents.
   b Why do you think Berry chose to write the poem in the Creole dialect? Consider his identity and the effect of the language on the reader.

▶ Glossary 2.4.1, 3.1

2. Look back at your answers to task C above, then analyse the poem's form. Consider the following aspects:
   a the role of the speaker in the poem and the person he is speaking to (and the effect on the reader);
   b how and why the poem focuses on a single event;
   c the structure of the poem (e.g. stanzas, lines);
   d the poet's use of repetition to emphasise certain points;
   e how and why the poet lists the items in his bag.

The poem is / takes the form of	a straightforward account of the event by the speaker a sort of dialogue between the speaker and the reader
For the reader this has the effect that …	
The speaker is …	
By focusing on just one event the poet …	
The poet uses one single event to …	
The poem is divided into verses. The effect of this is that …	
Berry uses certain devices in the poem to help get his message across. For example, …	
At one point in the poem, the speaker lists ...	
This has the effect of … (highlighting/contrasting / making very clear that …)	

E Reacting to the poem

1. Tell the story of the poem again from the viewpoint of the British policeman. It can be a report that the policeman writes afterwards or a dialogue between the policeman and one of his colleagues.

▶ Activity chest 8

✕ **Extra** Work in groups to show the class a 'Freeze-frame tableau' based on the poem. Be prepared to answer the class's question and to bring the characters to life to explain things.

2 BBC Video Nation (Two videos)

For many years, the BBC has run a project called Video Nation: people record short videos about their everyday lives, which are then put on the BBC website. You are going to watch two videos made by British Asians: Rana Miah, a young man who lives in Ipswich in the south east of England, and Vidya Thirunarayan from Portsmouth, a town on the south coast.

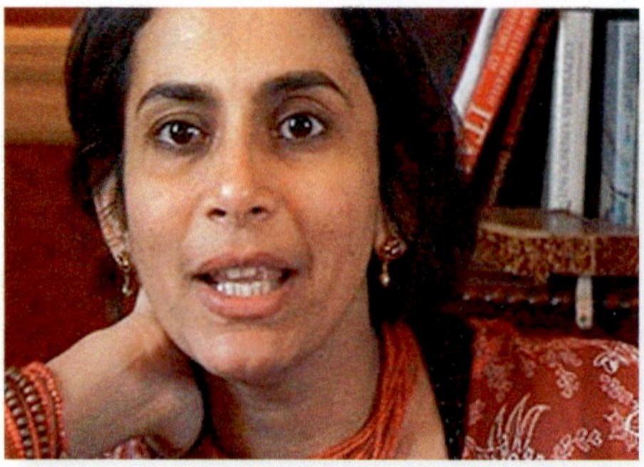

DVD 7, 8

A Understanding the videos

Copy the chart below and take notes as you watch the videos. Compare your notes with a partner's, then report to the class.

1. Note down the basic facts you learn about the two people – where they live, what they do, etc.
2. Write down the ideas and feelings that each person expresses, concentrating particularly on their special identity as a British Asian.
3. Sum up the main theme of each video and find a memorable quotation from each.
4. Point out any differences or similarities between Rana and Vidya.

	RANA	VIDYA
1. Basic facts		
2. Ideas/feelings		
3. Main theme & memorable quote		
4. Differences/similarities		

B Analysing the videos

► Glossary 1.2

The videos can be seen as case studies. Explain the term 'case study' and show why the videos belong in this category. Point out what effect this has on the viewer's attitudes.

C Reacting to the videos

1. Describe your personal reactions to the videos, focusing on the impression you get of Britain's Asian community. Compare this to the situation of ethnic minorities in Germany.
2. Imagine that you could make a similar video about an aspect of your life. Make notes on the following:

SITUATION/LOCATION	TEXT SPOKEN
...	...

3 Dancing to their tune? (Extracts from a novel)

Leicester ['lestə]

You are going to read some extracts from the novel *(Un)arranged Marriage* (2001) by the contemporary British Asian writer Bali Rai. Rai was born in 1971 in Leicester, in the West Midlands, but his family came from the Punjab (cf. KEY FACTS, p. 40). The novel's central character is Manny, whose family also originates from the Punjab. Punjabis are predominantly Sikhs, who have their own customs, religion and philosophy.

A Understanding and analysing the beginning of the novel

Rai begins his novel in a slightly unusual way. He starts with a short text. This is how this text begins and ends.

2 *disinfectant:* substance that kills bacteria
7 *succumb to sth.:* give in to sth.
8 *tearaway* (infml): young person who is difficult to control
philanderer: man who has many sexual relationships
10 *bother to do sth.:* make an effort to do sth.
11 *upset:* unhappy, worried
determined to do sth.: having made a decision to do sth.
12 *marker:* (here) pen with which sb. wrote sth. on the toilet walls
13 *suit:* Anzug
15 *have sb.:* trick sb.

The toilets in the motorway service station at Leicester Forest East stank of disinfectant. But at least they were warm compared to the biting cold wind that was kicking up outside in the car park – where my two brothers Harry and Ranjit were waiting for me. Waiting to take me to Derby, to a wedding – my wedding. A wedding that I hadn't asked for, that I didn't want, to a girl who I didn't know. They must have sat there waiting for me, laughing to themselves about how I had finally succumbed to their way of thinking, their way of life. A good Punjabi man at last, after years of being a tearaway, a rebel, a junkie and a philanderer. At least, that was what they had called me at various times. […]

You see, if they had bothered to open their eyes they would have seen me: seventeen, angry, upset but determined. Determined to do my own thing, to choose my own path in life. They would have seen the marker left in those toilets at Leicester Forest East and realised that, underneath my ill-fitting suit, I had on my real clothes. That in my head was a hip-hop tune that summed up exactly how I had them. They thought they were finally playing me, that I was dancing to their tune, when all the while I had them dancing to mine. It's kind of hard to explain the journey that I've made over the last few years, but I'll try because I believe that it's a story worth telling.

[From: *(Un)arranged marriage* by Bali Rai, 2001]

1. Sum up what you learn about Manny's situation and character.
2. Analyse the following aspects of the text:
   - What kind of narrator does Rai use? What is the effect on the reader?
   - What atmosphere does he create (think of where the action takes place and the events he describes)?

   ▸ Glossary 2.2.1, 2.1
3. In this text we learn about what will happen later in the novel. How do you think this affects the reader?
4. A text of this type at the beginning of a work of fiction is called a prologue. Using Rai's text as an example, describe possible functions of a prologue.

B Reading the extracts

You are now going to read four extracts from the novel.
Read all the extracts through, then outline the main events and explain the title of the novel.

Extract 1 (Four years earlier)

I was sitting in the lounge watching kids' TV and eating Frosties without milk, straight from the box. My dad walked in and belched twice. The sound echoed around the room like heavy thunder. I was so used to him doing it that all I did was pull a face and then carry on watching telly.

"Manjit," he began, pointing to the cereal box. "Getting bloody bowl for them."

"Yes, Daddy-ji." I always made sure that I was extra polite to him the morning after a real bender and using 'ji' after 'Dad' indicated respect for your elders and that was just what was required when he began one of his mega-hangovers. I went and got a bowl from the kitchen, but still didn't add any milk. On my return to the living room, my old man was sitting on the sofa, picking his ear with a forefinger.

"You don't want to come to your brother's wedding?" he asked, as I sat down and started watching TV again.

A Sikh bride on her wedding day

Through a mouthful of cereal I replied that he wasn't really my brother so it didn't matter if I went or not. Bad move.

"You young people," he said in Punjabi, "what do you know? Brother, cousin, it's all the same to us. We are Punjabis, Manjit, Punjabis. Not bloody *goreh*."

Here we go again, I thought to myself, as he began one of his tried and tested lectures about saving Punjabi culture from the grips of the white man and his filth, about being careful not to become too white for your own family.

"... and put their own mothers in homes. At least we look after our families," he continued. And then came the twist, stuck into the conversation like a knife, only casually. "We are Punjabis and proud of it. Good Jat Sikhs from a good family. Look at your brothers. Ranjit is a man now, working and married to a lovely girl and Bilhar will be doing the same. Sikh girls, beautiful and pure. What is wrong with them? Tell me?"

I stared straight at the telly, trying to look right into the picture like there was something hidden behind it.

"And when you are Bilhar's age, you will do just the same."

His age? But he was only just seventeen. SEVENTEEN! That gave me four years. Four! The thought hit me like a brick. I hadn't even had a girlfriend, never mind thinking about a wife. And I had all these things that I was going to do. I was going to be a top striker for Liverpool and score the winning goals in a league and cup double. I was going to be the first Asian pop star and write a bestseller, go out with supermodels and win an Oscar and stuff. Loads of stuff. *Loads*. None of which included getting married at seventeen to some girl who I didn't know. I mean, what if she had a moustache like my Aunt Sukhjit? No way!

2 *belch:* rülpsen
5 *getting:* (here) get a
7 *bender* (sl): evening where you drink too much alcohol
8 *hangover:* illness after drinking too much alcohol
19 *goreh:* (Hindi, derog): white person
23 *filth:* dirt
26 *twist:* unexpected change
27 *Jat:* ethnic group living in Punjab
37 *striker:* footballer

Extract 2 (A year later)

Manny is walking around Leicester during the school holidays with his best friend Adrian ('Ady'), who is from a black British family originally from Jamaica.

We walked on up the road as all around us the hustle and bustle of cars, buses, customers and shopowners continued. I was playing a game that I had invented called 'spot the white man'. The whole area was about ninety per cent Asian. All the shops were owned by Asians apart from a fish restaurant, a couple of hairdressers and a florist. Most of the people on the street were Asian too, or black. It was one of the things that I loved about Leicester. Some areas were nearly all white, some black and some Asian. And everyone kind of melted into the city centre so that it was all multicultural. I liked that – it was the way it should be – only it wasn't the way that my family saw it, or even Ady's when it came down to it. We used to say all the time, Ady and me, that it was down to us kids to sort things out. I mean, I was born in England. I liked being born in England. It was my home. If you stuck me on the streets of Delhi or Mumbai I wouldn't have a clue what to do or where to go. In England I knew how things worked. Man, England was my country and Ady's. Ours. [...]

Cathedral in Leicester

As we walked Ady told me about a girl at school, Sarah, who wanted to go out with him. I didn't really know what to say about it, mainly because I didn't have a girlfriend – and I didn't really want one either. I'd never even considered asking a girl out. In the end, just to shut him up, I told him that he should go out with her, which made him grin. [...]

We were wandering up into Silver Street which led into a pedestrianised square when I saw Lisa for the first time. Ady pulled on my sleeve and pointed at two blonde girls who were walking towards us on the opposite pavement.

"That's her, man!" he said excitedly, pointing at the taller of the two. I was too busy looking at the other one. She was wicked. Long hair in ringlets, a deep tan and wearing three-quarter length black combats with a black vest top.

"That's Sarah."

"Who?" I asked, not really paying attention to him.

"Sarah, man. The girl from school."

"So who's the girl with her?" Man, I was in shock. I couldn't stop looking at her. And as they both passed by, they smiled. I mean it was obvious that we were just gawping at them.

"Dunno, my yout', but you check that smile she gave me? Man, I'm in there."

"They were smiling at me, bwoi. Not you."

"Yeah, right," Ady laughed. "Because they really loved your Bollywood bad boy looks, innit?"

We didn't see them again that afternoon, but somehow I had gone from not

9 *melt into sth.:* become part of sth. so that you can no longer be seen
13 *come down to sth.:* auf etwas hinauslaufen
28 *pedestrianised:* forbidden for cars
32 *wicked* (sl): very good
33 *combat:* trousers with a military style
vest top: shirt with no arms
41 *bwoi* (infml): friend, pal
43 *innit* (infml): (here) didn't they?

being sure about wanting a girlfriend to wanting the girl with the ringlets in her hair in the space of about five minutes.

Extract 3 (Five months later)

"I can't believe it took us so long to talk to each other properly."

Lisa looked across the table at me. We were having coffee in an Italian bar in town, on what must have been our tenth date. Ady and Sarah had been good to their word, introducing me to Lisa the week after I overheard them discussing my love life in Sarah's bedroom. We hit it off straight away when Sarah introduced us, because Lisa had been holding a copy of the same book that I was reading. Our first conversation was all about books that we'd both read and ones which we wanted to recommend to each other. I also found out that she was a mad keen Liverpool fan thanks to her mum who was from that city. Well, after that it was plain sailing.

"I wouldn't have known what to say anyway," I replied tapping my cup. Lisa smiled and pushed my hand away from the cup.

"That's so annoying. What's the matter, do I make you nervous?"

"No," I replied, really quickly before looking away.

"Is something wrong?" She looked concerned.

I started topping my cup again and sighed. "It's just this thing about not being able to have you over to my house because of my old man."

"Manny, I told you the other day, it's not a problem. My parents would have no problem with you coming over to mine. Sarah and Ady practically live there."

"What do they do – your mum and dad?"

"Mum's a teacher at a school out in Loughborough and Dad lectures at the university."

"In what?"

"It's a mix of sociology and cultural studies – really interesting stuff."

"I love all that kind of thing."

"Well you should meet my dad. He can talk for hours. I'm sure he'd love it if you were interested."

"I'd like that." I looked away again, hoping she wouldn't ask about my parents but she had other ideas. I thought about what I wanted to say about my old man and my mum, not wanting to give too much away but something about Lisa made me tell her things that I'd never told anyone else apart from Ady, and sometimes not even him. In the end it all came out in a flood. I told her about my old man and his ideas about culture and tradition. About how racist he was and what he thought of my friendship with Ady. When I told her about his threat to arrange my wedding she took hold of my hand and held it until I'd finished talking.

I went on about my mum and the way in which she was this person that I didn't really know. She never asked me anything and never got involved, as if she had learnt early on not to question my father, being a good Punjabi wife and taking a back seat to her husband. I told her that I thought my mum's life was quite sad and that I spent hours sometimes dreaming that I wasn't really my parents' child. We talked all about my brothers, too, and then I told her in more detail about what my old man had said to me about getting married at seventeen. And all the way through, she held my hand and listened in a way that no-one had ever listened to me before.

3 *be good to your word:* do as you promised
5 *hit it off straight away* (ifml): get along very well with sb.
9 *plain sailing:* very easy
10 *tap sth.:* make a regular pattern of sound

Extract 4 (Two weeks later)

About two weeks after the date in the coffee shop my cousin Ekbal and his mum and dad came round to see us. I was up in my room when they arrived and Ekbal came straight up. I was sitting on my bed when he walked in and immediately I could tell he wanted to ask me something.

"Hey, Manny, is it true?"

"Is what true?" I said, looking up from my book.

"About you getting married?"

"You what?" I raised an eyebrow at him, wondering what he was on about.

"My dad was just on about it on the way over."

"Eky, you ain't making sense, man. On about what?"

"He said that your dad has some girl lined up for you, from India, and that he wants to get you sorted out as soon as you leave school."

"He said something about it a while back but it wasn't anything serious. He just told me that was what he wanted me to do."

"Man, I can't believe that. My old man would never think like that."

"Well the old man can say what he likes. I ain't doing it anyway," I said with false bravado.

"Yeah, like he's gonna let you. Come on Manny, even my old man is wary of him.

"He's just traditional, that's all. When the time comes he'll just have to chill out. After all, it is three years away.

"Man, you can't do it. You'll end up like your brothers."

"No way, Eky."

"Seriously though, you need to tell him straight. You know, about how you want to go to Uni and that, and be a writer."

"He wouldn't listen, Eky. He'd just give me all that crap about being a good Punjabi."

"My old man's Punjabi but he ain't nothing like yours."

"Yeah, I know. All those liberal parents out there and I get stuck with him."

"Well, if you ever wanna talk about it, give me a call, man. You gotta make sure you don't crack under the pressure."

"I won't, Eky. Believe me."

It was only after Ekbal and his parents left that I allowed myself to really react to what he had told me. If my old man and my mum were going round telling people what they had planned for me, then they were deadly serious about it. I mean, they weren't going to lose face over it, not their precious *izzat* (honour). And if they were deadly serious then I was in big trouble. Up until then I had let the whole arranged marriage thing bother me but in the back of my mind I had always believed that they weren't serious about me having to do it at seventeen. And it was still a long way in the future. What Eky had just told me made me see the light as far as my old man's intentions for me were concerned. I realised that I was going to have to go for it if I wanted all the things out of life that I'd always dreamed of. And there was Lisa to think of too. I wasn't about to let them mess up my relationship with her. No way.

There was only one thing for it. I'd have to make myself as unsuitable as possible. What father-in-law in his right mind would want a thief and a smoker for a son-in-law?

[From: *(Un)arranged marriage* by Bali Rai, 2001]

11 *line sth. up:* organise sth.
12 *sort sb. out:* solve sb.'s problems
17 *bravado:* confident way of behaving
18 *wary of sb.:* careful when dealing with sb.
25 *crap:* nonsense
27 *ain't* (ifml): (here) isn't
42 *mess sth. up:* damage sth.
45 *father-in-law:* Schwiegervater

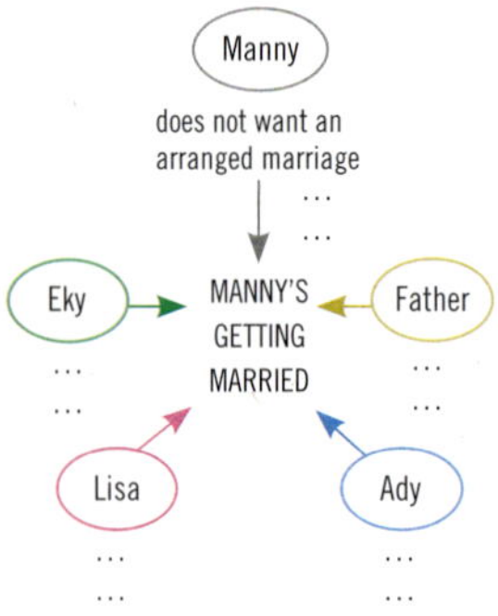

C Understanding the complete text

1. As a British Asian, Manny lives in two worlds. Point out which attitudes or which actions are more influenced by his Punjabi culture and which by his British culture.
2. In these extracts Rai introduces different characters that have different attitudes to Manny getting married. Draw a diagram that shows each character's function as regards Manny's marriage.

D Analysing the complete text

▶ Glossary 2.1

1. Characterisation

Writers can characterise people in two ways: either directly through what is said about them, or indirectly through how the characters behave, speak etc. Analyse the type of characterisation used in these extracts.

▶ Glossary 2.2.1

2. Telling the story

Writers can present their stories in two ways: They can tell what is happening or show what is happening through events, conversations etc. Analyse how Rai tells his story.

▶ Glossary 2.2.1, 3.2

3. The reader

Describe what kind(s) of reader the writer seems to have in mind. Analyse the means he uses to address his readership (think about the narrator, the style of language, the use of Punjabi words, the treatment of Punjabi culture, and the subject matter).

E Reacting to the complete text

Choose one of the following tasks.

1. There are several points in the story where it is possible to imagine conversations that are not actually in the text, e.g. between Manny and his mother (about his marriage), between Lisa and Sarah or her parents (about Manny), between Manny and Ady (about the talk with Lisa), between Manny and Lisa (about what Eky has told him). Choose one point and write the missing dialogue.
2. Thinking of the prologue and the last paragraph of Extract 4, speculate about what happens later in the book and how it might end.
3. Comment on the last sentence of the prologue.

IMPROVE YOUR WRITING Expressing an opinion

In your exams, you may be asked to express a personal opinion. Below are some useful phrases. Be careful also to remember the prepositions ('in', 'to' etc.)!

In my opinion, … / To my mind, … / From my point of view, …
I firmly believe that … / I am (totally) convinced that … / I am absolutely of the opinion that … / I am quite certain that …
I would (certainly) say that … / It seems to me that …
I am not at all convinced that … / I can't agree (at all) with people who say that … / I don't go along with the idea that … / The idea that … is totally wrong in my eyes. / I have to come down very firmly against the idea that …
I am somewhat undecided whether … / It seems to me that there are two sides to this argument. On the one hand, … On the other, … / I am afraid I have to sit on the fence on this / the idea that …

TOPIC 04

Finding a role in today's world

Speaking in 1962, Dean Acheson, one of America's most influential politicians at the time, famously said: 'Great Britain has lost an empire and not yet found a role.' In this topic, you are going to look at Britain's role in the world today and see whether the situation has changed since Acheson's speech.

Collect ideas

▶ Skills 2.2

1. Describe and analyse the cartoon: What idea is dealt with here, and how is it conveyed? (Tip: think of which countries are often represented by the eagle or the lion respectively).
2. Britain's role in the modern world depends on several factors. Work on the diagram below in small groups, collecting and adding ideas. You may have more questions than answers about some of the points. List these, too – you can find out more when you work on the topic. Report to the class at the end.

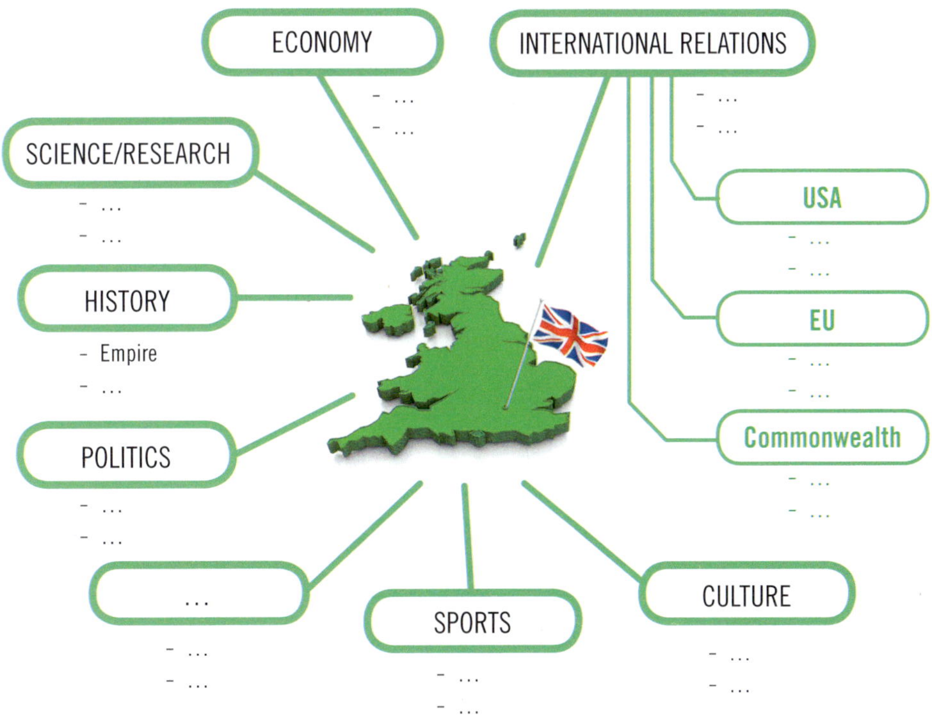

1 The Commonwealth (Videos)

Before you watch videos from the Commonwealth's official website, here is some information about this institution.

A Before you begin

Look at the map and the photo below. Collect and structure information about the Commonwealth that you already know and that you can deduce from the map and photo.

KEY FACTS The Commonwealth of Nations

The Commonwealth of Nations was officially created in 1949 as 'The British Commonwealth'.

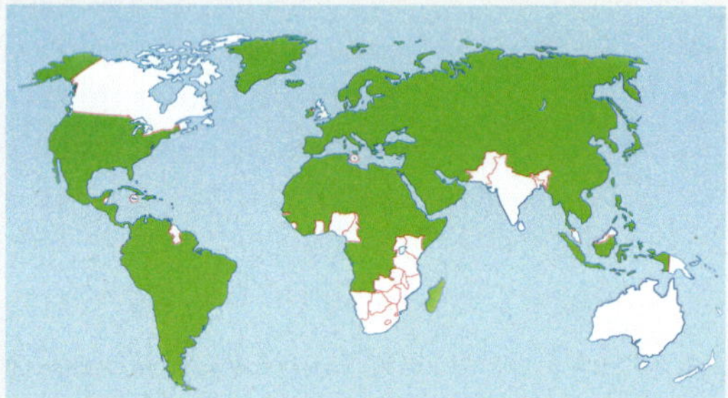

Even during the days of the British Empire, a difference developed between white settler colonies such as Canada, Australia and New Zealand and those colonies over which Britain ruled as a colonial power – India, for example. At the end of the 19th century, the white settler colonies became self-governing, although their Head of State was still the British monarch. After World War II, India became independent but also wanted to keep its links with Britain. To make this possible, the British Commonwealth was set up. Later, in the 1950s and 60s when other countries in the Empire also won their independence, they too joined the organisation. Today, the Commonwealth consists of 54 countries around the world. It is not a political union, but an intergovernmental organisation and it aims at promoting human rights, democracy, free trade and world peace. The British monarch is the head of the Commonwealth, but all the nations in it are independent and are free to leave if they wish. It does not, of course, include the USA.

Activities

▶ Activity chest 4

Use a 'Cheat sheet' to give an oral summary of the information in the KEY FACTS box.

B Watch the videos

DVD 9

1. Watch the first video called 'The Commonwealth family'. Sum up the main facts you learn about the Commonwealth.

▶ Skills 4

2. Describe the most important visual and sound techniques used in the video. Characterise the kind of audience the video seems to be addressing.

DVD 10

3. Watch the second video, which is also called 'The Commonwealth family', and compare it to the first video. Consider the information given, visual and sound techniques and the kind of viewer it is intended for.

2 London: a world city (A newspaper article)

With a population of more than 7.5 million, London is Europe's largest city. You are going to read an article about it from the *Times* newspaper.

A Before you read

Talk in class. Collect your ideas of London. Have you ever visited the city? What were your impressions?

A couple of years ago, a friend of mine bought a one bedroom flat in Chalcot Square in Primrose Hill, London NW1. He paid £480,000 — just less than one million dollars. As I was living in the States at the time and flabbergasted by the price, he explained: "Chalcot Square is the best place in Primrose Hill, which is the nicest part of London, which is the coolest city on earth." Location, location, location. "This is the best property on the planet." [...]

Why? Because London is, indeed, the coolest city on earth. The capital of the world. New York, like Paris, has become a mini-break destination, a playground for grown-ups who enjoy the same standard tourist menu: a walk around Central Park; a shopping trip in SoHo; an entertaining, if unsurprising, show on Broadway; and a very large steak.

The world loves a long weekend in New York but, these days, prefers to make its home in London. New York has the nostalgia, London the future. New York defines the metropolitan, London the cosmopolitan.

And the reason for this is that foreigners in New York are, always, just that. The city treats even its long-term residents from abroad as visitors [...].

"New York is always American," says Bill Roedy, the American who has spent the past 15 years in the UK running MTV world-wide. "Like Paris is French, Moscow is Russian, New York is American." London, on the other hand, is passport-blind. It does not have the luxury of being the de facto capital of a continental economy. So, it is international: it treats its visitors as citizens, as players. [...]

In business terms, London's claim to be the world's favourite marketplace is not just a boast, it's a statistic: in the past five years international companies have not been choosing to list on the New York stock exchanges but to float their businesses in London. In 2001 the US accounted for 57 per cent of all stock market floatations over $1 billion — otherwise known as initial public offerings (IPOs). By 2006 this had fallen to 16 per cent. In the same period, Europe's share of the world's big IPOs had risen from 33 per cent to 63 per cent. Small companies as well as big ones have been choosing London. [...]

But more than these technicalities, what matters is geography: London is the centre of the world. From London it is possible to work a normal day and talk to Tokyo in the morning and Los Angeles in the afternoon. A businessman can get on a plane from Moscow and be in London in five hours, from Bombay in seven, even from Beijing in nine. This is one of the reasons why, over the past 25 years, London

5 *flabbergasted:* very surprised
8 *location:* place where sth. is
9 *property:* (here) house or flat that you own
15 *SoHo:* district in New York with many shops and bars
18 *metropolitan:* way of living in a big city
cosmopolitan: way of living anywhere in the world
25 *de facto:* tatsächlich
29 *boast* (n): exaggerated claim
30 *list sth. on a stock exchange:* start selling shares in your business
float your business: start selling shares in your business
31 *stock market floatation:* Börseneinführung
33 *share* (n): part of sth. that you own

has turned itself into an international marketplace while New York has remained essentially a domestic financial capital.

The other factor is history. Since the late 1970s London, once the capital of a trading empire, has transformed itself into the hub of the foreign exchange markets. It became the place for European companies to borrow money, the home of the Eurobond.

And in the past decade it has extended itself beyond the Continent to companies from India, Russia and China. [...]

London has qualities: geography, history, culture and, more than that, a grudging embrace of all comers. Within a short walk from Trellik Tower in West London you can find a coffee, a cheese sandwich and a custard pie from Lisbon that make you feel as though you are in a provincial Portuguese café, and you can eat a plate of steamed dumplings from the Royal China that would satisfy a discerning Shanghainese. [...].

A weekend in London is like a world's greatest hits of city living: an English breakfast at Tom's on Westbourne Grove, a morning spent browsing vintage Americana on Portobello Road, an afternoon watching the best French footballers at Arsenal, Chekhov at the Royal Court or Puccini at the English National Opera.

[...]

It's hard to say which personality, New Yorker or Londoner, is preferable – the ballsy versus the stoic, the gruff versus the curmudgeonly, the sharp-tongued versus the quick-witted. But the real difference between the two is this: New Yorkers come from the five boroughs; Londoners from the five continents. They are Poles, Pakistanis, Brazilians, Americans, Nigerians and more. There are, it is said, 300 languages spoken in London.

[From: *Times online*, 13 March 2007]

44 *hub:* centre
exchange market: Devisenmarkt
46 *Eurobond:* Art internationaler Anleihen
49 *grudging:* done unwillingly
50 *embrace* (n): Umarmung
53 *steamed dumpling:* gedämpfter Kloß
discerning: anspruchsvoll

B Understanding the text

▶ Activity chest 12

1. Work in groups with a 'Placemat', then share your ideas in class.
- Look at each paragraph of the text and identify its main idea. List in your own words the reasons used by the author to support his opinion.
- State in one sentence the author's overall opinion of London.

2. Write an answer to one of the following questions. Be very careful to include only the aspects that are relevant for your specific task.
a Outline the writer's view of London as a world city.
b Compare London and New York as they are presented in this article.

C Analysing the text

▶ Skills 7.4

Read through the **SPOTLIGHT** box, then analyse the text about London:
- identify its topic and analyse how the author tries to get the reader's attention;
- examine the structure of the text;
- show how the writer makes his conclusion memorable;
- identify the supporting ideas he uses;
- analyse his use of stylistic means.

SPOTLIGHT ON Argumentative texts

Argumentative texts are among the non-fictional text types that you will often meet during your course. They are common in newspapers, magazines and academic papers. In an argumentative text, the writer's aim is to put forward an opinion and to argue that it is the correct view of something. A well-written argumentative text will convince the reader of the writer's viewpoint – or at least give the reader some interesting ideas with which to form their own opinion.

Techniques used in argumentative texts

1. *Introducing the topic*. The writer highlights an idea (or a problem) at the beginning of the text to arouse the reader's interest. This allows the reader to focus clearly on what the writer will say in the text.
2. *Clear structure and conclusion*. The writer writes as clearly as possible – using paragraphs to structure ideas – and ends with a conclusion or final paragraph which leaves the reader with a lasting idea of what the writer has said. All of this allows the reader to follow the argument and to remember what the writer wants to stress.

▶ Glossary 3.1

3. *Supporting ideas*. The writer must convince the reader, so it is important that there are concrete facts in the text to support his / her ideas. These can be statistics, quotes from experts, or generally agreed facts. The effect is that the text is believable and authoritative.
4. *Rhetorical devices*. Writers of argumentative texts may use many stylistic devices, e.g. rhetorical questions, repetition, imagery, antithesis, exaggeration, understatement, enumeration, etc. The effect of such devices is to make ideas clearer, more striking and more memorable for readers – and to hold their interest as they read.

USEFUL PHRASES FOR ANALYSING AN ARGUMENTATIVE TEXT	
The text is an example of an argumentative text.	
The writer's aim/intention/objective (in the text)	is to …
In order to do this,	the writer …
For example,	in the first paragraph / in line … , he/she …
Another device the author uses is …	
In paragraph …,	we can see a further way in which the writer …
The effect of … on the reader	is …

✕ **Spotlight task** Think of a topic that might be controversial. It could be related to London, e.g. the city as a media centre (the BBC, newspapers), the 2012 Olympics, the history of the city, tourism in London, etc. Collect and structure arguments, then write an argumentative text.

D Reacting to the text

▶ Skills 7.1

Work in pairs. Imagine one of you wants to go to New York on holiday, the other to London. Collect arguments, then act out a dialogue in which you have to agree on one place to visit.

- I'd love to … / I really want to see … / People say that … / What about you? / What do you think?
- I'm not so sure. / I don't think so. / I'm afraid … / OK, but listen to my idea.
- No way! / Well, actually, I … / I really don't agree that … / I've heard bad things about …
- Oh? I didn't know that … / Would you be happier if …? / Have you got a better idea?
- OK. I like your idea. / You've got a point there. / Great idea! / You've won me over! / Ah, I see.
- It's decided! We'll go to … / It's a difficult decision, but … / So you agree? We're going to …

3 Britain and Europe (An extract from an essay)

You are going to work with different materials on the relationship between Britain and the EU.

A Before you read

Every year, the EU surveys people's attitudes within the EU and produces a report called *Eurobarometer*. On the right, you can see some selected results for one of the questions from a recent report (autumn 2009).

1. Say what the results show about the UK's attitude towards the EU.
2. Speculate about the reasons.

✕ **Extra** Produce a bar chart of the results and write a short text to explain the graph.

(OUR COUNTRY)'s membership of the European Union is a good thing. Agree:	
EU 27	53%
Sweden	57%
Finland	51%
Ireland	72%
Austria	42%
Spain	64%
The Netherlands	74%
United Kingdom	30%
Poland	61%
Germany	60%
Belgium	64%
Luxembourg	74%
Italy	49%
France	49%

[From: *Eurobarometer* 72, 2009]

KEY FACTS Britain and Europe

General de Gaulle: 'Non!'

In 1957 the European Economic Community (EEC) or 'Common Market', the predecessor of the European Union, was founded by Belgium, France, Italy, Luxembourg, the Netherlands, and West Germany. Britain was not a member. Britain had strong ties with Commonwealth countries, with which it traded, and was suspicious of a union in which it felt it would lose its independence and its national identity. By 1961, however, it was clear to Britain that it could not remain isolated outside of Europe: the economies of the new Common Market countries were growing while that of Britain was declining. It applied for membership in 1961 and again in 1963. Both times, its application was vetoed by the French president General de Gaulle. De Gaulle was afraid that the US might gain too much influence on the common market through Britain. Only in 1973, after General de Gaulle had resigned, did Britain officially become a member of the European Community under the Conservative Prime Minister Edward Heath. Two years later, a referendum was held in the UK asking people if they wished to remain in the Common Market. 67% voted 'yes'. However, Britain has never introduced the Euro as its currency – a decision that is supported by the majority of Britons.

Activities

1. Based on information from the Key Facts and your own research make a timeline of the member states of the EEC/EU and the dates when they joined.
2. Collect the main arguments for Britain in favour of and against EEC membership. Characterise the kinds of reasons – e.g. economic, …

In this text, Charles Grant, a respected UK journalist and expert on the EU, examines British attitudes towards Europe.

When I travel around Europe, and people ask me why the British are eurosceptic, I offer four explanations – three of which are easily understood. The first of these is geography and the effect it has had on British history. The British people live on an island on the edge of the continent and have always been inspired by the oceans. The British talk of Europe as another place (as the Finns, Irish and Portuguese sometimes do). Britain's history has been very different to that of most continental powers. Its colonies, trade, investments and patterns of emigration and immigration have been focused on North and South America, Africa and Asia as much as on Europe. To some extent France, Holland, Spain and Portugal shared this maritime experience, while the other European states sought to build empires or wield influence mainly in their neighbourhoods. Although Britain has been involved in countless European wars, its history has been more orientated to other continents than that of any continental power. Even France, which had colonies all over the world, has focused its ambitions on Europe for much of its history.

Today, London is by far the most cosmopolitan city in Europe; more than 30 per cent of its population was born outside the UK. Although a little more than half of Britain's merchandise trade is now with the rest of the EU, many Britons believe that their country would flourish as a global hub for trade and investment, outside the EU, unencumbered by the rules and regulations of Brussels. Churchill famously told de Gaulle that, faced with a choice between the continent and *le grand large*, the British would always choose the wide open seas.

Britain's relatively glorious role in the Second World War plays a potent role in nourishing euroscepticism. Virtually every other major European nation has something to be ashamed of in that war. A lot of countries were on the wrong side. Others were conquered. And others stayed neutral. British popular culture is still

8 *pattern:* Muster
11 *wield sth:* use sth.
18 *merchandise trade:* Warenhandel
19 *flourish:* become successful, grow
hub: centre
20 *unencumbered by:* free from
22 *le grand large* (French): the open ocean
24 *nourish sth.:* make sth. grow

heavily focused on the Second World War as the country's 'finest hour'. Other countries have moved on, and supported the EU as means of ensuring that the horrors of the Nazi period can never be repeated. But the British do not want to forget the history of which they feel proud. Memories of the war give them a smug sense of moral superiority vis-à-vis most of the other peoples of Europe. Margaret Thatcher often said that the continent of Europe has been the source of most of Britain's ills, and that the Anglo-Saxon nations, and in particular the Americans, have repeatedly rescued Britain from those ills. Many Britons, especially the older generation, would agree with her.

In addition to geography and history, economics helps to explain British euroscepticism. Since the mid-1990s, the UK economy has outperformed the leading economies of Western Europe – France, Germany and Italy – by most measures. Britain has had relatively high growth and low unemployment. Its economy has some evident weaknesses, such as quite poor productivity. But Britain has appeared to benefit from the structural reforms of the Thatcher period, such as the liberalisation of labour markets, the openness to foreign investment and – though this is now open to some challenge – the fostering of vibrant financial markets. [...]

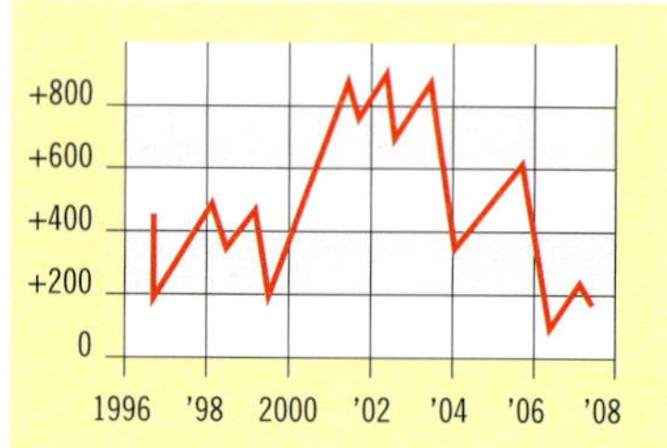

The fourth explanation for Britain's hostility to the EU, which is not easily understood outside the UK, is that Britain has a uniquely powerful and eurosceptic popular press. Ironically, some of the best media organisations that cover the EU, such as the *Financial Times, The Economist and Reuters*, are UK-based. But of the roughly 30 million people who read a daily newspaper in Britain, three-quarters read papers that are determined to make people dislike the EU. The remaining quarter read papers which, though broadly pro-European, still print much that criticises the EU. In the eurosceptic newspaper groups, journalists are expected to write stories that knock the Union. Articles which attempt to present a balanced account of an EU issue are unlikely to be published. *The Times* and the *Daily Telegraph*, two serious newspapers, almost never print an opinion piece that is supportive of the EU or what it is trying to do.

[From: *Why is Britain eurosceptic?*, 2008]

30 *smug:* arrogant
31 *vis-à-vis* (French): gegenüber
33 *ills* (pl): problems
37 *outperform sth./sb.:* be more successful than sb./sth.
39 *measure:* Maß
41 *evident:* easy to see
44 *Thatcher = Margaret Thatcher:* British Prime Minister 1979–1990
46 *foster sth.:* make sth. grow
56 *knock sb./sth.:* criticise sth.

B Understanding the text

1. Grant begins by saying he will give four reasons why Britain is eurosceptic. Name them and illustrate them in a few sentences in your own words.
2. Say whether the following statements are true or false.
   a Among the four reasons for British euroscepticism only one is easy to understand.
   b Just like Britain, countries such as Holland or Portugal also sought contact with countries overseas.
   c Britons are eurosceptic because they don't think that the EU will be able to prevent another Nazi regime.
   d According to the text, the Thatcher period helped the British economy.
   e There are no real pro-European newspapers in Britain.

C Analysing the text

▶ Skills 1.2.2
▶ Glossary 1.1

Analyse in how far this text is an argumentative text.

D Reacting to the text

Talk in class. Discuss how easy it is for you as a young European – and especially as a German – to understand Britain's attitude to Europe as described in this essay. How would you characterise the attitudes of British people as outlined in the text?

IMPROVE YOUR WRITING ▶ Using varied adjectives

Adjectives play an important part in producing a good written text. Having a store of varied adjectives enables you to express your ideas more interestingly and clearly.

1. The adjectives below could all be used to describe the aspects of Britain and the character of its people as described in the text above. Make sure you know their meaning, then find the missing words in the sentences below.
   proud – defiant – arrogant – traditionalist – self-reliant – backward-looking – superior – critical – isolated – independent – egoistic – sceptical – reactionary – sceptical – nihilistic – competitive – biased.
   a. *The British are exaggerating their role in WWII. I think they're (?).*
   b. *I like the way in which they concentrate on the good things they've achieved. They are very (?) of themselves.*
   c. *The article shows that British identity is shaped also by their past. They are a very (?) country.*
   d. *The British seem to think they are (?) to other nations because of their role in WWII.*
   e. *Britain misses out on all the good things happening in Europe because they are so (?) from it.*
2. Some pairs of adjectives may refer to the same objective fact, but express different attitudes towards that fact:
   a traditionalist person = person who values things from the past;
   a backward-looking person = person who seems to have lost contact with the present.
   Make pairs from the list above.

4 Britain's future role in the world (A web article)

You are going to read an extract from an article by the German journalist Jürgen Krönig in which he discusses Britain's future role in the world.

A Before you read

Discuss in class the picture on the right. Describe the situation and explain what aspect of modern Britain is illustrated.

Britain has to define a new, more modest role for herself. The UK can no longer continue "punching above her weight"; to use Douglas Hurd's way of describing the role she played in the past 30 years. One could argue that with the world-wide financial and economic crisis which erupted in 2007 a "mini golden age" came to an end. In this period a confident, more and more prosperous Britain, in alliance with the American superpower, was a global player with significant influence, underlined by a permanent seat in the UN Security Council, an independent nuclear deterrent and some of the best troops anywhere, experienced and regularly exercised in many parts of the world. The government in London did not even, in theory at least, need parliament to agree with a decision to send troops abroad. (Compare this with the German situation, in which even clear-cut battlefield decisions, which should be decided by officers in the field – asking for aerial support for troops on the ground, for example – are subject to lengthy parliamentary debates and majority votes).

The flow of oil from the North Sea and the relentless rise of the financial industries underpinned the special political status of the UK. Until 2007 these economic factors helped to deliver rising income for the government, which was used in the last 13 years to pump ever more money into the NHS, schools and welfare.

All this provided Britain with a special status among middle-sized European states. Tony Blair used these favourable conditions to define and argue for liberal interventionism in Kosovo, Bosnia, Sierra Leone and later on in Iraq and Afghanistan. In one of his last speeches as prime minister he warned the nation it would have to decide which role it would like to play in the world in the future, otherwise Britain would, "by default", end up in the "second league."

It seems that the financial crisis has taken the decision for the British: the state and the private sector are highly indebted, and it will take years to reduce and pay off the debt. The economy has shrunk in size. The country has become a net importer of oil and gas. Even when it recovers the financial industry will hardly be as big as it was before the crisis. Spending on the armed forces will be slashed. It is no coincidence that in the last months of the Brown government there was talk of possible military cooperation with France, a possibility also mentioned briefly during the first year of Tony Blair's government, but it never came to anything. Now even Trident, the independent nuclear deterrent, seems to be too expensive to keep, although both Conservatives and Labour, in contrast to the Liberal democrats, for the time being are determined not to give up this status symbol.

1 *modest:* bescheiden
2 *punch above your weight:* (in boxing) take on an opponent that is heavier than you
Douglas Hurd: British politician
8 *nuclear deterrent:* atom bombs used as a threat
13 *aerial support:* military planes to support ground troops
15 *relentless:* without stopping
16 *underpin sth.:* underline sth., emphasise sth.
18 *NHS = National Health Service:* British health system
22 *liberal interventionism:* doctrine which suggests democratic countries intervene in non-democratic countries
25 *by default:* as a natural reaction
27 *indebted:* verschuldet
28 *net importer:* country that imports more than it exports
30 *slash sth.:* reduce sth.
31 *Brown = Gordon Brown:* British Prime Minister 2007–10
33 *Tony Blair:* British Prime Minister 1997–2007

38 *hedonistic:* wanting fun or pleasure
41 *entail sth.:* have sth. as a consequence
44 *overdue:* later than it should have been
shift (n): *change*
45 *occur:* happen
devolution: act of giving more power to smaller political organisations
46 *electoral reform:* Wahlrechtsreform
fixed term parliament: parliament that is elected at regular intervals
47 *akin to sth.:* similar to sth.
48 *evolve:* develop

The British nation itself has changed as well: it has become more emotional, hedonistic and entertainment-driven than before, and more "post-heroic", a bit like the Germans and other continental European nations. To be sure the nation might have turned anyhow against continuing to play a role in world affairs that unavoidably would at some stage entail military engagements in far corners of the world. [...]

One may regret this development as a weakening of a proud nation state, or greet it as change which was overdue. What can't be denied is that a dramatic shift has occurred. Perhaps Britain is now getting a political system, including devolution, electoral reform, coalition governments and fixed term parliaments, which reflects her changed, post-imperial reality – a political system much more akin to the one that evolved in Germany after the war, which was underpinned by a desire to avoid a strong, powerful central government.

[From: www.policy-network.net, 25 June 2010]

B Understanding the text

1. Copy and complete the table below with Krönig's ideas from the text.

BRITAIN IN THE PAST	RECENT CHANGES
– *'mini golden age' (ll. 4–5)* – ...	– ... – ...

2. Sum up what the author says about Britain's future role.

C Analysing the text

▶ Glossary 1.1

1. Identify the text type of the article and support your answer with examples from the text.
2. Outline the kind of reader Krönig may have in mind. Illustrate how this affects the way he writes his article.

D Reacting to the text

Work with a partner. Jürgen Krönig has been invited by the BBC to give an interview about his view – as a German journalist – of Britain today. Write an interview and present it to the class. One of you is Krönig, the other a BBC interviewer. The phrases below will help you.

INTERVIEWER	INTERVIEWEE
– (Introducing a guest) ... is a German journalist based in London who ... – Welcome to the programme, ... – Can I begin by asking you ...? – I'd like to go on now to talk about ... – Could you explain a little what you mean by that? / Could you give an example? – In your opinion, would you say that / agree that ...? – So you're saying that ... – Thanks very much for coming on the programme today.	– It's nice to be here, thank you. – OK, well, ... – Certainly. ... – What I mean by that is ... – Yes, I would generally agree with that. – No, that's not really what I think. – Yes, that sums up my ideas very well. – Can I just add that ...? – I think it's important to stress that ... – The other point I'd like to make is ... – Thank you. It was a pleasure.

SEQUENCE

02

NORTH AMERICAN DREAMS

The North American experience has often been told through stories of presidents and powerful people. But a look at North America, that is the United States and Canada, must also include those millions of 'normal' Americans who built those countries – and those for whom the North American Dream was sometimes more of a nightmare. In this sequence we look at how these countries were born and at the hopes and ideals that have shaped them.

1

Collect ideas

1. Talk in class. In what ways might a country – like the United States or Canada – represent a dream for someone?

▶ Skills 2.1

2. Study the pictures on pp. 62 and 63 and fill in a 'K-W-L chart' like the one below. For each picture make notes on what you already know (K) about what is shown and what relevance the picture has for our topic. Then formulate questions to find out what you want to know (W) about each of the pictues.

Picture No	**K** (I know)	**W** (I want to know)	**L** (I learned)
1			
2			
3			
4			

▶ Skills 7.4

3. Adopt-a-picture: work in groups of three or four.
   a Choose one of the pictures, research what it depicts and present your findings to the class. Make your presentation as interesting as you can.
   b Listen to the presentations and complete the L-section of your K-W-L chart.

The picture shows / In the picture you can see … The caption reads … The picture stands for / symbolises / illustrates …	the Statue … / a row of … / horse-drawn wagons / a water fountain with a sign reading … a sense of freedom / … the exclusion of / discrimination against / frontier spirit
I would like to find out more about … I (re)discovered … I was surprised to hear/learn … I now realize …	

4. This sequence is called 'North American Dreams'. Write a short text describing in what way the pictures are related to this topic.

TOPIC 01

The USA: the making of a nation

1 Free and independent states (An extract from a historical document)

Long after the first settlers had arrived in North America, they continued to live in a colony governed by Great Britain. Around the middle of the 18th century, however, the colonies began to revolt against British rule. You are going to read an excerpt from the American Declaration of Independence, which was written in 1776 and which put an end to the British rule over the American colonies.

A Before you read

One of the key events in the development of the USA was the British colonies' independence from Great Britain. Which other key events can you remember between the arrival of the first settlers in North America and independence?

1. Match the events to the dates in the timeline and explain them.

1607 | 1620 | 1754 | 1765 | 1775 | 1776 | 1789

A. British Parliament imposes new taxes; colonists protest bitterly.
B. First permanent settlement is founded at Jamestown, Virginia.
C. George Washington is elected first President of United States.
D. Pilgrims land at Plymouth, Massachusetts.
E. Second Continental Congress adopts Declaration of Independence.
F. The American Revolution begins.
G. War between the British and the French begins.

2. Summarise in a few sentences the historical development of the United States between 1607 and 1789.

Writing the Declaration of Independence

When, in the course of human events, it becomes necessary for one people to dissolve the political bands which have connected them with another, and to assume among the powers of the earth, the separate and equal station to which the laws of nature and of nature's God entitle them, a decent respect to the opinions of mankind requires that they should declare the causes which impel them to the separation.

1 *in the course of sth.:* im Verlauf von etwas
2 *band:* connection, link
4 *station:* status
6 *impel sb. to (do) sth.:* force sb. to (do) sth.

8 *endow sb. with sth.:* give sb. sth.
unalienable (old use) = inalienable [ɪn'eɪliənəbl] (fml): that cannot be taken away
9 *pursuit of sth.* [pə'sjuːt] (fml): act of trying to achieve sth
10 *institute sth.* ['- - -] (fml): introduce sth., esp. a policy or a system
derive sth. from sb.: get sth. from sb.
consent [-'-] (n): agreement
11 *end* (n): purpose
12 *alter sth.:* change sth.
15 *prudence:* careful forethought
16 *transient:* lasting for a short time
hath (old-fashioned) = has
17 *disposed:* willing
right yourself: put yourself in the right position
19 *abuse* (n): bad treatment
usurpation [ˌjuːzɜː'peɪʃn] (fml): act of taking possession of a position of power without the right to do so
evince sth. (fml): show clearly that you have sth.
20 *design:* plan, intention
despotism: ruling of a country with cruelty.

We hold these truths to be self-evident, that all men are created equal, that they are endowed by their Creator with certain unalienable rights, that among these are life, liberty and the pursuit of happiness. That to secure these rights, governments are instituted among men, deriving their just powers from the consent of the governed. That whenever any form of government becomes destructive to these ends, it is the right of the people to alter or to abolish it, and to institute new government, laying its foundation on such principles and organizing its powers in such form, as to them shall seem most likely to effect their safety and happiness. Prudence, indeed, will dictate that governments long established should not be changed for light and transient causes; and accordingly all experience hath shown that mankind are more disposed to suffer, while evils are sufferable, than to right themselves by abolishing the forms to which they are accustomed. But when a long train of abuses and usurpations, pursuing invariably the same object, evinces a design to reduce them under absolute despotism, it is their right, it is their duty, to throw off such government, and to provide new guards for their future security. Such has been the patient sufferance of these colonies; and such is now the necessity which constrains them to alter their former systems of government. The history of the present King of Great Britain is a history of repeated injuries and usurpations, all having in direct object the establishment of an absolute tyranny over these states.

B Understanding the text

Summarise the text by putting the following sentences in the correct order.

A	Until recently, the American colonies have suffered quietly, but now the time has come to change their system of government.
B	It is every government's duty to protect its citizens' god-given rights and if a government fails to do so, the people have the right to change or abolish that government.
C	Governments should only be changed or abolished for good reasons.
D	The American colonies have often complained about their unfair treatment by Great Britain, but the British king has not in any way changed his way of dealing with the colonies.
E	If a people feels the necessity to cut its ties to another country, it is a sign of respect to declare the reasons for this decision.
F	History has shown that people tend to suffer very long before they decide to change their situation. But if sufferings become too severe, it is a people's right, even its duty to make such changes.
G	The writers believe that all human beings are equal and that they have a god-given right to life, liberty and the pursuit of happiness.

C Analysing the text

▶ Skills 1.2.2

1. Analyse Jefferson's line of argumentation. Consider especially:
   - why he points out human rights before describing the colonists' situation;
   - what evidence he cites to support his points.

✕ **Extra** The period in which this document was written is often referred to as the Age of Reason because of the emphasis on logic and discipline at the time. Assess how the Declaration of Independence reflects a faith in reason.

▶ Skills 2.1

D Reacting to the text

1. Have a look at the painting on p. 64, which shows the writing of the Declaration of Independence. Describe the painting and analyse the impression it creates of this historical moment.
2. Jefferson's biographer Joseph Ellis says,

   '[…] the 55 words of the *Declaration of Independence* that begin "We hold these truths to be self-evident, that all men are created equal," are probably the most important words in American history – and possibly all of modern history, as they continue to inspire the dream of freedom of people everywhere.'

   Comment on this statement.
3. Work in groups and discuss the following questions:
   - What motivates peoples to declare their independence?
   - Which people in the world today want more independence?
   - What are they doing to achieve it?

KEY FACTS The Bill of Rights

In 1791, fifteen years after the Declaration of Independence, another key document in American history came into effect: the Bill of Rights. It contained ten 'amendments' to the basic constitution – additions to it that were felt necessary to build the country and its democracy. It protects the individual's rights, e.g. the rights of life, liberty and property, and thus limits the power of the US government.
Like the Declaration of Independence and the Constitution, the Bill of Rights has not only served Americans well but has also been employed as a guide for democracies around the world to define the relationships between citizens, their governments and the rule of law. Many of the hot issues that divide Americans in the 21st century are addressed in this document, which is now more than two centuries old.

Activities

1. Talk in class. Collect ideas about the kind of 'rights' you might expect to find in a document like this.
2. Do research on the Bill of Rights and find out about the ten amendments. Sum them up in your own words.
3. Talk again in class. Did any of the rights surprise you? Could you imagine any of them causing problems today?

2 Europeans and Americans (A public letter)

The man who invented the now famous description of America as a 'melting pot' was a French immigrant, a farmer called Jean de Crèvecoeur. In 1782 he wrote a book of 'open letters' about his new life. You are going to read an excerpt from his book.

A Before you read

1. Talk in class. Look at the picture. Speculate about some of the things Crèvecoeur might write about in his letters, bearing in mind his situation.
2. The text contains the following key words that have to do with 'the American':

dependence – European – idleness – labour – mixture – prejudice – prince – religion – rewards

Make one sentence with each word, defining its relationship to 'the American'.

The American's … He might be called … His relationship to …	might be seen in his … in that he … can be described as …

… might refer to 'the American' … is expected of 'the American' … would not be considered a positive trait of 'the American' 'The American' might receive …	because (he) … despite his … if … for

What attachment can a poor European emigrant have for a country where he had nothing? The knowledge of the language, the love of a few kindred as poor as himself, were the only cords that tied him: his country is now that which gives him land, bread, protection, and consequence: *Ubi panis ibi patria*, is the motto of all emigrants. What then is the American, this new man? He is either a European, or the descendant of an European; hence that strange mixture of blood, which you will find in no other country. I could point out to you a man, whose grandfather was an Englishman, whose wife was Dutch, whose son married a French woman, and whose present four sons have now four wives of different nations. *He* is an American, who, leaving behind him all his ancient prejudices and manners, receives new ones from the new mode of life he has embraced, the new government he obeys, and the new rank he holds. He becomes an American by being received in the broad lap of our great Alma Mater.

Here individuals of all nations are melted into a new race of men, whose labours and posterity will one day cause great change in the world. Americans are the western pilgrims, who are carrying along with them that great mass of arts, sciences, vigour, and industry, which began long since in the East; they will finish the great circle. The Americans were once scattered all over Europe; here they are incorporated into one of the finest systems of population which has ever appeared, and which will hereafter become distinct by the power of the different climates they inhabit. The American ought, therefore, to love this country much better than that wherein either he or his forefathers were born. Here the rewards of his industry follow with equal steps the progress of his labour; his labour is founded

3 *kindred:* family member
cord: Band
4 *Ubi panis ibi patria* (Latin): Where there is bread, there is my country
6 *descendant:* Nachfahre
11 *ancient* ['eɪnʃənt]: very old
12 *embrace sth.:* (here) accept sth.
13 *lap:* Schoß
Alma Mater (Latin): nourishing mother
14 *labour:* hard work
15 *posterity* (fml): all the people who will live later
17 *vigour:* energy
industry: quality of being hard-working
finish the great circle: (here) move to the west like the sun
22 *forefather:* family member who lived long before you

24 *allurement:* attraction
25 *in vain:* vergeblich
26 *frolicsome:* enthusiastic and playful
whence (old-fashioned): from where
exuberant [ɪg'zju:bərənt]: plentiful
28 *abbot:* head of a monastery (= Kloster)
31 *involuntary:* unwanted
idleness: inactivity
32 *servile:* eager to obey and serve
penury ['penjəri]: poverty
toil (n): very hard work
33 *ample subsistence* [səb'sɪstəns]: state of having more than enough

on the basis of nature, self-interest; can it want a stronger allurement? Wives and children, who before in vain demanded of him a morsel of bread, now, fat and frolicsome, gladly help their father to clear those fields whence exuberant crops are to arise to feed and to clothe them all; without any part being claimed, either by a despotic prince, a rich abbot, or a mighty lord. Here religion demands but little of him; a small voluntary salary to the minister, and gratitude to God; can he refuse these? The American is a new man, who acts upon new principles; he must therefore entertain new ideas, and form new opinions. From involuntary idleness, servile dependence, penury, and useless labour, he has passed to toils of a very different nature, rewarded by ample subsistence. This is an American.

[From: *Letters from an American Farmer by Jean de Crèvecoeur*, 1782]

B Understanding the text

1. Working as a pair, answer the following questions. There should be one set of answers between you, but both of you should be able to substantiate your answers.
   a Why does Crèvecoeur assume Europeans have no attachment to the countries they have just left?
   b How does the American population differ from that of Europe?
   c What character traits does Crèvecoeur hold up as being both typically American and admirable?
   d In what ways does Crèvecoeur believe the world will be affected by Americans?
   e What reasons might have motivated an eighteenth-century European to relocate to the United States?

▶ Skills 1.1, Step 2

2. In your own words, summarise Crèvecoeur's definition of an American.
3. Go back to your results to A. Which of your ideas were correct, which weren't?

C Analysing the text

▶ Glossary 3

Crèvecoeur calls the texts in his collection 'letters'. Point out Crèvecoeur's aims and examine how he has tried to achieve them. Think especially about his language and style, how he contrasts Americans and Europeans, which rhetorical devices (e.g. alliteration) he uses and how they affect the reader.

D Reacting to the text

1. Compare the hopes and dreams of immigrants in the 18th century to those which immigrants to the United States might have today.
2. Crèvecoeur was the first writer to use the image of a melting pot (cf. l. 14). Describe this image and its consequences for immigrants, their identity and their way of becoming part of their new society.

✕ **Extra** Imagine that you are living in Europe in 1782 and have read Crèvecoeur's letter. Write (in modern English, of course) a letter to him describing your reactions to it. Would it maybe encourage you to emigrate to America yourself? Why (not)?

3 Moving west (A first-hand account)

Around 60 years after independence, the United States extended from the East Coast, where the original colonies had been, to as far west as the Mississippi River, and people began moving further westwards to settle the rest of the country. You are going to read a first-hand account by a young woman who was one of those who made the journey.

KEY FACTS Moving west

Throughout American history, the frontier as a place or an idea was constantly changing. Westward movement lasted for more than 300 years, from the founding of the first settlement in Jamestown in 1607 until settlers crossed the continent and reached the Pacific Ocean.

First came the expeditions, whose aim was to explore and map the West. Businessmen followed. Seeking trade with the Native Americans, the mountain men, the Spanish in the Southwest and the English in the Northwest, these men were the next link in the opening of the West. By the 1840s large segments of the American population began to move westward. To most, the frontier provided hope for the future. The seemingly endless lands and resources of the west were only waiting to be utilised. Pioneers sought to improve social and economic conditions, but many also considered conquering the continent as a patriotic duty. All of them felt they had a right to settle the land, that this was a natural development – referred to as 'Manifest Destiny'.

However, this westward expansion collided with the way the Native Americans used their land. To them, the vast open territories were necessary to maintain traditions of hunting and migration, while the settlers wished to settle and to build permanent towns. Though the Native Americans put up enormous resistance against those driving them from their land, they could do little to halt the migration of thousands of settlers. By the end of the 19th century, most Native Americans had been resettled on reservations, their own land having been given to farmers.

13 *Manifest Destiny:* (here) offenkundige Bestimmung

Activity

▶ Activity chest 4

Use a 'Cheat sheet' to sum up orally why Americans went west and how this affected the people living there already.

A Before you read

1. Work with a partner. Discuss the following points and explain your answers to each other. If you find it difficult to make choices, explain why.
   - Are you a home person or an outdoors person?
   - Are you a risk-taker or do you prefer safety?
   - Are you a head person or a hand person?
   - Do you feel more comfortable alone or in a group?
   - Do you want to fulfil your dreams or are you content with what you have?
2. Now look at the picture on p. 70. How do you think each of the people would answer these questions?

JANUARY 5th, 1856. We are going to Kansas. The Vegetarian Company that has been forming for many months, has finally organized, formed its constitution, elected its directors, and is making all necessary preparations for the spring settlement ... We can have, I think, good faith to believe, that our directors will fulfill on their part; and we, as settlers of a new country, by going in a company will escape the hardships attendant on families going in singly, and at once find ourselves surrounded by improving society in a young and flourishing city. It will be better for ourselves pecuniarily, and better in the future for our children.

MAY 2nd. A lovely day. Our husbands are loading the ox-wagons. ... Women and children walk along up the hill out of this 'Great City', wait under a tree – what a beautiful country is spread out before us! Will our Kansas scenery equal this ...?

MAY 6th. Dined on the prairie, and gathered flowers, while our tired beasts filled themselves with the fresh, green grass. Have driven 18 miles to-day ... so here we are, all huddled into this little house 12 by 16 – cook supper over the fire ... fill the one bed lengthwise and crosswise; the family of the house take to the trundle-bed, while the floor is covered ... with women and children, rolled in Indian blankets like silk worms in cocoons.

MAY 11th. 'Made' but a few miles yesterday. Forded the Little Osage; the last river, they say, we have to ford ... our 'noble lords' complained of the great weight of the wagons ... That our wagon is heavily loaded, have only to make a minute of what we have stowed away in it – eight trunks, one valise, three carpet bags, a box of soda crackers, 200 lbs. flour, 100 lbs. corn meal, a few lbs. of sugar, rice, dried apple, one washtub of little trees, utensils for cooking, and two provision boxes – say nothing of mother, a good fat sister, self, and two children, who ride through the rivers ...

At nightfall came to a log-cabin at the edge of the wood, and inquired of the 'Lord of the Castle' if some of the women and children could take shelter under his roof for the night; the masculine number and whichever of the women that chose, couching in the wagons and under them. He said we could. His lady, who was away,

6 *attendant on sb.:* accompanying sb.
8 *pecuniary* [pɪ'kjuːniəri]: with respect to money
15 *huddle:* gather closely together
12 by 16: 12 feet wide, 16 feet long
16 *lengthwise:* längs
crosswise: quer
19 *ford* (a river): cross a river by walking through it in a shallow place
21 *make a minute* (old-fashioned): make a list
22 *trunk:* large box in which you store things
valise (old-fashioned): small bag for carrying clothes
23 *lbs:* pounds
27 *log-cabin:* small hut made from wood

presently came, with bare feet, and a white sack twisted up and thrown over her shoulder, with a few quarts of corn meal in the end that hung down her back. I said to myself – 'Is that what I have got to come to?' She seemed pleased to have company – allowed us the first chance of the broad, Dutch-backed fireplace with its earthy hearth, and without pot hooks or trammels, to make ready our simple evening repast …

Arrive at Elm Creek – no house to lodge in tonight – campfire kindled – supper cooked, and partaken of with a keen relish, sitting in family groups around the 'great big' fire. Some will sleep in wagons, others under the canopy of the blue vault of Heaven. The young men have built some shady little bowers of the green boughs; they are looking very cosily under them, wrapped in their white Indian blankets.

We ladies, or rather, 'emigrant women,' are having a chat around the camp-fire – the bright stars are looking down upon us – we wonder if we shall be neighbors to each other in the great 'Octagon City …'

MAY 12th. Full of hope, as we leave the smoking embers of our camp-fire this morning. Expect tonight to arrive at our new home.

Have sent three men in advance to announce our coming; are looking for our Secretary, (Henry S. Clubb) with an escort to welcome us into the embryo city. If the booming of cannon is not heard at our approach, shall expect a salute from the firing of Sharp's rifles, certainly.

No escort is seen! no salute is heard! We move slowly and drippingly into town just at nightfall – feeling not a little nonplused on learning that our worthy, or unworthy Secretary was out walking in the rain with his dear wife. We leave our wagons and make our way to the large camp-fire. It is surrounded by men and women cooking their suppers while others are busy close by, grinding their hominy in hand mills.

Look around, and see the grounds all around the camp-fire are covered with tents, in which the families are staying. Not a house is to be seen. In the large tent here is a cook stove – they have supper prepared for us; it consists of hominy, soft Johnny cake (or corn bread, as it is called here), stewed apple, and tea. We eat what is set before us, 'asking no questions for conscience' sake.'

The ladies tell us they are sorry to see us come to this place; which shows us that all is not right. Are too weary to question, but with hope depressed go to our lodgings, which we find around in the tents, and in our wagons.

MAY 13th. Can anyone imagine our disappointment this morning, on learning from this and that member, that no mills have been built; that the directors, after receiving our money to build mills, have not fulfilled the trust reposed in them, and that in consequence, some families have already left the settlement …?

As it is, we find the families, some living in tents of cloth, some of cloth and green bark just peeled from the trees, and some wholly of green bark, stuck up on the damp ground, without floors or fires. Only two stoves in the company …

[From: *Went to Kansas* by Miriam Davis Colt, 1862]

34 *Dutch-backed fireplace:* Kachelofen
35 *trammel:* hook used to hang a pot over the fire
hearth [hɑːθ]: Feuerstelle
36 *repast:* meal
38 *partake of sth.* (old-fashioned): eat sth.
relish (n): enjoyment
39 *canopy* ['– – –]: Baldachin
40 *vault* [vɔːlt]: Gewölbe
bower: place under trees
41 *bough* [baʊ]: large branch
42 *blanket:* Decke
53 *nonplused:* perplexed
56 *hominy* ['– – –]: dry corn, usually ground and boiled for food
64 *weary* ['wɪəri]: very tired, exhausted
71 *bark* (n): outer skin of a tree

B Understanding the text

1. Compare Colt's expectations about life at Octagon City to the reality she finds.
2. Copy the axis below and draw a line graph which illustrates the changing mood of the writer. Label the most distinctive points on the graph with phrases from the text. Work in groups of three or four, compare your graphs and discuss any differences.

► Skills 5.1, Step 3

3. Using your graphs, summarise the text. Make sure to connect your sentences and avoid enumerating statements.

At the beginning When they set off … The mood changes when … After a while / gradually /… When they arrive at their destination …	she is … happy/optimistic/stoical/hopeful/determined she expects … she looks forward to … she realises … she becomes disappointed/disillusioned/…

C Analysing the text

► Glossary 2.2.1

1. Analyse the point of view this text is written from and describe the effect on the reader.

► Glossary 2.2.1

2. Thinking of your answers in B, analyse, with examples, how Colt's language changes with her mood.

D Reacting to the text

1. Moving west was risky and dangerous for pioneers. Suggest why so many were willing to move west despite the dangers.

► Skills 7.1

2. American politicians often refer to the 'frontier spirit', e.g. in speeches. Define what this is and why Americans might mention it so often. Suggest contexts in which it could be relevant.

► Activity chest 9

✕ **Extra** Work in groups. During these years, the government or businesspeople often produced posters to encourage Americans to go west. Think of how you might appeal to people with words and pictures. Design a poster, then organise a 'Gallery walk'.

Creating dreams in the US

Immigrants waiting to enter the U.S. at Ellis Island, New York in 1907

Today's immigrants taking the Oath of Allegiance in Los Angeles

The USA has always been a nation of immigrants. Many came in great waves at the beginning of the 20th century and people continue to move there today. In this topic we look at why people are so attracted to the USA and what they experience when they arrive there.

Collect ideas

Work in groups on the tasks below, then report to the class.

1. Collect what you know from your previous English lessons about Ellis Island and immigration to the USA in the early 20th century (why? how? experiences?)
2. Look at the picture of modern immigrants. In what ways may they be similar to – or different from – those earlier immigrants (why? how? experiences?)
3. Brainstorm words that you could use when talking about immigration: *immigrant, journey, arrival, poverty, escape (from), opportunity, …*

1 My dream realised (An autobiography)

The family of the Irish-American writer Frank McCourt came to the United States as immigrants. He was born there, but when he was five, his father died and the family returned to Ireland. In 1949, he landed again in New York and served in the American army as a GI. You are going to read an extract from his autobiography. The year is 1953. He has left the army and has to decide what to do with his life.

A Before you read

1. Work in small groups. The following three sentences are events taken from the text you are going to read. In your group choose one event and brainstorm at least five possible reasons why it might have happened. Remember: he is 23 and has just left the army.
   - McCourt unloads meat from freezer trucks.
   - He sits in a bar with artists all around him.
   - He buys textbooks.

Maybe he does it because ... Perhaps ... It could be that ... He might have ... / He could ... It's just possible that ...

Frank McCourt

2. Look out for these events as you read the text and compare your ideas to what really happened.

It's a nickel for the Staten Island Ferry and the sight of the Statue of Liberty and Ellis Island reminds me of the morning in October 1949 I sailed into New York on the *Irish Oak*, past the city and up the river to anchor that night in Poughkeepsie and on the next day to Albany where I took the train back down to New York.

That was nearly four years ago and here I am on the Staten Island Ferry with my tie stuffed in the pocket of the jacket hanging from my shoulder. Here I am without a job in the world, my girlfriend gone, and the little red flag waving on my name. I could go back to the Biltmore Hotel and take up where I left off, cleaning the lobby, scouring the toilet bowls, laying carpet, but no, a man who was a corporal can never sink that low again.

Looking at Ellis Island and an old wooden ferry rotting between two buildings makes me think of all the people who passed here before me, before my father and mother, all the people escaping the Famine in Ireland, all the people from all over Europe landing here with their hearts in their mouths for fear they might be caught with diseases and sent back and when you think of that a great moaning moves across the water from Ellis Island and you wonder if the people sent back had to return with their babies to places like Czechoslovakia and Hungary. People who were sent back like that were the saddest people in all of history, worse than

1 *nickel:* coin used in the US, value 5 cents
3 *anchor* ['æŋkə] (v): ankern
8 *little red flag:* symbol of left-wing or communist politics
10 *scour sth.* ['skaʊə]: clean sth. by using a rough cloth
14 *Famine* ['fæmɪn]: period in the middle of the 19th century where roughly 1 million people died of hunger in Ireland
15 *for fear* (that): afraid (that)
16 *moan:* make a low sound as if suffering

people like me who might have bad eyes and the little red flag but are still secure with the American passport. [...]

A few blocks away is Merchants Refrigerating Company and they need a platform man to fill in for men on summer vacation. They tell me, We might be having a heat wave but dress warm.

My job is unloading meat from the freezer trucks that bring sides of beef from Chicago. It's August on the platform but inside where we hang the meat it's freezing. The men laugh and say we're the only workers who travel so fast from the North Pole to the equator and back.

Peter McNamee is platform boss while the regular man is on vacation and when he sees me he says, What in the name of the crucified Jesus are you doing here? I thought you had a brain in your head.

He tells me I should be going to school, that there's no excuse for me humping sides of beef in and out in and out when I could be using my GI Bill and moving up in the world. [...]

On a slow day at Merchants Refrigerating Company we're told we can go home. [...] There's nothing to do but sit at the bar tormenting myself with questions. What am I doing here with this knockwurst and beer? What am I doing in the world at all? Will I spend the rest of my life hauling sides of beef from truck to freezer and vice versa? Will I end my days in a small apartment in Queens while Emer is happy raising a family in a suburb completely protected by insurance? Will I ride the subways all my life envying people carrying books from universities?

I shouldn't be eating knockwurst at a time like this. I shouldn't be drinking beer when I don't have an answer in my head. I shouldn't be in this bar with poets and artists all sitting there with their serious whispered conversations. I'm weary of knockwurst and liverwurst and the feel of frozen meat on my shoulders every day.

I push the knockwurst away and leave a half stein of beer and walk out of the door, across Hudson Street, along Bleecker Street, not knowing where I'm going but knowing I have to keep walking till I know where I'm going, and here I am in Washington Square and there's New York University and I know that's where I have to go with my GI Bill, high school or no high school. A student points to the admission office and the woman gives me an application. She says I didn't fill it in properly, that they need to know my high school graduation, where and when.

I never went.

You never went to high school?

No, but I have the GI Bill and I've been reading books all my life.

Oh, my, but we require high school graduation or the equivalency.

But I read books. I've read Dostoyevsky and I've read *Pierre, or the Ambiguities*. It's not as good as *Moby Dick* but I read it in a hospital in Munich.

You actually read *Moby Dick?*

I did and *Pierre, or the Ambiguities* got me thrown out of the hospital in Munich.

I can see she doesn't understand. She goes into another office with my application and brings out the Dean of Admissions, a woman with a kind face. The

31 *Peter McNamee:* a fellow immigrant whom McCourt knows from before
37 *hump sth.* (infml): carry sth.
side: (here) one of two halves of an animal
38 *GI Bill:* law passed in the US in 1944 which provides for education for people who have served in the armed forces
41 *torment sb.:* (here) cause mental pain or suffering to sb.
45 *Emer:* girl the narrator once met and found very attractive
46 *envy sb.:* jdn. beneiden
56 *admission office:* office where you apply to attend classes at a university or college
61 *equivalency:* sth. with equal value
62 *Dostoyevsky* (= Fyodor Mikhaylovich Dostoyevsky): Russian writer (1821–1881)
Pierre, or the Ambiguities: novel by Herman Melville (1852)
63 *Moby Dick:* novel by Herman Melville (1851)
67 *dean:* head of a department

dean tells me I'm an unusual case and wants to know about my schooling in Ireland. It's her experience that European students are better prepared for college work and she will allow me to enroll at NYU if I can maintain a B average for a year. She wants to know what kind of work I do and when I tell her about the meat she says, My, my, I learn something every day.

Since I'm not a high school graduate and work full time I'm allowed to take only two courses, Introduction to Literature and the History of Education in America. I don't know why I have to be introduced to literature but the woman in the admissions office says it's a requirement even though I've read Dostoyevsky and Melville and that's admirable for someone without a high school education. She says the History of Education in America course will provide me with the broad cultural back-ground I need after my inadequate European education.

I'm in heaven and the first thing to do is buy the required textbooks, cover them with the purple and white NYU book jackets so that people in the subway will look at me admiringly.

[From: *'Tis* by Frank McCourt, 1999]

70 *enroll:* sich einschreiben
NYU = New York University
B: second best mark in American schools or universities
maintain sth.: etwas aufrechterhalten

B Understanding the text

In this extract, McCourt describes an important decision he makes. Sum up what situation he is in, what his decision is and which events lead up to it.

C Analysing the text

1. The climax is the high point of interest in a story where decisions are made, situations are changed etc. Identify the climax of this part of the memoir, list events that lead to the moment of decision and that follow the decision.
2. Characterise McCourt as he presents himself in this extract.
3. The text is from an autobiography. In groups, suggest who might write an autobiography and who might be interested in reading it. Now look at McCourt's text. Identify those features which are typical of an autobiography and explain their effect on the reader. Think, for example, about the narrator, the style and language of the text, how events or the writer's thoughts are presented, any use of humour or irony, …

► Glossary 2.2.2; 3.1

D Reacting to the text

1. Talk in class. People often talk about America as a land of opportunity where anything is possible. Comment on how far this text supports this idea (or not).
2. McCourt writes a letter home to his mother in Ireland. He thinks about his family's whole history (they first came to the USA in dire poverty) and the situation he is in now. Write his letter.

KEY FACTS Immigration to the USA

The United States was built by immigrants who came to the country to begin a new life. After 1820 four great periods of immigration, or 'waves', can be identified. The immigrants in those periods came mostly from three regions:

- 1820–1860: Great Britain, Ireland and Germany. The most powerful 'push factor' for most immigrants were hardships such as hunger and poverty in their homelands;
- 1860–1890: many immigrants still came from the countries above, but people from Scandinavian countries also began to immigrate to the US;
- 1890–1910: the majority of immigrants now came from Austria, Hungary, Italy, and Russia. Political storms swept through Europe and drove many people to seek a better life on the other side of the Atlantic.
- since 1965: the fourth wave of immigration has brought immigrants mainly from Latin America and to a lesser extent also from Asia and Europe.

Limits to immigration

Before 1882, the United States was open to anyone. But as the population swelled, the federal government decided to control immigration. Laws were passed in the late 1800s and early 1900s that set limits on the number of immigrants from particular countries who could enter the US. In 1965, these quotas were replaced by laws that limited not only the number of immigrants from countries *outside* the Western Hemisphere but also the number of immigrants from countries *within* the Western Hemisphere. These laws included Latin Americans, who had been coming to the United States for years. Many Latin Americans ignored the laws and came illegally. In 1986, the US government decided to offer amnesty to these illegal immigrants.

At the US-Mexican border

Immigration today

Today, the United States limits immigration to 600,000 newcomers a year. However, officials estimate that millions of people live illegally in the United States. Many illegal immigrants cross the US-Mexican border to escape poverty in Latin America.
These days there is a bitter debate over illegal immigration among policymakers and citizens in the United States. How big is the problem? An estimated 12 million people are living illegally in the US today; that's roughly 1 out of every 25 people. Some policy-makers contend that the government should create pathways to citizenship for those living in the US illegally. They say illegal immigrants can have a positive impact on society by working jobs, paying taxes, buying homes, taking out loans and purchasing US-made goods. Others believe that the government should focus on deporting illegal immigrants, claiming that the negative consequences of illegal immigration, such as increased crime, gang activity and pressure on social services, outweigh the positive effects. The answers that today's leaders give to this question will determine tomorrow's immigration policy.

Activities

Make notes about how immigration has changed (or not) over the years – e.g. reasons for immigrating, the kinds of people who immigrate, attitudes towards immigrants. Give a short talk.

2 Zeitoun's story (An extract from a biography)

You are now going to read an extract from a biography by the American writer Dave Eggers about a man called Zeitoun, published in 2009.

A Before you read

The biography is of the man in the picture, Abdulrahman Zeitoun. Talk in class. What can you guess about him – his background, his job and status? What first impression does he make on you? Why?

Kathy and Zeitoun worked harder than anyone they knew, and the work and worry never ended. Nights, weekends, holidays – respite never came. They usually had eight to ten jobs going at any one time, which they oversaw out of a home office and a warehouse space on Dublin Street, off Carrollton. And that was to say nothing of the property-management aspect of the business. Somewhere along the line they started buying buildings, apartments, and houses, and now they had six properties with eighteen tenants. Each renter was, in some ways, another dependent, another soul to worry about, to provide with shelter, a solid roof, air-conditioning, clean water. There was a dizzying array of people to pay and collect from, houses to improve and maintain, bills to deal with, invoices to issue, supplies to buy and store.

But she cherished what her life had become, and the family she and Zeitoun had created. […]

Across town, Zeitoun was at his first job of the day. He loved this place, a magisterial old house in the Garden District. He had two men on the job and was stopping by to make sure they were there, that they were busy, that they had what they needed. He jumped up the steps and strode into the house. It was easily 120 years old.

He saw Emil, a painter and carpenter from Nicaragua, kneeling in a doorway, taping off a baseboard. Zeitoun snuck up behind him and grabbed his shoulders suddenly.

Emil jumped. Zeitoun laughed.

He wasn't even sure why he did things like this. It was hard to explain – sometimes he just found himself in a playful mood. The workers who knew him well were unsurprised, while the newer ones would often be startled, thinking his behavior a bizarre sort of motivational method.

Emil managed a smile.

In the dining room, applying a second coat to the wall was Marco, originally from El Salvador. The two of them, Marco and Emil, had met at church and had gone looking for work as a team of housepainters. They'd shown up at one of Zeitoun's job sites, and because Zeitoun nearly always had more work than he could handle, he'd taken them on. That had been three years ago, and Marco and Emil had worked for Zeitoun consistently since then.

3 *respite:* short break from something unpleasant
4 *oversee sth.:* make sure that sth. is done properly
5 *warehouse:* building where large quantities of goods are stored
6 *property-management:* Immobilienverwaltung
9 *tenant:* Mieter
12 *dizzying:* making you lose your orientation
array [- '-]: large collection of sth.
13 *issue an invoice:* eine Rechnung ausstellen
supply: Lieferung
17 *magisterial:* showing authority
22 *tape off sth.:* etwas abkleben
baseboard: board fixed along the the bottom of a wall where it meets the floor
30 *coat:* layer of paint

Outside of employing a number of New Orleans natives, Zeitoun had hired men from everywhere: Peru, Mexico, Bulgaria, Poland, Brazil, Honduras, Algeria. He'd had good experiences with almost all of them, though in his business there was an above-average rate of attrition and turnover. Many workers were transient, intending only to spend a few months in the country before returning to their families. These men he was happy to hire, and he'd learned a fair bit of Spanish along the way, but he had to be prepared for their short-notice disappearances. Other workers were just young men: irresponsible and living for today. He couldn't blame them – he'd been young and untethered once, too – but he tried, whenever he could, to instill in them the knowledge that if they kept their heads down and saved a few dollars a week, they could live well, could raise a family doing this kind of work. But he rarely saw a young man in this business who had an eye to the future. Just keeping them in food and clothing, chasing them down when they were late or absent – all of it was exhausting and occasionally disheartening. He felt, sometimes, as if he had not four children but dozens, most of them with paint-covered hands and mustaches. [...]

When he began working in New Orleans, eleven years earlier, Zeitoun labored for just about every contractor in the city, painting, hanging Sheetrock, tiling – anything they needed – until he was hired by a man named Charlie Saucier. Charlie owned his own company, had built it from scratch. He'd become wealthy, and was hoping to retire before his knees gave out on him. [...]

At the time, Zeitoun didn't have a car, so he rode to Charlie's work sites on a bike – a ten-speed he bought for forty dollars. One day, when Zeitoun was already in danger of being late, the bike blew a tire. After riding on the rim for half a mile, he gave up. He needed to get four miles across the city in twenty minutes, and it was looking like he would be late for work for the first time in his life. He couldn't leave the bike and run – he needed that bike – and he couldn't ride on the flat tire, so he threw the bike over his shoulders started jogging. He was panicking. If he was late for this job, what would happen to his reputation? Charlie would be disappointed, and he might not hire him again. And what if Charlie talked to other contractors, and found he couldn't recommend Zeitoun? The consequences could be far-reaching. Work was a pyramid, he knew, built on day after solid day.

He ran faster. He would be tardy, but if he sprinted, he had a shot at being no more than fifteen minutes late. It was August and the humidity was profound. A mile or so into his run, already soaked in sweat, a truck pulled up next to him.

'What are you doing?' a voice asked. Without breaking stride, Zeitoun turned to see who it was. He figured it was some smart aleck poking fun at the man running along the road with a bike over his shoulders. But instead it was his boss, Charlie Saucier.

'I'm going to the job,' Zeitoun said. He was still running; in hindsight he should have stopped at this point, but he was in a rhythm and he continued, with the truck puttering beside him.

Charlie laughed. 'Throw your bike in the back.'

As they drove, Charlie looked over to Zeitoun. 'You know, I've been at this for thirty years, and 1 think you're the best worker I've ever had.'

---

39 *attrition:* Abnutzung
turnover: rate at which workers leave a company and are replaced by new workers
42 *short-notice* (adj): kurzfristig
44 *untethered* [ˌʌnˈteðəd]: free
45 *instill sth. in sb.:* gradually fill sb. with a belief in sth.
53 *hang Sheetrock:* die Wände verkleiden
tile sth.: etwas fliesen
55 *build sth. from scratch:* start sth. from nothing
59 *blow a tire:* einen Platten haben
67 *reputation:* general opinion of one's character
71 *tardy:* late
72 *humidity:* Feuchtigkeit
profound: deep
74 *break stride:* slow down
75 *smart aleck:* person who annoys others by claiming to know everything

They were driving to the job site and Zeitoun had finally managed to relax, knowing he wouldn't be fired that day.

'I have one guy,' Charlie continued, 'he says he can't come to work because his car won't start. I have another guy, he doesn't come because he slept late. He slept late! Another guy, his wife kicked him out of the house or something. So he doesn't show. I have twenty or thirty employees, and ten of them show up to work any given day.'

They were at a stop sign, and Charlie took a long look at Zeitoun. 'Then there's you. You have the perfect excuse. All you have is a bike, and the bike has a flat. But you're carrying your bike on your back. You're the only guy I've ever known who would have done something like that.'

After that day, things moved quickly forward and upward for Zeitoun. Within a year, he had saved enough to buy his own truck. Two years later, he was working for himself and employing a dozen men. [...]

Zeitoun headed to the West Bank to get a look at the tangerine bathroom. He tried to be amused by the fickle nature of clients' tastes; it was part of the job, and if he got exasperated every time someone changed their mind, he'd never survive. The upshot was that it ensured no day was dull. The intensely personal nature of his business, the subjectivity of taste, the variables of light and curtains and carpets, guaranteed that minds would reevaluate and work would have to be redone.

Still, the most unusual requests often came from the most normal seeming people. One customer, a Southern belle in her sixties, had called Zeitoun Painting and had been happy to talk with Kathy, with her chatty demeanor and familiar accent. But when the painters showed up to begin work on the exterior of her home, the woman immediately called Kathy.

'I don't like these men,' she said. 'What's wrong with 'em?' Kathy asked.

'They're swarthy,' she said. 'I only want white people working on my house.' She said it like she was choosing a kind of dressing for her salad.

'White people?' Kathy laughed. 'Sorry, we're fresh out of those.' She convinced the woman that the men who had been sent – all of them Latino, in this case – were skilled professionals who would do an excellent job. The woman assented, but continued to call. 'He's too short to be a painter,' she said about one worker, Hector, who was over six feet tall. Realizing that no matter how much she complained, she would not be able to replace these painters with taller, Caucasian ones, the Southern belle resigned herself to watching the men, checking on them frequently.

Of course, every so often, would-be clients could not get past Zeitoun's last name. They would call for an estimate and ask Kathy, 'Zeitoun, where's that name come from? Where is he from?' And Kathy would say, 'Oh, he's Syrian.' Then, after a long pause or a shorter one, they would say, 'Oh, okay, never mind.' It was rare, but not rare enough.

Kathy sometimes told Zeitoun about such incidents, sometimes not, and never at dinner. Usually he just laughed it off, but occasionally it got under his skin. His frustration with some Americans was like that of a disappointed parent. He was so content in this country, so impressed with and loving of its opportunities, but then why, sometimes, did Americans fall short of their best selves? If you got him started on the subject, it was the end of any pleasant meal. He would begin with a

98 *tangerine* [ˌtændʒə'riːn]: mandarinenfarbig
99 *fickle:* often changing
100 *exasperated:* very annoyed
101 *upshot:* outcome
106 *belle:* beautiful woman
107 *demeanor* [dɪ'miːnə]: way of behaviour
111 *swarthy:* dark skinned
115 *assent* (fml): agree
118 *Caucasian:* (here) belonging to the races of people who have pale skin
130 *fall short of sth.:* not reach sth.

140 *convenience store:* small shop that sells a range of everyday items
141 *ancestry:* origin of your people

defense of Muslims in America and expand his thesis from there. Since the attacks in New York, he would say, every time a crime was committed by a Muslim, that person's faith was mentioned, regardless of its relevance. When a crime is committed by a Christian, do they mention his religion? If a Christian is stopped at the airport for trying to bring a gun on a plane, is the Western world notified that a Christian was arrested today and is being questioned? And what about African Americans? When a crime is committed by a black man, it's mentioned in the first breath: 'An African American man was arrested today ...' But what about German Americans? Anglo Americans? A white man robs a convenience store and do we hear he's of Scottish descent? In no other instance is the ancestry mentioned.

[From: *Zeitoun* by Dave Eggers, 2009]

B Understanding the text

1. Compare the ideas you formed about the character before reading the text to what you've found out now.
2. Sum up Mr Zeitoun's experiences as an immigrant to the USA pointing out both positive and negative aspects of it.

C Analysing the text

▶ Glossary 2.2.1

1. The writer, Dave Eggers, uses flashbacks to tell his story. Point out how and why they are used, and describe their effect on the reader.
2. Because he is writing a biography, Eggers wants to build up for the reader a picture of Mr Zeitoun's character. One of the ways he does this is by showing how his protagonist interacts with other characters. In groups, make a diagram of the characters in this extract and point out what the different relationships tell us about Mr Zeitoun. Report to the class.

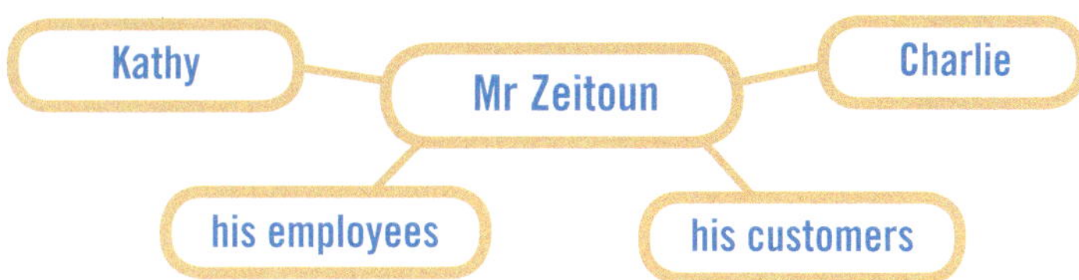

3. Juxtapose the positive and negative aspects of different cultures as they are presented in this passage. Decide who considers them positive or negative: the author, the customer, Kathy or Zeitoun? How would you evaluate them?

D Reacting to the text

1. Choose one of the people below and retell some of the events in the story from their perspective.
   a Mr Zeitoun's wife
   b Charlie
   c The 'Southern Belle'

✕ **Extra** In the last paragraph (ll. 132–141) Eggers refers to a subtle but powerful form of racial discrimination. Describe it and point out if you've experienced something similar. Write a letter to a newspaper in which you describe your experiences and voice your opinion

3 The new immigrants (A book extract)

The book extract that you are going to read paints a general picture of immigrants in the USA today. You are going to use the information from the text to make a short radio programme about this topic.

A Before you read

Talk in class. What have you learned so far about the immigrant experience in the USA and what further information would you like to have for your radio programme? List the kinds of questions about immigrants in the USA that you would like to be answered (for example: what percentage of the population do they make up?)

The immigrant influx of the last forty years is a demographic shift of historic proportions. The percentage of the population that was born abroad is slightly lower than it was when the last great wave of immigrants arrived, at the beginning of the twentieth century: 11 percent now compared to 15 percent then. But the absolute number of newcomers living in the United States today is the highest it has ever been: One in nine Americans is an immigrant. And half the laborers entering the American workforce in the 1990s were foreign-born. Add in their families and extended families and the picture glows more dramatic still. Together, immigrants and their children now account for one in five Americans. Hispanics, at nearly 14 percent of the population, are already the largest minority, outnumbering blacks. Asian-Americans are still a relatively small share of the nation – at only 4 percent. But despite their numbers, they, too, are going to play a major part in the country's future: already, they make up between 15 and 20 percent of the students at most Ivy League colleges.

Where do these new arrivals come from? Just over half the foreign-born are Hispanic and a little more than a quarter are Asian. They hail from all the corners of the globe, though more from some countries than from others. Mexicans, by far the largest category, account for roughly one in three first-generation immigrants – almost ten times more than any other nationality. The next largest groups are Filipinos and Indians, followed by Chinese, Vietnamese, Koreans, Cubans and Salvadorans – but none of these account for more than 3 or 4 percent of the total.

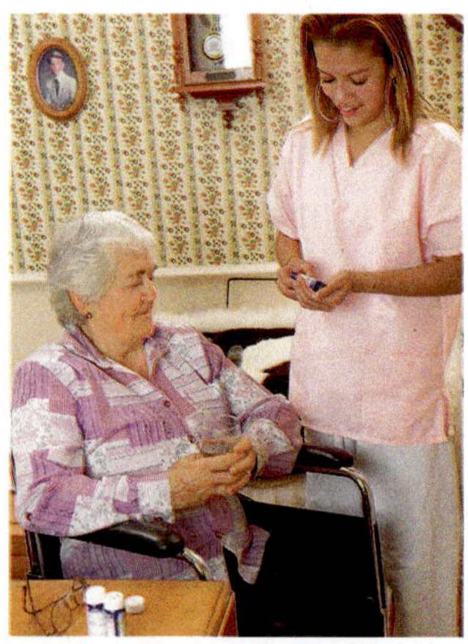

What do the newcomers do for a living? They tend to be clustered at both the top and the bottom of the job ladder. A large percentage work in dirty, demeaning, low-paid jobs that native-born Americans no longer want to do: busboys, chambermaids, farmhands, nurses' aides, sweatshop workers, on the assembly-line in meatpacking plants. But a large number also work at the top of the job pyramid: as scientists, engineers, nurses, high-tech

1 *influx:* Zustrom
demographic shift: Wandel in der Zusammensetzung der Bevölkerung
8 *laborer* (AE = BE labourer): person who does unskilled physical work, usually outside
11 *account for sth.:* etwas ausmachen
16 *Ivy League college:* one of the eight best American universities
28 *clustered:* grouped together
29 *ladder:* Leiter
30 *demeaning:* making you feel less respectable
33 *plant:* factory

entrepreneurs and the like. Two of the statistics that paint this picture most vividly are the percentage of U.S. farmhands who are foreign-born (an astonishing 80 percent) and the percentage of patents that are held by foreigners (an equally astonishing 26 percent). Social scientists call this a 'barbell pattern,' and it has some predictable corollaries. Not surprisingly, today's newcomers are either quite rich or quite poor, and they are either very well educated or hardly educated at all. Roughly a quarter have less than nine years of schooling, while an equal percentage have university degrees – a much larger share than the proportion of native-born Americans who have stayed in school that long.

Where in the United States do most immigrants settle? Until about ten years ago, they were concentrated in what demographers call 'gateway cities': New York, Los Angeles, Miami, Houston, Chicago. But this is changing dramatically and with profound consequences for the country. States such as New York and California and New Jersey are still home to the largest numbers. But the states with the fastest growing immigrant populations are places like North Carolina, Georgia, Arkansas and Tennessee. Even Iowa more than doubled its share in the 1990s. The cities where the immigrant population expanded the most in the past decade are equally surprising: Greensboro, N.C., Charlotte, N.C., Raleigh, N.C., Atlanta and Las Vegas. Still more of a departure, while some of today's new arrivals still gravitate to urban areas, many head straight for the suburbs, and roughly half of all Asians and Latinos now live outside the center city. True, these are often older, less affluent, inner-ring suburbs: Port Chester rather than Scarsdale, say, in the New York metro area. But all around the country, from New York to California, suburban America is increasingly ethnic.

Whether or not they are assimilating is harder to quantify. Becoming an American is a complex, personal process – the kind of transition that can take a lifetime, even two. A Mexican farmhand with a sixth-grade education takes a different path into the mainstream than an Indian engineer working on an MBA, and the sometimes mind-boggling diversity of today's immigrants can make it difficult to generalize. What's more, even when one focuses on one group, it can be hard to assess just how well or how fast they are integrating. Economic success or failure, for example, is reflected in countless and sometimes contradictory statistics, and in today's polarized immigration debate, any statistical portrait is sure to be controversial. Nevertheless, a lot is known about today's immigrants, and on the whole it adds up to an encouraging story.

Most foreigners, whether they arrive legally or illegally, come to the United States to work. Most do not come in the expectation of living on welfare: most are not entitled to most kinds of benefits for at least five years. Thanks to modern technology, they generally know from other immigrants who have preceded them from their regions whether or not work is available. And in economic downturns, when there are fewer jobs to be had, fewer immigrants seem to make the trip. After

35 *entrepreneur* [ˌɒntrəprəˈnɜː]: person who starts their own business
38 *barbell pattern:* pattern that looks like a barbell (= Hantel) with great numbers on either side and very few in between
39 *corollary:* consequence that follows from sth. else
54 *share* (n): Anteil
61 *gravitate to:* be attracted by
63 *affluent:* wealthy
69 *MBA* (= Master of Business Administration): university degree for the study of economics
70 *mind-boggling:* very surprising
78 *on welfare:* on state money
79 *benefits:* money paid by the state e.g. to the unemployed
81 *available* [əˈveɪləbl]: verfügbar

TOPIC
03
Dreams and doubts

For many Americans, the American Dream is (or was) just that: a dream. Topic 3 is going to look at the fights, frustrations and setbacks experienced by those people in search of their American Dream.

Collect ideas

▶ Activity chest 12

1. The picture above shows the Civil Rights Memorial in Richmond, Virginia. Describe and analyse it. Consider especially what message the statue conveys and how both the text at the top and the figures help to convey it. Think, for example, about how they are standing/walking, their faces, the attitudes or feelings they seem to have, etc.

▶ Skills 7.4

2. Work in pairs, exchange ideas and add to your notes so that you can use them to present your ideas, then practice and give your presentation.

In the sculpture there are … / The sculpture consists of … / It depicts/shows…	
The people/figures in the sculpture … One figure … They appear … They create an impression of …	stand tall / in an upright position look ahead / move forward hold hands / support each other put arms around shoulders / with interlocking arms very dynamic/fearless/determined move as one / hold their heads high / stride onwards
I think / I suppose it might … I'm (quite) convinced/sure/certain … This is all beyond me. / I have no idea. My interpretation is …	express/indicate/mean/ … its meaning/intention is … it shows/portrays/illustrates/represents …

✕ **Extra** Imagine yourself as one of the figures. Write a speech bubble in which you express your idea of the American Dream.

1 Frederick Douglass (A poem)

Robert Hayden (1913–1980) was a US-American writer who often protested against the social and economic conditions of African Americans in his writing. You are now going to read his poem 'Frederick Douglass' (1966).

A Before you read

4 *diastole* [dʌɪ'astəli]: phase in the cardiac cycle when the heart fills with blood
systole ['sɪstəli]: phase in the cardiac cycle when the heart contracts and pushes out blood
6 *gaudy:* showy and overly bright
mumbo jumbo: complicated, but meaningless words or actions
9 *alien* ['eɪliən]: fremd
11 *rhetoric* ['– – –]: Rhetorik, Phrasendrescherei
12 *wreath* [ri:θ]: ring of flowers or leaves used to honour or respect a dead person

Find out who Frederick Douglass was. Give a one-minute report, then read the poem.

When it is finally ours, this freedom, this liberty,
this beautiful and terrible thing, needful to man as air,
usable as earth; when it belongs at last to all,
when it is truly instinct, brain matter, diastole, systole,
reflex action; when it is finally won; when it is more
than the gaudy mumbo jumbo of politicians:
this man, this Douglass, this former slave, this Negro
beaten to his knees, exiled, visioning a world
where none is lonely, none hunted, alien,
this man, superb in love and logic, this man
shall be remembered. Oh, not with statues' rhetoric,
not with legends and poems and wreaths of bronze alone,
but with the lives grown out of his life, the lives
fleshing his dream of the beautiful, needful thing.

[From: *Collected Poems* by Robert Hayden, 1966]

▶ Skills 1.2.4

B Understanding the poem

1. Point out how the poem describes the freedom that will some day be reached.
2. What do you learn about Frederick Douglass from this poem? Compare this information to your own research.
3. Describe how, according to the poem, Douglass will be remembered.

▶ Glossary 2.4.1, 3.1

C Analysing the poem

1. Collect words and images from the poem used to characterise freedom. Describe their connotations and associations and examine their meanings.

WORDS AND IMAGES	CONNOTATIONS AND ASSOCIATIONS	POTENTIAL MEANING

2. Analyse the sentence structure of this poem and describe its effect.

D Reacting to the poem

Evaluate the poet's message. Judge it critically against the background of what you know about the American Dream and decide whether you do or do not agree with it.

KEY FACTS The fight against discrimination of African Americans

Slavery

Slavery existed in America for over 250 years. From the foundation of the first British colony in 1607 until slavery was finally made illegal in 1865, some 12 million black Africans were brought to the USA, mostly to the southern states where they worked on cotton plantations. It is impossible to exaggerate the horrors of slavery. The separation of families, constant beatings and starvation were part of a slave's everyday life. From the 1770s on, slavery became a topic of debate in US politics and it lead to growing tension between northern states, which were against slavery, and southern states, which wanted to keep it.

First steps

The American Civil War (1861–1865) was fought between the northern and southern states of the USA. After the north had won, three constitutional amendments gave former slaves the full rights of citizenship: the thirteenth Amendment, which abolished slavery; the fourteenth Amendment, which guaranteed civil rights; and the fifteenth Amendment, which granted black males the right to vote. However, the deep-seated racial prejudice within society could not be erased by legislation so easily. Southern leaders implemented 'Jim Crow' laws, which segregated public facilities by race. These laws affected restaurants, theatres, schools, and even water fountains.

Martin Luther King

Barack Obama

The Civil Rights Movement

The second half of the 20th century saw considerable progress in the civil rights movement. The Black Power Movement, which was active between about 1966 and 1975, aimed not only at equal rights, but also at racial dignity, social equality, and freedom from oppression by white Americans. Its campaigns were non-violent and concentrated on civil resistance, e.g. boycotts or marches. The most prominent leader of the Civil Rights Movement was Martin Luther King, Jr. King campaigned for changes to civil rights laws with passive resistance, sit-ins, civil disobedience and large demonstrations. He was one of the leaders of the March on Washington in 1963, a large political rally for the rights of African Americans, where he delivered his famous 'I Have a Dream' speech. In 1964 he was awarded the Nobel Peace Prize. Tragedy struck when he was assassinated in Memphis, Tennessee in 1968. As a result of the Civil Rights Movement, several laws were enacted that curbed discrimination and granted more freedom to African Americans. For example, in 1964, the Civil Rights Act was passed. It prohibited discrimination based on 'race, color, religion, or national origin' in public places such as restaurants and hotels. The Voting Rights Act of 1965 aimed to eliminate practices that prevented African Americans and other minorities from voting. It forbade literacy tests for voters, poll taxes, and intimidation of voters in any state. Additionally, the Fair Housing Act of 1968 banned discrimination in the sale or rental of housing.

Growing African American influence

After the Civil Rights Era, African Americans gained considerably in the political and economic arena. For example, in the years between 1970 and 2000, the number of African Americans holding political office increased by around 600 percent. When in 2008 Barack Obama (born 1961) became the first President of the United States to have African American heritage, this clearly marked the climax of this development.

Activities

Describe the way in which the African American movement towards equality is reflected in the poem.

2 Hunger in New York City (A poem)

You are going to read a poem by Native American writer Simon Ortiz, who reflects on his experience of the American Dream.

A Before you read

H …
U …
N …
G …
E …
R …

1. Ortiz's poem is about hunger. Write an acrostic poem based on this word, i.e. a list of words that begin with the letters of the word 'hunger'.
2. Form small groups and explain your acrostics to each other.
3. Now read the poem and see if you can identify aspects of your acrostic in it.

Hunger crawls into you
from somewhere out of your muscles
or the concrete or the land
or the wind pushing you.

It comes to you, asking
for food, words, wisdom, young memories
of places you ate at, drank cold spring water,
or held somebody's hand,
or home of the gentle, slow dances,
the songs, the strong gods, the world
you know.

That is, hunger searches you out.
It always asks you,
How are you, son? Where are you?
Have you eaten well?
Have you done what you as a person
of our people is supposed to do?

And the concrete of this city,
the oily wind, the blazing windows,
the shrieks of automation cannot,
truly cannot, answer for that hunger
although I have hungered,
truthfully and honestly, for them
to feed myself with.

So I sang to myself quietly:
I am feeding myself
with the humble presence
of all around me;
I am feeding myself
with your soul, my mother earth;
make me cool and humble.
Bless me.

[From: *Woven Stone* by Simon Ortiz, 1992]

Simon Ortiz

3 *concrete* ['- –] (n): substance used for building
12 *search sb. out:* look for sb. until you have found them
19 *blazing* (here): very bright
20 *shriek:* wild high cry, usually resulting from excitement or fear
automation: use of machines for work that used to be done by people
31 *humble:* of low rank or position

► Skills 1.2.4

B Understanding the text

1. One way to appreciate poetry is to read it aloud in sentences rather than in poetic lines. Practice reading the poem aloud: avoid pausing at the end of each line, but follow the punctuation as if you were reading prose. Pause briefly after commas, and pause longer after full stops. Experiment with different moods and intonations.
2. Work in groups and complete the following tasks.
   a Formulate four questions which the poem inspires you to ask. Write answers to them, then write each question on a separate sheet of paper and give the questions to another group.
   b In your group discuss the questions you have been given and agree on answers to them. Write an answer under the question on each sheet of paper.
   c Display all the questions and answers on a classroom wall for everybody to read.
   d Use ideas from the wall display to summarize the poem.

KEY FACTS Native Americans

Conflict on the new continent arose when European pioneers moved their settlements further west, hindering the nomadic lifestyle of the Native Americans. The latter half of the 19th century saw a series of 'Indian Wars' which led to Native Americans giving up much of their land to live on reservations established for them in western states. But the land there was poor and they were unable to maintain their traditional way of life, which included a close spiritual connection to nature.

Today about one fifth of the Native American population still lives on reservation land where they suffer extremely high levels of unemployment and poverty. They tend to be poorly educated and are faced with various health problems and poor nutrition. Many feel they have lost their spiritual ground, their roots and heritage; there are very high rates of depression and alcoholism on reservations.

However, from a legal point of view, the situation of Native Americans has seen considerable improvements. For example, in 1975 Native American tribes were given the right to self-determination. They were allowed to establish tribal governments, to enforce laws and levy taxes. But, despite greater freedom and acceptance, the situation for many Native Americans remains grim when compared to the rest of America.

Activity

Sum up orally the situation of Native Americans in modern America and point out how this situation came about.

C Analysing the text

Work in pairs or small groups. Discuss the following tasks and make notes on possible answers. Then report your answers back to the class as a whole.

► Glossary 2.4.1
► Glossary 3.1

1. Examine who the speaker is and look for clues to his attitude or outlook on life.
2. One of the main devices Ortiz uses in the poem is personification. Point out how, where and to what effect he uses it.
3. Contrast the world the speaker once knew – the world of his homeland – and the city he lives in now. List the images he uses for both worlds and explain them.
4. Compare the concept of hunger in this poem to your own ideas on the subject.

SPOTLIGHT ON Elements of poetry

Poems are a very special kind of literary text: they are generally quite short and their form contributes a lot to their overall meaning. Since poems are short, each word or phrase has to be chosen with care; there is no room for redundant or imprecise words. Moreover, like plays, poems are written primarily not to be silently read but to be heard, so it is very important to listen to them or imagine how they might sound. When analysing a poem, it is therefore essential to consider its form and sounds. Poems use imagery, lines, stanzas, rhyme, rhythm, and sounds of letters to communicate emotions, ideas, sounds, and even stories.

- **Images** are words or phrases that describe how something looks, sounds, feels, tastes, or smells.
- **Rhetorical devices** are techniques poets use to produce a particular effect. They can refer to sound (e.g. in alliteration), structure (e.g. in repetition) or meaning (e.g. in similes or metaphors).
- **Stanzas** are groups of lines in a poem. Poets don't always use stanzas, however.
- **Rhyme** means the repetition of sounds at the ends of words, as in 'moon' and 'balloon'.
- **Rhythm** is the beat of poetry created by combinations of stressed and unstressed syllables. Poetry that is not written in a regular rhythmical pattern is known as free verse.
- **Sound** is important, as poems are meant to be heard. The sounds of words or of combinations of words create feeling and music in a poem. For example, if words starting with the same consonants at are used, we call this alliteration. Assonance is the repetition of vowel sounds within words. Of course, rhyme also influences the sound of a poem.
- The **speaker** of a poem is the character from whose viewpoint the poem is told and whose ideas are expressed in it. The speaker and the poet are not necessarily the same person, e.g. the speaker may be a person living in another time or place, an animal, an insect or even an object.

If you analyse poetry, make sure not only to list its features, such as images or rhyme scheme, but always ask yourself to what effect these features are employed. Remember: poems are short so each word is chosen with extra care!

▶ Glossary 3.2

✕ **Spotlight task** Based on your acrostic on hunger (A1), write a few lines of poetry: decide on a rhetorical device (e.g. rhyme, alliteration, metaphor) and try to integrate it into your poem.

D Reacting to the text

1. Work in groups and make a collage to illustrate the concept of 'hunger' as presented in this poem. You can use e.g. photos from magazines, picture postcards, snapshots, etc. Present them to other groups in a 'Gallery walk'

▶ Activity chest 9

✕ **Extra** You probably know someone whose life is centred on their cultural heritage. Together with a classmate, conduct an interview with such a person. To prepare, use the following tips:
- Formulate questions to establish the person's background and history.
- Determine what effect their background has had on their life.
- Create a list of suitable follow-up questions.

Write a report based on the interview.

▶ Skills 5.2

3 More than a storm (An extract from a non-fiction book)

For the city of New Orleans, hurricanes are quite a normal phenomenon. But in 2005, Hurricane Katrina had an especially devastating effect: It caused massive flooding in parts of the city and started a chain of events that had a lasting impact on the American psyche. You are now going to read about this disaster and its social consequences.

A Before you read

The photo below shows two victims of Hurricane Katrina.

1. Imagine how the couple's life was changed by the natural disaster. Consider when, why and from whom they might need help – e.g. neighbours, friends, the authorities, etc.
2. Imagine yourself as the man or woman below, brainstorm and structure ideas, and prepare to tell your story.
3. Get together in groups and tell your stories. Ask questions about each other's stories to find out more details.

During the tropical storm season 2004, the state of Florida was hammered by a series of four hurricanes – Charley, Frances, Ivan, Jeanne – in a period of only six weeks. [...] Those four hurricanes were a rapid-fire assault on the state of Florida and mighty manifestations of nature's power. Yet even so, they did not threaten the future of one of America's most beloved and influential

cities; expose racial and economic divisions too often ignored in the US; undermine the credibility of authorities from city hall to the statehouse to the White House; rock the presidency of George W. Bush; and challenge the country's vision of itself. Hurricane Katrina did all that, and more.

Why was this storm more than a storm? Although Katrina ranks as one of the most powerful disasters ever to strike the U.S., it was in the hours and days after the storm struck the nation's coast that its lasting effects began to be felt. The storm's own power was so great that it seemed to leave a vacuum of power in its wake, suspending the citizens of the Gulf Coast in a new and different America,

3 *rapid fire assault:* attacks that follow after each other very quickly
6 *undermine sth.* [ˌʌndəˈmaɪn]: make sth. weaker
7 *credibility:* Glaubwürdigkeit
city hall: Rathaus
statehouse: capitol building of a US state
8 *challenge sth.:* question whether sth. is true
13 *in its wake:* following it
14 *suspend sb.:* (here) leave sb. hanging

one in which the daily norms of social civility and 21st century technology went absent without leave, and one's life suddenly became a series of urgent questions: How high will the water rise? Which family pictures should I try to save? If I tie myself with my belt to this pine tree, can I survive the storm surge? Do I have time to heed my neighbor's call for help?

In the great majority of cases, [...] the response to those questions was honorable, even heroic. But in New Orleans, citizens found themselves coping with a second, equally harmful shortage: the failure of those in power to assist Americans in need. Thanks to the hurricane's last-minute swerve to the east, the grand old city of jazz and Mardi Gras was spared a direct hit. But much of New Orleans is built on land that lies well below sea level, and when the hurricane's storm surges breached the levees that keep the city dry, the brackish waters of adjacent Lake Pontchartrain filled the city's streets.

In the days that followed, Americans watched in horror as one of the nation's major cities descended into a state that recalled scenes from the Third World. As the waters rose and kept rising, New Orlanians scrambled to reach high ground. Many of them ended up stranded on the rooftops of homes, scanning the skies and the waters for help. That help was disgracefully late in arriving. Elsewhere, TV cameras showed crowds of 25,000 people suffering in the hot, fetid Superdome, where there was no power, little food and, apparently, no one in charge – while the local, state and federal authorities of the world's richest nation couldn't manage to get a convoy of buses to the site to get them out of there.

Even as Katrina was exposing the flaws of our government, it was also exposing racial and social inequities in the nation's life that had been swept aside for far too long, for those hit hardest by the storm were society's least fortunate citizens. Katrina's winds took a scalpel to this city – famed as a wonderfully diverse mosaic of cultural influences – and dissected it, revealing that the story of New Orleans is also a tale of two cities. Economic divisions that didn't seem to mean so much in everyday life suddenly emerged as matters of life and death: if you owned a car, you had the means to leave the city; if you didn't, you stayed to face the floods.

The story of Hurricane Katrina's effect on our nation is in some ways only beginning. On Sept. 15, two weeks after the storm, President George W. Bush addressed the nation from Jackson Square in New Orleans. The President's image as a strong, effective leader with a feel for the plight of the common man had taken a direct hit from his Administration's fumbling response to the storm. Now he proposed a sweeping federal program to rebuild the city. [...]

Yet more than a city must be rebuilt in Katrina's wake. Just as important are the lives that must now be reconstructed from scratch. Evicting some 1.3 million people from their homes, Katrina created a storm surge of a different kind, a floodtide of internal migrants not seen since the days of the depression. As these individuals create new lives in new surroundings, or return to build a new future for the Gulf Coast, they will write the final pages of the story of how Hurricane Katrina changed America.

[From: *Hurricane Katrina – The Storm That Changed America*, 2005]

15 *civility:* good manners
16 *absent without leave:* fahnenflüchtig
18 *surge* [sɜːdʒ]: Woge, Brandung
22 *cope with sth.:* deal with sth
25 *Mardi Gras:* a carnival in New Orleans
27 *breach sth.:* make sth. break
levee ['levi]: wall at the side of a river to keep it from flooding
28 *brackish:* having a salty taste
37 *fetid:* smelling very bad
Superdome: sports arena in New Orleans
38 *in charge:* responsible
41 *flaw:* small mistake
42 *inequity* [ɪn'ekwəti]: injustice
45 *dissect sth.:* look very carefully into sth, e.g. a problem
52 *plight:* very bad situation
53 *fumbling:* mishandling
56 *from scratch:* von Grund auf

B Understanding the text

1. Describe the effects Katrina had on both the city of New Orleans and American society in general, and give reasons for them.

▶ Skills 8.3

2. Explain, using quotes from the text to support your answer, how the storm exposed 'racial and social inequities' (l. 42).

C Analysing the text

To make this text effective, the writer uses words which are likely to produce a strong emotional response in the reader. Analyse the text to find words and phrases which appeal to sentiments. Use a chart like the one below to help you.

WORDS AND PHRASES	→	CONNOTATIONS	→	EMOTIONS
'rapid-fire assault' (l. 3)	→	war, planned military operation, violence	→	fear, helplessness, feeling under attack
'brackish waters ... filled the city's streets' (ll. 28–29)	→	dirt, decay, destructive power	→	disgust, fear, being threatened
...		...		...

The writer of the text clearly feels ... about what happened in New Orleans	
His intention in the text is to convey / communicate these emotions to ...	
share these feelings with ...	
One of the main techniques he employs to do this is to use ...	
For example, in l. XX	he writes ... / we read the word/phrase
This word/phrase	has connotations of ... / makes the reader think of ...
The effect is to	arouse feelings of ... in the reader.
A further example is to be found / There are several more cases like this / Similarly, in l. XX we read ...	
To sum up,	the general tone of the text is / the overall effect is ...

D Reacting to the text

1. The writer believes that the storm 'challenge[d] the country's vision of itself' (l. 8). From what you now know about Katrina's impact on the USA, explain how this might be so. Describe what happened to America's self-image after Katrina.

▶ Skills 5.2

2. Write an outraged letter about the effects of Hurricane Katrina. You may address the letter to any person in authority who is somehow connected with the disaster, such as the mayor of a city, the editor of an American newspaper, etc. In your letter, focus on social attitudes and aspects of racism.

4 America and the world (A radio interview)

Today the USA is without doubt one, if not *the* dominant world power – and not just regarding politics and international diplomacy. But this may not always be the case. Even now, voices predicting a decrease in American influence are becoming louder. You are going to listen to a radio interview with the American journalist Fareed Zakaria on this subject.

A Before you listen

1. Have a look at the word cloud below and make sure you know all the words. Then in small groups, use it to discuss the role the USA has, used to have or should have in the world.

2. Give examples of the US acting as a military superpower in the present.

B Understanding the text

CD 3

▶ Skills 6

Listen to the interview and take notes. Then work on the following tasks:

1. Describe the new relationship between the USA and the rest of the world as discussed by Zakaria in his book.
2. Zakaria mentions three criteria by which he measured the power shift in the world. State and explain them.
3. Point out how important superpower status is for the USA, according to Zakariah.

C Reacting to the text

Discuss how the role of the USA as an international superpower may be considered a reflection of the American Dream.

D Reacting to Topics 1 to 3

▶ Skills 7.5

Consider what you have found out in Topics 1 to 3 about the USA. Collect and structure your ideas, then prepare an oral presentation to discuss which aspects of the USA make it a dream and which make it a nightmare. Come to your own conclusion.

TOPIC

04

The Canadian Mosaic

Collect ideas

▶ Activity chest 2

1. Brainstorm the topic 'Canada' to find out what you know or feel about the country.
2. Describe the pictures and point out what aspects of Canada they highlight.
3. Develop a mindmap about Canada, using the words and ideas you have collected.

1 A promised land? (An extract from a novel)

At the end of the eighteenth century, the colonies in North America that are now Canada were a safe haven for many black people who had escaped slavery in the American colonies. But the atmosphere soon began to change.
You are now going to read excerpts from the novel *The Book of Negroes* (2010). They tell of Aminata Diallo, a former slave who escapes to Nova Scotia where she watches her dream of a sanctuary in Canada begin to crumble.

A Before you read

▶ Activity chest 2

For thousands of former slaves Nova Scotia was their promised land (cf. the **KEY FACTS** box below). Working with a partner, brainstorm about the phrase 'the promised land' with reference to Black Loyalists moving to Nova Scotia.

KEY FACTS Black Loyalists

In contrast to African Americans in the USA, the majority of Canadian black people weren't brought to Canada as slaves. They came from the USA through voluntary migration.
Most of them were Black Loyalists – former American slaves who were granted freedom by the British for fighting on their side in the 1776 War of Independence. When the British lost the war, a few Black Loyalists went to England or Germany, but most of them landed in what was later to become Canada (in Quebec and especially Nova Scotia). For their loyal services to the British, they were promised lands and rich forests just begging to be converted into farmland.
But more than a thousand Black Loyalists gave up on Nova Scotia after ten years of miserable treatment by the British to form the first Back-to-Africa movement of the Americas. To this day, the Black Loyalists of Nova Scotia are still known as some of the founders of the modern state of Sierra Leone.
It was not until August 1, 1834, that slavery itself was formally abolished in Canada. Another thirty-one years passed before the Thirteenth Amendment of the United States Constitution officially abolished slavery in the USA in 1865.

Extract 1:

Aminata Diallo is talking to her employer, Mr Witherspoon.

'Why are so many businesses closing?' I asked Mr Witherspoon.

'They built this port in too much of a hurry,' Mr Witherspoon said. 'Everybody was convinced it would become the next New York. But the jobs never came. The people have no money to spend, and the businesses can't sell their goods. This town will collapse nearly as quickly as it was built.

An unusual heat wave settled over Shelburne and Birchtown in the month of July. The mosquitoes were meaner than any I had met in South Carolina, and bears came to the edge of town to eat berries off the bushes and to root through our garbage. Few of the Negroes had received land, and the British had cut off our provisions. Men hunted deer and moose to salt as much meat as they could for the winter. Most of the healthy men and women of Birchtown looked every day for work in Shelburne, but jobs were becoming harder to find. Mr Witherspoon's whaling operation was just one of many businesses to close. Wages were dropping – especially for the Negroes. At nine pence a day, Negroes carrying crates on the wharves made less than one-third the pay of whites. Businesses that did have work were often happy to hire the Negroes at the cheaper rate, but that left growing groups of white labourers – many of them disbanded soldiers who, like the Negroes, had come to Shelburne after serving the British in the war in the Colonies – gathering angrily in the alehouses. From their ragged clothing and worn faces, I could see that many of the white men endured difficulties too, and I knew that for the Negroes, these were the most dangerous people of all.

One evening in late July, May and I had finished at the Witherspoons' house and were walking down Charlotte to Water Street. […]

'Mama, what are they doing?'

'They're hurting people,' I said. I wanted to hurry back to Birchtown. But the angry mob was growing outside the alehouse to my right, and another crowd was forming to my left on Water Street. I pressed May flat against the side of the building.

'Let's burn their homes,' one man shouted. 'Let's torch Birchtown,' another said.

'It's time to teach the niggers a lesson,' said one man.

'Let's start with that big bastard down there.'

Many of the men were drinking beer, and others carried muskets. The two groups of white men merged as they moved away from May and me, crossed Water Street and headed toward a Negro who was well known in Birchtown. Ben Henson, a tall, thick-set man, was stationed at his usual post to the side of Water Street, sawing logs at the rate of one penny a foot. Ben had the biggest arms in Birchtown, but I wished that he would take off and run before they got to him. I didn't want him to prove his strength. I wanted him to be safe. But as the men advanced, Ben kept working on his thick log.

'Why don't you haul them logs back to Nigger town?' a man leading the crowd called out.

Ben did not look up from his sawing. The leader walked closer to him, musket pointed at Ben's waist. Ben kept working until the man was within reach. In a flash, Ben grabbed the musket, seized the man and flung him to the ground. Two more men jumped him, but Ben tossed them off like cats. While he was dodging the

8 *root through sth.:* search sth. with the snout
15 *wharf:* place where ships are unloaded
17 *disband sth:* break up sth. (esp. an organised army)
33 *merge:* become one
39 *log:* Baumstamm
40 *haul sth.* [hɔːl]: pull sth.
45 *dodge sth.:* move quickly to avoid sth.

knife of a fourth man, yet another slid behind him, raised a musket and shot him through the head. [...]

Mrs Witherspoon fed us and put us up for the next three days. Her husband brought more news: the white men were still rampaging. Roaming bands of unemployed workers had killed at least four Negroes and beaten many others. There was talk of rape. When the whites descended on Birchtown, they had been beaten back, but they had only returned in larger numbers to tear down some houses and set fire to others, attacking anyone who resisted. [...]

Every evening, I asked Mr Witherspoon for a report. Four days after the riots began, he told me that they had stopped. There were no more bands of men roaming the streets, he said, and no more reports of violence in Birchtown.

49 *rampage:* rush about angrily
roam: walk around randomly

B Understanding extract 1

1. List all the information you can find to describe the situation in Birchtown.
2. Label each point as either positive or negative. Explain.

Extract 2:

Over the next four years [...] Shelburne's heyday had come and gone, and many Loyalists closed their businesses and returned to the United States. The blacks of Birchtown stayed, however, and I stayed with them. [...]

In the spring of 1790, the Methodists crammed into Daddy Moses' chapel to listen to a visitor from Annapolis Royal. He was a short, stocky fellow who looked a little older than me, and he spoke in a tone so flat that some parishioners fell asleep. But he seemed to have something urgent to say, so I slipped into the first pew to hear him better.

'My name is Thomas Peters,' he said. 'Fourteen years ago I ran from the man who owned me in North Carolina. During the war I served the British in the Black Pioneers, and anybody who doesn't believe me can come on up here and see my regimental papers. I'm just the same as the rest of you: I came to Nova Scotia seven years ago and I'm still waiting for my land. But now I'm tired of waiting and I'm going to do something about it.'

Thomas Peters said he was taking up a collection to travel to England. There, he said, he hoped to speak to members of the British Parliament about the landless Black Loyalists and the perpetuation of slavery in Nova Scotia. None of us imagined that anything would come of it, but contributed what we could. I admired Peters' determination, and gave him ten shillings. After the meeting, I helped him write the conclusion to what he called his Memorial. 'The poor friendless Slaves have no more Protection by the Laws of the Colony ... than the mere Cattel or brute beasts ... and ... the oppressive Cruelty and Brutality of their Bondage is particularly shocking, irritating and obnoxious to ... the free People of Colour who cannot conceive that it is really the Intention of the British Government to favour Injustice, or tolerate Slavery in Nova Scotia.' [...]

A few days later, while reading the *Royal Gazette*, I came across a notice from the chairman and twelve directors of the Sierra Leone Company in London, England: FREE SETTLEMENT ON THE COAST OF AFRICA.

The notice claimed that the Sierra Leone Company was willing to receive into its African colony Free Negroes who could produce testimonials of their character,

1 *heyday:* time of greatest prosperity
8 *pew* [pjuː]: bench in a church
17 *perpetuation* [pəˌpetʃu'eɪʃn]: (here) continuation
22 *bondage:* (here) slavery
23 *obnoxious* [əb'nɒkʃəs]: nasty

'more particularly as to their honesty, sobriety and industry.' It said that every 'Free black' who could produce such a written testimonial would have a grant of twenty acres of land in Sierra Leone for himself, ten for his wife and five for every child. Blacks and whites would have the same civil, military, personal and commercial rights and duties in Sierra Leone, and it would not be lawful for the Sierra Leone Company to hold any person in slavery or to traffic in the buying or selling of slaves.

FREETOWN, SIERRA LEONE: PADEMBA ROAD.

Once I started reading the notice to people in Birchtown, others asked me to read it over and over again. I read it in Daddy Moses' Methodist chapel. I read it in the Baptist church. I read it anywhere and everywhere that folks wanted to hear about it. I read the document aloud enough times to memorize it. Still, I could not understand who would be allowed to travel to Africa, how they would get there, how they could pay for the journey, or who was behind this scheme and why they were offering it. Everybody asked me where Sierra Leone was, but I did not know.

We soon discovered that it was unsafe to discuss the scheme publicly. In Shelburne, three men beat up a Negro cooper who stepped into a coffee house with a copy of the Gazette in his hand. Some people in Birchtown worried that all the talk of moving to Africa would amount to nothing more than an excuse for white people to riot against the Negroes again.

A few days later, an Englishman named John Clarkson rode into Birchtown on his horse, wearing his full uniform as a lieutenant in the Royal Navy. He was a young-looking man. I was about 46 that year, and he appeared to be half my age. Young, but earnest. He had a boy's face, small nose, pursed lips. He was clean shaven but with wildly bushy sideburns. He asked to address Daddy Moses' congregation. Hundreds of people crammed into Daddy Moses' chapel and just as many crowded outside the doors, so we all moved outside. John Clarkson stood with his back to the ocean, brushing the hair out of his eyes. We gathered around him in a giant horseshoe shape, looking out at the bay.

John Clarkson had a high-pitched voice but it carried well. We stood motionless and silent so as not to miss a word.

'Reverend Moses, ladies and gentlemen, my name is John Clarkson, and I am a lieutenant with the British Navy. I am not here, however, on a military mission. I am here on a civilian purpose, which is to offer those of you who are interested and eligible passage to Sierra Leone, in Africa.'

The people cheered so loudly that Lieutenant Clarkson had to wait for the roar

31 *sobriety* [sə'braɪəti]: (here) serious and sensible nature
43 *scheme:* plan
46 *cooper:* maker of tubs (= Wannen), barrels (= Fässer), etc.
64 *eligible* ['elɪdʒəbl]: suitable to be chosen

to subside. I was stuck by his paleness, and could see a blue vein near his temple. His eyes were lively, however, and appeared to study all the people before him while waiting for them to settle down. His gaze fell on me. I imagined that his eyes were lingering on the orange scarf wrapped around my head. John Clarkson's own hair was blond and receding. Bald spots extended back from the top of his forehead. He wiped sweat from his brow and buried his eyes in his palms, like a man who was fighting sleep because he had too much work to do.

When the crowd had grown quiet once again, Clarkson said that he had been born in Wisbech, a small port some ninety miles from London. He and his relations believed that the slave trade was a stain on Christianity. He said that he had become acquainted with the fact that Negroes who had served the British in the war against the rebellious Colonies had been denied land and opportunities in Nova Scotia and New Brunswick.

'I am here to tell you today that I have been authorized by the proper authorities in England to offer loyal Negroes passage to a new life in Africa.'

75 *stain:* Schmutzfleck

[From: *The Book of Negroes* by Lawrence Hill, 2010]

C Understanding extract 2

1. List the events that lead up to the offer of passage to Africa by filling out a sequence chart like the one below:

Event 1: … → Event 2: … → … → … → a new life in Africa

2. When the narrator informs others about the passage, she asks herself the same questions again and again, but cannot answer them (cf. ll. 41–44). Answer the questions for her. For those you cannot answer, speculate.

D Analysing both extracts

Have a look at the **SPOTLIGHT** and the **IMPROVE YOUR WRITING** boxes on pp. 102–103, then work on the following tasks.

▶ Glossary 2.1

1. Write a character study of the narrator based on her actions, thoughts and language in both extracts. Explain her contrasting feelings at the beginning of extract 2.
2. Describe the atmosphere in the extracts.
3. Analyse the description of Clarkson and examine how it adds to the effectiveness of the scene (ll. 50–60).

E Reacting to the text

1. In pairs, act out a conversation between the narrator and Thomas Peters about the opportunity to travel to Africa. Record it (e.g. with your mobile phone) and use it as a basis to write either a play script of the conversation (including stage directions) or a narrative account of the meeting.
2. Referring back to your speculations in task C2, finish Clarkson's presentation. Make sure to address your audience and to try to convince them.
3. Research this relocation of black Nova Scotians to Sierra Leone and present your results. Make sure to answer the questions from C2 that are still unanswered.

SPOTLIGHT ON Analysing narrative texts

When analysing narrative texts, it is essential to a) identify the characteristic properties of the text and b) describe and analyse to what effect they are used. In other words, don't just identify the kind of narrator, but say, for example, what it means for the story that it is told from the perspective of an eight-year old girl (who possibly does not fully understand what grown-ups say). And never forget to support your observations from the text.

Properties	Possible features to analyse	Your analysis	Proof from text
Characters	- the use of monologue/dialogue / reported speech; - explicit or implicit characterisation; - round or flat characters		
Point of view	- the kind of narrator used and to what effect		
Language and style	- the tone of the text; - the use of rhetorical devices		
Action and plot	- order or events told; - turning point and climax; - ending and solution		
Mode of presentation	- the use of telling or showing		
Theme/ context	- the theme; - the (historical) context		

IMPROVE YOUR WRITING Formulating a text analysis

In order to present the results of your text analysis in a coherent form, you need to know special words and ways of integrating them into a sentence – actually, it's a special type of English you are using, just like English for doctors or engineers!

Theme/context

The short story is set in … / takes place in / at the time of … / The action takes place at a time when …
The story deals with / explores the theme / confronts the issue of …

Characters

… is characterised/presented as … / a … person … acts impulsively / in a very silly manner / like a child … … talks more than … / does all the talking / interrupts … / asks questions / dominates the conversation There is no dialogue. / The writer uses monologues to … The narrator explicitly describes/characterises him as …

She is a … person.	This becomes obvious when she … You can conclude this from the way …
… is a fairly flat character. However, … is very rounded.	He represents … She is/acts … first, but then … / There are changes and contradictions in his behaviour. This makes it easy/difficult to identify with …

Point of view

… is told from …'s perspective / uses a first-person-narrator	so the reader doesn't learn / only knows … Hence, the perspective is limited.

Language and style

The writer takes a very … tone. / The article's tone is / can be described as / comes across as … The writer uses / makes use of / employs … In the text you can find many examples of …	
The frequent use of …	makes the text … / contributes to the impression that …
Apparently, the writer is critical of / is in favour of …	You can conclude this from the way he … / the use of …

Action and plot

The events follow / are told in a chronological order. There are / The writer uses many flashbacks / frequently shifts between layers of time. The action shifts between present and past/future.
This is when the story reaches its climax. / The climax is the moment when … The ending is open as we don't know … / The ending solves the conflict between …

Mode of presentation

The narrator calls the protagonist … / describes … as … … tells the readers directly what kind of person … is.	
When characterising the protagonist, the writer lets the reader experience … / prefers showing … The reader has to draw their own conclusions about…	because she / the writer rarely …

2 A dream of multiculturalism (A book extract and a newspaper article)

Canada is often praised for its multiculturalism. Immigration has always been strong there, and Canada has faced relatively few of the problems that are associated with high immigration by other countries. You are now going to read two texts with different perspectives on multiculturalism in Canada.

KEY FACTS Canada as a multicultural society

Canada became the first country in the world to officially introduce an agenda for multiculturalism into its legislative system. Because of such recognition of the importance of immigration, Canada's multiculturalism policies are generally regarded as exemplary. 20% of its 34 million citizens can be identified as foreign-born, so Canada is widely regarded as a nation of immigrants.

Canada's history of multiculturalism is strongly bound to its history of immigration. From the British explorers of the 18th century through the gold rushes in the 19th century to settlements out west in the late 19th and early 20th century, Canadian society has been defined by immigration. The **cultural mosaic** (the Canadian counterpart to the USA's 'melting pot') involves the collaboration of all ethnic and cultural groups which simultaneously retain their own various features within the society.

In 1967, Canada introduced a **points system** as the core of its immigration policy. This meant that immigrants were judged on various merits: whether they could speak English or French, had arranged jobs in Canada, had relatives there, and what education or training they had already received. If they had enough points, they were able to apply for immigration. This removed any formal discrimination from the process: no one could be denied immigration to Canada based on their ethnicity, religion or nationality. However, critics point out that levels of education vary between countries, so the Canadian policy invariably favours those from more developed states.

In more recent years, the source of Canadian immigration has changed significantly, shifting from Europe (particularly Britain) to Asia, which now represents the largest region of origin for new Canadians. Other important sources of immigration include Africa, the Middle East and South and Central America.

A Before you read

Canadian society is often called a 'cultural mosaic'.

1. Remembering what you already know about Canada, say what pieces make up this mosaic, i.e. which ethnic groups live there.
2. Compare the image of a mosaic to the American idea of a melting pot. What implications does this have for multiculturalism in Canada and in the US?

A mosaic consists of …	which don't change in shape / retain their shape	when they are put together / connected / …
So the individual parts stay the same / are unchanged / still recognisable		
In a melting pot, however, the parts/ingredients	are heated / become liquid / lose their shape	
In the end, the original substances cannot be told apart / no longer exist / become indistinguishable		
If we transfer the two images to multiculturalism, the concept of a mosaic implies / means that …	separate communities are able to … / society is made up of …	

Text 1: A post-national state

Why is Canada such a successful country? Simple: we are the product of a fortunate historical accident. In the late 1700s, once the dust had settled from the Seven Years' War and the American Revolution, the British found themselves with a unique problem in managing their remaining North American possessions. Apart from the aboriginal population, the territory consisted of a large and entrenched French colony in what used to be known as New France, alongside mostly British colonies in the Atlantic region, with yet more British, along with American loyalists, flooding into the wilderness to the west. British North America was evolving into a political space consisting of discrete French and British populations. It should have been a recipe for war, which is what the French and the British had been at, more on than off, in Europe since the Middle Ages.

The British solution – one the empire employed with varying degrees of success around the world – was to ignore the problem. The French in Lower Canada went their own way, under the watchful but mostly passive eye of an appointed governor, while Upper Canada, the Maritimes and Newfoundland did the same. The one attempt, in 1840, at uniting Upper and Lower Canada under responsible government was a miserable failure – the resulting assemblies were even more unstable than some of our recent Parliaments – and so in 1864 local politicians proposed dissolving that union and instead confederating the colonies into a collection of self-governing jurisdictions, with a general government charged with administering areas of joint concern. In that sense, Confederation was a divorce as much as a marriage: an agreement by the English and the French to create a minimalist state in which, as far as possible, each left the other alone.

It wasn't much of a recipe for nation building, but there was nothing for it. The chasm between British and French cultures made a Canadian nation impossible, despite the longings of editorialists and the best efforts of cultural reformers. However, the good news was that having no particular notion of nation meant that there was no precious culture to protect, which is one reason – filling an empty land was another – that Canadian governments encouraged immigration, with the general consent and approval of the population. We brought in waves of it, decade after decade. [...]

Today, roughly a quarter of our intake comes from China and environs, and a quarter from India and environs, with the rest hailing from the Caribbean, Latin America, the Middle East and Africa. We even take in a few from Europe, though not many want to leave there anymore.

We ask only of our immigrants that they embrace the principles of liberal democracy embodied by our governments and our Constitution – which are an amalgam of English and French political traditions – that they abide by the laws and accept the legal philosophy underpinning those laws [...] and that they respect the uniqueness of other peoples and cultures, just as others respect them,

5 *aboriginal:* (here) First Nations
6 *entrenched:* firmly established
11 *American loyalist:* American who supported British rule
14 *discrete:* separate, independent
21 *appointed:* chosen for a position of responsibility
22 *Maritimes:* New Brunswick, Novia Scotia and Prince Edward Island
24 *assembly:* (here) parliament
26 *dissolve sth.:* break sth. up
confederate sth.: unite sth.
27 *jurisdiction:* area with its own laws and authority
28 *concern:* (here) interest
32 *chasm* ['kæzəm]: big difference between two groups
37 *consent:* agreement
39 *environs:* surrounding areas
40 *hail from:* come from
45 *amalgam:* mixture
46 *underpin sth.:* form the basis of sth.

which is the essence of Canadian multiculturalism. The overwhelming majority of immigrants have had no difficulty living by these rules, because it was those rules, and the society that created those rules, that drew them here in the first place.

Sadly, this policy has done nothing to help unify Canada as a national entity; we remain as fractured and fractious as we were in the days of Brown and Cartier, King and Duplessis, Trudeau and Levesque. It has, however, fitted Canada splendidly for its emerging role as the world's first truly cosmopolitan, post-national state [...]

Yes, this is overly simplistic. Yes, it glosses over real problems. Not all communities are integrating successfully. Race-based crime is frontpage news in Toronto and Vancouver and Montreal, though it does not begin to compare with that in many other North American and European cities. Militant Islam infects Canadian society too: at least one gang of young men, Canadian born, allegedly conspired to wage their own jihad by assaulting the Parliament buildings.

As Canada evolves into one of the world's most urban and diverse nations, its rural regions remain monochromatic and monocultural – cut off from the urban state of mind, their populations and economies generally in decline, and their citizens bewildered and resentful of the big cities that seem to have a monopoly on the attention and resources of government.

Far more worrying, generations of neglect and failed experiments have left Canada's aboriginal people – status and non-status Indians, Inuit and Métis – too often confined to isolation, poverty and exclusion. This is not the place to analyze the causes of, and possible solutions to, this national disgrace. But it remains our most compelling and urgent dilemma.

Yet within a global context, Canada is comparatively the most peaceable of kingdoms, seemingly immune from the cultural stresses that are threatening the fabric of too many other states in both the developed and developing world. Not only immune – we are visibly thriving by pursuing the very policies that have led other countries into turmoil.

[From: *Uneasy partners* by Janice Stein et al., 2007]

51 *entity:* sth. that has its own identity
52 *fractious:* easily troubled by small things
67 *bewildered:* confused
72 *Métis:* people with mixed European and Aboriginal backgrounds
79 *thrive:* be successful

B Understanding the text

On the basis of the text, collect information on the following:
- How could Canada develop into a multicultural society?
- In what way has it been successful?
- What are the downsides of Canada being a multicultural society?
- What problems have arisen?

C Before you read

Take notes on the aspects you examined in text 1 (cf. task B1) when reading text 2.

Text 2: A basic Canadian value?

In recent weeks, the debate in Britain over the wearing of the niqab or face veil has crossed the north Atlantic to Canada. It came on the heels of claims that the leaders of the large Indo-Canadian population in British Columbia were turning a blind eye to widespread domestic violence. Last year saw an acrimonious dispute in Ontario over whether Muslims could use Islamic sharia courts to settle family disputes. (The provincial government eventually decided that they could not.)

In themselves, fights over cultural practices and symbols are nothing new in Canada. Sikhs went to the Supreme Court to win the right for uniformed policemen to wear turbans and students to wear ceremonial daggers known as kirpans. What is new about the latest arguments is an underlying tension between some cultural practices of recent immigrants and the mainstream values of Canadian liberal democracy, such as sex equality.

This comes as a small minority of Muslim immigrants seek to emphasise their separation from, and even hostility to, the wider society. In June 17 Canadian Muslims were arrested on charges of plotting terrorist attacks on targets including the national Parliament. 'Muslims are the first group to seriously challenge our notions of multiculturalism and tolerance,' says Neil Bissoondath, a writer on the subject.

Similar debates have raged in Europe. Two things give them a different edge in Canada. First, even more than the United States, Canada is nowadays a nation of immigrants. Immigration is both increasing and increasingly non-European. Second, from its birth as a self-governing nation in 1867 Canada was a multicultural mixture of British and French settlers and the indigenous people they called Indians. A century later, this was officially recognised.

In 1971 Pierre Trudeau, a Liberal prime minister, declared Canada bilingual and multicultural. The Multiculturalism Act of 1988 replaced the previous policy of assimilation with one of acceptance of diversity.

Multiculturalism has since sunk deep roots in government, reflected in everything from broadcasting to education policy. It has itself become a basic Canadian value. Polls show that a majority support continued immigration and do not want it limited to whites. Almost half believe that immigrants should be free to maintain their cultural and religious practices. But a poll published this week reflected the new

1 *niqab:* piece of cloth worn by some Muslim women to cover the face
2 *come on the heels of sth.:* quickly follow sth.
4 *turn a blind eye to sth.:* ignore sth.
acrimonious: angry
5 *sharia:* system of Muslim laws

Religious practices: Mosque in Canada

disquiet: when asked whether those practices should be tolerated if they infringe women's rights, a large majority said No. Some feminists counter that Canada tolerates other practices that they see as demeaning, such as cosmetic surgery.

One school of thought says that it is time to set firmer rules for what is expected of citizens and to define more clearly what it means to be Canadian. Adherents to this view gleefully seized on a comment by Yann Martel, a novelist, that 'Canada is one of the greatest hotels on earth – it welcomes everyone from everywhere.' (Mr Martel claims that he was misunderstood.)

But most commentators still subscribe to multiculturalism as not just a worthwhile aspiration but as the only way of holding Canada together. To preserve it, some trust in muddle-through. [...]

Others worry that laissez-faire is a recipe for rising tension. They say there is no alternative but to negotiate solutions to cultural clashes, new or old. Rudyard Griffiths of the Dominion Institute, a think-tank concerned with Canadian identity, points to a long history of finding ways to accommodate seemingly intractable differences of language, culture and religion, such as those between English and French speakers or Catholics and Protestants.

Some of the new disputes will doubtless be resolved in the courts. Politicians, who until a few years ago were happy to talk up multiculturalism, have mainly fallen silent. [...] Officially, then, Canada still stands squarely behind multiculturalism. But the silences are eloquent.

[From: *The Economist*, November 16, 2006]

46 *demeaning:* humiliating
48 *adherent:* sb. who supports sth.
53 *aspiration:* (here) aim, sth. to be acheived
54 *muddle-through:* (here) continuing without a plan
58 *intractable:* very difficult to deal with
63 *squarely:* firmly

D Understanding the texts

▶ Skills 5.1, 5.2

Structure the notes you have taken for Text 1 and 2 and write a summary on Canadian multiculturalism.

E Analysing the texts

1. Problems with multiculturalism in Canada are mentioned in both texts but they are weighed differently. Compare the writers' attitudes to the problems.
2. Text 1 is taken from a chapter with the title 'Success? We failed!' Explain and analyse this title.

The title refers to Canada's success in ...	and its failure to ...	
Because Canadians were unable / did not try to ...	establish ... / create ...	they laid the foundations of ... / enabled people from ... to ...
The title contains / is made up of two words	that mean/express ... / contain a contradiction / a paradox / are contradictory	

F Reacting to the texts

In Canada, the majority of immigrants become Canadian citizens. Find out what conditions they have to meet to become Canadian citizens and compare them to those in your country.

3 A better life in the suburbs (A newspaper article)

Since the 1990s, more than 200,000 immigrants have come to Canada each year. An increasing number decides not to live in the big cities but to move to the suburbs. The following text explores the reasons for this.

A Before you read

Try to collect possible reasons why most immigrants tend to move to big cities. Then speculate what might make up their 'suburban dream', as the text calls it.

Recent immigrants in smaller suburban communities are faring better than those setting roots in big cities when it comes to jobs, incomes and homeownership, says a new study that measures newcomers' life quality across Canada.

The report shows immigrants to the Greater Toronto Area are increasingly choosing the 905 regions as their destination over Toronto. Even those initially settling in the city are then moving on to the suburbs.

The study, conducted by the Federation of Canadian Municipalities, compared how newcomers who have been in the country for five years or more and living in the suburbs fared against their counterparts in the city. It found those living outside big cities were less likely to be living off social assistance, less likely to be unemployed, twice as likely to have a university degree and more likely to own homes.

The Shukla family outside their Mississauga home

Jyoti Shukla, her lawyer husband, Kamen, and their 12-year-old daughter, Vishwa, were drawn to Mississauga to live their suburban dream – and for its relatively lower costs of living when the family moved here from India in 2004.

'There are actually plenty of job opportunities for newcomers in the suburbs,' said Shukla, 42, who has a master's degree in marketing and 18 years of business experience. 'The city's job market is pretty saturated and it is too competitive. We are close enough to the city but out of the city. There is more stability and we feel more safe here.'

The suburbanization trends, partially a result of Ottawa's push to spread immigrants evenly across the country, have led to a lose-lose situation for large and small communities alike: While big cities are finding it harder to meet their labour needs with the exodus of well-educated and highly skilled immigrants, their smaller counterparts struggle to accommodate the influx.

'While most immigrants continue to live in large urban centres, a growing number of our most educated and highly skilled immigrants are settling in suburban and smaller communities,' said the municipal federation's president, Jean Perrault, mayor of Sherbrooke, Quebec.

1 *fare well:* jdm. geht es gut
6 *905 regions:* suburban areas of Toronto
8 *municipality:* area with its own local government
12 *social assistance:* financial aid from the government
25 *saturated:* (here) full
31 *counterpart:* Ebenbild
influx: Einströmen

'Those who remain in large centres face greater socio-economic challenges.

'Large cities are losing the skilled immigrants their labour markets need while (they are) bearing a disproportionate share of the cost of assisting immigrants with special challenges such as language and skills training needs.

'Municipal governments are where immigrants go first for help, but we are not consulted on immigration policies or programs and we do not have the resources to provide the needed services. It's time for a change,' he said. [...]

Evelyn Myrie, director of the Peel Newcomer Strategy Group, said while newcomers in smaller communities may fare better than those in big cities, they still have settlement needs, such as language upgrading and employment counselling, to be met. Issues such as poverty and homelessness are also slowly emerging in the suburbs, too, she added.

'Some smaller communities like Caledon just don't have the resources in place to serve those needs,' said Myrie, whose group was formed four years ago by the United Way of Peel to involve community players in immigration and settlement planning.

Alykhan Velshi, a spokesperson for Immigration Minister Jason Kenney, said the department will review the report.

Toronto city councillor Janet Davis, chair of the city's now-defunct immigration and settlement working group, said Toronto is still the No. 1 recipient of new immigrants, despite its dwindling share.

[From: *Toronto Star*, 20 March, 2009]

39 *disproportionate:* unangemessen
55 *defunct:* no longer existing
56 *recipient of sth.:* receiver of sth.
57 *dwindling:* decreasing

B Understanding the text

1. Point out the advantages that living in the suburbs may have for immigrants to Canada.
2. Describe the problems that arise when more immigrants choose to live in the suburbs.

C Analysing the text

▶ Glossary 1.1

1. Examine the author's intention when writing this text and identify the text type.
2. This text mostly consists of information or opinions from other sources. Examine how the writer manages all the same to express an opinion despite this.

D Reacting to the text

▶ Activity chest 9

1. Imagine you were going to live in Canada. Do some research about the country and decide where you would want to live. Design a poster about your favourite place and present it in a 'Gallery walk'.

▶ Activity chest 14

2. The question of where to live does not only affect immigrants. Would you prefer to live in a city, in a suburb or in the countryside? Discuss this in a 'Silent discussion'.

4 Volunteering in Canada (A newspaper article)

An English friend of yours is about to finish school and is thinking about some kind of voluntary work. You have just read the following article about Anelia D'Souza, a volunteer in Canada, and (in English) tell her about it.

D'Souza leistet gemeinnützige Freiwilligenarbeit in den Wäldern Kanadas. Trotz Regens ist sie an diesem Morgen einige Kilometer an den Minnewanka-See gewandert, um den Uferweg in Stand zu setzen. Sie rollt umgestürzte Baumstämme weg, liest Unrat auf und befreit den Wegrand von überflüssigem Gestrüpp. Was eben nötig ist, um den Pfad nach dem Winter wieder begehbar zu machen. Zwei Dollar bekommt sie dafür am Tag. Doch darum geht es ihr nicht.

„Ich will etwas Sinnvolles für die Allgemeinheit tun und herausfinden, welche Richtung ich in meinem Leben einschlagen soll," erklärt Anelia D'Souza. Nahe der westkanadischen Kleinstadt Canmore absolviert die 21-Jährige in einer Gruppe mit acht weiteren Jugendlichen ein soziales und ökologisches Jahr. Zum ersten Mal ist sie für mehrere Monate weg von zu Hause, ohne Eltern oder Freunde. Es ist eine Herausforderung. [...] Trotzdem hat sich Anelia für den Freiwilligendienst entschieden – wie immer mehr junge Menschen in Kanada. Sechs von zehn Kanadiern arbeiten schon in jungen Jahren als „Volunteers", so nennt man die Freiwilligen. Mal neben Schule oder Studium, mal dazwischen, mal danach. In der Altersgruppe zwischen 15 und 24 Jahren sind das etwa doppelt so viele wie noch vor zehn Jahren. Es sind auch deutlich mehr als in Deutschland, wo sich laut Bundesfamilienministerium etwa jeder dritte Jugendliche schon ehrenamtlich betätigt hat.

Der Boom bei der Freiwilligenarbeit hat kulturelle und politische Gründe. In Kanada sind die Sozialsysteme dünner gestrickt als in Europa, ehrenamtliches Engagement und Nachbarschaftshilfen spielen traditionell eine größere Rolle als in Europa. In jüngerer Zeit kommt die Wirtschaftskrise hinzu, die auch Jugendliche trifft und ihnen den schnellen Berufseinstieg oft erschwert. Da ist „Volunteering" ein willkommener wie sinnvoller Zeitvertreib. Das Schulsystem spielt ebenfalls eine Rolle: In Kanada verlassen viele Jugendliche bereits mit 17 Jahren die High School und es gibt keinen Wehr- oder Zivildienst. Den Bachelor, eine Art Grundstudium mit Abschluss, haben sie manchmal schon mit 20 oder 21 in der Tasche. Auf der Suche nach Orientierung gehen viele junge Kanadier danach auf Reisen, sammeln in einfachen Aushilfsjobs Erfahrung – oder werden Freiwillige.

„Volunteering wird immer populärer, weil die jungen Leute dabei ihr Land und vor allem sich selbst entdecken können," erklärt die Sozialarbeiterin Marie-Maude Hamelin, die Betreuerin der neunköpfigen Freiwilligen-Gruppe. [...]

Einfach gemacht wird es den Volunteers nicht: Im Haus in Canmore gibt es einen Küchen- und Putzdienst. Wenn alle zusammen sind, gilt ein Handy-Verbot. Alkohol ist tabu. An zwei Abenden der Woche müssen alle Computer ausgeschaltet werden, einmal die Woche wird der Strom abgeschaltet. An manchen Tagen wird nur Englisch gesprochen, an anderen Französisch. Die Jugendlichen sollen lernen, sich mit sich selbst zu beschäftigen.

[From: *Berliner Zeitung*, 4 July, 2011]

SEQUENCE

03

GOING GLOBAL

No other generation has ever lived in a globalised world. Yours does, and the world around you continues to grow increasingly globalised. In this sequence we ask: what is globalisation, what are its advantages and disadvantages, and what kind of world will it lead us to?

Collect ideas

► Skills 2.1

1. Work in groups of three or four. Each of you choose three pictures and prepare descriptions of them. Then share descriptions in your group. If you are not sure about details of a picture you can speculate.

I am not (totally) sure, but …	
I think … / I would guess that …	*this picture (probably) shows … / is (possibly) set in …*
I would say that / It is quite likely that …	*the person/people in this picture …*

► Activity chest 15

2. Do a 'Walk-talk-write':

a Divide the class into eight groups. Each group chooses one picture and collects ideas on the following question: Which aspects of globalisation does the picture illustrate?

b Write your results on a big sheet of paper and hang it up in the classroom.

This picture illustrates/highlights	*the fact/idea that …*
If we look at picture … and then at picture …,	*we can see that … / they show …*

war

clothe from everywhere

nature katastrophen

natural disasters

c Go around the classroom, reading what others have written. Comment on or add to their work. Discuss the results in class. Try to come up with other aspects of globalisation.

childwork

Travel around the world

TOPIC

01

Living in a globalised world

1 Multinational companies (A text from a company's website)

When looking for a job after school or university, you may think of applying to one of the 'MNCs' (or multinational companies). You are going to look at the careers website of one of the world's largest MNCs.

1 *foremost:* most important
nutrition: provision of food
3 *operation:* company consisting of many parts
strive to do sth.: try to achieve sth.
8 *Chief Executive Officer:* Generaldirektor
11 *Market Head:* employee who leads the marketing department
14 *Sales and Division Functions:* company department that is responsible for customer relationship and sales analysis
17 *supply chain:* Lieferkette
procurement (fml): process of getting all the materials to produce goods
R&D: research and development
19 *integrity:* quality of having high moral standards
21 *prospect:* possibility that sth. is going to happen
22 *outstanding:* excellent
ambitious: determined to be successful
23 *recruitment:* Anwerbung, Einstellung

A Before you read

Collect ideas about MNCs: list companies you know, say where their headquarters are and what products they make.

Nestlé is the world's foremost Nutrition, Health and Wellness Company, committed to serving consumers all over the world. [...]

We have operations in almost every country in the world, and strive to help our employees to achieve their full potential wherever they are. At Nestlé our commitment to your development can lead to an exciting career that takes you all over the world, as it did for me.

CAREER OF PAUL BULCKE	
Since April 2008	**Chief Executive Officer of Nestlé S.A.**
2004–Jan 2008	**Executive Vice President for Zone Americas**: United States of America, Canada, Latin America, Caribbean
2000	**Nestlé Germany**, Market Head
1998	**Nestlé Czech** and **Slovak Republic**, Market Head
1996	**Nestlé Portugal**, Market Head
1980	**Nestlé Peru**, Ecuador and Chile Marketing, Sales and Division Functions
1979	**Nestlé S.A.** Marketing Trainee (Switzerland, Spain, Belgium)

We have opportunities across all business disciplines including Sales, Marketing, Supply Chain and Procurement, Manufacturing, R&D, Engineering, Finance and Human Resources. We expect you to be dynamic, pragmatic, a team player, a person of integrity, and an achiever. These are the qualities which are the basis of strong management, financial discipline and social responsibility for our company.

We have great plans for our future growth. If you're excited by the prospect of outstanding career opportunities in a global company with ambitious goals, in a truly international culture, Nestlé provides just that. Contact our Recruitment teams to discuss your next steps; we look forward to hearing from you!

Paul Bulcke
Chief Executive Officer,
Nestlé S.A.

[From: www.nestle.com]

B Understanding the text

Outline what Paul Bulcke says about his career, his company and about future employees.

C Analysing the text

▶ Glossary 1.1

▶ Glossary 3

1. Make notes on the following tasks:
   a Describe the writer's intention and identify the type of text he has written.
   b Analyse the techniques he uses to achieve his objectives.

The text is (mainly / primarily / first and foremost) informative / instructive / …	
The writer's aim / purpose / intention is to … / He sets out to / aims to …	
He / The writer begins by	describing / pointing out / informing the reader that …
He goes on to	list / enumerate / highlight / emphasise …
The writer uses words such as …	in order to …
A picture / photograph of the writer is used to …	The effect on the reader is …
By including details of his own career,	the author shows the reader (that) …
In the final part of the text the writer … The aim of this is to …	
To sum up, the general / overall effect of the text on the reader is …	

2. Work on the task in the box below. Then write down your results to task 1 in a coherent text. Use the structures from the box at least three times.

IMPROVE YOUR WRITING *'by doing sth.' / '(in order) to do sth.'*

Two structures that you can use when writing a text analysis are 'by + -ing' and '(in order) to'. 'By' tells you *how* someone does something (= *indem*); '(in order) to' tells you *why* (= *um … zu*). Combine the pairs of sentences below, using one of the structures to make a single sentence.

1. The writer emphasises this idea. He gives an example.
   The writer emphasises this idea by giving an example.
2. The writer writes this text. (He wants to) persuade the reader to apply for a job.
3. He uses facts about the company. (He wants to) show the reader how big it is.
4. The writer makes the text easier to follow and understand. She divides it into sections and uses headings.
5. Songwriters often highlight their main theme in a song. They repeat certain lines in a 'chorus'.
6. This text was published in a left-wing newspaper. Its aim is to criticise the government.

D Reacting to the text

▶ Activity chest 14

Work in small groups to hold a 'Silent Discussion' on the theme: could you imagine working for a multinational company? Why (not)? If so, which countries would you like to work in and why? What kind(s) of job would you hope to have? Give reasons.

▶ Skills 7.4

✕ **Extra** Find out about a multinational company and present it to the class. You could also look for jobs at one of these companies and write a letter of application.

2 Sharing knowledge (Listening text)

You are going to listen to four people speaking about the online encyclopedia Wikipedia: first the founder of Wikipedia, Jimmy Wales, then three young men from around the world who use or contribute to the encyclopedia.

founder: Gründer/in

A Before you begin

State when and why you sometimes need to get information. Give a recent example. Where do you usually look? What is good about this source of information? What may be bad?

B Understanding the texts

CD 4

CD 5

▶ Skills 6

collective wisdom: broad knowledge that all members of a society share

1. Listen to Jimmy Wales. Note down why he is speaking on this occasion and what you learn from him about Wikipedia.
2. Listen to the three other speakers. You will hear speaker 1, then speaker 2, then speaker 1 again, and finally speaker 3. Note down what each says in a copy of the chart below.

speaker 1	
speaker 2	
speaker 3	

3. Sum up the key facts and opinions given by all the speakers in one short text.

C Reacting to the texts

1. Below are some remarks from online reviews of Wikipedia. What do they tell you about it? Discuss how they correspond to any personal experiences that you have had.

The Knowledge Of The World At Your Fingertips!

Advantages: Extensive site with a little about lots and lots
Disadvantages: Detail varies greatly depending on the item

Easy reference for nearly anything, if it's the truth!

Advantages: Quick to update. Easy to find reference. Clear design of site.
Disadvantages: User generated content maybe not wholly accurate.

2. A term sometimes used when speaking about globalisation is democratisation. Explain what this means and discuss how relevant it is to Wikipedia. Give reasons.

3 The changing world map (An online article)

You are going to read an online article about globalisation and its effects worldwide.

A Before you read

What makes a city a 'global' city? Collect ideas, then name some cities that would fall into this category.

Shanghai: a global city in the making

Shanghai is the ultimate poster-child for the effects of globalisation on cities and regions.

China's largest city languished for 30 years as the Chinese economy was closed to outside influence and the country went through the political turmoil of the cultural revolution.

All this was dramatically changed when the country opened up its markets to the West in the 1980s, and Shanghai was given the green light to 'get rich'.

In the last 15 years, the city has been transformed into a glittering metropolis of 21 million people, with more skyscrapers than New York and a public transport system that will soon overtake London's in size.

The city has tripled in size and its influence now extends throughout the whole Yangtze Delta region, the richest area in China.

But it is not just the size and speed of its transformation, but also its glittering economic achievements that have grabbed the attention of the world. The Shanghai region, including the two adjoining provinces, accounts for 30% of China's foreign exports and attracts 25% of all foreign investment into the country, while 20% of its manufacturing output is produced here. […]

More than 500 multinational companies, ranging from General Motors to Volkswagen, have their regional corporate headquarters in Shanghai. And it has become one of the leading financial sectors in East Asia, with major Western banks flocking to its new financial centre, built from scratch in the new district of Pudong. […]

The growing urban middle-class also fuelled a consumer boom and a property boom in the city. Western shops dominate the pedestrianised shopping street of Nanjing Lu, while the more elegant shops of the former French concession include the world's busiest H&M women's clothing store. […]

The city government of Shanghai is nothing if not ambitious. To ensure Shanghai dominates foreign trade, it is building the world's largest container port on an island 30 km offshore, linked by a six-lane bridge. […]

But the biggest obstacle to Shanghai's future development may be political. Just as Shanghai's takeoff to growth was stimulated when Shanghai mayor Jiang Zemin took power in the 1990s, the new leadership of the Chinese Communist Party is

---

2 *poster-child:* thing that represents a particular quality
5 *languish* (fml): be forced to be in an unfortunate situation for a long time
7 *turmoil:* state of confusion
cultural revolution: political changes to advance socialism in China from 1966 to 1976
10 *glitter:* shine brightly
15 *triple:* become three times as big
17 *adjoin:* be next to
19 *manufacturing:* production of goods in large quantities in factories
21 *corporate headquarters:* company's central office
22 *flock* (v): move in great numbers
23 *build sth. from scratch:* build sth. where there are no buildings yet
24 *fuel sth.:* make sth. grow
property boom: extreme rise in prices for houses, flats and land
26 *former French concession:* part of Shanghai governed by the French until 1946
29 *container port:* harbour where goods arrive to be distributed
31 *obstacle:* situation that makes it difficult to achieve sth.

34 *curb sb.'s wings:* prevent sb. from doing what they want
35 *arrest sb. on corruption charges:* arrest sb. who is supposed to be corrupt
37 *shift sth.:* move sth.
38 *narrow sth.:* make sth. smaller
39 *income disparity* (fml): difference concerning the amount of money people earn
41 *entrepreneurial tradition* [ˌɒntrəprəˈnɜːriəl]: tradition of people with their own businesses
45 *bounce back:* return to a high level after a time of difficulty
chances are: it is very likely that

attempting to curb its wings. In October, the party secretary for Shanghai, Chen Liangyu, was arrested on corruption charges and was only replaced in March by an outsider, Xi Jinping. Analysts believe that the move was intended to curb Shanghai's power, and was also related to the policy of the new party leadership to shift development from the rich coastal regions further inland, in order to narrow income disparities.

But Shanghai, with its entrepreneurial tradition and focus on getting rich, has always bounced back. This time, chances are it will do more than just that.

[From: www.bbc.co.uk, 7 May 2007]

B Understanding the text

Say if the statements below are true or false. Where you think a statement is false, correct it. Finally, sum up in your own words why Shanghai may be called a world city and what might be the opportunities and obstacles concerning its future.

a Shanghai has been a major world city since the 1950s.
b Since 1980, the city has grown to be larger than London.
c The city has become more westernised.
d The organisation which controls the city is not ambitious.
e The central Chinese government has some concerns about Shanghai.
f The writer is optimistic about Shanghai's future.

C Analysing the text

Examine the author's attitude towards the global city Shanghai.

D Reacting to the text

1. Comment on the picture of Shanghai as it is painted in this article.
2. In 2010, an international estate agent ranked the world's cities according to four criteria and gave them points from 1 (worst) to 40 (best). Below are some results. Try to explain the criteria and comment on what you think are interesting findings – including what the data tells you about Shanghai.

estate agent: Immobilienmakler

City	New York	Tokyo	Berlin	Washington DC	Sydney	Shanghai	Zurich
World rank	1	4	8	12	16	19	20
Economic activity	40	38	19	10	28	34	16
Political power	39	34	29	40	7	24	1
Knowledge & influence	40	36	26	32	30	12	28
Quality of life	32	36	39	29	27	12	34
Total points	**151**	**144**	**114**	**111**	**92**	**83**	**79**

[From: www.knightfrank.com]

3. If you had to choose where to live, which criteria would be important for your choice? Why? Are there other criteria you would add?

▶ Skills 5

Extra Categorise your home town according to the criteria given above, then write a newspaper article about it.

4 Globish around the world (A video)

You are going to watch a video about a language called Globish. The speaker is Jean-Paul Nerrière, its promotor.

A Before you watch

1. Read the **KEY FACTS** and complete the following tasks.
   a Make a timeline of the development of the English language.
   b It is often said that English is a world language because it is easy to learn and use. Say whether the text supports this view.
2. Talk in class. Speculate about what you think Globish may be.

KEY FACTS The development of the English language

Origins

People on the British Isles have not always spoken English. When the Romans conquered Britain in 43 AD and brought their Latin language with them, the inhabitants of the island spoke Celtic languages, and echoes of these languages can still be heard today in the Welsh and Gaelic languages. An early form of the English language was brought to Britain in the 5th century by the Angles and Saxons – Germanic peoples from what is now Northern Germany and the Netherlands. The Anglo-Saxon English that emerged was later influenced by the Viking language, which was brought to England through a Scandinavian invasion in the 9th century. One more invasion did even more to change English. In 1066, the Normans (from Northern France) conquered Britain and for the next three hundred years Norman French was the official language of the court and the nobles. Of course the language also influenced the English spoken by the common people. So in the 15th century, modern English emerged as a mixture of Norman French and Old English. Today we would be able to recognise it as English – although we would find it hard to understand. So the English language has many sources, and this helps to explain why today it has such a huge vocabulary. For example, modern English often has multiple words (e.g. the three adjectives 'kingly', 'royal' and 'regal' or the verbs 'ask', 'question', 'interrogate') that mean roughly the same.

English goes global

At the time of Shakespeare (1564–1616), English was only spoken by around 3 million people, all living in England. Its spread around the world and its first steps towards becoming the global language that it is today are a result of the British Empire. Beginning in the 17th century, the English language was carried around the world as countries were added to the Empire. By 1920, this covered a quarter of the globe and affected over 400 million people. The way in which English was spoken in the Empire varied. It was brought to the white settler colonies (America, Canada, Australia, New Zealand and parts of South Africa) as the first language of most settlers. In these cases it came to be used by the ruling classes and the common people. In other countries such as India, Africa and parts of Asia, English was used mainly by the ruling classes and became the official language. So many of the native inhabitants learned and used it as a second language, but they still retained their own languages. These two types of English (as a native versus a second language) are still evident around the world today.

The modern era

It was Britain's first colony, America, that would lead the way in many respects for the further spread of English during the 20th and 21st century. American culture and the country's economic and political power combined with technological advances such as cinema and the internet, have helped to make English today's global language – for culture, business, science and technology. Exact numbers of speakers of English today can only be estimated. One of the world's leading authorities on global English is the Indian academic Braj Kachru. He divides English speakers into three groups: native speakers (around 380 million), second language speakers (between 150 and 300 million). But the largest number are those like you, who have no background in English but are learning it because it is the world language, today's lingua franca. There are about 100 million to 1 billion of these speakers already.

'Englishes'

English has always been spoken by native speakers with different accents and there are some words and phrases which are unique to each country (think of American English). As it is spoken more and more around the world, however, many variants of the language have begun to evolve. They differ from the standard form normally taught at school, e.g. because they are influenced by the first language of the (non-native) speakers. They are sometimes given names such as Spanglish, Chinglish, or Indish. This may make them difficult to understand at times. But even if they differ from the standard, this does not necessarily make them wrong. Many experts agree that the English spoken in Britain or the USA is not the only correct form and that other forms are also acceptable as long as they are understandable. Thus today we talk increasingly of 'Englishes'.

DVD 11

executive: Vorstandsmitglied
limitations: (here) imperfect knowledge of sth.
codify sth.: write sth. down, e.g. a law
return on investment: profit you get after having invested sth.

B Understanding the video

1. Watch and take notes, then organise your ideas in a copy of the chart below.

What is Globish?	– … – …
How was it invented?	
What are its advantages?	
How can you learn it?	

2. Outline how, according to its inventor, Globish can play a role as a world language.

C Analysing the video

▶ Glossary 1

▶ Skills 4

1. The video is an example of a presentation. Explain what this means, pointing out the speaker's intention and classifying the text as a non-fictional text type.
2. Analyse the techniques used by the speaker to achieve his goals. Consider the setting of the presentation, the speaker's tone, his language, the use of visual aids, the beginning and end of the presentation.

D Reacting to the video

1. In class, discuss your views of Globish.
2. Write an email to the Globish website expressing your opinion of Globish.

5 A globalised world

In this topic you have looked at some key aspects of a globalised world. You are now going to sum up your ideas by completing a KEY FACTS box.

1. Work in groups. Look through the sections 1–4 in this topic and point out what aspects of a globalised world are discussed in the texts. Key words such as technology or business might come to mind, but you should add others. Complete the table below.

SECTION	ASPECTS OF A GLOBALISED WORLD
Multinational companies	
Wikipedia	
Shanghai	
Globish / The English language	

▶ Activity chest 11
▶ Skills 5.1

2. Use your findings from 1 to complete the KEY FACTS box below in a structured way. Use 'Peer review' to correct and improve your text.

KEY FACTS Aspects of globalisation

There have been many times in history when various empires – Greek, Roman, Islamic etc. – have linked countries through trade and politics. We can say that a first important step towards our modern world was taken in the 15th century when European explorers first began exploring the world at large and establishing colonies. Eventually, Britain came to be the most important world power and the British Empire played a vital role in making the world a smaller place.

However, there is much debate among experts about whether we should call such empires global powers. The general opinion is that what we now understand by the term is something more recent. It began in the 1950s when governments took measures to make international trade easier.
So what are some of the key aspects of this modern globalised world?

One aspect that is very clear is (that) …
One of the most striking aspects of globalisation is (that) …
An example of this is … / We can see this in action if we look at …
Another characteristic / feature of a globalised world is (that) …
Globalisation would not be possible if … not / without …
… has played a key role / has been an important influence in the globalisation process.
To sum up, … We may define a globalised world in the following way / in the following terms.
A general definition of a globalised world could be that it is one in which …

TOPIC

02

Challenges of globalisation

Imagine that the world was a village in which 100 people lived. Imagine that their lives in that village mirrored conditions in the real world exactly. What would the village be like?

mirror sth.: be an exact representation of sth. / represent sth. precisely

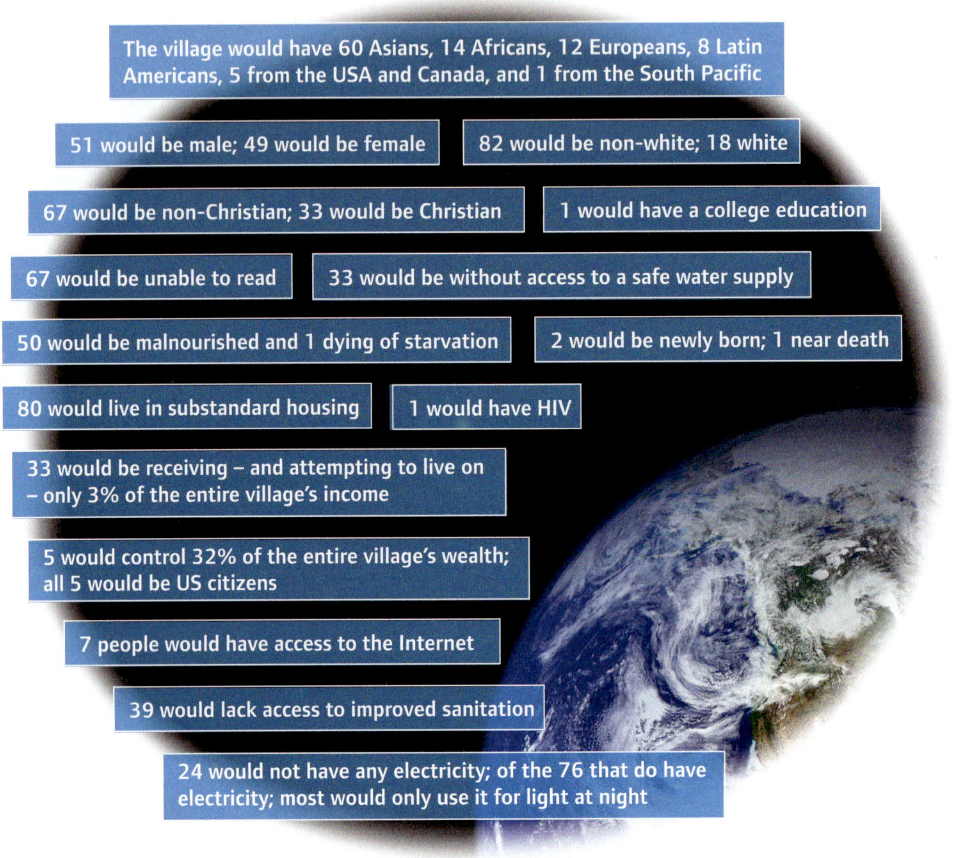

The village would have 60 Asians, 14 Africans, 12 Europeans, 8 Latin Americans, 5 from the USA and Canada, and 1 from the South Pacific

51 would be male; 49 would be female

82 would be non-white; 18 white

67 would be non-Christian; 33 would be Christian

1 would have a college education

67 would be unable to read

33 would be without access to a safe water supply

50 would be malnourished and 1 dying of starvation

2 would be newly born; 1 near death

80 would live in substandard housing

1 would have HIV

33 would be receiving – and attempting to live on – only 3% of the entire village's income

5 would control 32% of the entire village's wealth; all 5 would be US citizens

7 people would have access to the Internet

39 would lack access to improved sanitation

24 would not have any electricity; of the 76 that do have electricity; most would only use it for light at night

malnourished: not getting enough food
starvation: death caused by having no food
sanitation: system of pipes used to get rid of dirty water, esp. from toilets

Collect ideas

1. Copy the table below and add more categories, then complete it with facts from the text.

SEX	NATIONALITIES	TECHNOLOGY	
- 51 male - ...	- 60 ... -	- ...	

2. This topic deals with the challenges of globalisation. Thinking about the facts in this text, what challenges can you imagine?

Extra Imagine you could interview people from the village. What would you ask them? What would they answer? Choose one or two and act out dialogues.

1 Rich and poor (Maps and a video)

We may live in a globalised world, but that does not mean that all countries in it are equal. You are going to look at two world maps, then watch a video.

A Understanding the maps

Work in groups to interpret the maps below, then make a presentation of your ideas to the class.

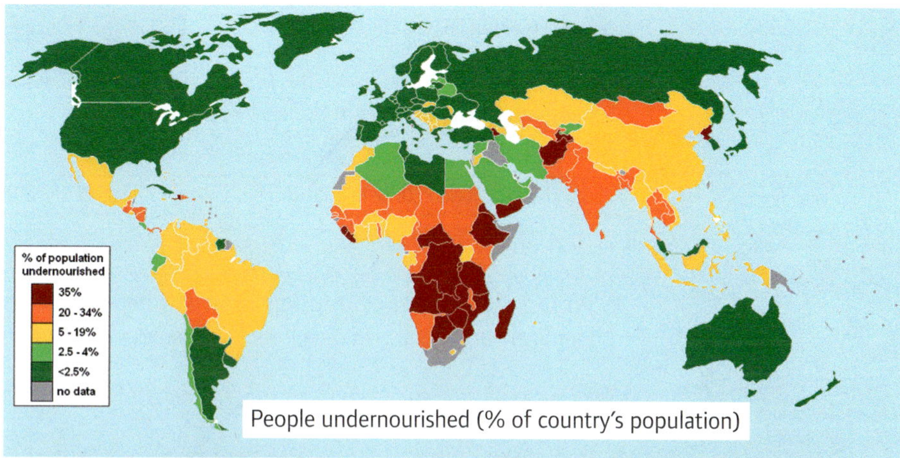

People undernourished (% of country's population)

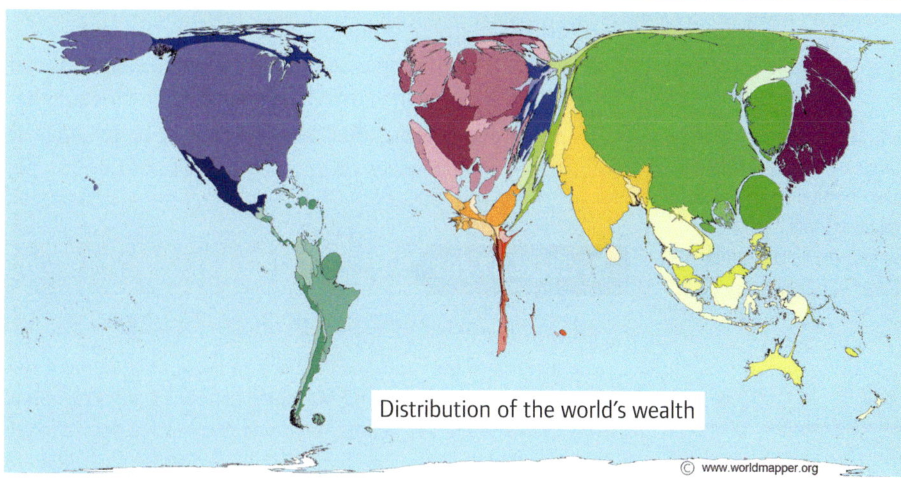

Distribution of the world's wealth

The first map shows … It uses colours to show … These are grouped into … categories.		
The second map is unusual / more difficult to understand at first. It is called a 'cartogram'.		
On it, the size of the countries … / the countries are distorted according to … / to show …	The … a country is, the … it is (and vice versa).	
From the first map	it is clear that …	the largest number of …
There are also significant numbers of …		
It is perhaps not surprising that	countries such as … have the fewest …	
The second map makes it clear that	the distribution of wealth around the world is …	
Countries such as … appear very large on the map while/whereas countries such as …		
The world's wealth appears to be	concentrated in / owned by …	
A very noticeable aspect of the map is	how big / how small … is/are	
Summing up the two maps,	we can say that …	

You are now going to watch a video made in Australia.

B Before you watch

Describe the still from the video on the right. What impression do you get of the girl, Erin? Speculate about what may be happening in the scene.

DVD 12

hound sb.: follow and ask sb. again and again to do sth.
plea (for sth.) (fml): urgent request
cereal: Getreideflocken
milk bar (AustrE): small general store
endure sth.: etwas ertragen
gruelling: very difficult and tiring
brass bombshell casing: Granatenhülse aus Messing
forage for sth.: look for sth., esp. using the hands
morsel: small piece of sth., esp. food
dump sth.: get rid of sth.
suffer sth.: etwas erleiden
branded: made by a well-known company and having that company's name on it
dye sth.: colour your hair
abduct sb.: kidnap sb

C Understanding the video

1. Watch the video. Explain what is happening in the scene in the still.
2. Take notes to fill in the following table. You may work and compare with a partner.

PROBLEMS OF YOUNG PEOPLE IN AUSTRALIA	PROBLEMS OF YOUNG PEOPLE IN POOR COUNTRIES
– … – …	– … – …

3. Write 5-8 sentences contrasting in specific detail the lives of average Australian teenagers and people in developing countries you see in the video.

D Analysing the video

1. Define the central message of the video. Also explain the title 'Teenage affluenza' (hint: 'affluenza' is a mix of 'affluence' and 'influenza').
2. In order to get their message across the makers of the video use irony. Look at the SPOTLIGHT box below, then explain how this video makes use of irony.
3. Examine other means the video uses to get its message across. Think e.g. of the speaker's tone of voice or the inclusion of poor young people. How effective do you think this video is?

SPOTLIGHT ON Irony

Irony in real life
We sometimes use 'irony' to describe an event or situation if someone does something with a particular purpose in mind, but what happens is just the opposite. So if, for example, you are late for a doctor's appointment and you quickly decide to take the underground rather than your old bike to speed things up – and if then the underground breaks down and leaves you stuck in the tunnel for hours, this might be called ironic.

Irony as a rhetorical device
As a more technical term, 'irony' is used to refer to a rhetorical device. Irony here means that a speaker says just the opposite of what they really mean. So if you're in a café and your friend praises the lively atmosphere there, it may well be that she thinks it's so noisy you can hardly understand what you're saying.

✕ **Spotlight task** Rewrite parts of the video's voiceover without using irony. You can start like this: 'Erin wakes up in her single bed that her parents bought when she was 10. She doesn't like it because she finds it too narrow and because she thinks it's too old and no longer fashionable.'

2 Rich multinationals, poor people (A video and other materials)

For this activity you are going to work in groups. You will use a short video as a starting point for developing your own ideas about a topic, then do some research and finally present your results to the class.

DVD 13

Step 1 Understanding and researching the video

In 2008, the Danish journalist Frank Piasecki Poulsen made a documentary called *Blood in the mobile*. This is the trailer for his film.

1. In your group, watch the trailer and take notes for a summary. Compare your notes and write a summary of what you learn from the trailer.

▶ Activity chest 9

2. Do research to find out more about the background to Poulsen's film. First brainstorm possible aspects of your research (you might want to start with the Democratic Republic of Congo, the role of minerals in the mobile phone industry etc.). Divide up your research so that each student looks at a different aspect. Present your ideas to the class using a 'Gallery walk': make a poster in your group that sums up what you have found out.

fuel sth.: make sth. stronger / keep sth. going
revolt sb.: make sb. feel disgusted
abduct sb.: kidnap sb

Step 2 Finding out more about multinationals and presenting your ideas

▶ Skills 8

1. In your group, brainstorm other problems you have heard about multinationals and how they sometimes operate in poorer countries. Do some research, then choose one specific example that you would like to make a presentation about. Remember to relate your topic to the general theme of globalisation. Divide up the research among the students in your group again, and thoroughly plan your work in a group.

▶ Skills 7.4

2. Present your ideas to the class. Use visuals wherever possible and divide up your talk so that everyone in your group has a chance to speak. Be prepared to answer questions at the end.

We have chosen to focus on … for the following reasons: …
The consequences for people living in this particular developing country are that …
This makes the situation in … much worse because …
It is too simple to blame one multinational / The West's reliance on cheap … means that …

✕ **Extra** Work in your group still. Make a documentary radio programme about your topic. Include interviews with people concerned and experts on the issues.

3 The economics of global warming (A newspaper article)

You are going to read an article by Thomas C. Schelling, a Nobel Prize winning economist.

A Before you read

In class, collect some key information about global warming: its causes, its effects on people around the world, possible measures against it.

The real global challenge facing us will be organizing to reduce carbon emissions and provide help to poor countries coping with climate change. The worst, but not the most likely, consequences of climate change could be rising sea levels: there is grounded ice in Antarctica that, if loosed from its moorings, is worth five or six meters of sea level, enough to sink Stockholm, Manhattan, or London, or to oblige them to build levees to escape inundation, and to oblige millions of Bangladeshis and others to abandon their homes and workplaces and to migrate. […]

The most likely consequences of climate change will be severe impacts on food production in the developing world. We can worry about urban heat waves, polar bears, and forest fires, but the worst effects are almost certainly going to be on food production in the poor countries, where half or more of the population depends on growing its own food.

Estimates of lost world product due to climate change are moderate because the poor have so little to lose. More than a billion people, maybe 2 billion, are estimated to live on less than the equivalent of $2 per day. If a billion of those poorest people lost half their income, it would be an overwhelming tragedy, a true catastrophe, worse than all the earthquakes, floods, tsunamis, landslides, and fires of the past decade happening every year. But those billion people together would lose only $365 billion per year. That is less than 1 percent of world income! They have so little to begin with that what they can lose doesn't amount to much of a statistic. But they can lose tragically.

In a developed nation like the United States, or most of Europe, agriculture is less than 5 percent of gross national product; nearly all the rest of Western income is substantially impervious to climate, or may benefit slightly from warming. The U.S. has scientific assistance to agriculture and experience with climates and crops across the country, and can respond with appropriate changes in crops and techniques of cultivation. Developing countries currently have little, if any, such capacity to adapt.

World incomes will surely continue to rise, as will population. One of the notable changes in consumption with rising incomes is demand for meat. Already demand for meat in China is hugely increased in urban areas. The production of a single calorie of meat, depending on whether it is beef, pork, or chicken, requires four to 10 calories in animal feed. The shift toward meat will raise food prices everywhere; the rich may have to eat a little less meat, the poor will have to pay more for their rice and bread. Consumption inequalities between the world's rich and poor will increase.

2 *cope with sth.:* deal successfully with sth. difficult
5 *moorings* (pl): Verankerung
6 *levee:* low wall built at a water's edge to prevent it from spreading onto the land
inundation: Überflutung
8 *migrate:* move from one town or country to live in another
9 *impact* [' - -]: powerful effect
14 *due to sth.:* caused by sth.
moderate (adj): neither very large nor very small
17 *overwhelming:* überwältigend
18 *landslide:* Erdrutsch
24 *gross national product:* Bruttosozialprodukt
25 *substantially impervious to sth.:* mainly uninfluenced by sth.
28 *cultivation:* preparation and use of land to grow plants
31 *notable:* important
demand (n): Nachfrage

39 *demographer:* person dealing with information on the population and its different groups
41 *shift in sth.:* change in sth.
42 *uniform:* the same in all parts and at all times
fertility: Fruchtbarkeit
44 *shortfall in sth.:* lack of sth.
45 *shrink* (v): become smaller in size
glacier ['glæsiə]: Gletscher
48 *snowpack:* mass of snow on the ground that is compressed and hardened by its own weight
49 *irrigation:* Bewässerung
50 *crucial:* very important
51 *Fertile Crescent:* area in western Asia which is very fertile *(= fruchtbar)*

Population continues to increase in the developing world, though less than predicted. Unpredicted by demographers a couple of decades ago, declining population in almost every developed country leads not only to smaller populations, but to a shift in age structure toward the elderly. Even the developing world is undergoing, not uniformly, unexpected declines in fertility and birthrates. But still the populations of the developing world are increasing: more people to feed, and a likely shortfall in food production.

As an example, there is much alarm about the shrinking of glaciers worldwide, especially in Greenland, but also in the Alps and the Andes. But the problem is not glaciers. It is that what ought to be snowfall is sometimes coming as rain, and the snowpack that ought to wait until late spring or early summer to melt is, in fact, melting earlier; the result is that what traditionally has been available for irrigation is lost to the oceans before food crops can use the water. This is crucial in China, South Asia, Chile, Peru, Colorado, and California, and even the Fertile Crescent of the Middle East.

Climate change will be primarily a threat to the poor in poor countries. Understanding this may make it hard to persuade the non-poor in the developed world to take the problem seriously. Maybe I shouldn't be explaining this.

[From: *Newsweek*, 23 January 2011]

B Understanding the text

1. Point out what consequences of global warming developed countries and developing countries will have to face.

The effects of … will be greater/worse/ more devastating	for … than for … because …
Many poor people in developing countries will have to …	
Developed nations are able to …	

2. State which of the consequences the author finds worst and why.

C Analysing the text

▶ Glossary 1.1

1. Examine which category of non-fictional texts this article belongs to. Give reasons, also explaining the meaning of the last sentence.
2. This article is written in a factual tone. There are some instances, however, where the writer uses enumerations and exclamations. Find them and say why and to what effect the writer uses different sentences here.

D Reacting to the text

▶ Skills 7.5

Collect arguments why we in the developed countries should do something about global warming. Write a speech to persuade your fellow students.

The chief causes of climate change are … / We are in a better position to do something		because …
It is up to us / the Western world / citizens in developed countries …	to help those less fortunate / to use our knowledge / economic power	to reduce carbon emissions.
We cannot deny that / avoid the fact that / continue to …		
It is our responsibility to It is very important that we	take action improve the situation give support to …	by …

4 Global culture (Two online articles)

You are going to read two short texts from an online magazine for learners of English around the world.

A Before you read

Look at the headlines of the texts and the pictures. Speculate about who the writers are and what the texts are about.

Text 1

The Americanisation of Brazilian Culture

YARA BERG FROM BRAZIL

Almost all aspects of American pop culture such as McDonald's, American films, and blue jeans can be seen in Brazil. My father, who had leftist orientated ideas, used to say that all kinds of American cultural icons were distasteful. When I was a child, it was forbidden to drink coke and to chew chewing gum in my house. Both actions were representative of the American dominance to my father. Incongruently, he had an American Ford car.

My father died 32 years ago, and I wonder how he would feel seeing his daughter politically centered, a diet coke addict, sometimes chewing Wrigley's juicy fruit gum, and living in the United States. He didn't live long enough to see this and the spread of American culture in the last decades. He would probably be convinced that American pop culture was swamping Brazil.

I think it is difficult to curb American cultural hegemony. Many years ago, there was an attempt to reduce the number of American films in Brazil. The government imposed a law that all cinemas should show a higher percentage of Brazilian movies. However, we didn't have enough good films, or even enough films, to show. So, in spite of government subsidies, this measure failed soon after.

American music is, of course, present in Brazil [...] but Brazilian music has never lost its first place in the Brazilians' preferences. I read once that my country and some Asian countries are among the few which listen mostly to their own music.

I think we don't need to be afraid of cultural free trade. People tend to be selective, and not everything that is imported is necessarily bad. Our native Brazilians also protest against the dominance of imported culture in their lives while they wear watches and shorts and use tape recorders. We can't avoid the process, but we could learn to be more critical and as selective as possible.

4 *leftist:* person with left-wing political ideas
6 *distasteful* (fml): unpleasant or offensive
9 *incongruent:* not suitable for or appropriate in a particular situation
18 *curb sth.:* limit or control sth., esp. sth. bad
hegemony (fml): influence of one country or group over another
22 *subsidy:* Subvention
27 *cultural free trade:* kultureller Freihandel

Text 2

Korean Resistance to Starbucks

HENRYETTA HA FROM KOREA

Like in other countries around the world, the dominance of American popular culture is strong in Korea. Establishments such as McDonalds, Pizza Huts, and Starbucks are found everywhere in Korea, and they are increasingly popular. Several months ago, a Starbucks was opened in Insadong, a traditional Korean Street, where there are many Korean antique stores.

The owners of the stores and the residents in Insadong protested against the new Starbucks and tried to get the store closed.

Surprised by the response, Starbucks decided to change the atmosphere of the store into a traditional Korean one. They changed the logo which consisted of nine letters 'S, T, A, R, B, U, C, K, S' into Korean characters. They also changed the interior of the coffee shop, which is always the same around the world, to make it look like a Korean place. Moreover, they replaced the staff uniforms with new uniforms.

A Starbucks official said it was a really unusual situation. He said they had never changed the logo or the interior design of any of their stores before.

However, the citizen groups and the owners of the stores were not satisfied; they petitioned for signatures and held demonstrations to get Starbucks out of Insadong.

Although the resistance was strong, it does not seem that this Starbucks will be closed because most young Koreans still enjoy going to it. At the stands, they sign the petitions against Starbucks, and then they go into that same Starbucks store to drink coffee.

[From: www.topics-mag.com]

20 *stand:* Stand
21 *petition:* collection of signatures to show that many people want sth. to change

B Understanding the texts

▶ Activity chest 12

Work in groups with a 'Placemat'. Collect the reasons for and against the Americanisation of countries such as Brazil and Korea given in the two texts. Sum these up in a text of your own.

C Analysing the texts

Both texts are personal accounts. Identify, with examples, the characteristics of such texts (personal pronouns, level of formality etc.) and their effect on the reader.

D Reacting to the texts

1. The texts have given you a few ideas in what areas one culture may influence another. Make a mindmap in which you structure those areas. Add examples.
2. Not everybody welcomes elements of another culture in their own. Divide the class in two groups. One group collects ideas on why this process of acculturation is a good thing, the other collects arguments against it. Carry out a 'Panel discussion'.

▶ Activity chest 10

TOPIC 03

Keeping the world's peace

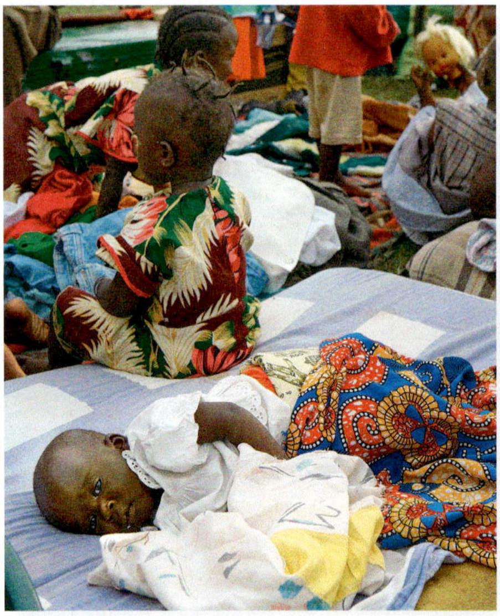

Collect ideas

1. Get together in small groups and collect ideas on the following:
   a In today's world, there is conflict or war in many places. Name some.
   b Briefly state what the conflict is about.
2. Say what sorts of people suffer in a war. How and why? Characterise the people who suffer most in your opinion.
3. Define what you understand by the term 'peacekeeping'. What sorts of people may be involved and why?

KEY FACTS Conflicts around the world

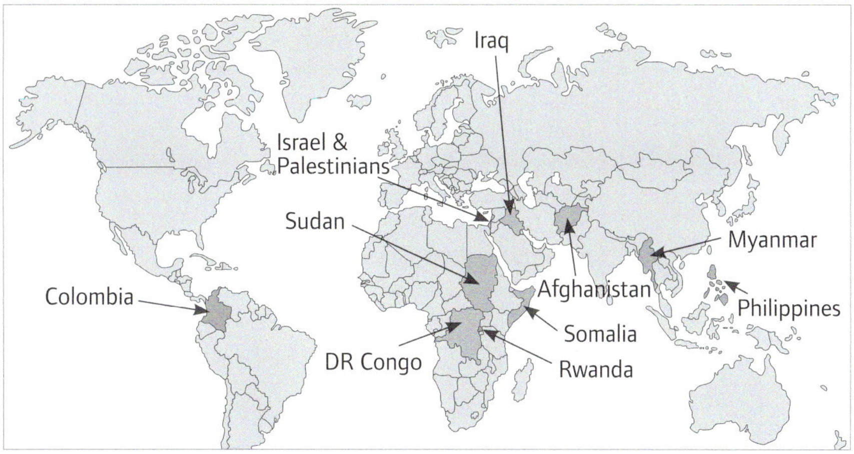

Two people die every minute somewhere in the world as a result of conflict. The map above shows just some of the war zones – there are others and by the time you read this, new conflicts will certainly have broken out. Amazingly, some of the conflicts have been going on for many years – sometimes almost unnoticed by the outside world.

Colombia Communist rebels have been fighting the government since 1966 with an estimated loss of 35,000 lives. Their aim is to set up a Marxist state.

Israel and the Palestinians The conflict between the Israelis and the Arab Palestinians goes back to the end of World War II. The new Jewish state of Israel was created in 1948 by dividing Palestine into two. Since then, however, Israel has occupied and claimed territories especially on the borders to Jordan and Syria. Since 2000, some 3,000 Palestinians and 900 Israelis have been killed. Of these around 1,400 Palestinians and 600 Israelis have been civilians.

Iraq Western forces led by the U.S. invaded Iraq in 2003 to depose the man they saw as a dangerous dictator, the head of state Saddam Hussein (later executed). However, various Muslim fundamentalist groups are still fighting against the new government and the country is far from peaceful. It is difficult to say exactly how many Iraqis have died but some estimates say between nine and ten thousand. In addition 700 American soldiers and 100 British and other soldiers helping them have also been killed.

Sudan has been torn by war for more than 20 years. The conflict is between the black African (Christian) population and an Islamic Arab government and is centred in the south of the country and in the region of Darfur in the east. The struggle is partly about religion but more importantly also about land and oil and many think that the government is trying to completely get rid of black African residents ('ethnic cleansing'). About 2 million have died in the south. In Darfur, 10,000 have died and 1 million have fled their homes and are refugees. In July 2011, Southern Sudan became an independent state.

Democratic Republic of Congo The Congo region has scarcely known peace since it became independent in the 1960s. The latest fighting, however, began after the Rwandan genocide. The Hutus responsible for the killing fled to Congo. In 1996, Rwanda invaded the country to pursue them and eventually replaced the leader of Congo with their own leader. In 1998 other African countries joined the conflict on the side of the

13 *civilian:* Zivilist
14 *depose sb.:* remove sb. from power
28 *ethnic cleansing:* policy of removing all members of an ethnic group from an area, sometimes by killing them
30 *refugee* [ˌrefju'dʒiː]: Flüchtling
34 *genocide* ['dʒenəsaɪd]: killing of a whole ethnic group

government. The result is that the whole of the country is continually being fought over by armed groups. One of the true reasons for the conflict is that Congo is rich in many natural resources including gold, diamonds and minerals for e.g. mobile phones. At least 3 million people overall have died or been killed.

Somalia Amazingly, Somalia has had no central government since 1991 – when the last leader of the country was deposed. Instead, several rival warlords have been fighting for power and 1 million people have died in the conflicts. The situation is worst in the capital Mogadishu. As a consequence, 'modern pirates' and terrorist networks like Al-Quaeda have started operating from Somalia.

Rwanda The Rwandan genocide is one of the most tragic events of modern times. Rwanda is a small country high in the mountains of East Africa. Throughout its history, Rwanda's population has consisted of two tribal groups, the Hutus and the Tutsis, and during much of this time the minority Tutsis governed the country. In 1994, Hutu rebels began massacring Tutsis and Tutsi sympathisers. Neither Western powers nor the United Nations intervened to stop the killing. In 100 days, 800,000 Rwandans were killed – roughly 10% of the country's total population. This happened as has often been said 'while the world stood by and watched'.

Afghanistan has been torn by war since 1978 but the latest phase of the fighting began in October 2001. The current war is a result of the attack on 11 September 2001 when the Islamist terrorist organisation al-Qaeda, crashed two planes into the World Trade Center in New York killing 3,000 people. The U.S. government suspected that al-Qaeda's leader, Osama bin Laden, was in Afghanistan and was being protected by the country's governing Muslim fundamentalist group, the Taliban. When the Taliban refused to hand over bin Laden, the USA led an invasion of the country. A new Afghan government was set up but fighting has continued until now with 120,000 NATO soldiers from around the world (80,000 of them from the USA) on one side and the Taliban (and some other groups) on the other. We will probably never know how many Afghans have died, but the latest estimates are around 14,000 up to the end of 2010 and almost 2,000 foreign soldiers in the same period. More Afghans are killed by the Taliban than by NATO troops.

Nepal, Myanmar, the Philippines Conflicts in these countries have been going on for many years. Maoist rebels have been fighting the Nepalese government since 1996 resulting in the deaths of over 9,000 people. An ethnic minority in Myanmar has been fighting to become a separate state ever since the end of World War II. In the Philippines, between 15 and 100 people die every year as various groups in the south fight for independence.

42 *warlord:* leader of a military group that has no official status

Activities

1. Draw a timeline of the wars in the text. Add the number of deaths.
2. List the various reasons you can find for the wars mentioned and put them into categories.

✕ **Extra** Use the text to develop a word cloud (cf. p. 28) about war and conflict. Add other words that you think may be useful.

1 The experience of war (An extract from a short story)

In 2008, a refugee help organisation in New Zealand put on a writing workshop for young refugees who had come to New Zealand. It then published their stories in a collection called *Earthless Trees*. You are going to read an extract from one of the stories. It is by a young man, Hajar Ali, and is set in Kabul, Afghanistan.

A Before you read

Look at the picture on the left and go back to the KEY FACTS on p. 131. Speculate about Ali's experience of war and explain the background to it.

The story begins with Ali's brother Najeeb giving him a letter: Ali has got a place at Kabul University. He must organise a visit to the university as soon as possible.

We were busy arguing over the procedures of the next few days when we heard a bomb explode. We all fell to the ground with glass shattering around us. Everyone ran to the basement to save their lives. Najeeb and I were the only ones left.

"Hurry up, let's get down to the basement," Najeeb yelled.

"Let's go and save the injured," I replied. "Better to die brave than live a safe fraud's life."

Najeeb followed me. There were bodies on the ground struggling to breathe, pieces of meat strewn across every inch of the ground. Everyone on the street was whimpering and crying. Moments like these are easier to talk about than to live through. I was here and there taking corpses to the trucks to be transferred to hospitals. Among those crying was a woman who had found two of her sons dead.

"Where is the other one?" I heard her saying.

It was like a sword striking into my heart. She ran into the street calling for her son. A mother who dreams every night of her sons becoming brave men of this country was running around madly to find her only surviving son.

"You're the only one left. Please don't leave me. Mama will die if you go. Please tell me where you are," she sobbed out aloud.

"Yosef, please don't go, please don't leave Mama. Your brothers left without me. Please take me with you if you've already left. I can't live without you three."

I couldn't stop and help her as there were others with serious injuries. Five people were running around putting the puzzles of body parts together in the right places. [...] Suddenly I heard a girl crying out: "Brothers, my dad is alive. Please save him, please don't let him die." I ran towards her and saw the old man's body on the young girl's knees. [...] One of the nurses on the scene came to help me carry him.

"Yae Ali," I said lifting the man up. The only thing I was left with was his legs. [...]

"Let's leave him here. He won't last in the hospital anyway," the nurse said, turning her face away.

"Please, don't leave my Baba, he's my only family. Save my dad," the girl wailed

7 *fraud:* person who cheats by pretending to be a different person
9 *strew sth.:* spread sth. over a surface
11 *corpse* [kɔːps]: dead body
31 *wail:* cry in a high voice out of despair

hitting herself again. What could I do? I found a piece of cloth from a woman's burqua lying on the ground and carefully placed him on it putting in his body parts before wrapping him like a child. In my arms he pressed his face against my chest, his body light and weak as if he was only a few kilograms. I put him on the truck and turned back to find more wounded.

[From: *'Ominous Day'* by Hajab Ali in *Earthless Trees*, 2008]

B Understanding the text

1. Sum up the events you read about in the story.
2. Characterise Ali as he is presented in this excerpt.

C Analysing the text

1. Analyse the way the writer refers to the injured or dead people he finds. Explain what effect this may have on the reader and what it may tell us about the writer.

<table>
<tr><td colspan="3">Ali is characterised as a … person / acts in a … way / makes a quick decision</td></tr>
<tr><td rowspan="2">While other bystanders …, he …</td><td>proves to be brave/courageous/responsible</td><td rowspan="2">when he …</td></tr>
<tr><td>shows courage / takes responsibility …</td></tr>
<tr><td colspan="3">… can tell important from unimportant / … can quickly decide what needs to be done because …</td></tr>
<tr><td colspan="2">but he also acts somewhat irrationally / but his emotions do waste valuable time</td><td rowspan="2">when he …</td></tr>
<tr><td colspan="2">… he shows his compassion / is full of compassion …</td></tr>
</table>

✕ **Extra** The writer describes the events in a fairly factual way; only when he describes the woman's reaction to her sons' deaths does he express a mild criticism. Look at ll. 15–16 again and explain his criticism.

D Reacting to the text

► Skills 5.2

1. A few days later, Ali writes an email to a friend, telling him about these experiences and what they make him feel about war. Write his email.

SPOTLIGHT ON Creative writing

When you are asked to write a text from another person's point of view, it is important to really get into this role. This means that you should …
- stick to the language and style that your person would use. An uneducated person would, for instance, never use the word 'inebriated', they would simply say 'drunk';
- be careful to stick to the facts you know about the character and their situation. If she is a young schoolgirl, you had better not let her have her own car;
- make sure that your character's actions, thoughts and feelings don't contradict the way they have acted before. If he is a shy and easily confused person, it won't be convincing to see him give a spontaneous, well-formulated speech in front of his teachers.

✕ **Spotlight task** Look at the following examples and say why they would not be suitable in a text written as a reply to the creative writing task above:
- 'I wanted to go inside where it would be safe, but Najeeb pushed me.'
- 'I perceived the awfully tragic sound of a wretched woman howling for her youngster.'
- 'The sight of all that suffering was too much for me. People screaming, blood everywhere, body parts on the street – I just didn't know what to do.'

2. The text is taken from a collection called *Earthless Trees*. Discuss this title.

2 The victims of war (A report and statistics)

You are going to find out about the UNHCR – the United Nations High Commission for Refugees, more often just known as the United Nations Refugee Agency.

A Before you begin

Talk in class. Give some reasons why people become refugees. Where do you think most refugees go to and how do they get there? Where do they come from? What possibilities are there for them in the long run?

B About the UNHCR

► Activity chest 4

Use the text below to sum up briefly and in your own words the key facts about the UNHCR. Prepare a 'Cheat sheet' and give an oral summary.

OUR STORY

The UNHCR was founded in 1950, in the wake of World War II, to help Europeans displaced by that conflict. The agency was given a three-year mandate to complete its work and then disband.

By 1956, UNHCR was facing its first major emergency, the outflow of refugees when Soviet forces crushed the Hungarian Revolution. It soon became apparent that UNHCR had a long future. In the 1960s, the decolonization of Africa produced the first of that continent's numerous refugee crises needing UNHCR intervention. Over the following two decades, UNHCR helped with displacement crises in Asia and Latin America. By the end of the century there were fresh refugee problems in Africa and, turning full circle, new waves of refugees in Europe from the series of wars in the Balkans.

The start of the 21st century has seen UNHCR helping with major refugee crises in Africa, such as the Democratic Republic of the Congo and Somalia, and in Asia, especially the 30-year-old Afghan refugee problem. At the same time, UNHCR has been asked to use its expertise to help many people internally

1 *in the wake of sth.:* after sth. that still is influential
2 *displace sb.* (fml): force sb. to go and live in another place
5 *crush sth.:* use violence to defeat sth., esp. a rebellion
Hungarian Revolution: a revolt in 1956 against the Hungarian government and the Soviet influence on it

displaced by conflict. It has also expanded its role in helping stateless people, a largely overlooked group numbering millions of people in danger of being denied basic rights because they do not have any citizenship. We will soon be celebrating our 60th anniversary, and we are aware that the refugee crisis we exist to solve is unlikely to disappear in the near future.

OUR WORK

Today, UNHCR is one of the world's principal humanitarian agencies with 6,650 national and international members of staff working in 118 countries. Our budget has grown from US$300,000 in its first year to more than US$2 billion in 2009, and with this money we help more than 34 million people: 14.4 million internally displaced people, 10.5 million refugees, 2 million returnees, 6.6 million stateless people and more than 800,000 asylum seekers.

As well as providing life-saving shelter, food, water and medical care, we strive to improve refugees' quality of life and future opportunities, providing infra-structure, schools and income-generating projects in established refugee camps and communities.

[From: www.givethemshelter.org]

17 *deny sb. sth.:* refuse to give sb. sth.
26 *internally displaced:* forced to go and live in another part of your country
returnee: former refugee who was able to return to their country
27 *asylum seeker:* Asylsuchende/r
28 *strive to do sth.* (fml): try very hard to do sth.

C A report and statistics by the UNHCR about refugees

You are going to look at a text and charts from a UNHCR report dealing with the countries that refugees come from (Chart 1), the countries that refugees go to (Text 1) and the economic situation of those countries (Chart 2 – here, the number of refugees in a country is compared to its average income level. This income level is measured by the gross domestic product GDP per person in US Dollars.)

Chart 1: Major source countries of refugees, end-2009

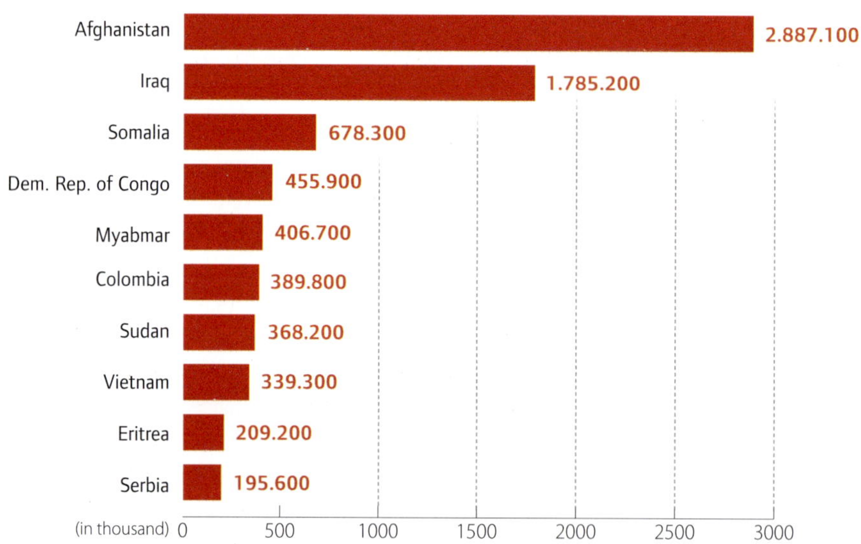

Chart 2: Number of refugees per 1 USD GDP (PPP) per capita 2009

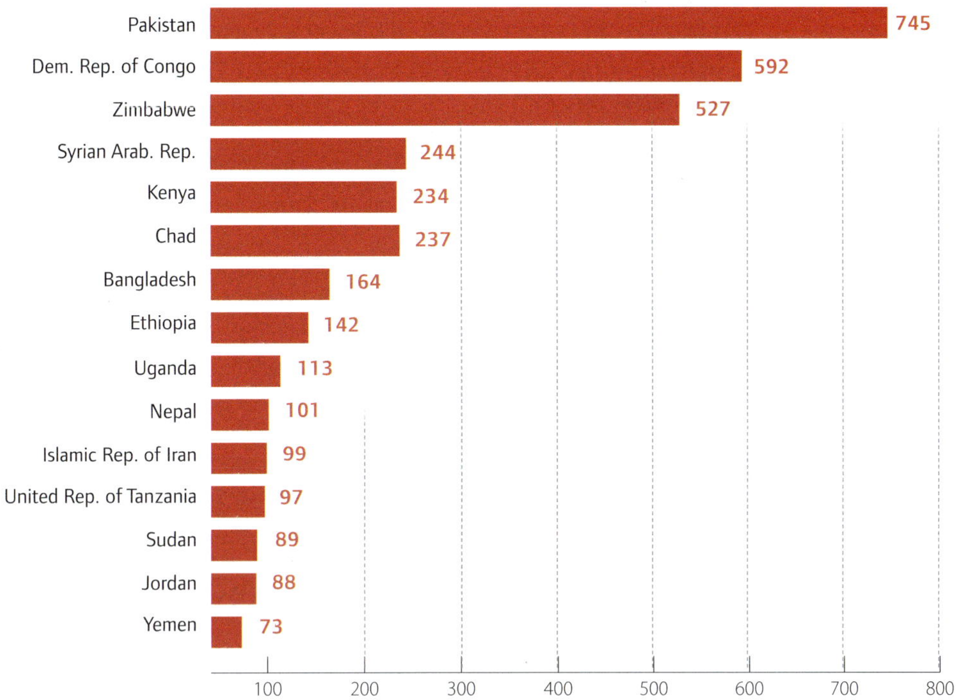

Text 1: Refugee-hosting countries

The five major refugee-hosting countries in 2009 were the same as those in 2008 [...]. Together, these countries accounted for almost half (47%) of all refugees under the UNHCR mandate. Pakistan was again the country with the largest number of refugees (1.7 million), nearly all from Afghanistan. The total refugee population in Pakistan decreased by 40,000 people from the previous year as a consequence of demographic factors, voluntary repatriation, registration and resettlement. The Islamic Republic of Iran hosted slightly over 1 million refugees, almost all Afghans [...]. The Syrian Arab Republic was host to 1.05 million Iraqi refugees according to government estimates, making it the third largest refugee hosting country. [...] Germany and Jordan reported 594,000 and 451,000 refugees, respectively, at year end.

[From: *2009 Global Trends* by United Nations High Commissioner for Refugees, 2010]

▶ Skills 3

1. Summarise the most important information of the charts in your own words.
2. Visualise the most important information of the text in a suitable form.
3. Discuss the findings of the UNHCR, referring to the **KEY FACTS** (p. 131) and the ideas you collected about refugees.

3 What is peacekeeping? (Extracts from a speech)

You are going to read parts of a speech given in 1999 by the then Secretary General of the United Nations, Kofi Annan. Before that, have a look at the KEY FACTS below.

KEY FACTS – The United Nations Organisation

The UN headquarters in New York

The United Nations Organisation (UNO), or more often simply the United Nations (UN), was founded after World War II to stop future wars between countries and to be a platform for international discussions. It is based on the UN Charter which sets out its rights and duties and all member countries have to agree to this. There are now 192 member states – every sovereign nation on Earth except the Vatican. Its main headquarters is in New York. The person at the head of the organisation and its spokesperson is the 'Secretary General'. Kofi Annan, a diplomat from Ghana, was Secretary General from 1997 until 2006.

In fact, the UN is not one single organisation but is made up of several different parts. You have already learned about the UN Refugee Agency. Other important parts are the General Assembly, which is like the UN's parliament; the Economic and Social Council, which works closely with the World Bank and the International Monetary Fund (IMF) to promote the global economy; and the International Court of Justice, which is based in The Hague in the Netherlands.

UN peacekeepers in the familiar light blue berets

One of the times when we hear most about the UN, however, is when there is a conflict and it is at these times that the UN acts as the 'world's peacekeeper'. It does this through its Security Council in New York. The Council consists of 5 permanent member states – China, France, Russia, the UK and the USA – and 10 non-permanent members that change. How does the Security Council act as a peacekeeper? The UN does not have its own army, but it has 'peacekeepers' – volunteers from its member states whose main duty is to go into a country where there has recently been a war and to make sure that fighting does not restart. When wars break out, however, the UN's job is to allow soldiers, ships and aeroplanes from countries such as the USA and various European nations to take action. It does this by issuing a Security Council Resolution – a statement that such countries may act. Any action without this resolution is illegal under international law.

6 *charter:* written document listing the rights and duties a group of people or organisations should have
8 *sovereign:* independent

Activities

1. Summarize why the UN was originally founded and how its role has developed since then.
2. Describe in your own words how the UN acts in times of war.

A Before you read

In early 2011, people in a number of North African countries rebelled against their countries' leaders. In some countries, the rebellions were peaceful and led relatively easily to a change of regime. In others, however, the leaders fought back against the rebels. What should the world community do in this situation? Should the countries decide for themselves or should other countries intervene?

1. Talk in class. Discuss reasons for and against intervention and try to decide when it is right or not to intervene in a conflict.
2. Now read the following speech about peacekeeping held in 1998 by the UN Secretary General Kofi Annan at that time.

The United Nations is [...] an association of sovereign states, and sovereign states do tend to be extremely jealous of their sovereignty. Small states, especially, are fearful of intervention in their affairs by great powers. And indeed, our century has seen many examples of the strong 'intervening' – or interfering – in the affairs of the weak, from the Allied intervention in the Russian civil war in 1918 to the Soviet 'interventions' in Hungary, Czechoslovakia and Afghanistan.

Others might refer to the American intervention in Viet Nam, or even the Turkish intervention in Cyprus in 1974. The motives, and the legal justification, may be better in some cases than others, but the word 'intervention' has come to be used almost as a synonym for 'invasion'.

The Charter of the United Nations gives great responsibilities to great powers in their capacity as permanent members of the Security Council. But as a safeguard against abuse of those powers, Article 2.7 of the Charter protects national sovereignty even from intervention by the United Nations itself. I'm sure everyone in this audience knows it by heart. But let me remind you – just in case – that that Article forbids the United Nations to intervene 'in matters which are essentially within the domestic jurisdiction of any state'.

That prohibition is just as relevant today as it was in 1945: violations of sovereignty remain violations of the global order. Yet in other contexts the word 'intervention' has a more benign meaning. We all applaud the policeman who intervenes to stop a fight, or the teacher who prevents big boys from bullying a smaller one. And medicine uses the word 'intervention' to describe the act of the surgeon, who saves life by 'intervening' to remove malignant growth, or to repair damaged organs. Of course, the most intrusive methods of treatment are not

2 *sovereign* ['sɒvrɪn]: independent
3 *jealous of sth.:* protecting sth. because it is very valuable to you
8 *interfere:* influence a situation that is not your concern
18 *safeguard* (n): protection
abuse (n): use of sth. in a way that is harmful or damaging
23 *domestic jurisdiction:* (here) laws of a specific country
26 *benign:* kind and gentle

always to be recommended. A wise doctor knows when to let nature take its course. But a doctor who never intervened would have few admirers, and probably even fewer patients.

So it is in international affairs. Why was the United Nations established, if not to act as a benign policeman or doctor? Our job is to intervene: to prevent conflict where we can, to put a stop to it when it has broken out, or – when neither of those things is possible – at least to contain it and prevent it from spreading. That is what the world expects of us, even though – alas – the United Nations by no means always lives up to such expectations. It is also what the Charter requires of us [...].

The purpose of Article 2.7, which I quoted just now, was to confine such interventions to cases where the international peace is threatened or broken, and to keep the United Nations from interfering in purely domestic disputes. Yet even that article carries the important rider that 'this principle shall not prejudice the application of enforcement measures under Chapter VII'. In other words, even national sovereignty can be set aside if it stands in the way of the Security Council's overriding duty to preserve international peace and security. On the face of it, there is a simple distinction between international conflict, which is clearly the United Nations' business, and domestic disputes, which are not. The very phrase 'domestic dispute' sounds reassuring. It suggests a little local difficulty which the state in question can easily settle, if only it is left alone to do so.

We all know that in recent years it has not been like that. Most wars nowadays are civil wars. Or at least that is how they start. And these civil wars are anything but benign. In fact they are 'civil' only in the sense that civilians – that is, non-combatants – have become the main victims.

This year we celebrate the fiftieth anniversary of the Universal Declaration of Human Rights. [...] And the day before it adopted the Universal Declaration, the General Assembly had adopted the Convention on the Prevention and Punishment of the Crime of Genocide, which puts all states under an obligation to 'prevent and punish' this most heinous of crimes. [...]

58 *obligation:* moral duty to do sth.
59 *heinous* ['heɪnəs]: terrible

Since genocide is almost always committed with the connivance, if not the direct participation, of the state authorities, it is hard to see how the United Nations could prevent it without intervening in a state's internal affairs. [...]

State frontiers [...] should no longer be seen as a watertight protection for war criminals or mass murderers. The fact that a conflict is 'internal' does not give the parties any right to disregard the most basic rules of human conduct. Besides, most 'internal' conflicts do not stay internal for very long. They soon 'spill over' into neighbouring countries. [...]

Can we really afford to let each state be the judge of its own right, or duty, to intervene in another state's internal conflict? If we do, will we not be forced to legitimize Hitler's championship of the Sudeten Germans, or Soviet intervention in Afghanistan?

Most of us would prefer, I think – especially now that the cold war is over – to see such decisions taken collectively, by an international institution whose authority is generally respected. And surely the only institution competent to assume that role is the Security Council of the United Nations. The Charter clearly assigns responsibility to the Council for maintaining international peace and security. I would argue, therefore, that only the Council has the authority to decide that the internal situation in any state is so grave as to justify forceful intervention. [...]

In French law [...] there is a crime called 'failure to assist a person in danger' *(non-assistance à personne en danger)*. I am sure this is what the late François Mitterrand had in mind in April 1991, when he congratulated the Security Council on its decision to intervene in the internal affairs of Iraq, in order to save the Kurds. 'For the first time', President Mitterrand declared, 'non-interference has stopped at the point where it was becoming failure to assist a people in danger.'

That [...] is what 'intervention' is all about.

[From: www.un.org, 26 June 1998]

60 *genocide:* murder of a complete group of people
connivance: help in doing sth. wrong
63 *watertight:* wasserdicht.
70 *legitimise sth.:* declare sth. morally right that isn't
championship: position of being a champion
78 *grave:* serious
81 *François Mitterrand (1916–1996):* fourth President of France (1981–1995)

B Understanding the text

1. Sum up Annan's definition of intervention and its aims.
2. The UN Charter describes the limits of intervention. Name them and point out what dilemma may arise from them. What is Annan's suggestion to solve this dilemma?

▶ Glossary 1.2; 3

C Analysing the text

Analyse Annan's aim in making this speech and the means he uses to reach his objective. Have a closer look at ll. 21–23, 26–28, 68–71.

D Reacting to the text

Go back to your ideas about intervention before you read this speech. Say if and in what way this speech has changed your views.

4 Singing for peace (A rap)

In 2011, the Sudanese musician, writer and activist Emmanuel Jal released a rap on the internet entitled 'We want peace'. You are going first to listen to the rap, then your teacher will give you the lyrics to study in more detail.

A Before you listen

Look back at the **KEY FACTS** box on pp. 131–132 to remind yourself of the situation in Jal's country.

CD 6

B Understanding the rap

1. Listen to the rap and take notes. Try to identify Jal's message and his arguments.
2. Work with a partner or in a small group to improve your notes.
3. Sum up in a short text the message of the rap.

C Analysing the text

▶ Skills 1.2.4
▶ Glossary 2.4.1

cease: stop
baffle: confuse
genocide: killing of a whole race or group of people
wreak havoc: cause destruction or confusion
deaf: unable to hear
suck up to sb.: try to please sb. by praising or helping them
villain: bad person

Your teacher will give you the lyrics of the rap.

1. Have a look at Skills 1.2.4. Analyse in what way this rap follows the typical structure of a song.
2. A rap is a text type that is meant to be heard, not read, so its intention must be made very clear even when listening only once. Analyse by what rhetorical means Jal tries to do this.

Jal uses repetition / the song's structure to emphasise / draw attention to …
He uses rhyme to … . A specific example of this is when he connects the words … and …
The song employs / uses strong vocabulary, like … and …, which make it more …
Jal uses / makes use of the imperative / Jal addresses his listeners directly, e.g. in the chorus.
The song refers to 'we', 'you' and 'I' in order to …
In general, the effect on the listener is powerful / inspiring / accusatory / challenging / friendly.

3. The rap contains a number of allusions: 'silence of the lambs' (l. 28), 'Rwanda' (l. 30), 'Darfur' (l. 36), 'Jericho' (l. 48). Explain these allusions (do some research if necessary), then examine what kind of listener Jal apparently has in mind.

D Reacting to the text

1. Talk in class. Do you believe that music like this can influence people and the way they think and behave? Give your reasons.

▶ Skills 5

2. Write a message to be posted on Jal's website expressing your views about 'We want peace'.

✕ Extra

1. Write your own rap about a topic which you think important.

▶ Skills 7.4

2. Visit Emmanuel Jal's website and find out more about his life and music – for example, about his time as a boy soldier. Present your findings in class.

TOPIC
04

Into a global future

In this topic you are going to draw together what you have learned about globalisation. At the end, you will get the chance to debate your thoughts and feelings about it.

Collect ideas

1. Below and on the next page you can see some cartoons about globalisation. Look at them and say what aspects of globalisation they deal with – for example, the growth of large multinational companies in a global world.
2. Work in small groups. Each group should study and analyse a different cartoon, using the **SPOTLIGHT** box on the next page for help. Give a presentation about your cartoon to the class.

A

B

C

D

E

F

▶ Skills 2.2

SPOTLIGHT ON Cartoons

Cartoons are a way of expressing an idea through a drawing, often combined with language. The cartoonist's intention is to make fun of something or to voice serious criticism e.g. of social or political issues. The language in cartoons may be in the caption usually beneath the picture and/or in speech bubbles.

When working with cartoons, it is important to analyse the picture, the words and the effect both have together. You may have to use your background knowledge as many cartoons derive their humour from allusions.
First start with the picture. Analyse it precisely, trying to identify the aspects that are important for the cartoon's message. Then examine the language used: what style is it written in, what rhetorical devices are employed and to what effect? In what way do picture and language influence each other?
When analysing a cartoon in writing, start with some basic information about the cartoonist and possibly also its source. Identify the message of the cartoon, then describe very briefly what you can see in the picture. You shouldn't lose yourself in too much detail, but you should mention those details of the picture that contribute to the overall meaning of the cartoon. Point out how language and picture work together to express the cartoon's message.

We are going to discuss cartoon (A, B, C, …)
It deals with the topic of …
The cartoon shows a … In the centre there is/are … If you look closely, you can see…
The fundamental message of the cartoon is in the writing/image/detail of the …
The artist highlights … by showing/writing/placing … in the centre/foreground.
The … represents …, whilst the … stand for …
The artist's message is that … which is made clear by the …
The cartoon functions as a subtle/obvious/clever/humorous comment on globalisation.

1 Globalisation: for or against? (Different texts)

▶ Activity chest 6

On the following pages, there are a few texts about globalisation. You are going to work in 'Expert groups' to study them and sum up the information they contain.

A Share information

1. Divide the class into four groups. Each group looks at one of the texts.
2. Copy the grid below, then – on your own – read your text and fill in the grid.

Topic	
Source	
Key points	– … – …
To sum up …	

3. In your group, compare your notes.
4. Form new groups and share information about all the texts. Take notes.
5. Return to your home group and compare notes.
6. Write a text that summarises what you have learned about globalisation from the texts.

TEXT 1

This is an article from the British quality newspaper the *Daily Telegraph*.

9 *crunch sth.:* deal with sth., esp. large amounts of data
fertility: ability to have children
10 *HSBC:* large international bank
11 *provided:* if
16 *bipolar* [ˌbaɪˈpəʊlər]: having two directly opposite extremes
17 *condominium* [ˌkɒndəˈmɪniəm]: control of a country by another country
18 *slither:* (here) fall
oblivion: state of being forgotten
19 *vault* (v): jump
settle a score: do sth. bad to sb. who did sth. bad to you
Ottoman: (here) Turkish

China and America to lead global mega-boom

The greatest global boom of all time has barely begun. Over the next forty years, economic growth will quicken yet further as the rising powers of Asia, the Middle East, and Latin America reach their full stride.

Crunching everything from fertility rates to schooling levels and the rule of law, HSBC predicts that the world's economic output will triple again by 2050, provided the major states can avoid conflict - trade wars, or worse - and defeat the Malthusian threat of food and water limits. Growth will rise to 3pc on average, up from 2pc over the last decade.

In a sweeping report entitled *'The World in 2050'*, the bank said China would snatch the top slot as expected, but only narrowly. China at $24.6 trillion [...] and the US at $22.3 trillion will together tower over the global economy in bipolar condominium – or simply the G2 – with India at $8.2 trillion far behind in third slot, and parts of Europe slithering into oblivion.

Turkey will vault past Russia, settling an Ottoman score. Egypt, Malaysia and

20 *reassert:* have an effect again
21 *Caliphate* ['kælɪfeɪt]: Muslim government that ended in 1924
22 *exact a toll:* (here) have a bad effect
29 *fare well:* be successful
32 *inflate sth.:* make sth. larger
35 *doom sb. to sth.:* make sb. certain to have sth. bad
36 *open the floodgates:* let lots of people come in
38 *energy crunch:* crisis when there is not enough energy
39 *depletion:* reduction
40 *non-renewable asset:* sth. useful that can be used without risk of finishing
42 *derail sth.:* have a negative effect on sth.
47 *irrigate sth.:* supply water to sth.
plain (n): large area of flat land
51 *sit pretty:* be relaxed because you're in an good situation

Indonesia will all move into the top 20. Muslim societies may start to reassert an economic clout unseen since the late Caliphate. Yet Brazil may disappoint again, stalling at 7th place in 2050 as its birthrate slows sharply and bad schools exact their toll.

The surprise is how well the Anglo-Saxon states hold up under HSBC's model, which is based on the theoretical work of Harvard professor Robert Barro. America's high fertility rate (2.1) will allow it too keep adding manpower long after China's workforce has begun to contract in the 2020s and as even India starts to age in the 2040s. [...]

Britain at $3.6 trillion also fares well, slipping one rank to sixth place but pulling far ahead of Italy and France, and almost displacing Germany as Europe's biggest economy. This is chiefly due to the UK's healthy fertility rate (1.9), although sceptics might question whether a birthrate inflated by the EU's highest share of unmarried teenage mothers is a good foundation for prosperity.

The low fertility of Korea (1.1), Singapore (1.2) Germany (1.3), Poland (1.3), Italy (1.4), Spain (1.4) and Russia (1.4), more or less dooms these countries to aging crises and population decline unless they open the floodgates to immigration. [...]

HSBC works from the assumption that mankind will avoid the energy crunch and overcome the eco-deficit, a term used to describe the world's depletion rate of non-renewable assets. It calls for $46 trillion of investments in alternative forms of energy to break out of the carbon trap, and head off a supply crisis that could derail growth.

Feeding the world may be harder. The UN expects food demand to rise 70pc by 2050, yet the yield growth of crops has slowed to 1.5pc a year from 3.2 pc in the 1960s. The number of people living in areas experiencing 'severe water stress' will double from a third of the world population to two thirds between 1995 and 2025. The water basins irrigating the crops of the North China plain are being exhausted at an alarming rate.

HSBC admits that its economic projections are based on a 'rather rosy scenario'. Yet one thing seems clear. As superpowers of world food output, the US and Canada are sitting pretty.

[From: *Daily Telegraph*, 5 January 2011]

TEXT 2

This is an article from *Forbes*, a famous and important American business magazine.

1 *trash sth.:* strongly criticize sth.
3 *ragtag:* badly organized
4 *villain* ['vɪlən]: bad person
overwhelm sth.: have such a powerful effect that sth. can't react against it
5 *ominous:* suggesting that sth. bad will happen
7 *business-bashing:* very critical of big companies

Globalisation is good

Multinationals are trashed as exploiters of the poorest people on the planet. Wrong, wrong, wrong.

A ragtag army of save-the-world crusaders has spent years decrying multinational corporations as villains in the wave of globalisation overwhelming the Third World. This ominous trend would fatten the rich, further impoverish and oppress the poor and crush local economies.

The business-bashing group Public Citizen argued as much in a proclamation signed by almost 1,500 organizations in 89 countries in 1999. Whereupon hundreds of protesters rioted outside a conference of the World Trade Organization in Seattle, shattering windows, blocking traffic and confronting cops armed with tear gas and pepper spray. Six hundred people were arrested.

Cut to 2007, and the numbers are in: The protesters and do-gooders are just plain wrong. It turns out globalisation is good – and not just for the rich, but *especially* for the poor. The booming economies of India and China – the Elephant and the Dragon – have lifted 200 million people out of abject poverty in the 1990s as globalisation took off, the International Monetary Fund says. Tens of millions more have catapulted themselves far ahead into the middle class.[...]

As the Chindia revolution spreads, the ranks of the poor get smaller, not larger. In the 1990s, as Vietnam's economy grew 6% a year, the number of people living in poverty (42 million) fell 7% annually; in Uganda, when GDP growth passed 3%, the number fell 6% per year, says the World Bank.

China unleashed its economy in 1978, seeding capitalism first among farmers newly freed to sell the fruits of their fields instead of handing the produce over to Communist Party collectives. Other reforms let the Chinese create 22 million new businesses that now employ 135 million people who otherwise would have remained peasants like the generations before them.

Foreign direct investment, the very force so virulently opposed by the do-gooders, has helped drive China's gross domestic product to a more than tenfold increase since 1978. Since the reforms started, $600 billion has flooded into the country, $70 billion of it in the past year. Foreigners built hundreds of thousands of new factories as the Chinese government built the coal mines, power grid, airports and highways to supply them. [...]

Per-person income in China has climbed from $16 a year in 1978 to $2,000 now. Wages in factory boomtowns in southern China can run $4 a day – scandalously low in the eyes of the protesters, yet up from pennies a day a generation ago and far ahead of increases in living costs.

Middle-class Chinese families now own TVs, live in new apartments and send their children to private schools. Millions of Chinese have traded in their bicycles for motorcycles or cars. McDonald's has signed a deal with Sinopec, the huge Chinese gasoline retailer, to build drive-through restaurants attached to gas stations on China's new roads.

Today 254 Starbucks stores serve coffee in the land of tea, including one at the Great Wall and another at the Forbidden Palace. (The latter is the target of protesters.) In Beijing 54 Starbucks shops thrive, peddling luxury lattes that cost up to $2.85 a cup and paying servers $6 for an 8-hour day. That looks exploitative until you peek inside a nearby Chinese-owned teahouse where the staff works a 12-hour day for $3.75.

Says one woman, 23, who works for an international cargo shipper in Beijing: 'My parents were both teachers when they were my age, and they earned 30 yuan [$3.70] a month. I earn 4,000 yuan ($500) a month, live comfortably and feel I have better opportunities than my parents did.'

[From: *Forbes*, 16 April 2007. This article has been slightly modified from the original format for educational purposes.]

9 *World Trade Organization:* organization that manages international trade
16 *International Monetary Fund:* organization that oversees countries' economic policies
18 *rank:* number of people in a group
22 *unleash sth.:* let sth. start having an effect
seed: make it possible for sth. to start
28 *peasant* ['peznt]: poor person who works on a farm
31 *gross domestic product:* value of goods and services produced in a country every year
tenfold: multiplied by ten
36 *power grid:* electricity network
47 *Great Wall:* stone wall in northern China built in 5th century BC
Forbidden Palace: Palace in Beijing for the Chinese emperor, now a museum
48 *thrive:* be successful
peddle sth.: sell sth.

TEXT 3

Helium is an online magazine based in the USA. Anyone can write an article in the magazine about an issue that interests them.

The environmental impact of globalisation

Globalisation is the concept of each economy being intertwined with the economies of other nations. As technology improves, it has become much easier for nations to do business with other nations on a global basis. For example, it is not uncommon to see an American company doing business in China, or a Japanese business having a manufacturing plant in America.

As trade expands so quickly on a global basis, it creates a new set of challenges. Shipping of goods requires a plane, ship or delivery van to reach the long distances often required to transport these goods. This means that fuel is needed, and often this fuel comes in the form of oil. When businesses build manufacturing plants in new markets, it causes the burning of more oil, coal or nuclear power.

More economic output creates new jobs, but it also creates new sources of pollution from not only the factories that release burned off fuels, but from the people who now flock to the areas surrounding these new factories. How bad is the problem of air pollution? According to the European Union, only one percent of the people in China breathed air that was deemed safe.

Some scientists predict that due to the resource needs of powers like the United States, and emerging powers like China and India, that humanity could be heading toward a deflation of growth. It has been noted that humanity has hit peak oil and is looking at hitting peak grain, peak fish and peak water limits. This means that humanity has extracted as much oil as it could and will no longer be able to get as much oil as in the past. This contrasts with the fact that humanity will require as much as 50 percent more energy, water and food by 2030.

A few of the consequences of globalisation might be staring humanity in the face sooner rather than later. It is said that Indonesia could log out its entire forest in just a decade. Papau New Guinea might suffer the same fate in 15 years given current trends. Minerals like zinc could soon be gone if conservation strategies aren't devised.

Globalisation has brought about a higher standard of living and growing economies in countries that had been relatively poor in the past. However, the demand for goods, and the need for energy sources to sustain business has left a major impact on the environment. Not all is lost yet, but something needs to be done before the Earth is simply not able to sustain the demands of human resource needs.

[From: *Helium*, 26 January 2011]

1 *intertwine sth.:* connect sth.
18 *flock to:* move somewhere in large numbers
22 *deem:* consider
25 *deflation:* decrease
hit peak limits: use the maximum amount possible of sth.
31 *log out:* cut down trees
37 *sustain sth.:* make it possible for sth. to survive

TEXT 4

This text is from a brochure produced by Friends of the Earth, an international environmental organisation.

On corporate globalisation

Corporate globalisation is the spread of big business across the world. As big business gets bigger, it gets more powerful, meaning people and governments have less control over their lives. All over the world big business is putting profit before people and the environment. [...]

What is corporate globalisation?

Corporate globalisation is one kind of globalisation [...]. It includes these trends and examples:

- Big companies get bigger and small companies and family businesses struggle to stay open. For example US giant Wal Mart has taken over Asda and Starbucks is taking the place of small coffee shops on every high street;

- Wealth is concentrated in the hands of a few. The gap between poor and rich is growing both between and within countries. Of the 6 billion people in the world, 2.8 billion are living on less than $1.20 a day. More than 60 countries now have lower per capita income than they did in 1990. The 475 richest dollar billionaires have a combined wealth greater than the poorest half of humanity;
- Financial centres such as the City of London have huge amounts of money flowing through them and have control over where money such as our pension funds is invested;
- Governments are forced or persuaded to do what big business wants – money is power and big business uses its power to change laws so that it can carry on growing, even if this means damaging the environment or undermining human rights;
- Multinational companies have been given the right to operate wherever they choose. These rights are enforced by World Trade Organisation (WTO), which has the power to tell governments which laws they can make. [...]

What are the alternatives?

[...] Friends of the Earth is calling for national and international rules and laws to make companies answerable for their actions and to put power back in the hands of citizens and communities. We want citizens and communities to be able to hold multinational companies legally accountable for their bad practices. [...]

If companies were properly accountable for their actions, it would help to ensure that people's rights and needs and protection of the environment are given priority over the profits of big business. It would help to reverse the trend of political power moving away from people and into the hands of multinational companies. It would help ensure that companies operate in the public interest, not

1 *corporate:* to do with companies and business
9 *struggle:* try hard to do sth. difficult
Wal Mart: very large group of shops in the US that sells cheap goods
11 *Asda:* large group of supermarkets in Britain
19 *per capita:* per person
23 *pension fund:* money held by the government to be paid to retired people
27 *undermine sth:* make sth. less effective
30 *enforce sth.:* make sure people obey a law or rule
34 *make sb.answerable for sth.:* make sb. explain sth. they have sone
35 *hold sb. accountable for sth.:* make sb. responsible for sth. they have done

against it. It would help protect the environment against rapid destruction for short term profit. It would help uphold people's rights, livelihoods and ways of life. In short, it would revolutionise the way we do business. [...]

What you can do

Join our email activists list to take simple actions against the destructive activities of multinational companies and to help us challenge corporate power.

[From: *The World for Sale*, by Friends of the Earth, January 2003]

✕ Extra **Here's a German article from the internet platform Wikia, whose aim it is to collect information and tips for consumers.**

Alles Bio oder was?

Die meisten sogenannten Bio-Produkte kommen inzwischen aus dem Ausland und verbrauchen durch diese langen Transportwege eine Menge Ressourcen (Verpackung & Energie). Das heißt: Öko-Produkt ist relativ! Eine Bio-Weintraube aus Südafrika ist keine Bio-Weintraube, sondern eine ökologische Katastrophe. Sicher: Sie wird relativ unbelastet sein und daher evtl. gesünder als eine herkömmliche Weintraube aus der Nähe – und wer der Ansicht ist NACH MIR DIE SINTFLUT, der wird sie wohl trotzdem kaufen.

Weiteres Beispiel: Portion Krabben. Die Hochseefischerei holt Krabben aus der Nordsee. Diese werden gekühlt nach Nordafrika geschafft, wo sie durch billige Arbeitskräfte gepult (von der Schale befreit) werden. Anschließend kommen sie wieder den langen Transportweg zurück in unsere Kühlregale. Und das nur, weil die Arbeitsleistung daheim teurer als der weite Transport ist. Von der Ökobilanz mal ganz zu schweigen.

Fazit:

- Erstes Gebot: aus der Nähe kaufen
- Zweites Gebot: Bio-Produkte aus der Nähe kaufen
- Drittes Gebot: bei langen Transportwegen innerlich das ‚Bio' wegdenken.

Anders ausgedrückt: Regional und saisonal sind Trumpf.

[From: www.wikia.com]

2 This House believes ... (A debate)

You are going to organise a formal debate in class. The motion for the debate is: 'This House believes that continued globalisation will make the world a better place.'

▶ Skills 7.2

Read the entry on the Skills pages to find out the rules of a debate and some tips on how to conduct one. Then prepare and carry out your debate.

SPOTLIGHT ON Taking part in a formal debate

The more you can support your arguments, the better your speech will be and there are four main ways to do this:

- **Use examples:** Let me give you an example. For instance, ...
- **Refer to generally agreed facts:** Everyone knows that ... It is generally agreed that ... It is common knowledge that ...
- **Use statistics to prove your point:** There are a (large) number of facts and figures to support this.
- **Quote expert opinion:** According to ... / I'd like to quote X here.

Although you do not know exactly what the other team will say until they speak, you can also think about how you might disagree with certain points. Useful phrases here are:.
The other team says that ...
I/We cannot agree with this. / I/We disagree completely because ...
The reason we disagree is that ...
What the other team is overlooking is that ... / They are missing the point here.
It is therefore not true to say that ... It is therefore much closer to the truth that ...
That is why we are right when we say that ...

✕ Extra

1. Some of the students in the class should keep minutes of the debate and make these available to everyone. Use the minutes to summarise the debate.
2. If you can, use video to record the debate and discuss it afterwards.
3. Write an article for an e-zine about your debate saying how you voted, and how you felt about the experience of debating.

SEQUENCE

04

INDIA RISING

One in every six people on Earth lives in India. With a population of 1.3 billion, the world's seventh largest country is its second most populous – and its biggest democracy. Since the 1990s, India has boomed economically. Some say that by 2050, it could be the second biggest economy in the world. Yet it is also a country where millions live on less than a dollar a day. In this sequence we look at India and its contrasts.

Collect ideas

1. Work in groups on the tasks below, then report to the class.

▶ Activity chest 2

   a Brainstorm what you know already about India – for example, its capital city, any films about the country (or its own film industry), its history, its languages and religions, famous places or buildings, …
   b Look at the pictures. Find a title for each one and explain what aspect of India it illustrates. What other aspects of India could you add to those shown in the pictures?
   c In what ways do the pictures support the idea that India is a 'land of contrasts'?

▶ Skills 5.1

2. Make a mindmap of India based on the pictures and the ideas you collected above. Compare with a partner and add new ideas or change those already on your mindmap.

TOPIC 01 Birth of a nation

1 Modern India's many roots (Background information)

The modern state of India came into existence at exactly midnight on 15 August 1947 – when it left the British Empire and became independent. We are now going to look at the story of India before its independence.

A journey through India

India is a country of huge geographical diversity, from the Himalayan Mountains in the north to the tropical beaches of Kerala in the south, desert in the north-west, and the Ganges, the sacred river of India's Hindus, in the east. Situated at the meeting point of East and West, the country has been invaded many times and still today has a dizzying array of cultures, religions and languages today.

5 *dizzying:* (here) enormous, very large
array: group, collection

Indus Valley

The Taj Mahal

Mumbai's main rail station

Hindu temple in Bhubaneswar

A First civilisation in the Indus Valley

Ancient India, around the Indus Valley in what is now Pakistan, was one of the world's earliest civilisations. Beginning in around 5000 BC and reaching its height between 2500 and 1900 BC, the civilisation that developed there was highly sophisticated, with clean and well-organised cities, advanced crafts, trade links, and a written language. Although the people did not build pyramids like those in Egypt at the same time, their civilisation can be seen as equal to that of the Egyptians – but larger and longer-lasting. The Indus Valley civilisation began to decline after 1900 BC; it is believed this was due to climate change that caused floods and droughts.

Buddha. Buddhism began in what is now Tibet in the 5th century BC.

B The birth of a country and India's Golden Age

Shiva, a major Hindu god

In around 1500 BC, India was invaded from the north by a group of people who would lay the foundations of the nation as a whole, and bring with them a culture and religion that miraculously still remain today. These people were the Aryans, white nomads from an area which is roughly modern-day Iran. Speaking and writing a language called Sanskrit (and giving the world some of its earliest written texts) Aryans gradually spread across all of northern India until finally settling in the Ganges valley in the east. Their religion was Hinduism, still the religion of 80 per cent of Indians today. They also established an aspect of life that again still remains in India today: the caste system. It divided society into different levels, with priests at the top and workers at the bottom (cf. p. 166).

India grew and developed so that, by around 31 BC, under the great king Ashoka almost the entire sub-continent had been conquered. There were attacks by the Persians and the Greeks (under Alexander the Great), but their effect was short-lived, and India remained united. It was also Ashoka who helped to spread another of India's great religions, Buddhism, when he himself became a Buddhist.

In around 500 AD, an era began which is often called India's Golden Age. Divided into six strong, mutually peaceful kingdoms, India thrived culturally and economically. The greatest temples (like the Hindu temple in Bhubaneswar in picture B on p. 154) were built; art, music and literature flourished; mathematics advanced (India developed the world's first modern number system); and trade increased. This era started to come to an end, however, in around 1000 AD, when a new group of invaders came from the north.

C The age of the Taj Mahal

Arab Muslim armies came to northern India in 1001 AD, first just raiding towns and villages, but then by the 12th century, conquering the north of the country and the Ganges valley. But it was other Muslims who were to have the biggest impact. These were the Moghuls, a people descended from Gengis Khan, a wild nomadic tribesman who had conquered much of Asia from his home in modern day

---

10 *sophisticated:* cultured and experienced
craft: skilled activity of making things with one's hands
14 *decline:* become smaller and weaker
15 *drought* [draʊt]: long period of time without rain
18 *lay the foundations:* den Grundstein legen
29 *caste* [kɑːst]: division of society according to family origin
38 *mutual* [ˈmjuːtʃuəl]: (here) that benefits all groups equally
thrive: be successful and strong
40 *flourish:* develop quickly and be successful
45 *raid sb./sth.:* attack sb./sth.
48 *descend from sb.:* be related to sb. who lived a long time ago

The 17th century Red Fort, Delhi

Mongolia. The first contact between the Moghuls and the Indians was brutal and bloody, but then from 1527 onwards, the Moghul monarch Babur established a dynasty that would finally cover most of the Indian subcontinent. Babur, and later his grandson Akbar, were more scholars than warriors and they brought peace and religious tolerance (Akbar married a Hindu princess). Again, great architecture flourished, and it was Akbar's grandson, Shah Jahan, who built some of India's now most famous buildings, for example the Red Fort in Delhi (see left) and the Taj Mahal in Agra (a tomb for Akbar's beloved wife; cf. picture C on p. 154). Since these Muslim invasions, Muslims have made up a large part of the Indian population, especially in the Northwest in what was later to become Pakistan.

By the 17th century, India had become a great nation, trading over vast areas within and beyond the Moghul Empire, and with an economy equal to that of many European countries. However, it was one of these European countries that was to change India – again – for ever. Enter the British.

D British India

The 15th, 16th and 17th centuries were the age of European Discovery, when European maritime powers began sailing around the globe and were starting to found worldwide empires. The British first arrived in India to trade. A commercial company called the East India Company signed trade treaties with the Moghul princes in 1617. Trade began to turn into domination, however, as the company – which had its own army of Indian troops – began to take over more and more of the country. In 1857, the Indian soldiers rebelled. The revolt was put down by British soldiers, the East India Company was disbanded, and for the next 100 years, India became part of the British Empire, ruled as a colony directly from Britain. This period is known as the British Raj (cf. pp. 14–15).

A huge amount has been written about British India, and it is one of the most hotly debated periods of British history. Was it good or bad for India? In one way, Britain was just another invader in India's long history. For Britain, it was a colony which could provide it with wealth. Crops such as spices, tea and cotton, were grown there, leading in some cases to terrible famines as less and less crops were grown that could feed the Indians. The British also felt superior to the Indians (this was a time when it was believed scientifically that Europeans were superior to other races), and these ideas were reflected in how Indians were treated. On the other hand, however, historians point out that the British built roads and railways (cf. picture D on p. 154), kept the peace, established forms of government and law still used today, and, most of all, introduced the English language, all of which brought India into the modern world. What we will never know, however, is how India would have developed under the Moghuls without the British.

60 *vast:* huge
67 *maritime power:* Seemacht
68 *found sth.:* establish sth.
72 *treaty:* formal agreement, contract
76 *be disbanded:* be split up, be divided
82 *crop:* plant grown in large numbers for food
83 *famine* ['fæmɪn]: Hungersnot

A Understanding the text

Work in groups to study the text. Write eight questions about the text and put them to your fellow students in a class quiz (with your books closed!).

2 Partition (A web article)

At the end of World War II, Britain was bankrupt as a country and was more than ready to let its (expensive) empire go. The first country to get independence was India, in 1947. But before the British left, there was one final event that would shape the country we know today. It was called 'Partition'. You are going to read an explanation of it in an article from the American website About.com.

A Before you read

► Activity chest 4

1. Look up the word *partition* in your dictionary. Looking back at the map of India on p. 154 and the information you got about Indian society, speculate about what it might mean in the context of Indian history.

The Partition of India was the process of dividing the subcontinent along sectarian lines, which took place in 1947 as India gained its independence from the British Raj. The northern, predominantly Muslim sections of India became the nation of Pakistan, while the southern and majority Hindu section became the Republic of India.

Background to Partition

In 1885, the Hindu-dominated Indian National Congress (INC) met for the first time. When the British made an attempt to divide the state of Bengal along religious lines in 1905, the INC led huge protests against the plan. This sparked the formation of the Muslim League, which sought to guarantee the rights of Muslims in any future independence negotiations.

Although the Muslim League formed in opposition to the INC, [...] the two political parties generally cooperated in their mutual goal of getting Britain to 'Quit India.' Both the INC and the Muslim League supported sending Indian volunteer troops to fight on Britain's behalf in World War I; in exchange for the service of more than 1 million Indian soldiers, the people of India expected political concessions up to and including independence. However, after the war Britain offered no such concessions.

In April of 1919, a unit of the British Army went to Amritsar, in the Punjab, to silence pro-independence unrest. The unit's commander ordered his men to open fire on the unarmed crowd, killing more than 1,000 protesters. When word of the Amritsar Massacre spread around India, hundreds of thousands of formerly apolitical people became supporters of the INC and Muslim League.

Mohandas Gandhi (1869–1948) *leader of the Indian Independence movement*

In the 1930s, Mohandas Gandhi became the leading figure in the INC. Although he advocated a unified Hindu and Muslim India, with equal rights for all, other INC members were less inclined to join with Muslims against the British. As a result, the Muslim League began to make plans for a separate Muslim state.

2 *sectarian* [sek'teərɪən]: defined by religion
3 *predominantly:* mostly
9 *spark sth.:* start sth., cause sth.
10 *seek (sought, sought) to do sth.:* try to do sth.
13 *mutual* ['mjuːtʃuəl]: (here) shared, common
15 *on sb.'s behalf:* for sb., representing sb.
16 *concession:* Zugeständnis
27 *advocate sth.:* support sth.
29 *be inclined to do sth.:* want to do sth.

Independence and Partition

World War II sparked a crisis in relations among the British, the INC and the Muslim League. The British expected India once again to provide much-needed soldiers and material for the war effort, but the INC opposed sending Indians to fight and die in Britain's war. After the betrayal following World War I, the INC saw no benefit for India in such a sacrifice. The Muslim League, however, decided to back Britain's call for volunteers, in an effort to curry British favor in support of a Muslim nation in post-independence northern India.

Before the war had even ended, public opinion in Britain had swung against the distraction and expense of empire. Winston Churchill's party was voted out of office, and the pro-independence Labour Party was voted in during 1945. Labour called for almost immediate independence for India, as well as more gradual freedom for Britain's other colonial holdings.

Jawaharlal Nehru (1889–1964) *India's first prime minister*

Mohammed Ali Jinnah (1876–1948) *leader of the Muslim League and Pakistan's first Governor General*

The Muslim League's leader, Mohammed Ali Jinnah, began a public campaign in favor of a separate Muslim state, while Jawaharlal Nehru of the INC called for a unified India. (This is not surprising, given the fact that Hindus like Nehru would have formed the vast majority, and would have been in control of any democratic form of government.)

As independence neared, the country began to descend towards a sectarian civil war. Although Gandhi implored the Indian people to unite in peaceful opposition to British rule, the Muslim League sponsored a 'Direct Action Day' on August 16, 1946, which resulted in the deaths of more than 4,000 Hindus and Sikhs in Calcutta (Kolkata). This touched off the 'Week of the Long Knives,' an orgy of sectarian violence that resulted in hundreds of deaths on both sides in various cities across the country.

Lord Louis Mountbatten (1900–1979) *the last Viceroy of India*

In February of 1947, the British government announced that India would be granted independence by June 1948. Viceroy for India Lord Louis Mountbatten pleaded with the Hindu and Muslim leadership to agree to form a united country, but they could not. Only Gandhi supported Mountbatten's position. With the country descending further into chaos, Mountbatten reluctantly agreed to the formation of two separate states, and moved the independence date up to August 15, 1947.

With the decision in favor of partition made, the parties next faced this nearly impossible task of fixing a border between the new states. The Muslims occupied two main regions in the north on opposite sides of the country, separated by a majority-Hindu section. In addition, throughout most of northern India members of the two religions were mixed together – not to mention populations of Sikhs, Christians and other minority faiths. […]

In the wealthy and fertile region of the Punjab, the problem was extreme with a nearly-even mixture of Hindus and Muslims. Neither side wanted to relinquish

37 *benefit:* positive consequence
sacrifice (n): (here) act of giving up an important or valuable thing
38 *curry sb.'s favour.:* try to get sb. to like you
41 *distraction:* thing that takes your attention away from what you should be concentrating on
expense: cost
44 *holding:* property
53 *descend towards sth.:* (here) approach sth. bad
54 *implore sb. to do sth.:* desperately encourage sb. to do sth.
58 *touch sth. off:* cause sth.
62 *grant sth.:* give sth., allow sth.
79 *relinquish sth.:* give sth. up

this valuable land, and sectarian hatred ran high. The border was drawn right down the middle of the province, between Lahore and Amritsar.

On both sides, people scrambled to get onto the 'right' side of the border, or were driven from their homes by their erstwhile neighbors. At least 10 million people fled north or south, depending upon their faith, and more than 500,000 were killed in the melee. Trains full of refugees were set upon by militants from both sides, and all the passengers massacred.

On August 14, 1947, the Islamic Republic of Pakistan was founded. The following day, the Republic of India was established to the south.

Aftermath of Partition

On January 30, 1948, Mohandas Gandhi was assassinated for his support of a multi-religious state by a young Hindu radical. Since August of 1947, India and Pakistan have fought three major wars and one minor war over territorial disputes. The boundary line in Jammu and Kashmir is particularly troubled. […]

In 1974, India tested its first nuclear weapon. Pakistan followed in 1998. Any exacerbation of post-Partition tensions today could be absolutely catastrophic.

[From: www.about.com]

85 *melee* ['meleɪ]: chaos
90 *assassinate sb.* [ə'sæsɪneɪt]: kill sb.
95 *exacerbation* [ig'zæsəbeɪʃən]: worsening

B Understanding the text

▶ Activity chest 11

Choose one of the questions below and write your answer. Use 'Peer-review groups' to check and improve your texts, then present your group's best text to the class.

a Sum up the parts played in the partition by the three main groups involved: Hindus, Muslims and the British.

b Outline how the partition of India affected the country and what effect it still has in modern India.

C Analysing the text

Analyse if this web article presents a neutral or biased view of the parties involved in Partition. Give evidence for your view.

The writer's aim in this article is	to give an overview of / help readers to understand …
The writer presents a	neutral/unbiased/objective/impartial/balanced view of the people and events involved
The writer's view is rather	biased/one-sided/partial/unbalanced
For example, in lines …	the writer shows both sides of the situation / balances the arguments for and against … (shows only one side of the argument / uses adjectives such as …)
The writer does / does not	comment personally on … / express a subjective view

D Reacting to the text

There are many dramatic photos of the Partition of India that help us to understand the drama and tragedy of the events. Find one online and present it to the class.

3 The birth of a nation (A speech)

You are going to read parts of the 'Tryst with destiny' speech made by Jawaharlal Nehru, modern India's first prime minister, shortly before midnight on 14 August 1947, i.e. the very minute the country gained its independence.

A Before you read

Talk in class. Use your dictionary to find out the meaning of the expression *tryst with destiny*. Speculate about what Nehru might mean with this in his speech. What other ideas and issues can you imagine he might deal with in the speech?

Long years ago we made a tryst with destiny, and now the time comes when we shall redeem our pledge, not wholly or in full measure, but very substantially.

At the stroke of the midnight hour, when the world sleeps, India will awake to life and freedom. A moment comes, which comes but rarely in history, when we step out from the old to the new, when an age ends, and when the soul of a nation, long suppressed, finds utterance. […]

At the dawn of history India started on her unending quest, and trackless centuries are filled with her striving and the grandeur of her success and her failures. Through good and ill fortune alike she has never lost sight of that quest or forgotten the ideals which gave her strength. We end today a period of ill fortune and India discovers herself again. […]

To the people of India, whose representatives we are, we make an appeal to join us with faith and confidence in this great adventure. […] The appointed day has come – the day appointed by destiny – and India stands forth again, after long slumber and struggle, awake, vital, free and independent. The past clings on to us still in some measure and we have to do much before we redeem the pledges we have so often taken. Yet the turning point is past, and history begins anew for us, the history which we shall live and act and others will write about.

It is a fateful moment for us in India, for all Asia and for the world. A new star rises, the star of freedom in the east, a new hope comes into being, a vision long cherished materialises. May the star never set and that hope never be betrayed!

We rejoice in that freedom, even though clouds surround us, and many of our people are sorrow-stricken and difficult problems encompass us. But freedom brings responsibilities and burdens and we have to face them in the spirit of a free and disciplined people.

On this day our first thoughts go to the architect of this freedom, the father of our nation, who, embodying the old spirit of India, held aloft the torch of freedom and lighted up the darkness that surrounded us.

We have often been unworthy followers of his and have strayed from his message, but not only we but succeeding generations will remember this message and bear the imprint in their hearts of this great son of India, magnificent in his faith and strength and courage and humility. We shall never allow that torch of freedom to be blown out, however high the wind or stormy the tempest. […]

The future beckons to us. Whither do we go and what shall be our endeavour? To bring freedom and opportunity to the common man, to the peasants and workers of India; to fight and end poverty and ignorance and disease; to build up a prosperous, democratic and progressive nation, and to create social, economic

2 *redeem a pledge:* do what one promised to do
7 *suppress sth.:* prevent sth. from developing
find utterance: discover the ability to speak
8 *dawn* [dɔːn]: Morgendämmerung
quest: long search
trackless: too many to be counted
9 *grandeur* ['grændʒə]: quality of being impressive
13 *representative* [ˌ– –'– – –]: Vertreter
appeal: request
14 *appointed:* chosen
15 *stand forth:* be strong, independent
16 *slumber (n):* sleep
cling on to sb.: (here) continue to have an effect for sb.
20 *fateful:* important for the future
22 *cherish sth.:* love sth.
betray sth.: (here) damage sth. that relied upon you
23 *rejoice in sth.* [rɪ'dʒɔɪs]: express happiness about sth.
24 *encompass sth* [–'– –]: completely surround sth.
28 *torch:* Fackel
30 *stray from sth.:* move away from sth.
31 *succeeding:* following, next
32 *bear the imprint of sth.:* das Gepräge von etwas tragen
33 *humility:* Bescheidenheit
35 *beckon to sb.:* jdm. zuwinken
whither (old use): where
endeavour [ɪn'devə]: (here) purpose

and political institutions which will ensure justice and fullness of life to every man and woman.

We have hard work ahead. There is no resting for any one of us till we redeem our pledge in full, till we make all the people of India what destiny intended them to be.

We are citizens of a great country, on the verge of bold advance, and we have to live up to that high standard. All of us, to whatever religion we may belong, are equally the children of India with equal rights, privileges and obligations. We cannot encourage communalism or narrow-mindedness, for no nation can be great whose people are narrow in thought or in action.

To the nations and peoples of the world we send greetings and pledge ourselves to cooperate with them in furthering peace, freedom and democracy.

And to India, our much-loved motherland, the ancient, the eternal and the ever-new, we pay our reverent homage and we bind ourselves afresh to her service. Jai Hind.

44 *be on the verge of sth.:* be about to do sth.
46 *obligation:* sth. that must be done
47 *narrow-mindedness:* inability to listen to new ideas and opinions
50 *further sth.:* make sth. stronger
52 *pay homage:* show respect
reverent: showing admiration
Jai Hind (Hindi): victory to India

B Understanding the text

1. Copy the chart below and note down the most important ideas from the speech.

India in the past	
India today	
Gandhi's role	
India in the future	
Tasks that India has to fulfill to create its future	

2. Sum up the main points of the speech in your own words.

C Analysing the text

Read the **SPOTLIGHT** box below, then analyse Nehru's speech. Don't forget to explain the image of a 'tryst with destiny'. Give concrete examples to support your ideas.

▶ Glossary 3.1

SPOTLIGHT ON Speeches

Speeches are given in many different situations and for many different reasons. One kind of speech that you will often come across is, as here, a political speech. The most important things to remember when you study a speech are:

- speeches are given live, usually by one person, to an audience, and this person often addresses the listeners directly, using the personal pronouns 'I' or 'we';
- speeches usually have a clear structure, with the ideas and emotions building up to a (dramatic) end. The speaker wants to leave the audience with a memorable message;
- the speaker often wants to persuade the listeners of a point of view, or to inspire them with her/his words;
- the speaker can use only words to get a message across and the way language is used is a key element. Look out constantly for rhetorical devices (which were first invented for public speaking and which make the speech more effective), and for poetic language (which makes the speech more emotional).

✕ **Extra** Do research to find out more about an aspect of this topic – Gandhi, for example, a famous city or building, the Indian religions, or the aftermath of this speech. Report to the class.

TOPIC

02

The new India

Modern India's booming economy is transforming the lives of many – but many more cannot enjoy the benefits. In this topic we look at how the lives of modern Indians are changing – or not changing.

Collect ideas

Work in groups, then report to the class.

1. Briefly describe each picture and explain which aspect of modern life in India it expresses. Say how the picture conveys this aspect.
2. In what ways would you expect life to change for the Indians who are becoming wealthier in today's India?
3. Speculate about the reasons why some Indians might not be profiting from the boom.

1 A visit to Infosys (A video)

You are going to watch part of a British TV series called *India with Sanjeev Bhaskar*. Baskhar (on the right in this picture) is a popular comedian and broadcaster in Britain, and in the series he visits India to find out what is happening there today. In this clip, he is at Infosys, a company based in Bangalore in south-eastern India.

DVD 14

oasis of calm: calm place in the middle of a busy area
heritage: (kulturelles) Erbe
gym: Fitnesscenter
snake charmer: Schlangenbeschwörer
tailored: made especially for you
loan: money that you borrow from a bank
mortgage: money that you borrow to buy a house
ATM (= automatic teller machine): Geldautomat

▶ Skills 4

▶ Skills 5.2d

A Before you watch

1. The picture with the pyramid on p. 153 shows Infosys. What kind of company might it be? What impression of it do you get from the photograph?
2. Speculate about the sort of people who might work there and about their attitudes.

B Understanding and analysing the video

1. Make a watching grid like the one below. Watch the video, divide it into sections, then fill in the left and middle columns.

SECTION OF VIDEO	CONTENT	FILM AND SOUND TECHNIQUES
Introduction	...	...
...	...	...

2. Watch a second time. Divide the group up so that each of you concentrates on a different section of the video. Note down the film and sound techniques used. Share your notes and complete the third column.
3. Sum up the video orally, commenting briefly on techniques that you found effective. Explain also why you think Baskhar was chosen to make the documentary and who might be the audience for his TV series.

C Reacting to the video

1. Talk in class.
   a What are your impressions of Infosys and the people who work there? What does the video tell you about modern India?
   b What do you think of Bhaskar and the way he presents the programme? Would you like to watch more of his series? Why (not)?
2. Several of the people Bhaskar interviews talk about their relationship with their parents. Imagine a dialogue between one of the people and their mother or father. Write the dialogue or role-play it with a partner.

2 India's new middle class

(A newspaper feature article)

Estimated at anything from 50 million to 300 million people, India's new middle class is growing fast. You are going to read part of an article by a British Asian journalist published in the British quality newspaper *The Guardian*. In this extract, he interviews three generations of the Aroras family.

Downtown New Delhi, India's capital and one of the world's fastest-growing cities

A Before you read

What differences would you expect to find between three generations (grandparents, parents and children) in any family, anywhere in the world? Speculate on differences between these generations that could be particular to an Indian family.

Nothing symbolises the ambitions of India's burgeoning middle class better than its love of cars. Outside a three-storey house in the north Delhi suburb of Mukherjee Nagar sit three sedans. Five years ago there would have been none. Inside, Govind Gopal Arora says that the changes in modern India are best measured by the changing size of wage packets.

After three decades as an engineer, the 51-year-old takes home 25,000 rupees (£300) a month. His eldest son, Ashutosh, joined one of India's multinationals as a management trainee last year. At 23, he is already earning nearly as much as his father. 'In a few years he'll be making double,' says Govind. 'That is progress.'

Govind, or 'GeeGee' as he is known at home, is happy that his children can take advantage of the opportunities he never had, but his own life, he says, was one of constant struggle. The eldest of five, GeeGee was born into a Hindu refugee family who fled from religious riots in Dera Ismail Khan, their home town on what is now the Afghanistan-Pakistan border, during the partition of British India.

Today three generations of the Aroras – GeeGee's family, his two brothers' families and GeeGee's parents – live in the family's dun-coloured house; 14 in total. But most of GeeGee's life was spent in squat brick one-bedroom homes that families who left Pakistan for India were given by the government. [...]

Like many middle-class Delhi families, the Aroras take their Hinduism seriously. When I visit GeeGee at his factory, he offers me prashad, sweetened rice flakes eaten to please Hinduism's pantheon of gods. 'Tuesday is Hanuman's day,' he explains, referring to India's revered monkey deity.

GeeGee's father, Devkinandan Arora, was a boy of 12 when he woke up in Dera Ismail Khan on the morning of April 13 1947 to the sound of rioting and the sight of plumes of black smoke rising from the countryside. These were the last few weeks of the British Raj, the empire going up in flames of religious hatred. 'We went to our terrace and could see the fire and the smoke,' recalls the retired civil

1 *burgeon* ['bɜːdʒən] (fml): start to grow rapidly
3 *sedan* [sɪ'dæn]: Limousine
5 *wage packet:* money paid for a job
13 *riot:* situation in which people behave in a violent way
17 *squat (adj):* (here) little and ugly
21 *pantheon* ['pænθiən]: group of gods
22 *revered* [rɪ'vɪəd]: respected
deity ['deɪəti]: god
25 *plume:* (here) cloud
27 *civil servant:* Beamter

servant. 'We were Hindus, but most of the people there were Mohammedans. We had lived in peace but that was over.'

The 40-strong Arora clan fled to Delhi in early August 1947, leaving behind their homes and farmland. Devkinandan, now 72, sits bolt upright when he talks of bringing up his young family in the aftermath of partition. These days he and his wife Sushil lament that their grandchildren no longer speak their 'mother tongue', Seraiki [...].

The patriarch of the Arora family has not been back 'home' in the past six decades. 'We have nothing but good memories of our home,' he says. 'Of the thousands of Muslims there, only a few families were bad. We were always welcome.'

These memories mean little to his grandson, Paritosh, an engineering student. Dressed in jeans and a T-shirt, he has his eyes on the future. 'My brother's best friend is a Muslim,' he says. 'My best friend is a Sikh. People say I look like a Muslim, and that's a compliment because the Pakistani cricket team are all pretty good-looking.' The 19-year-old says that while no one in his family has travelled outside India and Nepal, he would happily work abroad. His first preference, he says, is to work for an 'MNC' (multinational company). But he adds that India is the 'best place in the world to be born in right now'. In his evenings he goes out with friends and hangs out in coffee shops or malls. He also spends hours surfing the internet, a pastime that began only three years ago when the family bought its first computer.

With new ideas come new social patterns; Paritosh does not want to live in an extended family as an adult. 'It is inevitable that we will have nuclear families like the west,' he says. 'My mum stopped working to look after me and my brother. I want my wife to work.'

[From: *The Guardian*, 14 August 2007]

28 *Mohammedan* [-'- - -]
31 *bolt upright:* with a straight back
32 *aftermath:* Nachwirkungen
33 *lament sth.:* feel sad about sth.
49 *social pattern:* gesellschaftliche Strukturen
50 *nuclear family:* Kernfamilie

B Understanding the text

1. Copy and make notes from the text in the table below. Not all sections may be relevant to all the people.

	DEVKINANDAN	GEEGEE	PARITOSH
who			
personal details			
past life			
religious ideas			
ideas about modern India			
ideas about the future			

2. Use your notes to summarise what we learn about modern India from this extract.

C Analysing the text

▶ Skills 1.2.2

Point out what aims the writer has with this article. Analyse the techniques he uses to interest his readers.

D Mediation

▶ Skills 9.7

You and your parents visit India and meet GeeGee. They are keen to know about how family life is changing but speak no English. Write a conversation in which you mediate.

3 Poverty in India (An article and statistics)

While India's middle class continues to grow and the economy booms, there is another side of the country which stands in stark contrast. You are going to read a web article from the organisation *Economy Watch*, which collects economic data from around the world.

A Before you read

▶ Skills 2.1

1. Talk in class. Describe the pictures and describe the feelings they convey and how this effect is achieved.
2. Poverty in India is closely linked to the caste system. Read the **KEY FACTS** on castes below.
3. Try to work out a definition of 'poverty'.

KEY FACTS India's caste system

The caste system in India is made up of thousands of different groups ('Jatis') that cover the entire Indian population. It is supposedly based on Hindu texts that grouped people into four categories: the Brahmins were scholars and priests; the Kshatriyas were rulers and warriors; Shudras were builders and artists; Vaishyas were farmers and merchants. Dalits (those that dealt with human waste and dead bodies, cf. p. 169) and their various sub-groups were considered to be outside the caste system.
Under the caste system everyone belongs to a caste at birth, and they cannot move between castes. In theory, a person's caste determines what occupation they can take up, what their social status will be and even who they can marry.
Since independence, the Indian constitution prohibits discrimination based on caste and the system is slowly breaking down. In Tamil Nadu, for example, 70% of government jobs and state university places are reserved for people from lower castes. In fact, many Brahmins feel they have suffered a reversal of fortune and now find it hard to get good jobs. But for many Indians, especially in rural areas, the hierarchical element of the caste system is still very relevant and influences how they view themselves and others.

3 *scholar* ['skɒlə]: person who has studied and knows a lot
ruler: person who is in charge of an area
4 *warrior* ['wɒriə]: person who fights in wars
8 *determine sth.:* officially decide or arrange sth.
10 *prohibit sth.:* ban sth., not allow sth.
13 *reversal:* change to make a situation opposite of it was

Poverty in India is a major issue. Rural Indians depend on unpredictable agriculture incomes, while urban Indians rely on jobs that are, at best, scarce.

Since its independence, the issue of poverty within India has remained a prevalent concern. As of 2010, more than 37% of India's population of 1.35 billion still lives below the poverty line. More than 41% of the entire rural population and 25% of the urban population of India exists in this difficult physical and financial predicament. […]

The division of resources, as well as wealth, is uneven in India – this disparity creates different poverty ratios for different states. For instance, states such as Delhi and Punjab have low poverty ratios. On the other hand, almost half the population in states like Bihar and Orissa live below the poverty line.

A number of factors are responsible for poverty in the rural areas of India. Rural populations primarily depend on agriculture, which is highly dependant on rain patterns and the monsoon season. Inadequate rain and improper irrigation facilities can obviously cause low, or in some cases, zero production of crops.

Additionally, the Indian family unit is often large, which can amplify the effects of poverty. Also, the caste system still prevails in India, and this is a major reason for rural poverty – people from the lower castes are often deprived of the most basic facilities and opportunities. The government has planned and implemented poverty eradication programs, but the benefits of these programs are yet to bear fruits.

The phenomenal increase in population in the cities is one of the main reasons for poverty in the urban areas of India. A major portion of this additional population is due to the large scale migration of rural families from villages to cities. This migration is mainly attributed to poor employment opportunities in villages.

Since 1970, the Indian government has implemented a number of programs designed to eradicate poverty, and has had some success with these programs. The government has sought to increase the GDP through different processes, including changes in industrial policies. There is a Public Distribution System, which has been effective to some extent.

[From: www.economywatch.com]

unpredictable: unvorhersehbar
2 *prevalent* ['prevələnt]: very common
3 *below the poverty line:* unter der Armutsgrenze
5 *predicament* [prɪ'dɪkəmənt]: difficult situation
6 *disparity:* different in an unfair way
7 *poverty ratio* ['pɒvəti 'reiʃiəʊ]: Anteil an armen Menschen
12 *irrigation facilities:* Bewässerungsanlagen
14 *amplify sth.:* make sth. larger
16 *deprived of sth.:* without sth.
23 *attributed to:* linked to
24 *implement sth.* ['- - -]: start using sth. officially

B Understanding the text

► Skills 5.1, Step 1

Make a mindmap of the key ideas in the text. Compare with a partner.

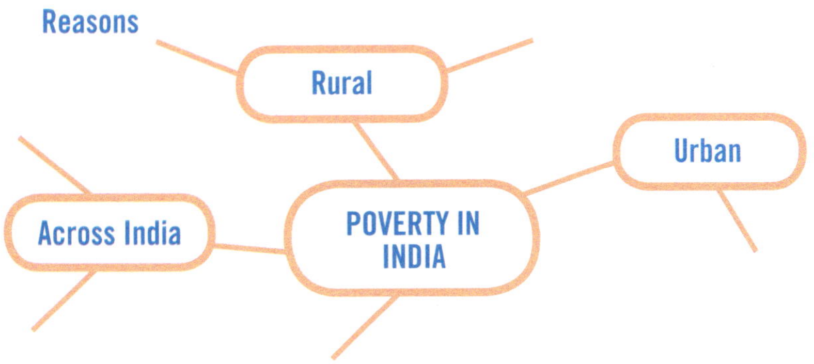

C Understanding and explaining statistics

▶ Skills 3

The two diagrams below give additional information about the kinds of poverty described in the text.

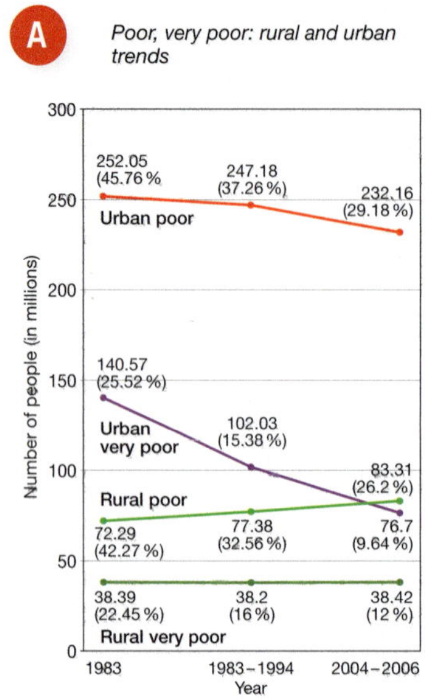

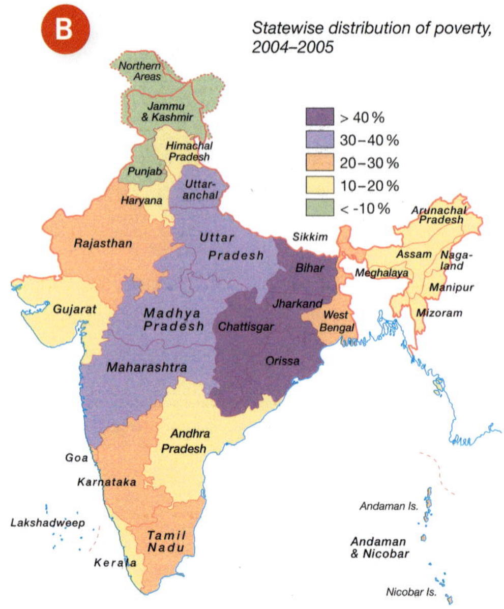

[From: www.downtoearth.org]

IMPROVE YOUR WRITING Connecting sentences

When working with statistics, you often compare numbers and developments. Therefore, when formulating your results, it is necessary to express these comparisons – mainly through connecting sentences. Compare the following texts that describe two imaginary line graphs. Identify the ways the sentences are connected to establish a logical connection between them. Make sure you use such connectors when analysing statistics:

Export and import have risen considerably. Up to the year 2000 their development was almost parallel. Between 2000 and 2006 the export rate grew steeply. During that time, the import rate grew only slowly. After 2006, the number of imports fell marginally and the export rate took a steep decline.	Both export and import have risen considerably. However, while up to the year 2000 their development was almost parallel, the export rate grew steeply between 2000 and 2006 in comparison to the import rate. In contrast to the number of imports, which only fell marginally after 2006, the export rate took a steep decline.

D Reacting to the material

Poverty has been identified as a major issue in India. But it is a phenomenon that also exists in other western countries, also in Germany. Looking back at your definition of poverty, describe the difference between poverty in countries like India and in western countries.

4 Untouchable (Listening)

You are going to listen to two extracts from the autobiography *The Whole Truth and Nothing but the Truth* of B. Kesharvisham, a Dalit (cf. KEY FACTS). In the extracts, which are read by an actor, we learn about the writer's childhood. Unusually for a Dalit at the time (Kesharvisham was born in 1940), he went to school.

A Before you listen

Read the key facts box below. How do you feel about the situation it describes?

KEY FACTS Dalits

Dalits ('the oppressed ones') are a group of people in India that live outside the Indian caste system. They are of such a low status that they do not even properly belong to society.

In country areas, Dalits do not own land, so they most often work on other people's farms. In towns and cities, they are cleaners, sweepers and carriers of dead meat. Dalit men regularly work – without protection – in the sewers under the streets. Here, as in the country, Dalits rely for food on what they are given by others, often scraps left over after a meal.

A Dalit woman cleaning public toilets

Physical contact between Dalits and other castes is virtually impossible – hence, they used to be called 'untouchables'. Two reports recently quoted the following statistics:

- 48% of villages deny Dalits access to water;
- 73% of villages don't permit Dalits to enter non-Dalit homes;
- 33% of public health workers refuse to visit Dalit homes;
- 28% police stations ban entry to Dalits;
- 38% of government schools make Dalit children sit separately while eating.

A report published in 2010 also said that Dalit children in schools have to clean the toilets there and that teachers refuse to correct their homework because that would mean touching their exercise books.

6 *sweeper:* Straßenfeger
8 *sewers* ['suːəs]: Kanalisationsröhre
11 *scrap:* small piece of food
15 *deny sb. sth.:* jdm. etwas versagen
17 *public health worker:* Angestellte/r im Gesundheitswesen

CD 7

▶ Skills 6

B Understanding the texts

1. Listen to both extracts, take notes and then retell one of the stories orally.
2. State what unspoken rules exist that govern how Dalits and other Indians interact.

C Reacting to the texts

▶ Activity chest 9

You are a young Indian. Next week you are going to take part in a protest about the plight of Dalits. Design a poster and show it to the class with a 'Gallery walk'.

5 A British Indian's view of the new India (A newspaper article)

The article below was written by a journalist working in India for the British quality newspaper *The Guardian*.

A Before you read

Read the headline and strapline of the article. Speculate about what it will be about.

'I've witnessed the arrival of a golden age'

Randeep Ramesh, the Guardian's Delhi correspondent, spent his childhood apologising for having any connection with India. But how times change ...

A few years ago, I visited an Indian software millionaire at his headquarters in Bangalore for a story about the country's effervescent computer industry. Software is modern India's spice, a precious commodity craved by the rest of the world. The businessman took great pleasure in showing me around. [...] After an hour or two, the conversation got personal. In the unselfconscious, no-nonsense manner of many educated Indians, the entrepreneur quizzed me on which university I had gone to (Cambridge) and the subject I had studied (physics), before triumphantly declaring that I had been 'born in the wrong country'. When I protested, he raised his palm.

'The British system has come to this – taking scientists and making them journalists,' he said with a smile. 'What a waste. Just imagine the opportunities you missed by not being born here.'

In my youth I would have laughed that comment away as misplaced optimism in a country that could not even get its trains to run on time. I had grown up shuttling between my birthplace, London, and India, my parents' homeland. My earliest memories revolved around the open sewers and the endless slumlands of my father's Mumbai, or Bombay as it was then known, and the tropical sloth of my mother's home in Kerala. [...]

I spent my childhood apologising for having any connections with India, a country that in my lofty opinion needed major surgery. But a decade ago, while the rest of the world was looking the other way, India reached some kind of tipping point, and change began to happen – fast.

The signs were easy to spot. By the mid-90s, the Marks & Spencer underwear and ovenproof CorningWare dishes my parents had always brought as gifts for relatives were politely returned, or left unopened. 'We can buy this here,' sniffed my auntie in Bangalore.

My Indian cousins, who had diligently studied science subjects, began to leave India for jobs with management consultants and computer companies in places such as Singapore and California. Friends in Britain started to climb the social ladder by having arranged marriages with Indian women who were often smarter, more sophisticated and better-looking than they perhaps deserved.

Since I pitched up in 2003 to live and work in Delhi, I have witnessed firsthand the arrival of a golden age. The making and spending of money has become respected in a country where poverty was once revered. Middle-income westerners now feel poor in the upmarket postcodes of India's big cities.

Yet it would be wrong to think that India has become just like everywhere else. Yes,

3 *headquarters (pl):* Hauptsitz, Zentrale
4 *effervescent* [efə'vesnt]: full of energy
5 *commodity:* sth. that is useful
crave sth.: want sth. very much
7 *unselfconscious:* unbefangen
8 *entrepreneur* [ˌɒntrəprə'nɜː]: person who starts new businesses to make money
11 *palm:* Handfläche
15 *misplaced:* not appropriate or correct
18 *sewers* ['suːəs]: Kanalisationsröhre
19 *sloth:* laziness
22 *lofty:* (here) arrogant
surgery ['sɜːdʒəri]: Operation
23 *tipping point:* time of extreme change
27 *sniff:* speak in a disapproving way
29 *diligent:* careful and serious
33 *sophisticated:* cultured and experienced
34 *pitch up:* casually arrive somewhere
36 *revered* [rɪ'vɪəd]: respected
37 *upmarket:* for rich people
postcode: Postleitzahl

an economic miracle is under way. Yes, there is now an elite as capable as any in the west. The paradox is that this is a modernising nation, but one still steeped in myth and legend. Indians tend to ascribe the country's rise to its unique, ancient civilisation and in the process tend to be rather dismissive of anywhere else.

This does tend to blind Indians to the real problems faced by the country. Venality abounds, and the widespread acceptance of corruption tarnishes the pride that Indians take in their most tangible achievement – democracy – and saps the energy with which they express it. [...]

Hanging in the air, too, is desperate poverty. To the naked eye, India appears not just an underdeveloped society, but an extremely unjust one. There are 260 million poor people in the country, and more than 1,000 children die of diarrhoea every day. [...]

Living in India sometimes feels like living in the midst of a cult, with hundreds of millions of souls convinced of the country's inevitable rise to global, nuclear-armed power. [...] During my time here, I have come to realise that Indians have little interest in the British now, or in a British Asian like me who has returned to his parents' land. [...] America, the first British colony to break free, is the model now. [...] Like the American people, Indians have become more confident and assertive, citing stories of those who triumph against the odds to balance their nation's shortcomings. They see glasses half-full, not half-empty, here. India wakes up with a smile on its face each morning, because its people know that the past may have been yours, but the future belongs to them.

[From: *The Guardian*, 14 August 2007]

40 *steeped in sth.:* full of
42 *be dismissive of sth.:* not think sth. is important
44 *venality* [viːˈnæləti]: (here) people doing dishonest things for money
abound: be present in large numbers
tarnish sth.: (here) have a negative effect on sth.
45 *tangible:* (here) clearly in existence
sap sth.: make sth. weaker
49 *diarrhoea* [daɪəˈrɪə]: Durchfall
57 *assertive:* expressing opinions strongly
against the odds: entgegen allen Erwartungen

B Understanding the text

1. Say whether the following statements about the text are true or false.
   a The Indian software millionaire mentioned at the beginning believes that the writer would not be a journalist if he had grown up in India.
   b When the writer visited India as a child, he thought it was better than Britain.
   c He says India began to change in 2003.
   d He believes India is changing in a unique way.
   e He claims that there are severe problems in India that Indians ignore.
   f The model, he says, for Indians today as they develop as a nation is Britain.
   g The writer thinks that Indians are pessimistic rather than optimistic people.
2. Summarize how the writer describes India today.

C Analysing the text

▶ Glossary 1.1
▶ Skills 1.2.2

1. Identify the text type and the writer's goal when writing. Analyse the techniques he uses to achieve it.
2. The writer sees India as a very successful country, but he also admits the country's weaknesses. Analyse how he deals with the negative sides and how he manages to support his positive view.

D Reacting to the text (Mediation)

▶ Skills 9.7

A German friend of yours maintains that former colonies almost always remain dependent on their former mother country and continue to feel inferior. On the basis of this article, write an email commenting on this idea – in German.

TOPIC

03

Women and men in India today

As India itself is changing, so are the roles of men and women – but again, not for everyone. In this topic, we look at gender issues in modern India.

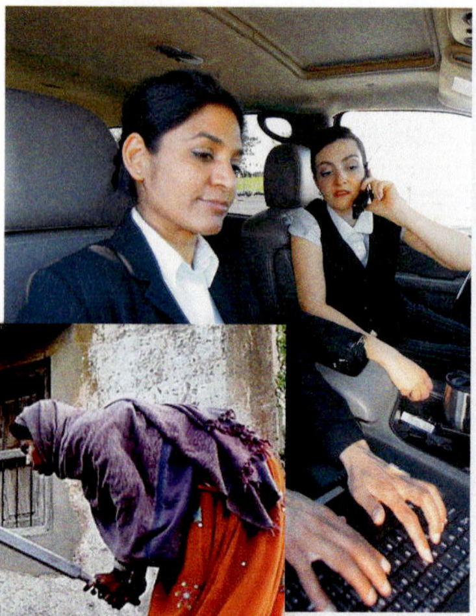

Collect ideas

In groups, work on the tasks below, then report to the class.

1. Look at the pictures. Describe them and find a title for each. Discuss what ideas and issues they raise concerning women and men in India.
2. Using the word cloud below, collect what you know or expect about marriage in India.

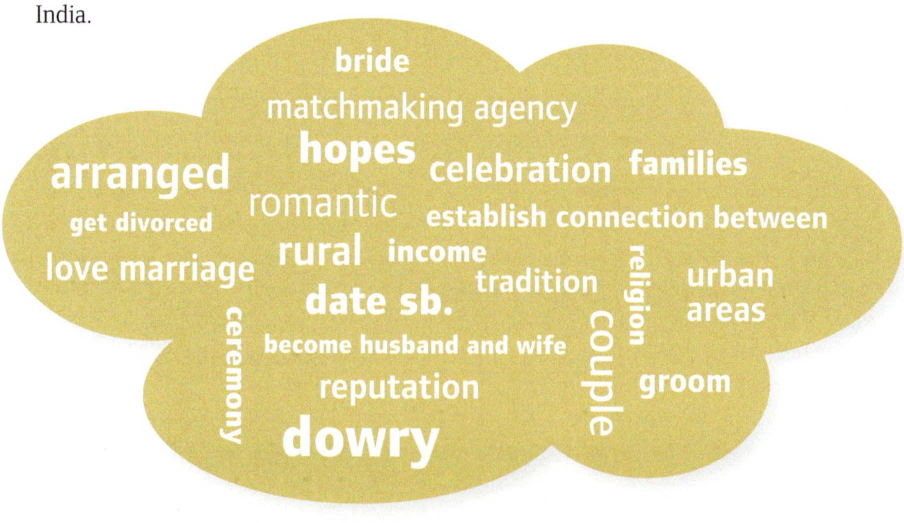

3. From what you have learned in this sequence about how India is changing, what sorts of gender issues do you think might come up in this topic?

1 Marriage in India (Marriage ads)

In this activity you are going to consider the idea of arranged marriages. You are going to look at some marriage ads and at the end you will organise a talk show.

A Before you read

Every day, Indian newspapers and online marriage agencies publish literally thousands of marriage advertisements (in India called 'matrimonials').
Look at the examples below and on the next page. Point out what kind of information is given and who placed the ad on the website. What do the ads tell you about marriage in India? What are your first reactions to this?

US ID: rainriver

Age: 35 **Height:** 5'4"
Marital Status: Never Married
Name: Rhia
City: Calcutta 700019
Personal Details: Non-Vegetarian, Non-Smoker

Education: MA/MSc/MBA
Country of Residence: India **Passport:** India
Country of Origin: Bengali **Religion:** Hindu
Employment: Media

I am slim, fair and what I look like is for you to judge. I wouldn't know but people say I am beautiful. I have a post graduate degree in Political Science and I am in corporate communications working for a reputed firm in Calcutta. My interests are reading, writing, theatre, dancing, visiting art galleries, watching films, meeting new people and cooking exotic dishes. At heart an incurable romantic, I believe I can make a man happy. I am looking for an educated, professionally qualified and well established man who is gentle, understanding with a progressive and liberal outlook who can be my friend and lover.

7 *MA:* master's degree
MSc: postgraduate university degree in science
MBA: postgraduate university degree in business
19 *incurable:* unheilbar

US ID: goyal85

Age: 24 **Height:** 5'4"
Marital Status: Never Married
Name: Shikha Goyal
City: Nangal Township
Personal Details: Vegetarian, Non-Smoker, Teetotaler

Education: BSc/MPhil
Country of Residence: India **Passport:** India
Country of Origin: Punjabi **Religion:** Hindu
Employment: Education

My daughter is a very happy-go-lucky girl and fun loving. She is simple, strong willed, cultured, respects elders and caring. She has a charming personality who loves to read and cook. She has graduated (BSc) from Govt. College (regular) from HP University Shimla, MPhil (Math) through distance education. She is currently working in an engineering college as lecturer and preparing for CSIR (UGC) net exam. She is sweet tempered and hopes that her professional aspirations will be supported. We are preferably looking for a groom who is well settled / vegetarian / nonsmoker / non drinker.

30 *BSC:* first university degree in science
30 *teetotaler:* person who doesn't drink alcohol
41 *distance education:* Fernstudium
47 *groom:* Bräutigam

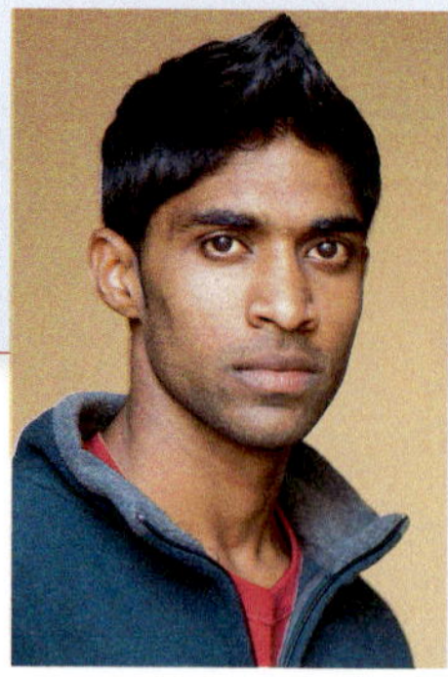

US ID: jagadishk

Age: 31 **Height:** 5'7" **Marital Status:** Never Married **Name:** K. Jagadish **City:** Bhubaneswar 751007 **Personal Details:** Non-Vegetarian, Non-Smoker, Teetotaler

Education: MA/MSc/MBA **Country of Residence:** India
Passport: India **Country of Origin:** North Indian
Religion: Hindu **Employment:** Business

I am a nice, simple, understanding guy with strong family values looking for a nice, simple, caring, understanding, jovial and beautiful girl as my better half.

B Understanding the texts

1. Find out exactly how marriages are arranged in India: by whom, how often, how successfully etc. and report to the class.
2. Describe which ideas a) about marriage and b) about the relation between the sexes are reflected in these ads.

C Reacting to the texts

1. Describe your personal reaction to the ads and the underlying concept of marriage.
2. Prepare a talk show in which you discuss the pros and cons of arranged marriages:
   a In groups, collect the pros and cons of arranged marriages – you could also go online again for more ideas. Compare your ideas in class.
   b Decide on the format of your talk show. It could be a chairperson with a panel of people who answer questions from the audience. Or a radio presenter who does a live phone-in programme with experts in the studio to answer the questions.
   c Collect possible questions and answers to them, then cast your roles and play

Welcome to … Today / This evening / our topic is … / we are going to be talking about …
In the studio with me / On the panel are …
Perhaps you'd like to introduce yourselves quickly to the audience? / On my right is … / (Name) is …
OK. Let's come to / take our first question. / …, perhaps you'd like to begin / start us off?
… would you like to reply to that / come in at this point?
Hang on! I'll let you have your say / come to you in (just) a minute.
In my opinion / view / to my mind / I'd say …
I'm not sure what you mean.
You're missing the point (entirely) / That's completely wrong, I'm afraid.
Well, this was a very lively / truly heated discussion. Thank you very much for sharing your views with us / for your questions/frankness.

2 Changing roles (A blog)

For some women – mainly those who belong to the new Indian middle class – life is changing. This is a post on the blog of one of these women.

A Before you read

Looking at the picture, write a short profile of the woman as you imagine her and her life to be (age? family? job? ...?). Compare your speculations in class.

The Role of Women in Indian Society

BY VIDYUT | 42 Comments

As a woman in India, I find that the society is changing a lot in terms of acceptance of the many roles of women as professionals, as bread-earners in families and as independent thinking individuals. Women have proved themselves as equals in many professions and even better suited than men in others. The situation for the changing role of women is improving fast.

On the other hand, female foeticide, dowry deaths and domestic abuse provide a macabre background of primitive barbarism. In the typical Indian society, you find that there are still expectations and assumptions about women that are not so much relevant to their current status, but a clear hangover from our suppressive past. This may be more obvious with traditional women or women in rural societies, but it is extremely prevalent in urban ones as well.

I am speaking of 'running the home' kind of stuff. Regardless of how hard the man and woman of the house work, when it comes to women and society, there are certain areas of the home that are the woman's province. [...]

'As the woman of the house, you should ...' is a familiar refrain for most women in India. Typical situations we see include the woman bringing a cup of hot tea for her man returning from work, or the woman returning home after her husband and heading straight to the kitchen to cook dinner, and so on.

The traditional role of a man has been the one of earning the money for the running of the home. This has changed to a great extent. Working women contribute to the expenses of running their homes as well. However, there has been little contribution from men in terms of shouldering some of the responsibilities of women. [...]

This is something that needs to be taken an honest assessment of. If we abandon the traditional perspective of division of responsibilities inside and outside the home (since it has already been broken in the outside the home area), we come to a situation where the couple are both inhabiting a home and earning and contributing toward its running. What we need to find is a sharing of responsibilities inside the home as well, that allows both some dignity. This would also help resolve many situations where a man feels threatened by a working woman. Why wouldn't he? She earns, she spends, she invests, and on top of that, she is independent in terms of being able to manage her own existence completely, including the running of her own home.

There is no point pushing women down. What needs to happen is the removal of

1 *in terms of sth.:* im Hinblick auf etwas
6 *female foeticide* ['fiːtɪˌsaɪd]: killing of an unborn girl
dowry death: murder or suicide of woman bullied by her husband to get a bigger dowry (= Mitgift)
domestic abuse: häusliche Gewalt
9 *hangover:* sth. left over from the past although it is no longer practical or suitable
suppressive: unterdrückend
22 *shoulder responsibility:* take responsibility
24 *assessment:* Bewertung
abandon sth.: give sth. up
33 *running (of home):* management of daily life in a household

the 'un-machoness' associated with responsibilities at home and recognise it as the actions of a responsible and independent individual, whether male or female. This would actually add some power to the increasingly 'lazy' image of men among women and empower them with some self-respect, while empowering the women with acceptance and support from the one source that matters the most.

Please note that I am not speaking of every man out there. There are many couples who are already on this journey and find themselves comfortable both inside and outside the home, and the mutual respect and closeness can be seen a mile off in such couples.

I sincerely think that this is an important adaption that is the need of today's times.

[From: http://aamjanata.com]

42 *mutual* ['mjuːtʃuəl]: (here) shared, common

B Understanding the text

1. Make notes about the text in a copy of the chart below.

THE ROLE OF WOMEN IN INDIAN SOCIETY	
DIFFERENT FROM IN THE PAST	SAME AS IN THE PAST
– *many now professionals*	...
...	

2. On the basis of your notes, summarise the writer's main argument and outline to what extent, in her opinion, the roles of women and men in Indian society have changed.

C Analysing the text

Choose one of the tasks below and write your answer. Compare ideas in class.

a How does the writer try to convince her readers that the roles of women and men need to change? Think of her use of examples from her life, how she constructs her argument and how she addresses the reader.

b Blogs are a common form of writing today. Explain what you think their main characteristics are and analyse how this text is (or isn't) typical of the genre. Think, for example, of who writes blog, for whom, the topics discussed, the tone and style of the language, and whether the writer expects answers.

D Reacting to the text

Work in groups to develop a role-play based on the text. Your central characters should be a young married couple, but you could include other people, too – in-laws, for example.

1. Decide on your scene and your characters: think of a situation and a conflict that may arise. Make role-cards for each character on which you decide about e.g. their age, job, interests, character, attitudes and especially about the role they are going to play.

2. Work out and practise your scene, then act it out to the class.

3 The dark sides of being a woman in India (A documentary video)

Walter Astrada is a photojournalist who is known for his hard-hitting stories from around the world. You are going to watch a documentary he made about women in India.

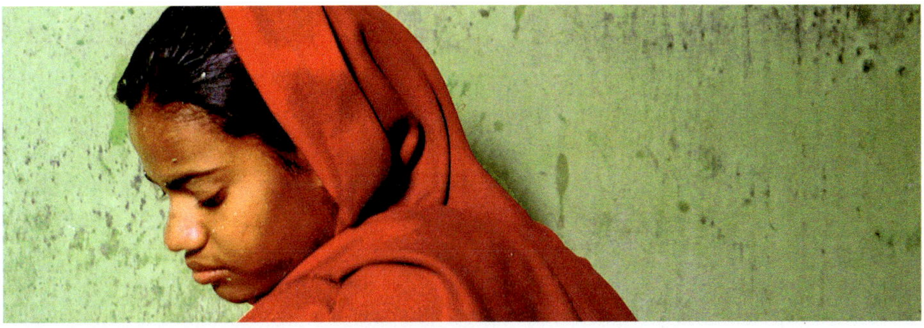

A Before you watch

Describe the picture, which is a still from the video. Speculate about what you might see in the video.

B Understanding the video

DVD 15

Work in groups.

1. Make a blank watching grid like the one below. Watch the video and fill in the left-hand column, dividing the documentary into sections. Compare your ideas and agree on one grid.
2. Watch again and fill in information in the middle column. Agree again on your final notes.
3. Summarise the main points of the video.

TIMECODE/SCENES	CONTENT	FILM AND SOUND TECHNIQUES

C Analysing the video

▶ Skills 4

In your groups again, divide up the sections of the video so that each person concentrates on a different section. Watch the video and note down the film and sound techniques used. Think especially about the following:

- the use of moving images and the use of stills;
- the role of Astrada himself (voiceover and straight-to-camera shots);
- the use of silent moving images and those with sound (e.g. interviews, background noise);
- the use of shocking/emotional/sad / (emotionally) moving / … images;
- the overall structure of the video.

Remember to point out the effect each device has on the viewer.

D Reacting to the video

▶ Skills 5.2d

Write a review of the video for a school magazine or website, expressing your own views and saying why (or why not) you think people should watch it.

4 Good advice is rarer than rubies

You are going to read a complete short story by the eminent and highly acclaimed British Indian writer Salman Rushdie. It was first published in 1987.

On the last Tuesday of the month, the dawn bus, its headlamps still shining, brought Miss Rehana to the gates of the British Consulate. It arrived pushing a cloud of dust, veiling her beauty from the eyes of strangers until she descended. The bus was brightly painted in multicoloured arabesques, and on the front it said 'MOVE OVER DARLING' in green and gold letters; on the back it added 'TATA-BATA' and also 'OK. GOOD-LIFE'. Miss Rehana told the driver it was a beautiful bus, and he jumped down and held the door open for her, bowing theatrically as she descended.

Miss Rehana's eyes were large and black and bright enough to not need the help of antimony, and when the advice expert Muhammad Ali saw them he felt himself becoming young again. He watched her approaching the Consulate gates as the light strengthened, and asking the bearded lala who guarded them in a gold-buttoned khaki uniform with a cockaded turban when they would open. The lala, usually so rude to the Consulate's Tuesday women, answered Miss Rehana with something like courtesy.

'Half an hour,' he said gruffly. 'Maybe two hours. Who knows? The sahibs are eating their breakfast.'

The dusty compound between the bus stop and the Consulate was already full of Tuesday women, some veiled, a few barefaced like Miss Rehana. They all looked frightened, and leaned heavily on the arms of uncles or brothers, who were trying to look confident. But Miss Rehana had come on her own, and did not seem at all alarmed.

Muhammad Ali, who was specialised in advising the most vulnerable-looking of these weekly supplicants, found his feet leading him towards the strange, big-eyed, independent girl.

'Miss,' he began. 'You have come for permit to London, I think so?'

She was standing at a hot-snack stall in the little shanty-town by the edge of the compound, munching chilli-pakoras contentedly. She turned to look at him, and at close range those eyes did bad things to his digestive tract.

'Yes, I have.'

'Then, please, you allow me to give some advice? Small cost only.'

Miss Rehana smiled. 'Good advice is rarer than rubies,' she said. 'But alas, I cannot pay. I am an orphan, not one of your wealthy ladies.'

'Trust my grey hairs,' Muhammad Ali urged her. 'My advice is well tempered by experience. You will certainly find it good.'

She shook her head. 'I tell you I am a poor potato. There are women here with male family members, all earning good wages. Go to them. Good advice should find good money.'

I am going crazy, Muhammad Ali thought, because he heard his voice telling her of its own volition, 'Miss, I have been drawn to you by Fate. What to do? Our

ruby: Rubin
1 *dawn bus:* (here) first bus at daybreak
headlamps: Scheinwerfer
3 *veil sth.:* cover sth.
4 *arabesque:* pattern formed by lines that circle around each other
5 *'Move Over Darling':* US movie and song (1963)
6 *Tata-Bata, OK. Good-Life:* advertising slogans
9 *antimony* ['æntiməni]: chemical substance used to make eyes shine more
13 *lala (Hindi):* guard
cockaded: decorated with ribbons, feathers, etc.
14 *Tuesday women:* (here) Tuesday is the day for giving women visas to Britain
15 *courtesy:* politeness
16 *gruff:* bad-tempered
sahib (Urdu): term used to refer to a European man esp. of higher social status
18 *compound:* area surrounded by a fence or wall, containing a group of buildings
21 *confident:* feeling sure about your ability to do things and be successful
23 *vulnerable:* verletzlich
24 *supplicant:* Bittsteller/in
26 *permit* ['– –] *(n):* Einreisegenehmigung
27 *shanty-town:* slum
28 *munch sth.:* eat sth. slowly and steadily
pakora: frittierte Teigtasche
29 *at close range:* seen from very near
digestive tract: Verdauungstrakt
33 *orphan:* child whose parents are dead
34 *temper sth.:* make sth. less severe by adding something that has the opposite effect
40 *volition* [və'lɪʃn]: will

meeting was written. I also am a poor man only, but for you my advice comes free.'

She smiled again. 'Then I must surely listen. When Fate sends a gift, one receives good fortune.'

He led her to the low wooden desk in his own special corner of the shanty-town. She followed, continuing to eat pakoras from a little newspaper packet. She did not offer him any.

Muhammad Ali put a cushion on the dusty ground. 'Please to sit.' She did as he asked. He sat cross-legged across the desk from her, conscious that two or three dozen pairs of male eyes were watching him enviously, that all the other shanty-town men were ogling the latest lovely to be charmed by the old grey-haired fraud. He took a deep breath to settle himself.

'Name, please.'

'Miss Rehana,' she told him. 'Fiancée of Mustafa Dar of Bradford, London.'

'Bradford, England,' he corrected her gently. 'London is a town only, like Multan or Bahawalpur. England is a great nation full of the coldest fish in the world.'

'I see. Thank you,' she responded gravely, so that he was unsure if she was making fun of him.

'You have filled application form? Then let me see, please.'

She passed him a neatly folded document in a brown envelope.

'Is it OK?' For the first time there was a note of anxiety in her voice.

He patted the desk quite near the place where her hand rested. 'I am certain,' he said. 'Wait on and I will check.'

She finished the pakoras while he scanned her papers.

'Tip-top,' he pronounced at length. 'All in order.'

'Thank you for your advice,' she said, making as if to rise. 'I'll go now and wait by the gate.'

'What are you thinking?' he cried loudly, smiting his forehead. 'You consider this is easy business? Just give the form and poof, with a big smile they hand over the permit? Miss Rehana, I tell you, you are entering a worse place than any police station.'

'Is it so, truly?' His oratory had done the trick. She was a captive audience now, and he would be able to look at her for a few moments longer.

Drawing another calming breath, he launched into his set speech. He told her that the sahibs thought that all the women who came on Tuesdays, claiming to be dependents of bus drivers in Luton or chartered accountants in Manchester, were crooks and liars and cheats.

She protested, 'But then I will simply tell them that I, for one, am no such thing!'

Her innocence made him shiver with fear for her. She was a sparrow, he told her, and they were men with hooded eyes, like hawks. He explained that they would ask her questions, personal questions, questions such as a lady's own brother would be too shy to ask. They would ask if she was virgin, and, if not, what her fiancé's love-making habits were, and what secret nicknames they had invented for one another.

Muhammad Ali spoke brutally, on purpose, to lessen the shock she would feel when it, or something like it, actually happened. Her eyes remained steady, but her hands began to flutter at the edges of the desk.

He went on: 'They will ask you how many rooms are in your family home, and

Pakoras

43 *fortune:* luck
50 *ogle sb.* ['əʊgl]: stare at sb. (esp. with sexual interest)
50 *fraud* [frɔːd]: Schwindler/in
53 *fiancée* [fi'ɒnseɪ]: Verlobte
Bradford: town in north England with a large Pakistani community
67 *smite sth. (fml):* hit sth.
68 *poof:* exclamation used to express sth. happening suddenly
71 *oratory* ['ɒrətəri]: rhetorical skills
captive audience: (here) person who is compelled to listen
73 *set speech:* speech that sb. knows by heart
75 *dependent (n):* relative who relies on another person; family member
chartered accountant: Bilanzbuchhalter/in
76 *crook (infml):* criminal
cheat (n; infml): Schwindler/in
77 *for one:* used to emphasise sth. about yourself or about your beliefs or attitudes
79 *hooded (adj):* covered
hawk: Falke
82 *nickname:* Spitzname
86 *flutter:* move nervously

what colour are the walls, and what days do you empty the rubbish. They will ask your man's mother's third cousin's aunt's step-daughter's middle name. And all these things they have already asked your Mustafa Dar in his Bradford. And if you make one mistake, you are finished.'

'Yes,' she said, and he could hear her disciplining her voice. 'And what is your advice, old man?'

It was at this point that Muhammad Ali usually began to whisper urgently, to mention that he knew a man, a very good type, who worked in the Consulate, and through him, for a fee, the necessary papers could be delivered, with all the proper authenticating seals. Business was good, because the women would often pay him five hundred rupees or give him a gold bracelet for his pains, and go away happy.

They came from hundreds of miles away – he normally made sure of this before beginning to trick them – so even when they discovered they had been swindled they were unlikely to return. They went away to Sargodha or Lalukhet and began to pack, and who knows at what point they found out they had been gulled, but it was at a too-late point, anyway.

Life is hard, and an old man must live by his wits. It was not up to Muhammad Ali to have compassion for these Tuesday women.

But once again his voice betrayed him, and instead of starting his customary speech it began to reveal to her his greatest secret.

'Miss Rehana,' his voice said, and he listened to it in amazement, 'you are a rare person, a jewel, and for you I will do what I would not do for my own daughter, perhaps. One document has come into my possession that can solve all your worries at one stroke.'

'And what is this sorcerer's paper?' she asked, her eyes unquestionably laughing at him now.

His voice fell low-as-low. 'Miss Rehana, it is a British passport, completely genuine and pukka goods. I have a good friend who will put your name and photo, and then, hey-presto, England there you come!'

He had said it!

Anything was possible now, on this day of his insanity. Probably he would give her the thing free-gratis, and then kick himself for a year afterwards.

Old fool, he berated himself. *The oldest fools are bewitched* by the youngest girls.

'Let me understand you,' she was saying. 'You are proposing I should commit a crime ...'

'Not crime,' he interposed. 'Facilitation.'

'... and go to Bradford, London, illegally, and therefore justify the low opinion the Consulate sahibs have of us all. Old babuji, this is not good advice.'

'Bradford, *England*,' he corrected her mournfully. 'You should not take my gift in such a spirit.'

'Then how?'

'Bibi, I am a poor fellow, and I have offered this prize because you are so beautiful. Do not spit on my generosity. Take the thing. Or else don't take, go home, forget England, only do not go into that building and lose your dignity.'

But she was on her feet, turning away from him, walking towards the gates, where the women had begun to cluster and the lala was swearing at them to be

97 *authenticate sth.:* prove that sth. is genuine
97 *seal (n):* Siegel
98 *rupee* [ru:'pi]: Indian money
bracelet: piece of jewellery worn around the arm
102 *gull sb. (old use):* jdn. täuschen
104 *wits (pl):* ability to think clearly
106 *betray sb.:* jdn. im Stich lassen
customary ['kʌstəməri]: usual
112 *sorcerer:* person with magic powers
115 *pukka (Urdu):* of very good quality
116 *hey-presto:* Simsalabim
118 *insanity:* madness
120 *berate sb.:* criticise sb.
bewitch sb.: jdn. verzaubern
123 *facilitation:* act of making sth. easier
125 *babuji (Urdu):* respectful form of address
126 *mournful:* very sad
129 *Bibi (Urdu):* affectionate form of address for a woman
133 *cluster (v):* gather

patient or none of them would be admitted at all.

'So be a fool,' Muhammad Ali shouted after her. 'What goes of my father's if you are?' (Meaning, what was it to him.)

She did not turn.

'It is the curse of our people,' he yelled. 'We are poor, we are ignorant, and we completely refuse to learn.'

'Hey, Muhammad Ali,' the woman at the betel-nut stall called across to him. 'Too bad, she likes them young.'

That day Muhammad Ali did nothing but stand around near the Consulate gates. Many times he scolded himself, *Go from here, old goof, lady does not desire to speak with you any further*. But when she came out, she found him waiting.

'Salaam, advice wallah,' she greeted him.

She seemed calm, and at peace with him again, and he thought, *My God, ya Allah, she has pulled it off. The British sahibs also have been drowning in her eyes and she has got her passage to England.*

He smiled at her hopefully. She smiled back with no trouble at all.

'Miss Rehana Begum,' he said, 'felicitations, daughter, on what is obviously your hour of triumph.'

Impulsively, she took his forearm in her hand.

'Come,' she said. 'Let me buy you a pakora to thank you for your advice and to apologise for my rudeness, too.'

They stood in the dust of the afternoon compound near the bus, which was getting ready to leave. Coolies were tying bedding rolls to the roof. A hawker shouted at the passengers, trying to sell them love stories and green medicines, both of which cured unhappiness. Miss Rehana and a happy Muhammad Ali ate their pakoras sitting on the bus's 'front mud-guard', that is, the bumper. The old advice expert began softly to hum a tune from a movie soundtrack. The day's heat was gone.

'It was an arranged engagement,' Miss Rehana said all at once. 'I was nine years old when my parents fixed it. Mustafa Dar was already thirty at that time, but my father wanted someone who could look after me as he had done himself and Mustafa was a man known to Daddyji as a solid type. Then my parents died and Mustafa Dar went to England and said he would send for me. That was many years ago. I have his photo, but he is like a stranger to me. Even his voice, I do not recognise it on the phone.'

The confession took Muhammad Ali by surprise, but he nodded with what he hoped looked like wisdom.

'Still and after all,' he said, 'one's parents act in one's best interests. They found you a good and honest man who has kept his word and sent for you. And now you have a lifetime to get to know him, and to love.'

He was puzzled, now, by the bitterness that had infected her smile.

'But, old man,' she asked him, 'why have you already packed me and posted me off to England?'

138 *curse (n):* Fluch
143 *scold sb.:* jdn. schelten
goof (infml): fool
145 *Salaam (Arabic):* form of greeting meaning 'Peace be with you'
wallah (Urdu): jemand, der für etwas zuständig ist
146 *ya Allah (Arabic):* Oh God
147 *pull sth. off:* be successful with sth. (which was very difficult)
150 *Begum (Urdu):* formal address for a female Muslim
felicitations (old-fashioned): congratulations
157 *coolie (old-fashioned):* worker in South and East Asian countries with no special skills or training
158 *hawker:* person who sells goods on the street
163 *mud-guard:* Schutzblech
bumper: Stoßstange
168 *Daddyji:* Father (the ending -ji demonstrates respect)

He stood up, shocked.

'You looked happy – so I just assumed … excuse me, but they turned you down or what?'

'I got all their questions wrong,' she replied. 'Distinguishing marks I put on the wrong cheeks, bathroom decor I completely redecorated, all absolutely topsy-turvy, you see.'

'But what to do? How will you go?'

'Now I will go back to Lahore and my job. I work in a great house, as ayah to three good boys. They would have been sad to see me leave.'

'But this is tragedy!' Muhammad Ali lamented. 'Oh, how I pray that you had taken up my offer! Now, but, it is not possible, I regret to inform. Now they have your form on file, cross-check can be made, even the passport will not suffice. It is spoilt, all spoilt, and it could have been so easy if advice had been accepted in good time.'

'I do not think,' she told him, 'I truly do not think you should be sad.'

Her last smile, which he watched from the compound until the bus concealed it in a dust-cloud, was the happiest thing he had ever seen in his long, hot, hard, unloving life.

[From: *East, West* by Salman Rushdie, 1994]

183 *distinguishing mark:* besonderes Merkmal
184 *topsy-turvy:* durcheinander
187 *ayah (Urdu):* female servant who looks after children
189 *lament:* complain
191 *on file:* in den Akten
cross-check: Gegenprobe
suffice: be enough
195 *conceal sth.:* hide sth.

A Understanding the text

Divide the story into sections, then fill in the chart below.

SECTION	WHAT WE LEARN ABOUT THE CHARACTERS	HOW I THINK THE STORY WILL CONTINUE	WHAT SURPRISED ME
I (ll. … to …) II (ll. … to …) …			

B Analysing the text

▶ Activity chest 6
▶ Glossary 2.1, 2.2.1, 2.2.2

1. Talk in class. What do you think was Rushdie's intention when writing this story? Explain.
2. You are now going to work in 'Expert groups' to analyse the various ways in which Rushdie attempts to meet his aims. Each group should study one of the following:
   a the story as a short story (e.g. its structure);
   b its narrative perspective;
   c the way in which the characters are presented and how the reader's perception of them is influenced;
   d the way in which events and thoughts are conveyed to the reader (cf. showing vs. telling) and the reasons for this;
   e Rushdie's use of language.
3. Describe the picture drawn in this story of women and their relationship to men.
4. Analyse the title of the story and explain whether the saying is true for the story.

C Reacting to the text

▶ Skills 5.2d

Write a letter from Miss Rehana to her fiancé after this incident.

India on screen

India has the world's biggest film industry. In 2008, it was also the setting for a British movie that became a blockbuster hit, *Slumdog Millionaire*. In this topic you are going to look at the movie and the book it was based on and at the Bollywood film industry.

Collect ideas

1. Talk in class.
   - Have you seen *Slumdog Millionaire* or any Bollywood film? Tell the class about it.
   - Look at the pictures and describe what image of India they present.
2. Collect words and expressions to do with films and the film industry. E.g. *movie – actor/actress – star – shoot a film – …*

1 The boy from the slums who wins a quiz show (Extracts from a novel, a radio play and a film script)

In 2005 Indian novelist Vikas Swarup published his novel *Q&A*. It tells the story of a young man from the slums of Mumbai who takes part in a TV quiz show and wins the top prize. In 2008, the book was turned into a movie by British director Danny Boyle. In the same year, *Q&A* was also adapted as a series of radio plays by the BBC. The episodes had been recorded in Mumbai with Indian actors. You are going to listen to and read the same scene from the novel, the radio play and the film script.

The stars of Slumdog Millionaire, *the British actor Dev Patel and Mumbai model Freida Pinto*

A Before you begin

Read the SPOTLIGHT box below and fill in the table.

SPOTLIGHT ON Fictional genres

It seems obvious that there are differences between the different forms of fiction – between a novel and a film, for example, or a play and a poem. It is worth thinking in some detail, however, about exactly what these differences are and why they exist. Essentially, each genre has its own characteristics. It does certain things in certain ways. And it is better at doing some of these things than others.

Task
In groups, copy and complete the table below, then report to the class.

GENRE	CHARACTERISTICS	STRENGTHS / WEAKNESSES
novel / short story	*written – can take long time to read …*	*writer can/can't … – reader can/can't …*
film	…	…
drama		
radio play		
poem		

✕ **Spotlight task** Imagine how an event, emotion etc. could be portrayed differently in different fictional genres. You could work on the following concepts: an escape, fear, a fight between rivals, frustration with the political situation in a country.

Text 1: *Q&A*: Escaping Maman (An extract from a novel)

KEY FACTS Vikas Swarup: *Q&A* (2005)

The central character in Vikas Swarup's novel is Ram Mohammad Thomas. He was abandoned by his mother at birth and lived first in an orphanage, then as a street child in Delhi. Now 18, he is taking part in the TV quiz show *Who wants to win a billion?* When he is one question away from the prize, the organisers of the show arrest him: they suspect him of cheating because they can't imagine that a boy with his background could have such vast knowledge. He is tortured by the police for a confession, but then a mysterious woman, the lawyer Smita, appears and listens to what Ram has to say. The chapters in the book consist of Ram telling his story to Smita.

In this extract, Ram is still a young boy. He and his friend Salim are with the gangster Maman, who is planning to blind them and put them on the streets to beg. Here we find them together with Masterji, their singing teacher, and Punnoose and Mustafa, Maman's fellow gangsters.

Vikas Swarup

Punnoose comes into the room to talk to Masterji. They speak in low voices, then Punnoose takes out his purse and begins counting out some money. He hands over a sheaf of notes to the music teacher, who tucks it gratefully in the front pocket of his *kurta*. They leave the room together, leaving me alone with Salim and a harmonium.

'I should never have left Delhi,' I tell Salim. 'You have at least become a good singer, but I have gained nothing from this trip.'

It is then that I notice a hundred-rupee note lying on the floor. Punnoose must have dropped it while counting the money. My first impulse is to pocket it, but Salim snatches it from my hand and insists that we must return it. So we go down the corridor to the room Maman uses as his office, where Punnoose and Mustafa hang out.

As we approach the door, we hear voices coming from inside. Maman is talking to Punnoose.

'So what did the Master say after finishing his lessons? He is getting more and more expensive.'

'He said that the older one is useless, but the young kid has a lot of potential. He says he's never trained a more talented boy before.'

'So you think he can bring in at least three hundred?'

'What is three hundred? When he sings it is magic. And his face? Who can resist his face? I would say easily a potential of four to five hundred. We have hit the jackpot, Maman.'

'And the other boy? The tall one?'

'Who cares? The bastard will have to fend for himself. Either he gets us a hundred each night or he remains hungry.'

2 *Masterji:* master (the ending -ji demonstrates respect)
4 *sheaf:* number of pieces of paper
6 *kurta:* loose shirt
9 *rupee* [ruːˈpiː]: Indian money

'OK. Send them out on the trains from next week. We will do them tonight. After dinner.'

A chill runs down my spine as I hear these words. I catch Salim's hand and rush back to our room. Salim is confused about the conversation we heard, and the reference to numbers. But the jigsaw is piecing itself together in my brain. 'Salim, we have to escape from this place. Now.'

'But why?'

'Because something very bad is going to happen to us tonight, after dinner.'

'I don't understand.'

'I understand everything. Do you know why we were taught the *bhajans* of Surdas?'

'Because he was a great poet?'

'No. Because he was blind. And that is what we are going to become tonight, so that we can be made to beg on local trains. I am convinced now that all the cripple boys we have met here have been deliberately maimed by Maman and his gang.'

But such cruelty is beyond Salim's comprehension. He wants to stay.

'Why don't you run away alone?' he asks me.

'I can't go without you.'

'Why?'

'Because I am your guardian angel, and you are part of my package deal.'

Salim hugs me. I take out the one-rupee coin from my pocket. 'Look, Salim,' I tell him. 'You believe in destiny, don't you? So let this coin decide our future. Heads we leave, tails we stay, OK?'

Salim nods. I flip the coin. It is heads.

Salim is finally reconciled to escaping from Maman's den, but his mind is full of doubt. 'Where will we go? What will we do? We don't know anyone in this city.'

'I know where we will go. Remember that actress Neelima Kumari that Radhey told us about? She needs a servant. I have her address and I also know which local train goes there.'

'How about going to the police?'

'Are you out of your mind? Haven't you learnt anything since Delhi? Whatever you do, wherever you go, never go to the police. Ever.'

29 *a chill runs down my spine:* es läuft mir kalt den Rücken runter
31 *jigsaw:* Puzzle
36 *bhajan:* religious Indian song
41 *maim sb.:* injure sb. seriously
46 *guardian angel:* person who protects and guides sb.
package deal: (here) set of things that must be accepted together
48 *destiny:* Schicksal
49 *heads ... tail:* Kopf oder Zahl
50 *flip a coin:* eine Münze werfen
51 *reconciled to sth.:* in agreement to do sth.
den: hidden home

60 *leaky tap:* tropfender Wasserhahn
61 *wire-mesh:* Drahtgeflecht
63 *closet:* wardrobe
64 *frayed nerves:* nervousness
68 *jammed:* not able to be moved
70 *urgency* ['ɜːdʒənsi]: Dringlichkeit
75 *mound:* pile
gravel: Kiesel
76 *rubble:* Trümmer

We are inside the bathroom in the basement, listening to the steady beat of water dripping from a leaky tap. Salim is on my shoulder with a knife in his hand, trying to work the bolts holding the wire-mesh window in place.

'Hurry,' I whisper through clenched teeth.

Upstairs, Maman's guards trample through our room, opening closets and cupboards. We hear shouts and abuses. A bottle crashes, jangling our frayed nerves even more. Salim is terrified. He is breathing quickly in short gasps. The beating of heart intensifies till I can almost hear its pounding. Footsteps come closer.

'Only one is left,' says Salim. 'But it is jammed. I don't think I can open it.'

'Please … please try again!' I urge him. 'Our lives depend on it.'

Salim tackles the bolt with renewed urgency, twisting the knife into it with all his strength. Finally, it gives way. He takes out the four bolts and lifts the wire mesh. We can see the palm trees outside swaying gently in the breeze. There is just enough space for us to crawl out. Maman's men are about to come down the stairs to the basement when Salim manoeuvres himself through the window. Then he grasps my hand and helps me slither out. We clamber on to a mound of gravel and rubble, gasping and panting. The moon is full, the night is calm. We take in deep gulps of fresh air. It smells of coconuts.

[From: *Q&A* by Vikas Swarup, 2005]

A Understanding the extract from the novel

Summarise the extract.

B Analysing the extract from the novel

▶ Glossary 2.1

1. Examine how the writer creates suspense in this extract.

In the first part When Ram and Salim listen to Maman and Punnoose	Swarup uses dialogue to … / The writer shows rather than tells us how …	… let the reader experience … by using …
	The reader experiences	… how the boys slowly become aware of …
In the second part When Salim first refuses to go	the boys are pressed for time / need to hurry/escape quickly	the writer makes Salim doubt … / the boys lose time because …
	the atmosphere is full of …	
In the final/third part When the boys try to escape	the writer introduces small obstacles / makes the boys hear …	so as to increase …
	the writer uses … sentences	to express/emulate their breathlessness / growing panic /

2. Outline how the writer gives this extract local colour, how he makes it feel Indian.

▶ Glossary 2.2.2
▶ Skills 1.2.3

✕ **Extra** Examine this extract as a genre of writing. Point out the features that are typical or not so typical of the genre.

Text 2: *Q&A*: 50,000 rupees (A radio play)

In the radio play version, Maman is called Babu.

CD 8

A Understanding the radio play

Listen to the extract from the play and note down what happens. In class, discuss how closely the play follows the book, pointing out any differences if you find them.

B Analysing the radio play

1. Thinking back to your ideas about fictional genres, analyse how this extract 'works' as a radio play. Think, for example, how suspense is created here. Consider also any differences between the book and the play and why the producers of the play may have made them.
2. The radio play was recorded on location in Mumbai. Say why this decision may have been made and what effect this may have on the episode and the listener.

Text 3: *Slumdog Millionaire* (An extract from a film script)

In the film, the lead character is called Jamal; Salim is his brother. In contrast to the novel, the movie revolves not only around the quiz show, but also around Jamal's search for his childhood love, Latika. In this extract, there is also another boy, Arvind. When reading the extract, watch out for differences to the novel.

61 INT. SHACK. NIGHT

In a shack, Arvind is singing one of Surdas' bhajans in front of Maman and an old man who by his ragged appearance must be a villager. Punnoose and Salim sit behind Arvind.

MAMAN Very good, very good. I am pleased, Arvind. He is ready.

ARVIND Ready?

Maman nods to Punnoose. Before Arvind can turn round, Punnoose has covered his mouth with a cloth and after the briefest of struggles, Arvind's body goes limp. The villager puts an old tin box on the table. Taking the lid from the tin, he brings out a cloth and unwraps it. Inside is a spoon. He checks the edge with his thumb. Sharp. Douses it with a clear liquid from a bottle and passes it over a candle flame. The spoon whooshes with a high flame for a moment. The villager wipes it with the cloth, nods to Punnoose.

PUNNOOSE

Salim!

Utterly bemused, Salim nevertheless helps Punnoose lay Arvind on the table. The villager takes hold of Arvind's eyelid and pulls it open. He brings the spoon close. Suddenly, Salim is being sick in the corner of the shack. By the time he has turned back, the villager is wiping the spoon on a blood-soaked rag.

MAMAN Okay. Take him out the back.

Punnoose picks up Arvind and carries him out.

MAMAN Now the other one. Salim, go get Jamal.

3 *ragged:* old and torn
7 *go limp:* lose all strength and become unable to stand
9 *douse sth.:* pour a lot of liquid on sth.

A frozen moment.

SALIM What?

MAMAN Gunfighter Number One, isn't that right, Salim? The money, the women, the cars ... you want them bad, huh? And why not?

Maman gets out of his chair. Approaches Salim.

MAMAN (CONT'D)

The time has come to choose, yaar. The life of a slum dog or the life of a man. A real man. A gunfighter, Salim.

Maman holds Salim's head in his hands.

MAMAN (CONT'D)

Your destiny is in your hands, bhai. You can be me. Or nobody. Understand?

SALIM Yes, Maman.

Maman nods.

MAMAN So, brother, go get Jamal.

Salim is frozen for another few seconds, then turns and walks out of the door. Punnoose appears at the door. Maman nods to him and he slips off after Salim.

62 INT. DORMITORY, ORPHANAGE. NIGHT.

All the children are asleep apart from Jamal, who is crouched underneath a couple of wash-basins. He is talking through a plate-sized hole in the crumbling masonry. Latika's eyes can be seen.

JAMAL ... weddings, government things, big parties. If Maman says my voice is ready. Big money.

LATIKA Enough for a room?

JAMAL Easily. Maybe an apartment.

LATIKA Really?

JAMAL That's what Arvind said. On Harbour Road. You, me and Salim. The three musketeers.

LATIKA Harbour Road! We can have ice cream from Babanji's.

JAMAL Every day if we want.

Salim appears at the door. Nods his head at Jamal.

JAMAL (CONT'D)

It's my turn.

LATIKA Good luck, Jamal.

Latika's hand comes through the gap. Jamal takes it for a moment. Salim hisses at Jamal. He lets go of the hand and heads out.

63 EXT. PATH. NIGHT.

Salim and Jamal walk along the path, Jamal humming happily. Salim checks behind him, sees Punnoose following.

JAMAL So, this is it, hey, bhai? The good life, here we come ...

SALIM (conversationally) Athos.

Jamal is suddenly alert. Slows.

JAMAL Porthos?

Salim nods. Big smile. Puts a hand on Jamal's shoulder.

SALIM When I say.

31 *destiny:* Schicksal
bhai (sl.): gangster
46 *the three Musketeers:* group of three French soldiers from Dumas's famous novel published in 1844
54 *hiss:* make a sound like a long 's'
60 *Athos:* one of the Musketeers
62 *Porthos:* one of the Musketeers

64 INT. SHACK. NIGHT.

Salim guides Jamal into the shack where Maman and the villager are waiting. Maman smiles. Punnoose slips in behind Salim.

MAMAN Jamal, hello. You have done well. It's time for you to – turn professional.
JAMAL Really?
MAMAN Sing me a song, yaar. How about Chalo Ri Murali, huh? My favourite.

Jamal opens his mouth, then closes it again. Holds out his hand.

JAMAL Fifty rupees.
MAMAN What?
JAMAL (shrugs) I've turned professional. What can I do?

Maman laughs.

MAMAN Sala ...!

He throws some notes at him.

65 EXT. SHACK. NIGHT.

Outside, a giggle. Latika is peering through a gap in the wall.

66 INT. SHACK. NIGHT.

Jamal begins to sing. Maman waits a while, then nods to Punnoose. Behind Jamal, Punnoose hands Salim the bottle of chloroform and the rag. Salim approaches the back of Jamal. Salim waits until he has finished the song. Raises his hand with the rag in it. Maman smiles, nods. Salim flings the contents of the bottle in Punnoose's face. Punnoose screams and stumbles back clutching his eyes, knocking over the table.

SALIM Go!

Salim and Jamal scramble for the door. The knocked-over candle catches the spilled chloroform and a curtain which whooshes up in flame.

LATIKA Jamal!
JAMAL Run!

66A EXT. SHACK. NIGHT.

They charge past the prone Arvind – a flash of bloodied bandages covering his eyes.

67 EXT. HILLSIDE. NIGHT.

Heavy, desperate breathing. Feet stumble on roots. Fall into holes. The three children are running. Branches smack into their faces. But they are so scared, nothing will stop them. Behind them, torches scour the undergrowth. Men shouting. They break out of the woods and are confronted with a train goods yard.

68 EXT. GOODS YARD. NIGHT.

They run over the tracks, between the trains, but the shouts are getting louder, the torches closer. A diesel engine is moving out of the station. Jamal, Latika and Salim sprint for the Guard's van at the very back of the moving train. Punnoose is closest to them. Salim is fastest and first to jump the train. He holds out his hand. Jamal grabs it and is hauled in. Jamal holds his hand out to Latika.

JAMAL Come on! Faster!

She reaches out to him. Their hands almost touch.

96 *torch:* Taschenlampe
scour ['skaʊə]: search

JAMAL (CONT'D)

Take it! Take it! I can't reach ...

Salim barges Jamal out of the way. Jamal stumbles back as Salim reaches his hand out to Latika, so he doesn't see Latika's hand grasp Salim's, nor see their eyes lock onto each other, nor see Salim very deliberately let go of her hand. Latika stumbles.

LATIKA Jamal!

Jamal scrambles to the rail. The train gains more speed. Jamal climbs on to the top rung, makes to jump, but Salim flings him backward. Jamal tries to scramble to his feet again, but Salim restrains him.

JAMAL Got to go back. We've got to go back.
SALIM He'll kill us if we go back. Jamal! He was going to take your eyes out – with a bloody spoon!

The train is speeding along. Jamal breaks free and stares back at Latika.

SALIM (CONT'D)

She'll be alright. She always is.

Latika stumbles again and stops running. They watch as Punnoose catches up with her and stops running. He smashes Latika to the ground.

[From: *Slumdog Millionaire* by Simon Beaufoy, 2008]

111 *barge sb.:* push sb.
112 *lock onto sth.:* make fixed contact with sth.
116 *scramble:* move quickly and with difficulty
117 *restrain sb.:* hold sb. to stop them moving

C Understanding the text

1. Look at the script. Explain its layout – thinking particularly of the amount of dialogue (the words the actors must speak) and the directions given.
2. Work in a group. Choose a scene and describe how you would film it. Using a large sheet of paper, make a storyboard for it. Then present it to the class.

D Analysing the text

1. Compare the events in this extract with those in the book. Say why you think those changes were made and to what effect. Consider especially how suspense is created here.
2. Point out the features which make this scene typical of the movie genre. Then take one part of the extract and explain the writer's intention and how he achieves his aim.
3. After examining how different genres present a similar content, compare the strengths of film, novel and radio play in general. Which would be your favourite genre for the scene you imagined in the **SPOTLIGHT** task (cf. p. 184)? Give reasons.

E Reacting to the texts

In class, discuss what you enjoyed – or did not enjoy – about the radio play, the novel and the film script. Which would be your favourite medium if you wanted to read, see or listen to more?

✕ **Extra** The film *Slumdog Millionaire* caused a certain amount of debate when it came out. In particular, the filmmakers were accused of promoting Western stereotypes of poverty in India. Watch the movie and do some research about the controversy, then discuss in class whether you agree with these criticisms.

2 Welcome to Bollywood (An informative text)

Even though *Slumdog Millionaire* is a film about India, it is a Western production. But India has its own very successful film industry, often referred to as 'Bollywood'. Find out more about it.

A Before you read

Collect all the information on or ideas you have about Bollywood – what kind of films are shot there, which actors you may know, etc.

What is 'Bollywood'?

Bollywood is the name given to the Mumbai-based Hindi-language film industry in India. When combined with other Indian film industries (Tamil, Telugu, Bengali, Malayalam, Kannada), it is considered to be the largest in the world in terms of number of films produced, and maybe also the number of tickets sold.

The term Bollywood was created by conflating Bombay (the city now called Mumbai) and Hollywood (the famous center of the United States film industry).

Bollywood films are usually musicals. Few movies are made without at least one song-and-dance number. Indian audiences expect full value for their money; they want songs and dances, love interest, comedy and dare-devil thrills, all mixed up in a three hour long extravaganza with intermission. Such movies are called masala movies, after the spice mixture masala. Like masala, these movies have everything.

The plots are often melodramatic. They frequently employ formulaic ingredients such as star-crossed lovers, corrupt politicians, twins separated at birth, conniving villains, angry parents, courtesans with hearts of gold, dramatic reversals of fortune, and convenient coincidences.

Bollywood song and dance

While most actors, especially today, are excellent dancers, few are also singers. Songs are generally pre-recorded by professional playback singers with actors lip-synching the words, often while dancing. [...] Playback singers are prominently featured in the opening credits and have their own fans who will go to an otherwise lackluster movie just to hear their favorites. The composers of film music, known as music directors, are also well-known. Their songs can make or break a film and usually do.

The dancing in Bollywood films, especially older ones, is primarily modeled on Indian dance: classical dance styles, dances of historic northern Indian courtesans (tawaif), or folk dances. In modern films, Indian dance elements often blend with Western dance styles (as seen on MTV or in Broadway musicals), though it is not unusual to see Western pop and pure classical dance numbers side by side in the same film. The hero or heroine will often perform with a troupe of supporting dancers, usually of the same sex. If the hero and heroine dance and sing a pas-de-deux (a dance and ballet term, meaning 'dance of two'), it is often staged in beautiful natural surroundings or architecturally grand settings. [...]

6 *conflate:* put two things together to make one new thing
10 *dare-devil:* Draufgänger
11 *extravaganza:* large, expensive and impressive entertainment
intermission: break, pause in a show
13 *formulaic:* (here) tried and tested
ingredient: Zutat
14 *star-crossed:* not able to be happy because of bad luck
15 *connive:* plan to commit an illegal act
villain: evil character
19 *lip-synch sth.* ['lɪp sɪŋk]: etwas synchronisieren
22 *lackluster:* glanzlos
30 *troupe:* group
32 *stage sth.:* organize and present sth. theatrical

Dialogues and lyrics

The film script (frequently credited as 'Dialogues') and the song lyrics are often written by different people. The dialogues are mostly written in Hindi, with use of Urdu in situations which require poetic dialogues. Contemporary mainstream movies also make great use of English. Dialogues are often melodramatic and invoke God, family, mother, and self-sacrifice liberally. […]

Cast and crew

Bollywood employs people from all parts of India. It attracts thousands of aspiring actors and actresses, all hoping for a break in the industry. Models and beauty contestants, television actors, theatre actors and even common people come to Mumbai with the hope and dream of becoming a star. Just as in Hollywood very few succeed. […]

Finances

Bollywood budgets are usually modest by Hollywood standards. Sets, costumes, special effects, and cinematography were less than world-class up until the mid-to-late 1990s. But as Western films and television gain wider distribution in India itself, there is increasing pressure for Bollywood films to attain the same production levels. Sequences shot overseas have proved a real box office draw, so Mumbai film crews are increasingly peripatetic, filming in Australia, New Zealand, United Kingdom, continental Europe and elsewhere. Nowadays, Indian producers are drawing in more and more funding for big-budget films shot within India as well, such as Lagaan, Devdas, and the current production *The Rising*. […]

What problems does Bollywood face?

Bollywood's biggest problem is piracy – where people copy the films and either sell them or show them to other people for free. […]. Another problem is that younger generations sometimes find the stories a bit predictable and get bored of the similar tales. Film-makers are trying to solve this by changing storylines to reflect real life – like the fact that children of Indian families now study abroad.
What's the future for Bollywood?
The future looks even brighter for Bollywood. Big US film companies such as Warner Bros and Twentieth Century Fox are setting up offices in India. Where Indian film makers have found it difficult to compete with Hollywood's special effects, this is seen as the next big area for Bollywood to develop.

[From: www.bollywoodworld.com]

39 *self-sacrifice:* Selbstaufopferung
41 *aspiring:* wanting to be successful
42 *break:* opportunity to be successful
beauty contestant: participant in a beauty competition
47 *modest:* small, not impressive
49 *distribution:* (here) act of being shown by cinemas and TV stations
51 *box office draw:* aspect of a film that attracts lots of people to watch it
52 *peripatetic* [peripə'tetɪk]: able to travel from place to place
59 *predictable:* exactly what you would expect

B Reacting to the text

Choose an aspect of Bollywood that interests you. It may be one of the topics mentioned above, or the following list may inspire you:
- a famous film;
- a famous actor or actress;
- a famous singer / musician in Bollywood movies;
- themes in Bollywood movies – especially if these are changing to reflect the times;
- how Indian audiences (in India / abroad) feel about the whole Bollywood scene and what websites are devoted to it;
- your own views of Bollywood movies (do you watch them? why?).

Do some research, then give a presentation to class.

SEQUENCE

05

SHAKESPEARE AND HIS WORLD

In the 52 years of his life, William Shakespeare (1564–1616) produced what is often considered the greatest literature ever written in English. He was that extraordinarily rare thing, a true genius.

In this sequence we look at the man and his times, his work and his legacy 400 years after his death.

Collect ideas

Even though Shakespeare has been dead for around 400 years, he is still very much alive in his works and we come into contact with him quite frequently – sometimes without realising it. Before you discover why this might be, work on the following tasks to find out where you may have already met him:

1. Have a look at the pictures, then say where people may encounter Shakespeare today. You may also do some research to find more examples.
2. You certainly know some things about Shakespeare, his times and his work. Collect your ideas in groups, then say how you know these things.
3. Try to find reasons why his plays are still studied in schools today and still regularly performed.
4. You will also encounter (and even use!) Shakespeare in your everyday language. The following are quotations from Shakespeare. Say what they mean and try to find their German equivalents:

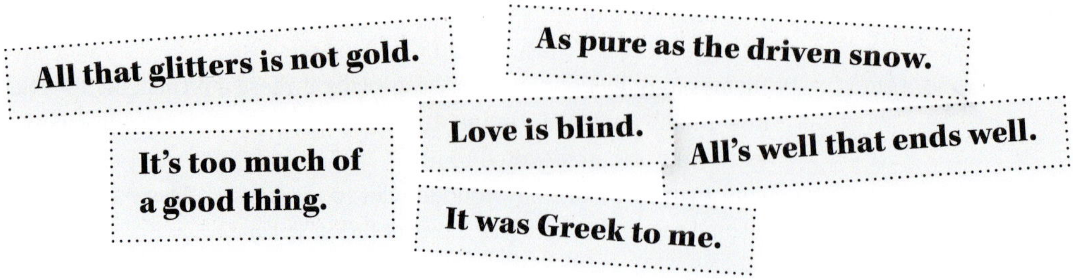

The young Will Shakespeare as played by the actor Joseph Fiennes in the film Shakespeare in Love

A modern performance of Macbeth

The Globe Theatre in Neuss, North-Rhine Westphalia, another reconstruction, where a Shakespeare festival takes place each summer

The modern Globe Theatre in London, an exact reconstruction

British students in a drama workshop. Shakespeare is studied in all British schools – and around the world including in the USA and Germany.

TOPIC

01

Shakespeare and his times

In this topic you are going to collect information from a number of different sources and then make a presentation about Shakespeare and his times.

1. Divide into groups, then as a group choose one text and study it. Collect the key information in note form and add any questions you think are important to answer. In the section Extra on p. 200 you will find some ideas for related topics you might like to add to your presentation.
2. In your group, discuss how you are going to present your results. Consider:
   - how you are going to show your information to your audience: via handout, a poster, a Powerpoint-presentation, etc.;
   - what visuals you are going to use to make your presentation interesting and lively;
   - who is going to present what (make sure that you all speak during the presentation).
3. Give your presentation, which should last around five minutes. Then discuss in class which presentation the class liked best and why.

▶ Skills 7.4

Text 1

This text is from the website of the Royal Shakespeare Company (RSC). It regularly performs all of Shakespeare's works.

Shakespeare's life

Very little is known for certain about William Shakespeare. What we do know about his life comes from registrar records, court records, wills, marriage certificates and his tombstone in Holy Trinity Church, Stratford-upon-Avon.

Shakespeare as he probably looked. Experts are not 100% sure this is a portrait of him – just one of the many mysteries about the man.

William Shakespeare was baptised on 26 April 1564 at Holy Trinity in Stratford-Upon-Avon. Traditionally his birthday is celebrated three days earlier, on 23 April, St George's Day.

William's father, John Shakespeare, was an affluent glove maker, tanner and wool dealer who owned property in Stratford. For a number of years he played a prominent role in the municipal life of the town. He served on the town council and was elected bailiff (mayor). However, around 1576 John Shakespeare was beset by severe financial difficulties and he was forced to mortgage his

2 *registrar:* person who looks after official records of births, marriages and deaths
court: Gericht
will: legal document stating what happens to sb.'s property after they die
3 *tombstone* ['tu:mstəʊn]: Grabstein
5 *baptise sb.:* jdn. taufen
8 *St George:* national saint of England
10 *affluent:* rich, wealthy
glove: Handschuh
tanner: person who makes leather
12 *municipal* [mju:'nisipl]: (here) urban
15 *beset (fml):* affected
16 *mortgage sth.:* etwas beleihen

wife's inheritance. William's mother, Mary Arden, was the daughter of a prosperous farmer, Robert Arden [...]. John and Mary Shakespeare had eight children: four daughters, of whom only one (Joan) survived childhood. William was the eldest of the four boys.

William almost certainly went to one of Stratford's 'petty' or junior schools [...]. From the age of seven or thereabouts, he would have progressed to the King's New School where the emphasis would have been on Latin, it being the international language still of Europe in the 1500s. Shakespeare probably left school at the age of 14 or 15.

In 1582, when he was 18, Shakespeare married Anne Hathaway. She was twenty six. Anne was the daughter of a well-to-do farmer. [...] Their first child, Susanna, was born in May 1583. Twins, Hamnet and Judith, were christened in February 1585.

Shakespeare's bust on his tomb in Stratford

From 1585 until 1592, very little is known about Shakespeare. These are generally referred to as 'The Lost Years'. But by 1592 we know that he was in London [...]. In 1594, Shakespeare became a founding member, actor, playwright and shareholder of the Lord Chamberlain's Men. Richard Burbage was the company's leading actor. He played roles such as Richard III, Hamlet, Othello and Lear. Under James VI/I, the company was renamed The King's Men. They performed at court more often than any other company.

Whereas John Shakespeare had lost a fortune, his son managed to amass great wealth in his lifetime. In 1597, he bought New Place, one of the largest properties in Stratford. [...]

Sometime after 1611, Shakespeare retired to Stratford. On 25 March 1616, Shakespeare revised and signed his will. On 23 April, his presumed birthday, he died, aged 52. On 25 April, he was buried at Holy Trinity Church in Stratford. Shakespeare's widow, Anne, died in 1623 and was buried beside him. Shakespeare's family line came to an end with the death of his grand-daughter Elizabeth in 1670.

In 1623, seven years after Shakespeare's death, John Heminge and Henry Condell (two actors from The King's Company) had Shakespeare's plays published [...]. This first folio contained 36 plays and sold for £1.

17 *inheritance:* Erbschaft
22 *King's New School:* a boys' grammar school in Stratford-upon-Avon
28 *well-to-do:* rich, wealthy
30 *christen sb.:* jdn. taufen
35 *shareholder:* owner of parts of a company or business
38 *James VI/I:* king of England and Scotland until 1625
42 *amass* [ə'mæs] *sth.:* collect sth. in large quantities
45 *retire:* stop working after a particular age
46 *presumed:* vermutet
48 *widow:* Witwe
52 *folio:* book made with large sheets of paper, used in early printing

[From: www.rsc.org.uk]

Text 2

England's golden age

The period of English history during which William Shakespeare lived is often described as England's Golden Age – or the English Renaissance. Under the reigns of both Elizabeth I and her successor, King James, England grew and changed at a pace that is sometimes compared to that of the Industrial Revolution in the 18th and 19th centuries.

3 *successor:* Nachfolger
King James I/VI: cf. picture on p. 198
4 *pace:* speed

The first reason for this is that it was a time of relative political stability. Before the arrival of Elizabeth on the throne, England had been torn by religious strife. Her father, Henry VIII (the king who had six wives) had made England a Protestant country with its own church – free from the control of the Catholic Pope in Rome (so that he could divorce his first wife). During Elizabeth's reign, and later that of James VI/I, England remained Protestant but Catholicism was tolerated. After James left the throne, England descended into a Civil War between king and parliament. For all of Shakespeare's life, however, England remained peaceful, with a strong, well-organised central government.

Elizabeth I, who reigned from 1558 to 1603 and who gave her name to the period known as the Elizabethan Age.

King James IV/I was the king of Scotland (where he was James VI) until Elizabeth's death. He then became also king of England (where he was James I). James ruled over both kingdoms but they were still legally two countries; England and Scotland were not fully united until 1707.

England began to become a world power and to grow economically at this time, too. In 1588, the British sea captain, Sir Francis Drake, defeated the Spanish Armada ('the greatest fleet the world had ever seen'), which had been sent to England by the Catholic Spanish king. The other European powers, the French and the Italians, had their own problems. England rose dramatically in power and importance.

Drake played an important part in an-other factor that made the Golden Age so golden. This was the age of discovery. Between 1577 and 1579 Drake sailed around the world. Other explorers sailed to America (already discovered, of course, by the Spanish) to set up England's first colonies there and bring valuable imports back into the country. Under James, a large commercial company (the East India Company) began trading with India and China.

It is perhaps in the intellectual life of England at this time, however, that we see the most signs of growth and change. And it was Shakespeare himself who played such an important role in this process. In painting, architecture, music, philosophy, literature, there was a blossoming of culture that had never been seen before – and was maybe never seen so dramatically again. Shakespeare was the towering genius of his age, but he was not alone. His contemporary, the playwright Christopher Marlowe, is considered by many to have been almost Shakespeare's equal – indeed, Shakespeare learned much from him in his early years. Another playwright was Ben Johnson, whose plays are still acted today. Composers, artists and poets of this time are still considered to be among England's greatest. And in philosophy, Francis Bacon developed the basics of the modern scientific way of thinking.

Christopher Marlowe (1564–1593). He was killed tragically young in a fight at an inn.

London was the centre of this explosion of culture. It had grown in size by 400% to a

9 *strife:* anger and violence
42 *sb.'s contemporary* [kən'tempərərɪ]: person who lives at the same time as sb.
playwright: person who writes plays

population of 200,000 just before Shakespeare arrived there. Coming from the village of Stratford, he would have seen nothing like it: a huge, filthy, noisy place alive with amazing energy. Theatre was truly the great entertainment in the city and there were several theatres of which the Globe was to become the grandest. Plays were performed every day to huge audiences – the Globe had room for three thousand spectators at a time. Elizabeth I herself adored plays and James VI/I became the patron of Shakespeare's theatre company, The King's Men.

England's Golden Age was not, of course, wonderful in all aspects. Around 80% of its population of 3–5 million lived on the land, and there, as well as in the country's few cities, there was enormous poverty and terrible disease. In Shakespeare's day, the difference between rich and poor was absolute. What is surprising, however, is that both rich and poor came to see plays. It seems that, for the English, the theatre had no social barriers.

59 *adore sb./sth.:* love, really like sb./sth.
60 *patron* ['peɪtrən]: person who gives money to artists

Text 3

The text below is from the book *Shakespeare* by the American writer and academic Bill Bryson.

Performing plays in Shakespeare's time

A play at the modern Globe theatre gives a good idea of a performance in Shakespeare's time. The cheapest seats were for those standing round the stage, the groundlings.

Plays were performed at about two o'clock in the afternoon. Handbills were distributed through the streets advertising what was on offer, and citizens were reminded that a play was soon to start with the appearance of a banner waving from the highest part of the structure in which the performance was to take place and a fanfare of trumpets that could be heard across much of the city. General admission for groundlings – those who stood in the open around the

1 *handbill:* small printed advertisement
4 *banner:* poster

stage – was a penny. Those who wished to sit paid a penny more, and those who desired a cushion paid another penny on top of that – all this at a time when a day's wage was one shilling (12 pence) or less. The money was dropped in a box, which was taken to a special room for safekeeping – the box office.

For those who could afford an additional treat, apples and pears (both apt to be used as missiles during moments of disappointment) and nuts, gingerbread and bottles of ale were on offer, as was the newly fashionable commodity tobacco. A small pipeful cost 3 pence – considerably more than the price of admission. There were no toilets – or at least no official ones. Despite their large capacity, theatres were reasonably intimate. No one in the audience was more than fifty feet or so from the edge of the stage.

There was little scenery and no curtains (even at the Curtain), no way to distinguish day from night, fog from sunshine, battlefield from boudoir, other than through words. So scenes had to be set with a few verbal strokes and the help of a compliant audience's imagination. As Wells and Taylor note, 'Oberon and Prospero have only to declare themselves invisible to become so.' [...]

A particular challenge for audience and performers alike must surely have been the practice of putting male players in female parts. When we consider how many powerful and expressive female roles Shakespeare created – Cleopatra. Lady Macbeth, Ophelia, Juliet, Desdemona – the actors must have been gifted dissemblers indeed. Rosalind in *As You Like It* has about a quarter of all the lines in the play: Shakespeare clearly had enormous confidence in some young actor. Yet, while we often know a good deal about performers in male roles from Shakespeare's day, we know almost nothing about the conduct of the female parts. Judith Cook, in *Women in Shakespeare*, says she could not find a single record of any role of a woman played by a specific boy actor. We don't even know much about them in general terms, including how old they were.

11 *apt:* likely
12 *missile* ['mɪsaɪl]: weapon thrown through the air
13 *ale:* beer
16 *intimate* ['ɪntɪmət]: intim
18 *scenery:* Bühnenbild
19 *boudoir* ['bu:dwɑ:] (old-fashioned): woman's bedroom
26 *dissembler:* person who pretends to be sb. else

[From: *Shakespeare: The World as a Stage* by Bill Bryson, 2007]

✕ **Extra** Choose one of the areas below and find out more about it. Report to the class with a short talk:

- the modern Globe Theatre and the layout of the stage;
- the Neuss festival;
- the Royal Shakespeare Company;
- the Shakespeare plays most often performed around the world and where they are performed;
- the names of more plays and a bit about what they are about;
- another aspect of life in Shakespeare's time – for example, music, fashion or food;
- Shakespeare tourist attractions in Stratford.

TOPIC 02

Speaking in verse

When Shakespeare wrote his poems and dramas over 400 years ago, he used the English language of his day. You can certainly imagine how much his English differs from the English spoken today. In this topic we look at Shakespeare's English and his way of writing – both in his poetry and in his plays.

Collect ideas

Reading Shakespeare, you quickly learn some everyday words and phrases from his time. Can you match the Elizabethan terms on the left below and the modern English equivalents on the right?

Elizabethan English	Modern English
1. hither	a. hello
2. as you will	b. no
3. aye	c. you
4. farewell	d. goodbye
5. good morrow	e. yes
6. hark	f. listen
7. nay	g. please
8. oft	h. here (towards me)
9. peace	i. often
10 prithee	j. OK
11. thee/thou	k. that (over there)
12. wherefore	l. why
13. yond(er)	m. be quiet

1 A sonnet

Shakespeare wrote 154 sonnets – a special form of poem you will find out about soon. Most of them are addressed to a young man; later sonnets speak of a 'dark lady'. Researchers have tried to identify both subjects, but the actual person or people remains a mystery. You are now going to look at one of Shakespeare's most famous sonnets.

A Before you begin

In the sonnet, the speaker talks about how beautiful his lover is. Collect words and phrases that you personally might use to describe a beautiful person.

✕ **Extra** Find a picture of someone you think is beautiful. Write a text to go with the picture explaining why.

B Understanding the sonnet

CD 9

1. Listen to Bryan Ferry singing the sonnet. Without reading the text, try to understand what the sonnet is about.

Sonnet 18

Shall I compare thee to a summer's day?
Thou art more lovely and more temperate:
Rough winds do shake the darling buds of May,
And summer's lease hath all too short a date:
Sometime too hot the eye of heaven shines,
And often is his gold complexion dimm'd;
And every fair from fair sometime declines,
By chance or nature's changing course untrimm'd;
But thy eternal summer shall not fade
Nor lose possession of that fair thou owest;
Nor shall Death brag thou wander'st in his shade,
When in eternal lines to time thou growest:
So long as men can breathe or eyes can see,
So long lives this and this gives life to thee.

1 *thee (old use):* you (accusative form)
2 *thou (old use):* you (nominative form)
temperate: mild, pleasant; without extremes
3 *darling (adj.):* lovely, attractive
bud: Knospe
4 *lease:* legal agreement that allows sb. to use sth. for a period of time in return for money
hath (old use): has
date: (here) length of time for which something can be used
6 *complexion:* the natural colour and condition of the skin of a person's face
dim sth.: make sth. less bright
7 *every fair:* every beautiful thing
8 *untrim sth.:* take away the decorations from sth.
9 *thy (old use):* your
10 *thou ow'st (old use):* you own
11 *brag:* talk too proudly about sth. you own or sth. you have done

2. Listen again and read the sonnet. Then write out the key ideas in modern English. You could begin like this: 'Shall I compare you to a summer's day? No! You are more … and more constant. In May, there are often strong winds, and …'.
3. Shakespeare deals with two separate themes in this poem, first in lines 1–8, then in lines 9–14. Sum up the two themes.

C Analysing the sonnet

1. The form of the sonnet

▶ Glossary 2.4.1

A sonnet (the term means 'little song') is written according to strict rules. In other words, its form is always the same. Look at Sonnet 18 and find out what this form is:

- identify the rhyme scheme, which is the same in all of Shakespeare's sonnets;
- examine how the structure of thought reflects the rhyme scheme. Consider especially where there are thematic turns or where e.g. a summary or conclusion begins;
- count the number of lines – all sonnets have the same number.

2. Imagery

▶ Glossary 3.1

Shakespeare constantly uses images in his writing.

- Find and explain some of the images in Sonnet 18.
- Describe their effect on the listener or reader.

✕ **Extra** There are certain themes that Shakespeare returns to over and over again in his sonnets. Among them are love (of course), the ability of art to make people immortal or the speaker's feelings of being inadequate. The sonnet below deals with another of Shakespeare's major themes. Remember that in Shakespeare's time, people were old at forty – 80 percent of the population of London in his day were under 25.

▶ Glossary 2.4.1, 3.1

Work in groups to look at Sonnet 73, then talk about it in class.

1. Sum up its theme(s).
2. Analyse its structure, language and use of imagery and rhetorical devices.
3. Say what you feel about the sonnet.

Sonnet 73

That time of year thou mayst in me behold
When yellow leaves, or none, or few, do hang
Upon those boughs which shake against the cold,
Bare ruin'd choirs, where late the sweet birds sang.
In me thou seest the twilight of such day
As after sunset fadeth in the west,
Which by and by black night doth take away,
Death's second self, that seals up all in rest.
In me thou see'st the glowing of such fire
That on the ashes of his youth doth lie,
As the death-bed whereon it must expire
Consumed with that which it was nourish'd by.
This thou perceivest, which makes thy love more strong,
To love that well which thou must leave ere long.

3 *bough* [baʊ]: large tree branch
4 *choir* ['kwaɪə]: Chor
5 *twilight:* Dämmerung
8 *seal up sth.:* (here) hide sth., cover sth.
9 *glowing:* glühend
10 *ashes:* Asche
11 *expire:* die
12 *nourish sth.:* feed sth.
13 *perceive sth.:* notice sth.
14 *ere* [eə]: before

2 Thee's and thou's

You are now going to look at a piece of Shakespearean drama. The scene you you are going to read is the first scene from *Hamlet* – he is the character who, when thinking of suicide, makes the famous speech: 'To be or not to be, that is the question.' The setting is the walls of the castle at Elsinore in Denmark, where Hamlet is a prince.

A Understanding the scene

The best way always to understand Shakespeare is to speak the words aloud – better still, to act them out. You may not be completely sure of every word, but the general meaning will become clear the more you try.

1. Read the text and think about how you would present the scene on stage – who moves, when etc. Remember that in Shakespeare's day there was no scenery and you would be acting out the scene in daylight – so you must 'paint a picture' with the words alone.

SCENE I. Elsinore. Enter Barnardo and Francisco, two sentinels.

BARNARDO Who's there?
FRANCISCO Nay, answer me. Stand and unfold yourself.
BARNARDO Long live the King!
FRANCISCO Barnardo?
BARNARDO He.
FRANCISCO You come most carefully upon your hour.
BARNARDO 'Tis now struck twelve. Get thee to bed, Francisco.
FRANCISCO For this relief much thanks. 'Tis bitter cold,
And I am sick at heart.
BARNARDO Have you had quiet guard?
FRANCISCO Not a mouse stirring.
BARNARDO Well, good night.
If you do meet Horatio and Marcellus,
The rivals of my watch, bid them make haste.
FRANCISCO I think I hear them.

Enter Horatio and Marcellus

Stand, ho! Who is there?
HORATIO Friends to this ground.
MARCELLUS And liegemen to the Dane.
FRANCISCO Give you good night.
MARCELLUS O, farewell, honest soldier, who hath reliev'd you?
FRANCISCO Barnardo hath my place. Give you good night.

Exit

MARCELLUS Holla, Barnardo!
BARNARDO Say – what, is Horatio there?
HORATIO A piece of him.
BARNARDO Welcome, Horatio. Welcome, good Marcellus.

3 *answer me:* It is the sentry on duty who has the right to challenge.
unfold sth.: reveal sth.
4 *Barnado's response – perhaps an accepted password – shows him to be a friend.*
7 *carefully:* promptly
10 *I am … heart:* I've had enough
15 *rivals:* partners
19 *this ground:* this country
18 *the Dane:* the Danish king
20 *liegeman* ['li:dʒmæn]: servant
21 *give you:* may God give you
22 *hath:* has taken
27 *a piece of him:* Horatio perhaps extends a hand as a mock proof of his identity

MARCELLUS What, has this thing appear'd again tonight?
BARNARDO I have seen nothing.
MARCELLUS Horatio says 'tis but our fantasy,
And will not let belief take hold of him,
Touching this dreaded sight, twice seen of us.
Therefore I have entreated him along
With us to watch the minutes of this night,
That if again this apparition come,
He may approve our eyes and speak to it.
HORATIO Tush, tush, 'twill not appear.
BARNARDO Sit down awhile,
And let us once again assail your ears,
That are so fortified against our story,
What we have two nights seen.
HORATIO Well, sit we down.
And let us hear Barnardo speak of this.
BARNARDO Last night of all,
When yond same star that's westward from the pole
Had made his course t'illume that part of heaven
Where now it burns, Marcellus and myself,
The bell then beating one –

Enter Ghost

MARCELLUS Peace, break thee off. Look where it comes again!
BARNARDO In the same figure like the King that's dead.
MARCELLUS Thou art a scholar, speak to it, Horatio.
BARNARDO Looks it not like the King? Mark it, Horatio.
HORATIO Most like. It harrows me with fear and wonder.
BARNARDO It would be spoke to.
MARCELLUS Question it, Horatio.
HORATIO What art thou that usurp'st this time of night,
Together with that fair and warlike form
In which the majesty of buried Denmark
Did sometimes march? By heaven, I charge thee, speak!
MARCELLUS It is offended.
BARNARDO See, it stalks away!
HORATIO Stay. Speak, speak, I charge thee, speak.

Exit Ghost

MARCELLUS 'Tis gone and will not answer.
BARNARDO How now, Horatio? You tremble and look pale.
Is not this something more than fantasy?
What think you on't?
HORATIO Before my God, I might not this believe
Without the sensible and true avouch
Of mine own eyes.
MARCELLUS Is it not like the King?
HORATIO As thou art to thyself.

[From: *Hamlet*, Act I, Scene I]

29 *this thing:* Shakespeare begins to build up suspense
31 *but our fantasy:* just our imagination
33 *dreaded:* dreadful
34 *Therefore:* that is why. The audience needs to be told this – Barnardo already knows.
along: come along
37 *approve our eyes:* believe what we have seen
40 *assail your ears:* get you to listen
41 *fortified:* i.e. by reason. The imagery is appropriate for a soldier
46 *pole:* pole star
47 *illume* [ɪ'luːm]: light up
49 *beating:* striking
52 *figure:* shape
53 *a scholar* ['skɒlə]: Horatio would know Latin, the proper language in which to address any supernatural being (although theatrical convention permits English here)
55 *harrows me:* breaks me up
56 *would:* wants to be
A ghost could not start a conversation
58 *usurp'st:* Horatio challenges the Ghost's right to appear at that time and in that particular shape
59 *warlike:* martial
60 *majesty of buried Denmark:* dead king of Denmark
62 *offended:* The Ghost turns away because the questioner is not the man it seeks
71 *without … eyes:* if I had not seen for myself: his eyes give the evidence ('avouch') of his senses. Horatio's conversion helps the audience to accept the Ghost's reality

2. Get together in groups, discuss your ideas and take parts. (One student may have to read more than one part). Then act the scene out.
3. Summarise briefly what happens in this scene.
4. As with the sonnets, Shakespeare's language, especially his grammar, differs from modern English also in the plays. Now look in more detail at Shakespeare's grammar. Read the **KEY FACTS** box at the bottom of the page, then copy the table below and complete it with examples where Shakespeare's English is different. Re-write the examples in modern English.

LANGUAGE FEATURE	EXAMPLES	MODERN ENGLISH
personal pronouns	Thou art a scholar (l. 53), …	
shortened forms	appear'd (l. 27), …	
forms of *have*	…	
forms of *be*	…	
imperatives	break thee off (l. 49), …	
questions	…	
past tense	…	

B Analysing the scene

► Glossary 2.1, 2.3

1. Analyse how Shakespeare has written this scene to achieve the following goals:
   - quickly setting the scene, i.e. the place, time and atmosphere;
   - introducing the characters and their feelings.
2. The ghost is a key part of the scene. Explain what effect Shakespeare wants to achieve with the ghost and how he does so.

C Reacting to the scene

1. Talk in class. Did you enjoy acting out the scene? Did it help you to understand the scene? What have you learned about the use of *watching* rather than *reading* drama?
2. Using this scene as an example, speculate why the theatre was so immensely popular in Shakespeare's London.

KEY FACTS Shakespeare's English

Just as England was changing during its Golden Age, so was the English language. In fact, Shakespeare played a huge part in this, introducing many new words into the language. Essentially, English at this time was developing into the language we know today. Some of the traditional features of the language were becoming old-fashioned while newer features were beginning to become standard. One example was the use of the pronoun *you*, which was the modern form and in Shakespeare's time was used to address people of higher rank. Shakespeare used it often – alongside the old forms *thee* and *thou* that were reserved for more intimate situations. But he did not use them consistently, so in his dramas, close friends would sometimes call each other *you* and sometimes *thou* with no change in meaning. Modern English was still some way in the future, however, so in Shakespeare we still find many expressions that are more than a little unfamiliar to us today. Sometimes these are verb forms (e.g. *art* as a form of the verb *be*). Others are words and phrases we no longer use today or which mean something different (e.g. *peace* for *be quiet*). What we can say, however, is that reading a text written before Shakespeare's time is much more difficult than reading Shakespeare!

3 Shakespeare's verse

Shakespeare wrote large parts of his plays in verse. This means that his lines are rhythmical, they are based on a standard beat. The verse form Shakespeare mostly used is called blank verse (blank meaning that it does not rhyme).

Step 1: Counting the beats

Blank verse is a kind of verse in which each line has five double beats. The emphasis goes on the second beat:

de DUM	de DUM	de DUM	de DUM	de DUM
1	2	3	4	5

A good way to see how the line works is by using a simple English sentence:
I think I'd rather have a cup of tea.

I	think	I'd	ra	ther	have	a	cup	of	tea
de	DUM	de	DUM	de	DUM	de	DUM	de	DUM
1		2		3		4		5	

The following table displays the beat patterns of some lines from the scene from *Hamlet*.

That	if	a-	gain	this	ap-	-pa-	-ri-	-tion	come
de	DUM	de	DUM	de	DUM	de	DUM	de	DUM
1		2		3		4		5	
He	may	ap-	-prove	our	eyes	and	speak	to	it.
de	DUM	de	DUM	de	DUM	de	DUM	de	DUM
1		2		3		4		5	

Working with a partner, make a similar table and enter ll. 44–48. Tip: start with the words that have more than one syllable and identify their stress pattern – they will give you a good starting point. Be careful: you will already encounter examples of 'breaking the rules' (see below).

Step 2: Breaking the rules

As you will have noted, Shakespeare does not stick to blank verse all the time – he frequently breaks the rules, i.e. he varies the basic pattern. On the basis of your table, state where and how Shakespeare changes the beat pattern. Why do you think he does so?

In l. ... Shakespeare changes the beat pattern by ...	making the line shorter / ending the line with an unstressed syllable
The effect of this is that ...	an unexpected word is emphasised / a sense of urgency is created / the rhythm of the verse is less predictable.
For the audience, this ...	adds atmosphere to the situation / lets them know something important is being said

TOPIC 03 Looking at a play

In this topic you are going to look at one of Shakespeare's most famous plays: *Romeo and Juliet*. Shakespeare wrote the play in 1595 or 1596. At that time his plays about love were wildly successful with the London audiences of the time. However, *Romeo and Juliet* is not simply a happy love story, as you are soon going to find out.

Collect ideas

Above is a word cloud about the play *Romeo and Juliet*. In groups, use it to speculate (or to remind yourself what you already know) about the play. Present your ideas to the class.

1 The prologue

***Romeo and Juliet* begins with a prologue. In some productions this is spoken by one person, in others, by several (a chorus).**

2 *fair:* beautiful
3 *grudge:* quarrel (Shakespeare never reveals what the feud is about)
mutiny ['mju:tɪnɪ]: violence
4 *civil:* of or belonging to citizens
5 *from forth:* born of
loins: Lenden
6 *star-crossed:* ill-fated (due to the astrological stars)
7 *misadventured piteous overthrows:* unglückselige herzzerreißende Katastrophen
8 *doth:* do (plural)
strife: Streit, Konflikt
9 *passage:* course
death-marked: doomed to death
11 *but:* only; except for
end: death
nought [nɔ:t]: nothing
12 *two hours' traffic:* business of two hours
13 *the which:* (reference to the two hours' traffic of the stage)
attend sth.: listen to sth.
14 *here:* (reference to the prologue)
toil: work

Prologue

Enter Chorus

Two households, both alike in dignity,
In fair Verona, where we lay our scene,
From ancient grudge break to new mutiny,
Where civil blood makes civil hands unclean.
From forth the fatal loins of these two foes
A pair of star-crossed lovers take their life.
Whose misadventured piteous overthrows
Doth with their death bury their parents' strife.
The fearful passage of their death-marked love,
And the continuance of their parents' rage,
Which, but their children's end, naught could remove,
Is now the two hours' traffic of our stage;
The which if you with patient ears attend,
What here shall miss, our toil shall strive to mend.

[From: *The Tragedy of Romeo and Juliet*, Prologue]

A Understanding the text

Copy and complete the chart in note form in modern English. Compare with a partner, then write a short summary of the speech.

SETTING		
CHARACTERS	FAMILIES	who? relationship between them?
	LOVERS	who? 'star-crossed' (l. 6)?
PLOT		
OTHER INFORMATION		

B Analysing the text

1. Analyse the structure and rhyme scheme of the prologue and state what type of text this is.
2. Shakespeare sometimes inserts such poems into a play. Speculate why and when.
3. Shakespeare begins the play by telling the audience what will happen in it. Do you find this surprising? (Why) not? Try to find reasons why Shakespeare might open his play in this way.

C Reacting to the text

1. Read out the prologue.
2. Describe what Shakespeare must achieve with the prologue (for example, get the audience's attention in the theatre of the time). Remember that the audience often reacted to what happened on stage in Shakespeare's theatres.

2 Juliet's balcony (Act II, Scene II)

This is one of the most famous scenes in the play. Young men from the two warring families, the Montagues and Capulets, are engaging in constant street fights, breaking the peace of Verona. Romeo, Lord Montague's son, is depressed after being rejected by a girl he likes. To cheer him up, his friends suggest that they go secretly to a Capulet ball. At the party, Romeo sees Juliet, Lord Capulet's daughter. Their feelings for each other are instant – it is 'love across a crowded room'. But they know they can't be together because of the feud between their families. Besides, Juliet's family want her to marry Paris. Later that night, Romeo climbs the walls of Juliet's orchard and sees her on her balcony.

1 *yonder:* that … over there
3 *envious:* neidisch
5 *her maid:* the servant of Diana, the goddess of the moon and virginity
12 *wherefore:* why
13 *deny your father:* refuse to acknowledge who your father is
14 *be but sworn my love:* if you swear that you love me
17 *'tis but:* it is only
18 *though not a Montague:* even if you were not a Montague
25 *owes:* owns, has
26 *title:* name
doff sth.: get rid of sth., throw away sth.
27 *for:* in exchange for, in return for
30 *call me but love:* just call me your love
baptised [bæp'taɪzd]: getauft
31 *henceforth* [hens'fɔːθ]: from now on
32 *bescreened:* hidden
33 *stumblest on my counsel:* intrude on my private thoughts

Romeo — But, soft! What light through yonder window breaks?
It is the east, and Juliet is the sun.
Arise, fair sun, and kill the envious moon,
Who is already sick and pale with grief,
That thou, her maid, art far more fair than she:
[…]
See, how she leans her cheek upon her hand!
O, that I were a glove upon that hand,
That I might touch that cheek!

Juliet — Ay me!

Romeo — *[Aside]* She speaks.

Juliet — O Romeo, Romeo! Wherefore art thou Romeo?
Deny thy father and refuse thy name;
Or, if thou wilt not, be but sworn my love,
And I'll no longer be a Capulet.

Romeo — *[Aside]* Shall I hear more, or shall I speak at this?

Juliet — 'Tis but thy name that is my enemy.
Thou art thyself, though not a Montague.
What's Montague? it is nor hand, nor foot,
Nor arm, nor face, nor any other part
Belonging to a man. O, be some other name!
What's in a name? That which we call a rose
By any other name would smell as sweet;
So Romeo would, were he not Romeo call'd,
Retain that dear perfection which he owes
Without that title. Romeo, doff thy name,
And for that name which is no part of thee
Take all myself.

Romeo — I take thee at thy word:
Call me but love, and I'll be new baptised;
Henceforth I never will be Romeo.

Juliet — What man art thou that thus bescreened in night
So stumblest on my counsel?

Romeo — By a name
I know not how to tell thee who I am:
My name, dear saint, is hateful to myself,

Because it is an enemy to thee;
Had I it written, I would tear the word.

Juliet — My ears have not yet drunk a hundred words
Of that tongue's utterance, yet I know the sound:
Art thou not Romeo and a Montague?
[...]
How camest thou hither, tell me, and wherefore?
The orchard walls are high and hard to climb,
And the place death, considering who thou art,
If any of my kinsmen find thee here.

Romeo — With love's light wings did I o'erperch these walls;
For stony limits cannot hold love out,
And what love can do, that dares love attempt.
Therefore thy kinsmen are no stop to me.

Juliet — If they do see thee, they will murder thee.

Romeo — Alack, there lies more peril in thine eye
Than twenty of their swords: look thou but sweet,
And I am proof against their enmity.

Juliet — I would not for the world they saw thee here.

Romeo — I have night's cloak to hide me from their sight.
And but thou love me, let them find me here:
My life were better ended by their hate,
Than death prorogued, wanting of thy love.
[...]

Juliet — Thou know'st the mask of night is on my face,
Else would a maiden blush bepaint my cheek;
For that which thou hast heard me speak tonight
Fain would I dwell on form, fain, fain deny
What I have spoke: but farewell compliment!
Dost thou love me? I know thou wilt say 'Ay,'
[...]

Romeo — Lady, by yonder blessèd moon I swear
That tips with silver all these fruit-tree tops –

Juliet — O, swear not by the moon, the inconstant moon,
That monthly changes in her circled orb,
Lest that thy love prove likewise variable.

Romeo — What shall I swear by?

Juliet — Do not swear at all;
Or, if thou wilt, swear by thy gracious self,
Which is the god of my idolatry,
And I'll believe thee.
[...]

NURSE calls within.

Juliet — I hear some noise within. Dear love, adieu!
Anon, good nurse! Sweet Montague, be true.
Stay but a little, I will come again.

Exit, above.

---

40 *utterance:* Sprechen
47 *overperch:* fly over
48 *limits:* boundaries
52 *peril:* danger
53 *look thou … enmity:* if you look at me with sweetness, I am protected against their enmity (= Feindschaft)
55 *not for the world:* not for anything at all
56 *cloak:* Mantel
57 *but:* unless
62 *maiden:* young girl's
bepaint sth.: colour sth., paint sth.
64 *dwell on form:* observe the rules of proper behaviour
fain: gladly
65 *compliment:* phrases used between men and women who do not know each other well
70 *inconstant:* changing
71 *circled orb:* sphere in which the moon circles the earth
76 *idolatry* [aɪ'dɒlətrɪ]: Vergötterung; Götzenverehrung
81 *anon:* I am coming

84 *be afeared:* be afraid, fear
86 *flattering-sweet:* delightfully attractive *substantial:* real

Romeo
O blessèd, blessèd night! I am afeared.
Being in night, all this is but a dream,
Too flattering-sweet to be substantial.

[From: *The Tragedy of Romeo and Juliet*, Act II, Scene II]

A Understanding the scene

1. You are going to approach the scene again by acting it out.
   a Divide into groups of three and take the roles of Juliet, Romeo and nurse.
   b Read through the scene for a basic understanding. Don't worry about every word at this stage. Compare ideas and agree on the storyline.
   c Go through the text in detail and write stage directions for the scene. Think about the following:
   - the setting and how you can create this on stage without a whole lot of props;
   - the movements of the characters;
   - their emotions;
   - their way of speaking and who they're speaking to.

   d Act out your scene.
2. In your own words describe what Juliet and Romeo say about the meaning of names (cf. ll. 17–31).

B Analysing the scene

1. A situation where the audience knows something that the characters do not is a dramatic device often used in plays. A simple example in a film might be that we know someone dangerous is in a room, but a second character does not – and goes into the room. Explain how Shakespeare uses this device in this scene and describe its effect on the audience.

▶ Glossary 3.1

2. It is often said that Shakespeare 'paints word pictures' with his poetry – he constantly uses images, metaphors and similes.
   a Consider the following two examples from the scene, point out the image and its effect on the audience:
   - 'But soft! What light through yonder window breaks?
     It is the east, and Juliet is the sun.' (ll. 1–2)
   - 'What's in a name? that which we call a rose
     By any other name would smell as sweet.' (ll. 22–23).

   b Analyse how Shakespeare uses the image of the night in this scene.

C Reacting to the scene

You are Romeo or Juliet. Write your diary entry for this evening after the scene above.

3 Friar Laurence's plan (Act IV, Scene I)

With the help of Juliet's nurse, the young lovers are married in secret by Friar Laurence. Later, Romeo kills Juliet's cousin Tybalt who has killed his friend Mercutio in a duel. To evade the law, Romeo plans to escape to Mantua. Before he flees, he hides in Juliet's room where they spend the night together. Back in Verona, Lord Capulet accepts Paris's plans to marry Juliet sooner than expected. Juliet panics, and visits Friar Laurence.

2 *past hope:* jenseits aller Hoffnung
5 *it strains me … wits:* it upsets me beyond the limits of my mind
6 *prorogue sth.* [prə'rəʊg]: postpone sth., delay sth.
11 *resolution:* decision, determination
12 *presently:* immediately
14 *ere* [eə]: before
sealed: versiegelt
15 *label:* seal
deed: document
19 *merry:* happy, cheerful
give consent: agree
20 *look:* make sure
lie: sleep
22 *vial* ['vaɪəl]: small bottle
23 *distilling liquor:* liquid which penetrates the entire body
off: completely, all of it
24 *presently:* shortly
25 *drowsy:* that makes you want to sleep
humour: feeling
for: as
26 *native progress:* natural flow
surcease: stop
27 *testify sth.:* indicate sth.
29 *paly:* pale
eyes' windows: eyelids
31 *part:* part of the body
supple government: power of movement
33 *borrowed likeness:* false similarity
shrunken death: death that is not really death
38 *manner:* tradition, custom
39 *uncovered:* with your face uncovered
bier [bɪə]: movable stand on which a corpse is laid

Juliet
O shut the door! and when thou hast done so,
Come weep with me, past hope, past cure, past help!

Friar Laurence
Ah, Juliet, I already know thy grief.
It strains me past the compass of my wits.
I hear thou must, and nothing may prorogue it,
On Thursday next be married to this county.

Juliet
Tell me not, friar, that thou hear'st of this,
Unless thou tell me how I may prevent it.
If, in thy wisdom, thou canst give no help,
Do thou but call my resolution wise,
And with this knife I'll help it presently.
God joined my heart and Romeo's, thou our hands;
And ere this hand, by thee to Romeo sealed,
Shall be the label to another deed,
[...]

Friar Laurence
Hold, then. Go home, be merry, give consent
To marry Paris. Wednesday is tomorrow:
To-morrow night look that thou lie alone.
Let not thy nurse lie with thee in thy chamber.
Take thou this vial, being then in bed,
And this distilling liquor drink thou off.
When presently through all thy veins shall run
A cold and drowsy humour, for no pulse
Shall keep his native progress, but surcease.
No warmth, no breath, shall testify thou livest.
The roses in thy lips and cheeks shall fade
To paly ashes; thy eyes' windows fall,
Like Death, when he shuts up the day of life;
Each part, deprived of supple government,
Shall, stiff and stark and cold, appear like death:
And in this borrow'd likeness of shrunk death
Thou shalt continue two and forty hours,
And then awake as from a pleasant sleep.
Now, when the bridegroom in the morning comes
To rouse thee from thy bed, there art thou dead.
Then, as the manner of our country is,
In thy best robes uncovered on the bier

40 *borne:* carried
vault [vɔːlt]: Gruft
41 *kindred* ['kɪndrəd]: family
42 *against:* ready for the time when
43 *drift:* plan
48 *inconstant toy:* unbeständige Laune
49 *abate … acting it:* weaken your bravery in carrying through with it (= the plan)
52 *hold:* take it (= the vial)
prosperous: successful
53 *resolve:* Entschluss
55 *help afford:* provide help

Thou shalt be borne to that same ancient vault
Where all the kindred of the Capulets lie.
In the meantime, against thou shalt awake,
Shall Romeo by my letters know our drift,
And hither shall he come: and he and I
Will watch thy waking, and that very night
Shall Romeo bear thee hence to Mantua.
And this shall free thee from this present shame.
If no inconstant toy, nor womanish fear,
Abate thy valour in the acting it.

Juliet — Give me, give me! O, tell not me of fear!

Friar Laurence
Hold. Get you gone, be strong and prosperous
In this resolve: I'll send a friar with speed
To Mantua, with my letters to thy lord.

Juliet — Love give me strength, and strength shall help afford.
Farewell, dear father!

Exeunt.

[From: *The Tragedy of Romeo and Juliet,* Act IV, Scene I]

A Understanding the scene

1. Rewrite and act out this scene to get a general understanding of it.
   a Read through the scene to understand what happens, take notes.
   b Compare notes with a partner and agree on the basic storyline.
   c Rewrite the scene in modern English. Do this not by rewriting each of Shakespeare's lines, but by trying to find the essential ideas and expressing them in your own words. The best way to do this would be to close your book completely and use only your notes. Add stage directions to your script. You could begin like this:

Juliet — *(Sitting with her head in her hands in despair. Friar Laurence standing just inside door).* Father, what am I going to do? There's no hope for Romeo and me.

Friar — Poor Juliet. Yes, I heard the news about …

B Analysing the scene

► Glossary 2.1, 2.3

1. Thinking back to the prologue at the start of the play, describe the thoughts and emotions the audience will have in this scene. Analyse how Shakespeare is playing with their feelings.
2. In classical drama, the fourth act follows the climax and prepares the (tragic) ending. Explain how this scene fulfils this function.

C Reacting to the scene

Write Juliet's diary for today.

4 No happy ending (Act V, Scene III)

The Friar's plan goes wrong. His message that Juliet is only sleeping never reaches Romeo. Instead Romeo hears that Juliet is dead. He returns to Verona, buys poison and goes to the Capulet family vault where he meets Paris. Romeo kills him and drinks the poison.

Friar Laurence
Romeo!
Advances.
Alack, alack, what blood is this, which stains
The stony entrance of this sepulchre?
What mean these masterless and gory swords
To lie discoloured by this place of peace?
Enters the tomb.
Romeo! O, pale! Who else? What, Paris too?
And steeped in blood? Ah, what an unkind hour
Is guilty of this lamentable chance!
The lady stirs.

Juliet
JULIET wakes.
O comfortable friar! Where is my lord?
I do remember well where I should be,
And there I am. Where is my Romeo?

Noise within.

Friar Laurence
I hear some noise. Lady, come from that nest
Of death, contagion, and unnatural sleep.
A greater power than we can contradict
Hath thwarted our intents. Come, come away.
Thy husband in thy bosom there lies dead;
And Paris too. Come, I'll dispose of thee
Among a sisterhood of holy nuns.
Stay not to question, for the watch is coming;
Come, go, good Juliet, I dare no longer stay.

Exit FRIAR LAURENCE.

Juliet
Go, get thee hence, for I will not away.
What's here? A cup, closed in my true love's hand?
Poison, I see, hath been his timeless end.
O churl! Drunk all, and left no friendly drop
To help me after? I will kiss thy lips.
Haply some poison yet doth hang on them,
To make die with a restorative.

6 *what mean …:* what does it mean that … / why do …
masterless: that are not in their owners' (master's) hands
gory: bloody
7 *discoloured:* unnaturally coloured (with blood)
10 *steeped:* covered
unkind: unnatural
14 *comfortable:* providing spiritual comfort
20 *contagion* [kən'teɪdʒən]: ansteckende Krankheiten
unnatural sleep: death
21 *contradict:* argue with
22 *thwart sth.:* destroy sth.
24 *dispose of sth.:* put sth. away
31 *timeless:* occurring too early
32 *churl:* fool
33 *help me after:* help me follow you
34 *haply:* perhaps
35 *restorative:* a kiss that should have restored her to life

Kisses him.

Thy lips are warm.

[Within] Lead, boy. Which way?

Yea, noise? Then I'll be brief. O happy dagger!

First watchman — Taking ROMEO's dagger.

Juliet — This is thy sheath;

Stabs herself.

there rust, and let me die.

Falls on ROMEO's body, and dies.

[From: *The Tragedy of Romeo and Juliet*, Act V, Scene III]

39 *happy:* well placed
41 *sheath:* Scheide
43 *rust:* rosten

A Understanding the scene

▶ Activity chest 8

You are going to sum up this scene with a series of 'Freeze-frame tableaux'.

1. Read through the text, form groups and agree on what happens in the scene.
2. Find four or five points in the scene that you can illustrate with a freeze-frame. For example, the first might show Friar Laurence standing in the tomb with Romeo and Paris dead on the floor. Work out all your tableaux and who will take what parts.
3. Show your tableaux to the class and have the others explain them. They should say where you are, what is happening and what the characters may be feeling at this point.
4. Discuss your tableaux in class. Which were the most effective? Why?

✕ **Extra** Act out this scene.

B Analysing the scene

1. Shakespeare experts often point out that in *Romeo and Juliet* the two young lovers never have time – they are always under pressure: in the balcony scene, the nurse ends the lovers' time together; when Friar Laurence has married them, they have just one night and then Romeo has to flee to Mantua. Looking at this scene, explain how even here the lovers don't have time. Thinking of the whole play, what effect might this have on the audience?
2. The prologue tells us that the two lovers are 'star-crossed' (p. 209, l. 6). Explain again what this means. Examine where Shakespeare reminds us of this in this scene towards the end of the play and explain why.

C Reacting to the scene

There is one more important scene to come in the play. The heads of the two families, the Montagues and the Capulets, come together to consider what has happened. Shakespeare has told us in the prologue that their deaths 'Doth … bury their parents' strife' (p. 209, l. 8). In groups, imagine this scene and outline what might be said and done. You could act out the scene. Then read Shakespeare's final scene of the play (you can find the text quite easily online).

D Considering the play as a whole

▶ Glossary 2.1

1. You will know that the plot especially of dramas usually follows a certain structure. Describe it and illustrate how the scenes you've read fit into this structure.

▶ Glossary 2.3.2

2. The full title of the play is *The Tragedy of Romeo and Juliet*. Recollect how a tragedy is defined and show how *Romeo and Juliet* is a tragedy.
3. What part do the two families play in the story? What deeper message for the audience might Shakespeare wish to convey here?
4. Think back to what you have learned about the theatre in Shakespeare's day. Explain how in *Romeo and Juliet* Shakespeare might have been writing for two different audiences (the groundlings – who would probably be great lovers of today's soap operas – and more educated people).

✕ **Extra** Shakespeare's dramas are very often adapted to take place in other times. The central theme of the play is that the two lovers cannot be together because their families are enemies. Imagine how you could adapt the play yourself for another play or movie. What backgrounds might you choose? Who would the lovers be? What would happen to them? Outline your story. If you wish, you could work in a group and act out one scene.

▶ Glossary 3.1

SPOTLIGHT ON Rhetorical devices

When analysing a text you are regularly asked to point out the rhetorical devices the writer uses. These devices are used in every form of text – we even use some of them when we speak – but they are often most important in works of literature, speeches and argumentative texts.

What are rhetorical devices?
A rhetorical device is simply a way of using words or structuring sentences (or a longer piece of text) so that they have more impact on the reader, make the language more interesting or beautiful, or bring out the meaning more clearly. An example might be a repetition: 'We had **no** water, **no** food, and **no** idea where we were.' – which is more interesting than just: 'We didn't have water, food or any idea where we were.'
When you analyse the rhetorical devices used in a text, do not just list them, but also describe their effect and the purpose they may serve in the text.

▶ Glossary 3.1

✕ **Spotlight task** You can imagine that Shakespeare, one of the world's greatest ever poets, was a master at using rhetorical devices in his works. You are going to look now at some examples from the balcony scene (p. 210). In groups, copy and complete the table below. Each group should then look at a different text from this topic and add 4–5 more examples of rhetorical devices. The entry in the Glossary will help you.

EXAMPLE	DEVICE	EFFECT
'Juliet is the sun' (l. 2)	Metaphor	Illustration, vividness
'Arise, fair sun, ...' (l. 3)	Personification	Vividness
'What's Montague?' (l. 19)	Rhetorical question	...
'With love's light wings' (l. 47)	...	...
...	...	...

TOPIC 04

Shakespeare today

After more than 400 years, Shakespeare's plays are still performed – and not just in English. They have also been filmed many times, and adapted into every genre from novels to operas. But just how relevant can his works still be today when there are much more contemporary writers dealing with the issues that interest us? These are the questions we look at in this topic.

Lars Eidinger as *Hamlet*. Shakespeare is number 1 in German theatres.

The 1996 film of *Romeo and Juliet* starring Leonardo DiCaprio and Claire Danes

The 1997 film *A Thousand Acres* – an adaptation of the novel of the same name by Jane Smiley – is based on Shakespeare's *King Lear*.

Collect ideas

▶ Activity chest 12

Work in groups to collect ideas about the questions below, then report to the class. You could use a 'Placemat'.

1. List reasons why people should continue to read or watch Shakespeare today.
2. Now list reasons why he may be problematic for modern audiences. Think of ways to solve these problems.
3. Discuss if and how these ideas might be seen as being untrue to Shakespeare.

1 Why bother with Shakespeare? (A web article)

The text below is from an German online magazine called *Terasof.*

Shakespeare in love? ... In love with Shakespeare!

Da war er wieder, der monatliche Rundruf aus der Terasof Redaktion an die freien Mitarbeiter: Wer möchte einen Artikel über William Shakespeare schreiben? Ich entschied mich dafür und begann sofort zu überlegen, wie ich an diesen großartigen Meister herantreten sollte. [...] Was mir bei der Recherche als erstes klar wurde: das Leben des Schriftstellers von Weltruf ist eine Quelle von Mutmaßungen und Legenden. Keine der Biographien, die mir zur Verfügung standen, noch deren Quellen, verbürgen sich für ihre Aussagen. Teilweise heißt es gar, Shakespeare wäre ein Plagiator gewesen oder habe sich zumindest bei anderen Autoren mehr als nur inspirieren lassen. War Shakespeare eventuell eine Frau, die unter Pseudonym schrieb? Oder gar eine Gruppe von Schriftstellern, die im Namen des einen Dichters ihre Stücke verfasste? Da keine dieser Behauptungen zweifelsfrei belegt sind, entschied ich mich, für diesen Artikel von Shakespeare als eine männliche Figur auszugehen.

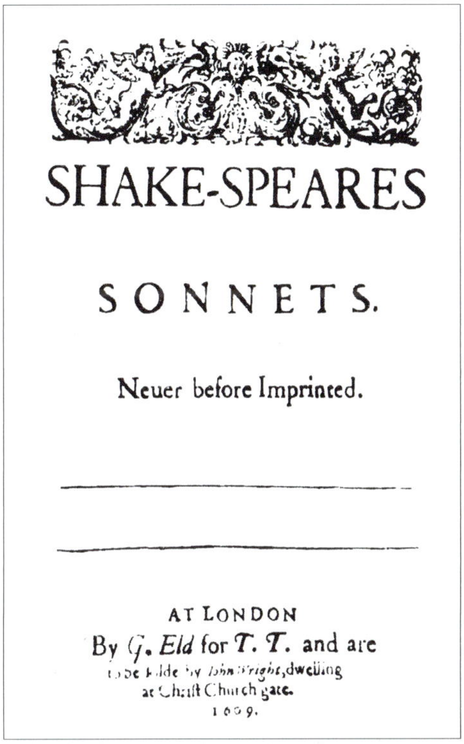
SHAKE-SPEARES

SONNETS.

Neuer before Imprinted.

AT LONDON
By G. Eld for T. T. and are
to be solde by Iohn Wright, dwelling
at Christ Church gate.
1609.

Denn, was schlussendlich auch immer der Wahrheit entsprechen mag, eines ist doch gewiss: William Shakespeare ist unbenommen der weltweit bekannteste Autor und wohl immer noch meistgespielte Dramatiker auf den Bühnen dieser Erde. An vielen Schulen ist er Pflichtlektüre und „Romeo und Julia" ist wohl eines der bekanntesten Liebespaare der Welt. Worauf gründet sich dieser Weltruhm? Auch dieser Frage möchte ich versuchen auf den Grund zu gehen.

Als ich mich letztens mit einem Schauspieler unterhielt, zitierte er eine längere Passage aus einem Stück von Shakespeare, die ihn an unsere momentane Situation erinnerte. „Magst du Shakespeare?", fragte ich ihn. Er antwortete, dass er ihm einer der, wenn nicht sogar DER liebste Bühnenautor wäre. Auf die Frage nach dem Warum antwortete er: „Der hat irgendwie ... alles ... und das in jedem Stück. Ich habe das Gefühl, dass es immer darauf hinausläuft, dass es kein Gut und Böse gibt und die Gegensätze aufgehoben bzw. miteinander vereint werden. Und dabei macht's auch noch verdammt viel Spaß." Nach längerem Überlegen fügte er hinzu: „Immer, wenn ich eines seiner Stücke lese, fühle ich mich, als würde ich mich von innen her säubern." [...]

Was macht die Faszination seiner Lyrik und vor allem der großartigen Theaterstücke bis zum heutigen Tag aus? Ich erachte am Shakespearschen Werk als besonders beeindruckend seine fortschrittliche Auffassung der Welt, die immer dazu mahnt, nach der Vereinigung der Gegensätze zu streben; das klassischste Beispiel ist auch hier wieder einmal „Romeo und Julia" – die Entzweiung der beiden Familien, die zu nichts anderem als Tod und Verzweiflung führt. [...]

Andererseits bieten die shakespearschen Komödien eine wunderbare Unterhaltung, die einen jedoch nie die inhaltliche Tiefe vermissen lassen und die seine

Stücke zu einem so außergewöhnlichen Erlebnis machen. Wahrscheinlich liegt hierin Shakespeares größte Qualität: Universelle Themen, die bis zum heutigen Tag Bestand haben – Mord und Todschlag, Liebe und Lust, die Frage nach unserer wahren Herkunft, unserer Bestimmung, das Streben nach der Wahrheit und natürlich eine starke Portion Humor. Eigentlich haben seine Stücke alle Zutaten, die sich eine große Hollywood Kinoproduktion nur wünschen kann. Dementsprechend lang ist auch die Liste seiner verfilmten Werke: Alleine vom „Hamlet" gibt es 12 Verfilmungen, „Romeo und Julia" wurde bereits sechs Mal als Kinofilm adaptiert und „Othello" erfuhr im Jahr 2000 mit der Hollywoodadaption „O" seine fünfte filmische Auferstehung, um nur einige zu nennen. Weit über hundert Maler haben sich von seinen Werken zu Illustrationen inspirieren lassen und auch in der Musik wird sein Einfluss deutlich: „Othello" und „Macbeth" wurden von Verdi als Oper vertont, ein wunderbares Ballett ist „Romeo und Julia" von Sergei Prokofiew, der „Sommernachtstraum" in der Vertonung von Henry Purcell ist ein weiteres bekanntes Exempel und später benutzte der Komponist und Dirigent Leonhard Bernstein das Thema von „Romeo und Julia" für sein weltberühmtes Musical, die „West Side Story". Auch bei modernen Komponisten finden sich einige von Shakespeare inspirierte Kompositionen, wie zum Beispiel der „Hamlet" von Hermann Reutter.

Obwohl zu Shakespeares Zeiten von dem Begriff Psychologie noch keine Rede war, ist die Zeichnung seiner Figuren auf eine Art und Weise psychologisch, die in der Literatur bis heute Seinesgleichen sucht. So sagte Thomas Mann in einem Interview einer schwedischen Tageszeitung: „Shakespeare ist meiner Meinung nach der größte Psychoanalytiker, der je gelebt hat."

Aber lassen Sie sich durch so hohes und durchaus qualifiziertes Lob nicht davon abschrecken, sich mit Shakespeares Werken zu beschäftigen: Shakespeare ist weit, tief und groß und Shakespeare macht Spaß. Für den Neueinsteiger ein kleiner Tip: geben Sie nicht so schnell auf, man muss sich erst einlesen, bis man den Stil und die phantastischen Geschichten genießen kann, aber ich verspreche Ihnen: Seine Werke sind eine wahre Freude, spannend und eine große Erbauung.

[From: www.terasof.de]

▶ Skills 9.7

A Mediation

In English outline the argument of the text.

B Reacting to the text

▶ Skills 7.4

1. Work in groups and prepare presentations on the following films, which are all adaptations of Shakespeare plays:
   Throne of Blood (1957) • *A Midsummer Night's Dream* (1999) • *O* (2001)
   The Merchant of Venice (2002) • *Coriolanus* (2011)
   Find out which plays they are based on and how the directors have managed to adapt the plots to modern times and topics.
2. Point out the ways in which these films support the ideas in the text you have just read.
3. Talk in class. Which of the films would you most like to see? Why?

2 Problems with Shakespeare (A newspaper feature article)

The following article by Emma Haughton from the British quality newspaper *The Independent* examines why it is difficult even for many English-speaking people to understand Shakespeare today.

A Before you read

Look at the picture below, which is from a modern production of *The Merchant of Venice*. Discuss whether you find it suitable as a modern version of a Shakespeare play.

Shakespeare's in danger. We have to act now to avoid a great tragedy

The Merchant of Venice

The other day I took my family to see one of my favourite Shakespeare plays. You'll love it, I told them. Nearly three hours later we tottered out into the night. Desperate to find something kind to say (there were friends involved), we praised one actor's Jim Carrey imitations and the flashing TV screens all over the postmodern set. And a costume made out of CDs that flashed like disco lights. And one character's use of a mobile phone. The rest was silence.

An American friend walked out of a Globe production recently, claiming that it was insulting her child's intelligence. That sums up the problem of so many contemporary productions; much of the Shakespeare we see now is unintelligent. The actors can't understand the words and compensate with silly antics. If the protagonist of the play I saw had lain down and kicked his legs in the air one more time I would have thrown a shoe at him. Directors, unable themselves, I suspect, to understand the text, resort to gimmicks, hiring designers to make the production more 'relevant' or 'meaningful'. […]. Boredom and Shakespeare go increasingly hand in hand.

At some point during the interminable evening, I found myself thinking the unthinkable: why bother with Shakespeare today? Why not relegate him to the dusty shelves along with Chaucer and the dozens of other Great Unreads in the literary canon? Why are we still so obsessed with Shakespeare that we insist on boring teenagers out of their minds with plays in a language they find foreign? Isn't it time to rethink our relationship with the Bard?

Now, I am not advocating the silly, elitist idea that Shakespeare is so irrelevant to today that students should study the cultural significance of Hollyoaks instead. I believe there is such a thing as great literature, and it is important that every generation should have access to it. I've always been a believer in the importance of Shakespeare for everyone, because not only did he create some of the most wonderful characters ever to grace a stage, but his language is truly marvellous. […] But my children don't have that language in their heads. All a bad production will do is deter them from going back to Shakespeare in the future.

The problem with Shakespeare today is linguistic. The language has become obsolete, Shakespeare's jokes are meaningless, his witticisms miss their target. It isn't the actors' fault: all they can do is struggle to make sense of a language that might as well be Tibetan. […]

2 *totter:* walk unsteadily
9 *contemporary:* (here) modern
10 *antics:* stupid behaviour
13 *resort to sth.:* make use of sth. when there is no other solution
16 *interminable:* long and boring
17 *relegate sth.:* move sth.
18 *Chaucer:* English poet (c. 1343–1400)
21 *the Bard:* nickname for Shakespeare
23 *Hollyoaks:* popular British TV soap opera
27 *marvellous:* great, fantastic
31 *obsolete:* no longer used
witticism: clever and funny remark

Some of the best productions I've seen have not been in English but in German, Spanish, Italian, Japanese and Czech. The plays have been lovingly dissected and translated. The directors don't have to resort to trick lighting and other gimmicks, because the actors understand what they're saying and the audience responds. There is an apocryphal story about a foreign director saying he pitied the English, because they could only read Shakespeare in the original. The other night the full truth of that came home to me. Shakespeare in other languages can have real significance, because people understand him. English audiences can only struggle.

What we need are good English translators to take Shakespeare in hand and liberate him for a new generation. [...] We need to throw away the outdated notion that everyone can understand Shakespeare if only they are exposed to his works, and get down to the business of making sure that people do understand him. Of course, some plays are more accessible than others: some of the tragedies still stand up reasonably well, as do some of the histories. The biggest problem is with the comedies. Maybe that is the best place to start. What we need are two versions of Shakespeare's plays: the original written version for anyone with specialist knowledge of Renaissance English; and the performance version, in good modern English. Shakespeare would doubtless be grateful. What writers want to feel that audiences can't understand their jokes? Please, someone out there, commission a good English translation of Shakespeare and save the Bard from extinction.

[From: *The Independent*, 14 November 2001]

35 *dissect sth.:* (here) study sth. in detail
38 *apocryphal* [ə'pɒkrɪfl]: well known but untrue
pity sb.: feel sorry for sb.
43 *outdated:* old-fashioned
53 *extinction:* Aussterben

B Understanding the text

1. Say whether the following statements are true or false according to the text. Correct the false sentences.
   a The writer doesn't like Shakespeare's plays.
   b The biggest problem with Shakespeare is that modern productions are 'silly'.
   c The writer's family were bored by the production they watched.
   d Some of the best productions the writer has seen were not in English.
   e The writer says the most difficult plays for modern English audiences to understand are Shakespeare's history plays because they are so out of date.
   f The writer tells a story about someone saying that non-English people have an advantage when it comes to watching Shakespeare plays.
   g The writer suggests we should throw away Shakespeare's plays and replace them with versions in contemporary English.
2. Summarise in your own words the main points of the article.

C Analysing the text

1. Identify the text type and the writer's intentions. Point out what devices she uses to achieve her aims and their effect on the reader.
2. Analyse the title of this article.

D Reacting to the text

Comment on the idea that it is easier for non-English readers to understand Shakespeare.

3 Helping to understand? (A modern translation and a comic book)

Reading Shakespeare is a demanding task, even for native speakers of English. You are going to look at two different approaches that might help.

A Before you read

1. The first approach is a kind of translation of Shakespeare into modern English offered by the American website No fear Shakespeare. Speculate who this website might be meant for. What might be the advantages and disadvantages of a modern English version?
2. For this text and the next, you are going to look at a scene from *Macbeth*. Look back to page 195. The picture of the man with blood on his hands shows Macbeth and his wife in this scene. Describe the picture and speculate about what is going on and how Macbeth is feeling.

Text 1: No fear Shakespeare: *Macbeth* Act 2, Scene 2

3 *deed:* Tat
4 *cricket:* Grille
10 *chamber:* room
11 *Donalbain:* the king's son
19 *Malcom:* the king's son

Macbeth has just murdered King Duncan while he slept. His wife, Lady Macbeth, is downstairs waiting for him. Their plan has been that Macbeth would use two daggers to kill the king, then leave them with the two servants who guard him, so that it looks as if they are the murderers. The two servants have been given a lot to drink so that they will sleep through the murder.

	ORIGINAL TEXT	MODERN TEXT
	Enter MACBETH, with bloody daggers	*MACBETH enters carrying bloody daggers*
Lady Macbeth	My husband!	My husband!
Macbeth	I have done the deed. Didst thou not hear a noise?	I have done the deed. Did you hear a noise?
Lady Macbeth	I heard the owl scream and the crickets cry. Did not you speak?	I heard the owl scream and the crickets cry. Didn't you say something?
Macbeth	When?	When?
Lady Macbeth	Now.	Just now.
Macbeth	As I descended?	As I came down?
Lady Macbeth	Ay.	Yes.
Macbeth	Hark! Who lies i' th' second chamber?	Listen! Who's sleeping in the second chamber?
Lady Macbeth	Donalbain.	Donalbain.
Macbeth	(looking at his hands) This is a sorry sight.	(looking at his bloody hands) This is a sorry sight.
Lady Macbeth	A foolish thought, to say a sorry sight.	That's a stupid thing to say.
Macbeth	There's one did laugh in 's sleep, and one cried. 'Murder!' That they did wake each other. I stood and heard them. But they did say their prayers, and addressed them Again to sleep.	One of the servants laughed in his sleep, and one cried, 'Murder!' and they woke each other up. I stood and listened to them, but then they said their prayers and went back to sleep.
Lady Macbeth	There are two lodged together.	Malcolm and Donalbain are asleep in the same room.

Macbeth	One cried, 'God bless us!' and 'Amen' the other, As they had seen me with these hangman's hands. List'ning their fear I could not say 'Amen,' When they did say 'God bless us!'	One servant cried, 'God bless us!' and the other replied, 'Amen,' as if they had seen my bloody hands. Listening to their frightened voices, I couldn't reply 'Amen' when they said 'God bless us!'
Lady Macbeth	Consider it not so deeply.	Don't think about it so much.
Macbeth	But wherefore could not I pronounce 'Amen'? I had most need of blessing, and 'Amen' Stuck in my throat.	But why couldn't I say 'Amen'? I desperately needed God's blessing, but the word 'Amen' stuck in my throat.
Lady Macbeth	These deeds must not be thought After these ways. So, it will make us mad.	We can't think that way about what we did. If we do, it'll drive us crazy.
Macbeth	Methought I heard a voice cry, 'Sleep no more! Macbeth does murder sleep' – the innocent sleep, Sleep that knits up the raveled sleave of care, The death of each day's life, sore labor's bath, Balm of hurt minds, great nature's second course, Chief nourisher in life's feast.	I thought I heard a voice cry, 'Sleep no more! Macbeth is murdering sleep.' Innocent sleep. Sleep that soothes away all our worries. Sleep that puts each day to rest. Sleep that relieves the weary laborer and heals hurt minds. Sleep, the main course in life's feast, and the most nourishing.
Lady Macbeth	What do you mean?	What are you talking about?
Macbeth	Still it cried, 'Sleep no more!' to all the house. 'Glamis hath murdered sleep, and therefore Cawdor Shall sleep no more. Macbeth shall sleep no more.'	The voice kept crying, 'Sleep no more!' to everyone in the house. 'Macbeth has murdered sleep, and therefore Macbeth will sleep no more.'
Lady Macbeth	Who was it that thus cried? Why, worthy thane, You do unbend your noble strength to think So brainsickly of things. Go get some water, And wash this filthy witness from your hand. Why did you bring these daggers from the place? They must lie there. Go carry them and smear The sleepy grooms with blood.	Who said that? Why, my worthy lord, you let yourself become weak when you think about things in this cowardly way. Go get some water and wash this bloody evidence from your hands. Why did you carry these daggers out of the room? They have to stay there. Go take them back and smear the sleeping guards with the blood.

[From: www.sparknotes.com]

27 *blessing:* Segen
36 *nourishing:* (here) healthy
43 *cowardly:* not brave
46 *smear sth.:* etwas beschmieren

B Understanding the scene

1. Complete the following sentences, then give an oral summary of the scene.
- a Macbeth comes down to where his wife is waiting and tells her that …
- b Macbeth looks at his hands and says …. This tells us that …
- c Lady Macbeth is … when he says this. She says that …
- d Macbeth tells his wife about the servants and that he could not …
- e Lady Macbeth gives him the advice that … and adds that …
- f Macbeth then talks at length about … He feels that … This tells us that …
- g Lady Macbeth responds by saying that …
- h At the end she talks very practically and tells her husband to …

2. One of the features of this scene is that Macbeth talks about hearing noises. Identify these passages. Point out what this tells you about his state of mind.

✕ **Extra** Divide the class into two. One half acts out the scene with the original text, the other with the modern text. Think as usual about stage directions, actions, conveying emotions etc. Compare the two versions.

C Analysing the scenes

1. Using your summary, compare Macbeth and Lady Macbeth in this scene. Who would you say is the dominant character? Explain. Comment also on the way they communicate (esp. ll. 10–25). Explain what this tells us about their characters and their relationship.
2. a Analyse Shakespeare's main intentions in this scene.

This scene takes place	just after Macbeth has …	
In it, Shakespeare now	wants to show us how Macbeth and his wife	feel / react to …
His main aim is	to explore / portray Macbeth's feelings of …	

b Looking at the original text, explain how he achieves his goals and what effect these techniques have on the audience. Consider the following aspects:
- the length of the lines, especially at the beginning;
- how the two characters speak and interact;
- the references to hearing noises;
- the images that Shakespeare uses to show us Macbeth's state of mind. Look especially at ll. 22, 31–36.

The short lines at the beginning	allow the audience to see / create the effect that …
In the scene	the two characters speak quite differently.
Lady Macbeth uses generally shorter sentences whereas Macbeth … She is also practical while Macbeth is … For example, … The effect on the audience of this is that …	
There are several references to hearing noises …	From these the audience understands that …
Shakespeare uses the following images to show Macbeth's state of mind. In lines …	
These give the audience a clear / concrete insight into his emotions. So, for example, …	

3. Compare the original and the modern version and say how helpful you find the modern one. Comment also on the layout of the modern text and what this might tell us about the writers' intention.

D Reacting to the texts

1. Imagine that you have been given this scene to study for homework or maybe that you are planning to put on a production of *Macbeth* (the original version) in your school. How exactly might you use the No fear Shakespeare website to help you? Explain.
2. Could you imagine putting on a production of the play using the No fear Shakespeare text (or a similar translation)? Why (not)?

Text 2: Comic Book Shakespeare: *Macbeth* Act 2, Scene 2

The text and pictures below are from a series of books published in the UK that present Shakespeare's most famous plays as comic strips.

A Before you read

Comics are a combination of (short) text and pictures. Go back to the extract from *Macbeth* and say which aspects of the text could be shown in the pictures and which text elements could be kept in the speech bubbles or captions.

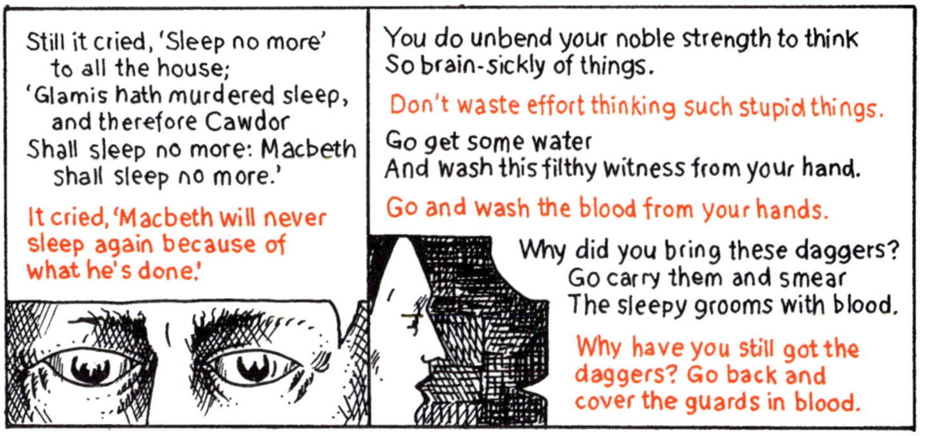

[From: *Comic Book Shakespeare: Macbeth* by Simon Greaves, 2003]

B Understanding the comic strip

Compare this version of the scene to how you imagined it and comment on it.

C Analysing the comic strip

Work in groups again, then present your ideas to the class.

▶ Skills 2.1

1. Analyse how the scene is presented as a comic strip. Think of text, visuals, etc.
2. The writer and artist of this and other Shakespeare comic books is British writer, designer and former teacher Simon Greaves. Speculate about his intentions with the books. What kind of reader do you imagine he writes them for? How does Greaves try to cater for their needs?

D Reacting to the comic strip

1. Talk in class. A few years ago, a British popular newspaper described this kind of comic book as 'dumbing down Shakespeare for bored schoolkids'. Comment on this statement.
2. Compare the comic book extract and the No Fear Shakespeare texts and say which you prefer and why.
3. Write an email to Simon Greaves at his website saying what you think of his comic book series and why.

SEQUENCE

06

FUTURE WORLD(S)

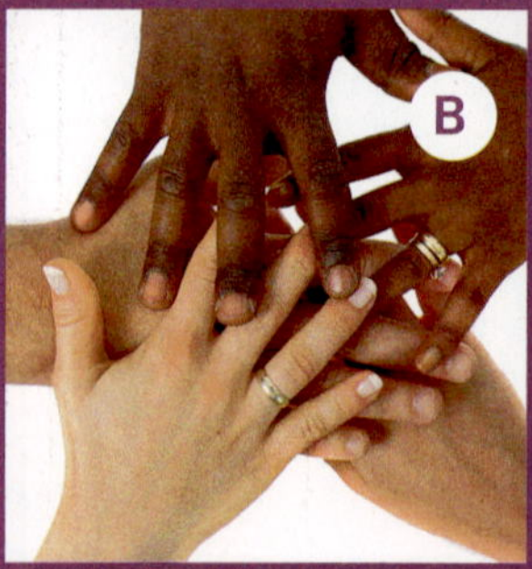

All of us would probably like to be able to look into the future. What will life be like in, say, 100 years from now? Of course, we hope it will be better – 'perfect' even. On the other hand, mankind has made plenty of mistakes in the past and sometimes with disastrous consequences. One thing is sure: the world of the future depends on what we do today.

Collect ideas

▶ Skills 2.1

1. Describe the pictures and find a suitable title for each one.
2. Now work in groups to look at the pictures in more detail.

   a Collect your ideas in a chart like the one below, then report to the class.

PICTURE	THEME	WHAT VISION OF THE FUTURE IS EXPRESSED?	WHAT AREAS OF LIFE ARE INVOLVED IN THESE VISIONS (SCIENCE, POLITICS, SOCIETY…?)?
A	e.g. future living (cities)	…	…
…			

   b Discuss whether the pictures shed a positive or negative light on the future.

3. Talk in class again. Explain why 'the world of the future depends on today'. What are some of the important issues for you that you need to be aware of – and should remain aware of during your lives?

Extra Make a mindmap to collect the most important vocabulary you will need in this sequence.

C

D

E

F

G

TOPIC

01

Imagining a different world

1 100 years from now (An old magazine article)

In December 1900, a popular American magazine, *The Ladies' Home Journal*, published an article in which experts wrote about how they imagined the world (America) 100 years in the future – in the year 2000. You are going to read some of the predictions.

New York, 1900

A Before you read

1. Describe the picture above. What does it suggest to you about how New York and life in general (in America or Europe) was different in 1900 from today? Think of things like technology, travel, lifestyle, ... You may also add aspects like health, communication or housing.
2. Speculate what predictions the experts back then may have made about life today.

2 *sanitation:* system that keeps everything clean
8 *cinder:* burnt wood or coal
11 *hay-wagon:* vehicle for transporting dried grass for animals
plow: equipment for digging soil on a farm
harrow: equipment to prepare farm land for plants
hay-rake: tool for collecting dried grass for animals
13 *sleigh:* vehicle that slides over snow
14 *substitute sth. for sth.:* replace sth. with sth.
harness: pieces of leather and metal that connect a horse to a carriage
15 *scarce:* rare
yoke: piece of wood attached to two animals so they can pull heavy weights

Life in the year 2000

Prediction #2: The American will be taller by from one to two inches. His increase of stature will result from better health, due to vast reforms in medicine, sanitation, food and athletics. He will live fifty years instead of thirty-five as at present [...].
Prediction #5: Trains will run two miles a minute, normally; express trains one hundred and fifty miles an hour. To go from New York to San Francisco will take a day and a night by fast express. There will be cigar-shaped electric locomotives hauling long trains of cars. Cars will, like houses, be artificially cooled. Along the railroads there will be no smoke, no cinders, because coal will neither be carried nor burned. [...]
Prediction #6: Automobiles will be cheaper than horses are today. Farmers will own automobile hay-wagons, automobile truck-wagons, plows, harrows and hay-rakes. A one-pound motor in one of these vehicles will do the work of a pair of horses or more. Children will ride in automobile sleighs in winter. Automobiles will have been substituted for every horse vehicle now known. [...] The horse in harness will be as scarce, if, indeed, not even scarcer, then as the yoked ox is today.
Prediction #7: There will be air-ships, but they will not successfully compete with surface cars and water vessels for passenger or freight traffic. They will be

maintained as deadly war-vessels by all military nations. Some will transport men and goods. Others will be used by scientists making observations at great heights above the earth.

Prediction #9: Photographs will be telegraphed from any distance. If there be a battle in China a hundred years hence snapshots of its most striking events will be published in the newspapers an hour later. Even today photographs are being telegraphed over short distances. Photographs will reproduce all of Nature's colors.

Prediction #13: Strawberries as Large as Apples will be eaten by our great-great-grandchildren for their Christmas dinners a hundred years hence. Raspberries and blackberries will be as large. One will suffice for the fruit course of each person.

Prediction #18: Telephones Around the World. Wireless telephone and telegraph circuits will span the world. A husband in the middle of the Atlantic will be able to converse with his wife sitting in her boudoir in Chicago. We will be able to telephone to China quite as readily as we now talk from New York to Brooklyn. By an automatic signal they will connect with any circuit in their locality without the intervention of a 'hello girl'.

Telephone operators ('hello girls') at a telephone exchange circa 1900

Prediction #20: Coal will not be used for heating or cooking. It will be scarce, but not entirely exhausted. The earth's hard coal will last until the year 2050 or 2100; its soft-coal mines until 2200 or 2300. Meanwhile both kinds of coal will have become more and more expensive. Man will have found electricity manufactured by waterpower to be much cheaper. Every river or creek with any suitable fall will be equipped with water-motors, turning dynamos, making electricity.

Prediction #23: Ready-cooked meals will be bought from establishments similar to our bakeries of today. They will purchase materials in tremendous wholesale quantities and sell the cooked foods at a price much lower than the cost of individual cooking. Food will be served hot or cold to private houses in pneumatic tubes or automobile wagons. The meal being over, the dishes used will be packed and returned to the cooking establishments where they will be washed.

[From: www.yorktownhistory.org]

18 *maintain sth.:* keep sth. in good condition
war-vessel: military vehicle used in war
27 *suffice:* be enough
course: specific part of a meal
29 *circuit:* path of wires through which electricity passes
span sth.: go around sth.
30 *boudoir:* bedroom
33 *intervention:* involvement
35 *exhausted:* used up
38 *creek:* very small river
41 *wholesale quantity:* large amounts that can be sold again to make a profit
43 *pneumatic tube:* Druckluft-schlauch

B Understanding the text

1. Look through the text and identify the different areas of life that it deals with. Make a mindmap and compare with a partner. There are some ideas below to get you started.

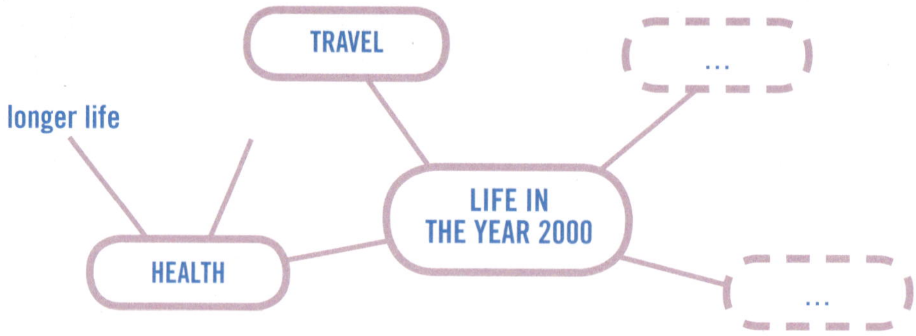

2. Point out whether the writers seem to be optimistic or pessimistic about life in a hundred years time.

C Analysing the text

▶ Glossary 1.1

▶ Glossary 3.2

▶ Skills 1.2.2; 3.2

1. Point out the authors' intention and say in which category (or categories) of text type it belongs. Bear in mind where the text appeared.
2. Examine how the writers put across their message and the effect these techniques might have on the reader. Take the following into account:
   - the structure and layout of the text;
   - the style of language used;
   - the use of tenses.

D Reacting to the text

▶ Activity chest 9

1. The most obvious thing about the text, of course, is that it contains predictions about the time in which we live today. So how accurate were the predictions? Work in groups, then report to the class. Identify the predictions which have become true (or nearly true) and which turned out to be wrong. Sum up by describing your reaction to their accuracy.
2. Talk in class:
   - Why might it be important to know about the future and for whom?
   - Looking at this text, how possible is it in your opinion to be accurate about the future? How would you say these predictions were made? What might we learn from this when we ourselves try to predict the future?
3. Working alone or in a group, write some predictions about how you imagine life will be in the year 2100. Remember to use the same format, style, tenses etc. as in the text above. Present your ideas to the class. You could do this by putting your predictions on a poster and organising a 'Gallery walk'.

2 Life in *1984* (Extracts from a novel)

One of the phrases from literature that has gone into everyday use in the English language is: 'Big Brother is watching you' – and Big Brother even gave his name to a popular reality TV show. The words are from the novel *1984*, written in 1948 by George Orwell. You are going to read two extracts. The first one is how the novel starts.

George Orwell

Extract 1

It was a bright cold day in April, and the clocks were striking thirteen. Winston Smith, his chin nuzzled into his breast in an effort to escape the vile wind, slipped quickly through the glass doors of Victory Mansions, though not quickly enough to prevent a swirl of gritty dust from entering along with him.

The hallway smelt of boiled cabbage and old rag mats. At one end of it a coloured poster, too large for indoor display, had been tacked to the wall. It depicted simply an enormous face, more than a metre wide: the face of a man of about forty-five, with a heavy black moustache and ruggedly handsome features. Winston made for the stairs. It was no use trying the lift. Even at the best of times it was seldom working, and at present the electric current was cut off during daylight hours. It was part of the economy drive in preparation for Hate Week. The flat was seven flights up, and Winston, who was thirty-nine and had a varicose ulcer above his right ankle, went slowly, resting several times on the way. On each landing, opposite the lift-shaft, the poster with the enormous face gazed from the wall. It was one of those pictures which are so contrived that the eyes follow you about when you move. BIG BROTHER IS WATCHING YOU, the caption beneath it ran.

Inside the flat a fruity voice was reading out a list of figures which had something to do with the production of pig-iron. The voice came from an oblong metal plaque like a dulled mirror which formed part of the surface of the right-hand wall. Winston turned a switch and the voice sank somewhat, though the words were still distinguishable. The instrument (the telescreen, it was called) could be dimmed, but there was no way of shutting it off completely. He moved over to the window: a smallish, frail figure, the meagreness of his body merely emphasized by the blue overalls which were the uniform of the party. His hair was very fair, his face naturally sanguine, his skin roughened by coarse soap and blunt razor blades and the cold of the winter that had just ended.

Outside, even through the shut window-pane, the world looked cold. Down in the street little eddies of wind were whirling dust and torn paper into spirals, and though the sun was shining and the sky a harsh blue, there seemed to be no colour in anything, except the posters that were plastered everywhere. The black-moustachio'd face gazed down from every commanding corner. There was one on the house-front immediately opposite. BIG BROTHER IS WATCHING YOU, the caption said, while the dark eyes looked deep into Winston's own. Down at street level another poster, torn at one corner, flapped fitfully in the wind, alternately covering

2 *nuzzle (v):* (here) push
5 *boiled:* cooked in water
rag mat: small carpet
11 *economy drive:* Sparprogramm
12 *flight:* series of steps
varicose ulcer: swollen, painful veins
15 *contrive sth.:* design sth.
18 *fruity:* deep and pleasant sounding
19 *pig-iron:* type of iron that is not pure
oblong: rechteckig
20 *plaque:* flat object attached to a wall
dulled: not bright or shiny
24 *frail:* weak and thin
meagreness: small amount
26 *sanguine:* cheerful
coarse: not soft
blunt: not sharp
29 *eddy:* circular movement

and uncovering the single word INGSOC. In the far distance a helicopter skimmed down between the roofs, hovered for an instant like a bluebottle, and darted away again with a curving flight. It was the police patrol, snooping into people's windows. The patrols did not matter, however. Only the Thought Police mattered.

Behind Winston's back the voice from the telescreen was still babbling away about pig-iron and the overfulfilment of the Ninth Three-Year Plan. The telescreen received and transmitted simultaneously. Any sound that Winston made, above the level of a very low whisper, would be picked up by it, moreover, so long as he remained within the field of vision which the metal plaque commanded, he could be seen as well as heard. There was of course no way of knowing whether you were being watched at any given moment. How often, or on what system, the Thought Police plugged in on any individual wire was guesswork. It was even conceivable that they watched everybody all the time. But at any rate they could plug in your wire whenever they wanted to. You had to live – did live, from habit that became instinct – in the assumption that every sound you made was overheard, and, except in darkness, every movement scrutinized.

Winston kept his back turned to the telescreen. It was safer, though, as he well knew, even a back can be revealing. A kilometre away the Ministry of Truth, his place of work, towered vast and white above the grimy landscape. This, he thought with a sort of vague distaste – this was London, chief city of Airstrip One, itself the third most populous of the provinces of Oceania. He tried to squeeze out some childhood memory that should tell him whether London had always been quite like this. Were there always these vistas of rotting nineteenth-century houses, their sides shored up with baulks of timber, their windows patched with cardboard and their roofs with corrugated iron, their crazy garden walls sagging in all directions? And the bombed sites where the plaster dust swirled in the air and the willow-herb straggled over the heaps of rubble; and the places where the bombs had cleared a larger patch and there had sprung up sordid colonies of wooden dwellings like chicken-houses? But it was no use, he could not remember: nothing remained of his childhood except a series of bright-lit tableaux occurring against no background and mostly unintelligible.

The Ministry of Truth – Minitrue, in Newspeak – was startlingly different from any other object in sight. It was an enormous pyramidal structure of glittering white concrete, soaring up, terrace after terrace, 300 metres into the air. From where Winston stood it was just possible to read, picked out on its white face in elegant lettering, the three slogans of the Party:

WAR IS PEACE
FREEDOM IS SLAVERY
IGNORANCE IS STRENGTH

37 *hover:* stay in the same place in the air
bluebottle: large blue fly
38 *snoop:* search for private things
42 *transmit:* send electronic signals
59 *scrutinize sth.:* carefully examine sth.
66 *baulk of timber:* rough piece of wood
68 *sag:* hang or bend due to weakness
69 *willow-herb:* Weidenröschen
70 *straggle:* grow in an untidy way
rubble: broken pieces of a destroyed building
71 *sordid:* dirty
73 *tableaux:* artistic image

A Understanding the text

1. Make notes about what you learn about Winston in this extract and the society in which he lives. Compare with a partner, then report to the class. Consider:
   - the setting of the novel;
   - physical characteristics (buildings, people's flats, …);
   - features of the society (politics, …);
   - Winston himself.
2. Characterise the world in which Winston lives.

Winston's world can be described as …	because …
Winston lives under/in a	dictatorship / totalitarian state / surveillance society
It is a society in which …	the state constantly … / people are always …
Its citizens are kept under strict surveillance / being watched all the time	because … by …
The political system seems to make citizens …	careful / depressed / robotic

B Analysing the text

▶ Glossary 2.1

1. Fictional texts usually follow a certain structure. Describe the properties and function of the beginning of a fictional text and examine how the beginning of *1984* is a typical example.

▶ Glossary 3.2

2. Orwell very quickly creates an atmosphere at the start of his novel. Describe it and examine how he does this, thinking of his use of detail, language, descriptions and repetitions.
3. Analyse the party slogans and explain their effect on the reader.

Extract 2

In this extract, also near the beginning of the novel, we see Winston at work.

A Before you read

Talk in class. What impression have you already formed of the Ministry of Truth from the first extract? Speculate about what kind of work is done there.

With the deep, unconscious sigh which not even the nearness of the telescreen could prevent him from uttering when his day's work started, Winston pulled the speakwrite towards him, blew the dust from its mouthpiece, and put on his spectacles. Then he unrolled and clipped together four small cylinders of paper which had already flopped out of the pneumatic tube on the right-hand side of his desk.

In the walls of the cubicle there were three orifices. To the right of the speak-write, a small pneumatic tube for written messages, to the left, a larger one for newspapers; and in the side wall, within easy reach of Winston's arm, a large oblong slit protected by a wire grating. This last was for the disposal of waste paper. Similar slits existed in thousands or tens of thousands throughout the building, not only in every room but at short intervals in every corridor. For some

6 *pneumatic tube:* Druckluftschlauch
7 *orifice:* hole
10 *wire grating:* Drahtfilter
disposal of sth.: act of throwing sth. away

John Hurt in the 1984 film version of the novel

reason they were nicknamed memory holes. When one knew that any document was due for destruction, or even when one saw a scrap of waste paper lying about, it was an automatic action to lift the flap of the nearest memory hole and drop it in, whereupon it would be whirled away on a current of warm air to the enormous furnaces which were hidden somewhere in the recesses of the building.

Winston examined the four slips of paper which he had unrolled. Each contained a message of only one or two lines, in the abbreviated jargon — not actually Newspeak, but consisting largely of Newspeak words — which was used in the Ministry for internal purposes. They ran:

times 17.3.84 bb speech malreported africa rectify

times 19.12.83 forecasts 3 yp 4th quarter 83 misprints verify current issue

times 14.2.84 miniplenty malquoted chocolate rectify

times 3.12.83 reporting bb dayorder doubleplusungood refs unpersons rewrite fullwise upsub antefiling

With a faint feeling of satisfaction Winston laid the fourth message aside. It was an intricate and responsible job and had better be dealt with last. The other three were routine matters, though the second one would probably mean some tedious wading through lists of figures.

Winston dialled 'back numbers' on the telescreen and called for the appropriate issues of *The Times*, which slid out of the pneumatic tube after only a few minutes' delay. The messages he had received referred to articles or news items which for one reason or another it was thought necessary to alter, or, as the official phrase had it, to rectify. For example, it appeared from 'The Times' of the seventeenth of March that Big Brother, in his speech of the previous day, had predicted that the South Indian front would remain quiet but that a Eurasian offensive would shortly be launched in North Africa. As it happened, the Eurasian Higher Command had launched its offensive in South India and left North Africa alone. It was therefore necessary to rewrite a paragraph of Big Brother's speech, in such a way as to make him predict the thing that had actually happened. Or again, *The Times* of the nineteenth of December had published the official forecasts of the output of

17 *furnace:* place where things are burnt
22 *rectify sth.:* make sth. right that was originally wrong
28 *intricate:* complicated, with lots of small details
30 *wade (v):* (here) sort with difficulty
34 *alter sth.:* change sth.

various classes of consumption goods in the fourth quarter of 1983, which was also the sixth quarter of the Ninth Three-Year Plan. Today's issue contained a statement of the actual output, from which it appeared that the forecasts were in every instance grossly wrong. Winston's job was to rectify the original figures by making them agree with the later ones. As for the third message, it referred to a very simple error which could be set right in a couple of minutes. As short a time ago as February, the Ministry of Plenty had issued a promise (a 'categorical pledge' were the official words) that there would be no reduction of the chocolate ration during 1984. Actually, as Winston was aware, the chocolate ration was to be reduced from thirty grammes to twenty at the end of the present week. All that was needed was to substitute for the original promise a warning that it would probably be necessary to reduce the ration at some time in April.

As soon as Winston had dealt with each of the messages, he clipped his speakwritten corrections to the appropriate copy of *The Times* and pushed them into the pneumatic tube. Then, with a movement which was as nearly as possible unconscious, he crumpled up the original message and any notes that he himself had made, and dropped them into the memory hole to be devoured by the flames.

[From: *Nineteen eighty-four* by George Orwell, 1948]

43 *consumption goods:* food
49 *pledge:* serious promise
65 *devour sth.:* (here) destroy sth.

B Understanding the text

1. Imagine that you could interview Winston about his job. Collect questions, including ideas about how he might feel about his work, and imagine how he would answer them. One student now comes to the front of the class and plays the role of Winston. Ask questions.
2. Describe what function Winston's work fulfils for the society in *1984*.

C Analysing the text

▶ Glossary 2.2.1

1. Analyse the point of view from which the novel is told.
2. Examine the meaning of Newspeak words such as 'malreport', 'doubleplusungood', 'unperson' (ll. 25–29) and describe how they are constructed. What do they suggest about the world Winston lives in?

▶ Glossary 2.1

✕ **Extra** The names 'Ministry of Plenty' and 'Ministry of Truth', and their abbreviations 'miniplenty' and 'minitrue', are examples of irony. Explain how they are ironic, considering the kind of job Winston does in the Ministry of Truth.

D Reacting to the text

▶ Skills 5.2c

Write a review of these two texts for a school website. Remember to point out your personal opinion of what you have read and what you feel it can (or can't) teach us about society.

3 Paradise on Earth? (A text from a website)

The text below is from the website of a real place called Auroville. People there have not only dreamed of a different world, they have begun to create it.

A Before you read

Imagine your perfect place to live. Make a sketch or drawing and explain it orally or write a text describing its features.

What is Auroville?

Auroville is a universal township in the making for a population of up to 50,000 people from around the world. [...]

Why Auroville?

The purpose of Auroville is to realise human unity – in diversity. Today Auroville is recognised as the first and only internationally endorsed ongoing experiment in human unity and transformation of consciousness, also concerned with – and practically researching into – sustainable living and the future cultural, environmental, social and spiritual needs of mankind.

When did Auroville start?

On 28th February 1968 some 5,000 people assembled near the banyan tree at the centre of the future township for an inauguration ceremony attended by representatives of 124 nations, including all the States of India. [...]

Who are the Aurovilians?

They come from some 45 nations, from all age groups (from infancy to over eighty, averaging around 30), from all social classes, backgrounds and cultures, representing humanity as a whole. The population of the township is constantly growing, but currently stands at around 2,160 people, of whom approx one-third are Indian.

Overview of the city plan

► **Peace Area**

At the centre of the township lies the Peace Area, comprising the Matrimandir and its gardens, the amphitheatre with the Urn of Human Unity [...], and a lake to help create an atmosphere of calm and serenity and to serve as a groundwater recharge area.

► **Industrial Zone**

A 109-hectare area to the north of the Peace Area, the Industrial Zone, a zone for 'green' industries, is focused on Auroville's efforts towards a self-supporting township. It will contain small and medium-scale industries, training centres, arts and crafts, and the city's administration.

2 *township:* place where people live
6 *endorse sth.:* officially support sth.
8 *sustainable living:* way of living that can go on for a long time
12 *inauguration ceremony:* show or speech to officially start an organization
18 *approx:* approximately
21 *Matrimandir:* golden dome building in the centre of Auroville
23 *serenity:* state of calm and peacefulness
groundwater recharge: absorption of water into the ground
27 *self-supporting:* able to produce everything necessary without help of outsiders

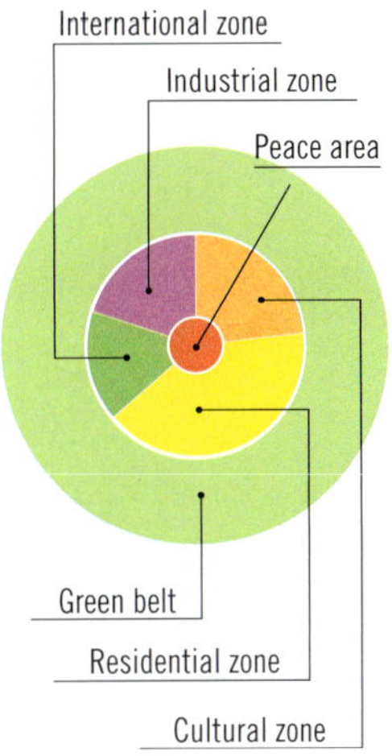

33 *radial:* going from a central point to the edge of a circle
34 *density:* Dichte
35 *habitat:* living environment
50 *dairy:* place where milk is kept and butter and cheese are made
orchard: land on which fruit trees are grown
51 *encroachment:* act of covering more and more of an area
54 *wasteland:* useless area of land

► **Residential Zone**

The largest of the four city zones, comprising of 189 hectares, the Residential Zone is bordered by parks on the north, south and west. Main access to the zone will be through the crown road with further traffic distribution via five radial roads that divide the zone into sectors of increasing densities. This zone wants to provide a well-adjusted habitat between individual and collective living. 55% of the area will be green and only 45% built surface, thereby creating an urban density balanced by nature.

► **International Zone**

The International Zone, a zone of 74 hectares to the west of the Peace Area, will host national and cultural pavilions, grouped by continents. Its central focus is to create a living demonstration of human unity in diversity through the expression of the genius and contribution of each nation to humanity.

► **Cultural Zone**

Planned on a 93-hectare area, situated to the east of the Peace Area, the Cultural Zone will be a site for applied research in education and artistic expression. Facilities for cultural, educational, art and sports activities will be located in this zone.

► **Green Belt**

The city area with a radius of 1.25 km. will be surrounded by a Green Belt of 1.25 km width. As a zone for organic farms, dairies, orchards, forests, and wildlife areas, this belt will act as a barrier against urban encroachment, provide a variety of habitats for wildlife, and serve as a source for food, timber, medicines etc. and as a place for recreation. Presently an area of 405 hectares, the Green Belt – though incomplete – stands as an example of successful transformation of wasteland into a vibrant eco-system. Its further planned extension with an additional 800 hectares will make it into a remarkable demonstration site for soil and water conservation, groundwater recharge, and environmental restoration. As lungs for the entire township, it will complete the healing process that Auroville started several decades ago.

[From: www.auroville.org]

B Understanding the text

Copy the chart below. Complete it in groups and then present your ideas to the class.

ZONES	FEATURES	INTENTION
Peace area	- area with an 'atmosphere of calm and serenity' (l. 23) - lake as a 'groundwater recharge' area (l. 57) - …	- relaxation, happiness - sustainability - …
Industrial zone	- small/medium 'green' industries - …	- self-support, business
…	…	…

C Reacting to the text

1. Imagine that you have just come to live in Auroville. Write an email to a friend back home explaining your decision and describing your everyday life.
2. Talk in class. Do you feel that Auroville is a model for a 'perfect world'?

4 Utopia

In 1516, the English philosopher Sir Thomas More wrote a book about an imaginary island on which life was ideal: there was no war, everyone had enough to eat, there was religious freedom, and the laws were fair for all. His island (and his book) was called *Utopia*. That term is still used today to talk about an ideal society.

Thomas More's island of Utopia – illustration from the original book

▶ Activity chest 15

You are going to use the activity 'Walk-talk-write' to collect and discuss your ideas about utopia.

1. In groups, collect ideas about what a perfect world would be characterised by, and imagine how this could be achieved. Think back to the texts you have read in this topic, but try to come up with some new ideas, too.
2. Write your ideas on a poster and position the posters around the classroom. Each poster should look like the one below – but at first, only fill in the two columns on the left.

CHARACTERISTICS	MEASURES	COMMENTS
… …	… …	… …

3. As a group, go round the classroom and discuss the other groups' utopias. Discuss them and add comments in the right column.
4. Discuss your results in class. Don't forget to consider the following points:
   - What sorts of utopias were there?
   - Was there a favourite utopia?
   - Do you feel now that it is possible to create a utopia at all?

✕ **Extra** Write a description of your idea of a perfect world and the measures to achieve it.

KEY FACTS Utopias and dystopias

The word *utopia* is a combination of the Greek prefix *eu-* ('good' or 'well') and the word topos ('place'). It was first used by Sir Thomas More in 1516 in his book *Utopia* to describe a perfect society.
Since then, the term *utopia* has been used as a literary term to describe fictional societies with faultless social, political and legal systems. However, literary utopias are extremely rare; the genre of dystopia is much more frequent. A dystopia presents a 'bad place', i.e. a society that relies on the extreme control of its members, often under the pretense of striving towards a utopian society. Dystopias often also explore the idea of abusing technology or the inability to cope with modern technology. Classic examples of dystopian novels are *Brave New World* by Aldous Huxley (1931), *Nineteen Eighty-Four* by George Orwell (1948) and *Fahrenheit 451* by Ray Bradbury (1953). Films such as *Never Let Me Go* (2010), *The Matrix* (1999–2003) or *Minority Report* (2002) are also examples of this genre.

TOPIC

02

Living in the digital society

The Industrial Age, which began with the Industrial Revolution, is now said to be over. Today, we live in a new era – the Information or Digital Age. There has been a new revolution and it, too, is changing how we live. It is people like you who will decide how this new age develops.

Collect ideas

1. Describe where, when and how you personally interact with the things you see in the pictures. What other devices, websites etc. can you also name that are part of the digital world in which you live?
2. Try to say how people led their lives before the things in the pictures were invented. For example, before there were mobile phones, people had to make concrete arrangements for meeting before they left the house.
3. Every massive change in society like the digital revolution brings with it advantages and disadvantages. Consider the technologies in the pictures again and say in what ways they could have positive and negative sides.

1 Living without your iPod (and the internet, and …)

(Extracts from a book)

In 2009, the author and journalist Susan Maushart decided to conduct an experiment. For six months, she and her three teenage children would all live without any digital technology – computers, TVs, mobile phones, iPods, video games, etc. She later wrote a book about their experiences. You are going to read two extracts from it.

Left to right: Bill, Susan Maushart, Sussy and Anni

A Before you read

1. When were the following technologies invented? Match them to the timeline below.

DVD – email – Facebook – laptop – mobile phone – mp3-player – PC – radio – telephone – TV – Twitter – World Wide Web – Youtube

1876 1896 1930 1971 1973 1976 1990 1991 1995 1997 2004 2005 '06

▶ Activity chest 5

2. Use the activity 'Double circles' to reflect about how you personally use digital technology, then report your ideas to the class.
   a How have family lives, friendships etc. been affected through the extended use of digital technology? List some ideas.
   b Imagine that you were going to take part in a similar experiment. List the three things you would find it hardest to give up with your reasons.

1 *pull the plug on sth.:* (here) no longer use sth..
5 *pond:* Becken
gracefully: in an attractive, controlled way
6 *unblinkingly:* (here) in a comfortable way
10 *dial-up:* internet that uses a telephone line
cordful: play on the word 'cordless' to mean 'with a cable'
11 *relic:* very old-fashioned object from the past
quaint: old-fashioned
inkwell: pot for holding ink for a pen
17 *molar:* big teeth used for chewing food
18 *syncopated:* shortened by deleting sounds or letters
19 *tribal tom-tom:* tall drum played with the hands
28 *shrug:* raise shoulders and then drop them to show lack of interest
32 *infuriating:* very annoying
33 *Magic Pudding:* a dessert in an Australian children's book that can never be finished
35 *nauseating:* sickening
36 *aka:* also known as
38 *force field:* barrier that cannot be seen
40 *dependency issue:* (here) problem of being unable to do basic things without electronic media
41 *recent:* that happened a short time ago
42 *sneak sth.:* take sth. secretly
43 *hooked:* addicted
44 *purge (n):* act of removing negative influences
45 *detox(n):* (here) process of removing harmful influences from one's life

Extract 1

This is a passage from the beginning of Maushart's book.

There were lots of reasons why we pulled the plug on our electronic media ... or, I should say, why I did, because heaven knows my children would have sooner volunteered to go without food, water or hair products. At ages fourteen, fifteen and eighteen, my daughters and my son don't use media. They inhabit media. And they do so exactly as fish *inhabit* a pond. Gracefully. Unblinkingly. And utterly without consciousness or curiosity as to how they got there.

They don't remember a time before e-mail, or instant messaging, or Google. Even the media of their own childhood – VHS and dial-up, Nintendo 64 and 'cordful' phones – they regard as relics, as quaint as inkwells. They collectively refer to civilization pre-high-definition flat screen as 'the black and white days'.

My kids – like yours, I'm guessing – are part of a generation that cut its teeth, literally and figuratively, on a keyboard, learning to say ''puter' along with 'Mama', 'Juice' and 'Now!'. They're kids who've had cellphones and wireless Internet longer than they've had molars. Who multitask their schoolwork alongside five or six other electronic inputs, to the syncopated beat of the Instant Messenger pulsing insistently like some distant tribal tom-tom.

Wait a minute. Did I say they do their schoolwork like that? Correction. They do their *life* like that.

When my children laugh, they don't say 'ha ha', they say 'LOL'. In fact, they conjugate it. ('LOL at this picture before I Photoshopped your nose, Mum!') They download movies and TV shows as casually as you or I might switch on the radio. And when I remind them piracy is a crime, they look at one another and go 'LOL'. These are kids who shrug when they lose their iPods, with all 5000 tunes and Lord-knows-what in the way of video clips, feature films and 'TV' shows (like, who watches TV on a television anymore?). 'There's plenty more where that came from,' their attitude says. And the most infuriating thing of all? They're right. The digital content that powers their world, like matter itself, can never truly be destroyed. Like the Magic Pudding of Australian legend, it's a dessert bar that never runs out of cheesecake.

There's so much that's wonderful, and at the same time nauseating, about that. The Winter Of Our Disconnect – aka The Experiment (as we all eventually came to call it) – was in some ways an accident waiting to happen. Over a period of years, I watched and worried as our media began to function as a force field separating my children from what my son, only halfironically, called RL (Real Life). But to be honest, the teenagers weren't the only ones with dependency issues. Although a relatively recent arrival to the global village, I'd been known to abuse information too. (Sneaking my iPhone into the toilet? Did I have no self-respect?) As a journalist, it was easy to hide my habit, but deep down I knew I was hooked.

The Winter Of Our Disconnect started out as a kind of purge. It ended up as so much more. Long story short: our digital detox messed with our heads, our hearts,

49 *self-imposed:* forced on one by oneself
50 *indelibly:* in a way impossible to forget or change

and our homework. It changed the way we ate and the way we slept, the way we 'friended', fought, planned, and played. It altered the very taste and texture of our family life. [...]

In the end, our family's self-imposed exile from the Information Age changed our lives indelibly – and infinitely for the better.

B Understanding the text

1. Summarise what Maushart says about her children in the extract.
2. Outline the experiment and what we learn about it from the text.

C Analysing the text

▶ Glossary 1.1

▶ Glossary 3.1, 3.2

1. Identify the writer, her intention when writing and the possible reader. Classify the text type.
2. Bearing in mind your answer to question 1, examine Maushart's writing style and its effect on the reader. Take the following into account:
   - the tone and style of the text;
   - the length of the sentences and paragraphs;
   - the use of quotations;
   - rhetorical devices such as alliteration, repetition and rhetorical questions.

IMPROVE YOUR WRITING ▶ Including examples and referencing

When writing an analysis of a text, it is essential not just to describe the results of your analysis, but to support them using the text. Basically, there are two steps in doing this:

1. Giving examples:
If, for example, you have found out that your text is fairly formal and probably written for an educated readership, you will have to justify why you think so. And to justify this, you should use examples:

The writer addresses an educated readership / obviously has a ... readership in mind. / This text is written for ...	
You can conclude this from the frequent use of .../ the way he/she ...	
For example, she often/frequently uses words such as ...	
The writer's attitude to ...	becomes obvious in words like ...

2. Referencing the lines:
Giving examples is not enough since your readers may want to go back to the text to see if they agree with your interpretation of the examples you give. So in order to make it easier for them to find the examples in the text, you need to reference the lines:

The writer uses many long/complex/short/incomplete sentences (cf. p.X, ll. Y–Z).
She refers to her children as '...' (p.X, ll. Y–Z).

D Reacting to the text

In class, discuss how accurate you think Maushart's description of today's teenagers is. Consider the following questions:
- Which of the things they do or the attitudes they have are also true for you?
- How realistic does she want to be and which effect does she want to achieve?

Extract 2

After three months of the experiment, Maushart talked to Bill, Anni and Sussy about how they felt. This is their conversation.

Midterm Interview

April 4, 2009

QUESTION Well, guys, we're at the halfway point. Three months! Can you believe it?

BILL It feels like longer.

ANNI To be honest, I haven't actually noticed it that much. I'm surprised how little I've missed it. I thought it would be just killing me. But it's been fine.

SUSSY The worst parts are there's never anything to do. I can't do homework when I want. And I can't go for walks 'cause I don't have my iPod.

QUESTION Because it's impossible to walk without an iPod?

SUSSY Yeah.

QUESTION You did some homework today, didn't you?

SUSSY Yeah, we had to go to McDonald's to use the Wi-Fi but they didn't have an electrical outlet so we went to the [...] Angel Café ... Yeah, it's hell nice in there. We stayed for three hours.

QUESTION Did you do homework all that time?

SUSSY MySpaced for a bit, but mostly, yeah.

QUESTION Has The Experiment affected the quality of your schoolwork?

BILL Nah.

ANNI Not really. It hasn't been a problem going to uni to get my work done.

QUESTION So all that stuff about 'I need the internet to do my homework' is ...

ANNI A total cover!

QUESTION Do you feel a different person in some ways?

BILL I'm not a different person but some aspects of my life have definitely changed. Basically, I'm playing sax more and reading more, yeah. But I think the technology thing was more of a trigger. Like, if everything went back on right now, I wouldn't change. Like, why would I? It's more fun than playing with the computer.

QUESTION Do you find you're listening to the radio more?

BILL Nah, radio is crap. I listen to my CDs, and that usually makes we want to play my sax, so ... [...]

QUESTION Would you say you spend more time thinking now?

ANNI Yeah. Like before I would spend heaps of time doing nothing, but it would take the form of maybe Facebook-stalking or something. Now, well, you find other ways to have fun. Going out more. Went through a big cooking phase for a while there, but that's died down now. Listening to the radio a lot more.

QUESTION What's that like?

ANNI Well, you miss the customization you have with your iPod. Like, you can't always have what you want when you want it – a song or a TV show or whatever. But you adjust.

12 *outlet:* Steckdose
22 *cover(n):* (here) reason that seems honest and true but hides true motivations
25 *sax* = saxophone
26 *trigger:* Auslöser
30 *crap:* (slang) really bad
33 *heaps:* lots, much
34 *stalking:* act of watching a person for a long period of time in a strange way
39 *customisation:* Anpassung

SUSSY I'm reading way more, and faster. I feel smarter. In the book section of MySpace most people are like, books? CBF!

QUESTION Yeah, but you've always been a reader.

SUSSY Yeah, but I'm reading more intense books now, and bigger ones. [...]

QUESTION Have there been any positives for you so far?

ANNI I think we're closer as a family, for sure.

QUESTION Why's that?

ANNI Because we talk more. It's like, 'There's people in this house ... Let's talk to them!' Suss and Bill come into my room now. It's been years since they've done that – just hang out and have conversations. Just to talk, you know?

QUESTION Has The Experiment changed your relationships at all?

SUSSY Anni and I are like we used to be. We're tight again.

QUESTION Is that out of desperation, or ...

SUSSY Probs! (Laughs)

QUESTION Seriously, how's it different?

SUSSY It's like, we chillax. We tell each other stuff now, like we used to. She helps me. I help her. [...]

QUESTION What about Bill? How's your relationship with him changed?

SUSSY Um, I want to kill him more, because of the sax. It's just. Soooo. LOUD!

[From: *The winter of our disconnect* by Susan Maushart, 2011]

43 *CBF = Can't Be Fucked (slang):* I don't care
54 *tight:* close, friendly
55 *desperation:* Verzweiflung
56 *probs* = probably
58 *chillax = chill + relax (slang):* calm down

E Understanding the text

1. Work in groups of three. Make a chart with three columns. Each of you collects what one of the children tells you in the interview. Then complete your chart with information from your group members.
2. Sum up the effect of the experiment on the family in a coherent text.

F Analysing the text

▶ Glossary 3
▶ Skills 1.2.2

Examine the format, language and style of the text and the effect it may have on the reader.

G Reacting to the two extracts

Work in groups of four. Imagine you are a family planning to do a similar experiment.

1. Make a role card for each player. The examples below may help you. Make sure to integrate opposing viewpoints so that you are going to have a lively discussion.

Family role	...
Your attitude to technology	frequent user, adores technology
Your intention in the discussion	to prevent the experiment

Family role	...
Your attitude to technology	frequent but critical user
Your intention in the discussion	...

2. Develop and practise your role play, then present it to the class.
3. Discuss all the role plays in class.

2 Virtual environments (Videos)

You are going to watch two videos about virtual reality.

DVD 16

Video 1: 'As real as it gets'

A Understanding the video

Watch the video and take notes. Give an oral summary of what kind of virtual reality the film deals with. Point out why the people in the video are doing what they are.

Oasis of the Seas: ship simulator
bridge (of a ship): part of a ship where the captain stands and steers the ship
refresher (course): course you do to repeat things you have learned before

B Reacting to the video

Simulations of this kind are already being used in many contexts. In groups, list areas that are using simulations already and point out exactly what their advantages could be. Then collect ideas for future applications of simulations.

DVD 17

Video 2: 'Be yourself'

A Before you watch

You are going to watch a video about Second Life. In class, describe what this is.

B Understanding the video

Watch the video and take notes on what you see and what you can read. Point out what you learn about Second Life here.

▶ Skills 4

C Analysing the video

1. Explain the intention of the video and examine how this is achieved. Consider the settings, the people and their actions, the background music.
2. Have a closer look at the captions. Describe their relationship to the pictures and examine the logical connection between the captions.

D Reacting to the two videos

Discuss both uses of virtual reality. Consider their functions, their advantages and their downsides.

3 Is Big Brother here already? (A newspaper article)

A Before you read

Talk in class.

1. Describe the picture on the right. Speculate about what it shows and explain its connection to the topic you're dealing with right now.
2. Would you say it gives a positive or negative impression? Explain.
3. Name other kinds of situations where the same sort of positive or negative effects might be felt.

data watchdog: organisation that checks that the government is acting legally with citizens' information
1 *commit social suicide:* (here) destroy connections between members of communities
5 *information commissioner:* head of an organisation that deals with how information is managed
6 *creeping:* gradual, slow
encroachment: act of taking over
civil liberty: laws established for the good of the community
7 *email monitoring:* act of checking other peoples' emails
CCTV (= closed-circuit television): Überwachungskamera
tracking of sth.: act of keeping records about sth.
10 *device:* Gerät
11 *combat sth.:* fight against sth., stop sth.
14 *benefit office:* Sozialamt
15 *pitch:* Tonhöhe
16 *pilot sth.:* test sth. by using it with a small group of people
18 *intrude into sth.:* (here) have an unwanted effect on sth.
20 *convenience:* Annehmlichkeit
affluent: rich
21 *vulnerable:* weak and easily hurt
23 *Home Affairs Select Committee:* committee that monitors the government

Britain becoming a Big Brother society, says data watchdog

Britain is in danger of 'committing slow social suicide' as such Big Brother techniques as surveillance cameras and recording equipment spread into every aspect of our lives, the nation's information watchdog will warn this week.

A new report from Richard Thomas, the information commissioner, will say that the public needs to be made more aware of the 'creeping encroachment' on civil liberties created by email monitoring, CCTV and computer tracking of our buying habits.

It is understood that one of the concerns in Mr Thomas's report is the use of special listening devices which can be placed in lamp posts, street furniture and offices. These are already widely used in the Netherlands to combat crime and anti-social behaviour.

More than 300 of the cameras with built-in microphones have been fitted in benefit offices and city centres. The equipment can pick up aggressive tones on the basis of decibel level, pitch and speed at which words are spoken.

Westminster council has already started piloting the listening devices, but experts say the use of these microphones raises questions about how surveillance can be used to intrude into the private lives of citizens.

He will also call for greater regulation of companies that supply surveillance technology which provides 'convenience or safety for the more affluent majority', but not for the vulnerable such as children, immigrants and the elderly.

His warning comes as MPs launch their first inquiry into the impact of surveillance in Britain. The Home Affairs Select Committee will investigate the use of video cameras to monitor high streets and residential areas as well as the holding of personal information on both government and commercial databases.

On Tuesday, Mr Thomas, who last year warned that Britain was 'sleepwalking into a surveillance society', will tell the committee at its first hearing that new safeguards must be introduced to protect the public from the increasing intrusion of surveillance into their daily lives.

Civil liberty campaigners have already warned that Britain is becoming a Big Brother society where its citizens are increasingly being watched. There are more than four million CCTV cameras in this country, one for every 14 people, and the national DNA database which was set up by police to combat crime now holds 3.5 million profiles.

[From: *The Independent*, 29 April 2007]

28 *safeguard (n):* Absicherung

B Understanding the text

Finish the sentences.

a It is Richard Thomas's job to ...
b In his new report he warns the public that ...
c The listening devices used e.g. in the Netherlands are meant to help combat crime by ...
d They have been criticised for ...
e At present the British government is investigating how ...

C Reacting to the text

Imagine the following scenario: your town council wants to put CCTV cameras in the town's park, where there have been several incidents lately of vandalism and two women have been attacked in the evenings.

1. Get together in groups and collect pros and cons.
2. Compare your arguments in class.
3. Then do one of the following:
   - Simulate a town council meeting where some councillors are putting forward their plea and other councillors react.
   - Write a letter to the local newspaper about the plan.
   - Organise a publicity campaign (poster, gallery walk) for or against the plan. Find a good slogan for your campaign.

It is ridiculous/tragic/strange/unfair/... that	the right to privacy is more important than safety.
	the community's fear is making it give up its privacy.
You cannot put a price on ...	the safety of individuals / feeling safe in the local area / ...
	the human right to privacy / feeling unwatched/free/...
If we say that ... is acceptable, then perhaps in a few years time ... will seem acceptable. We have to make a decision now.	
It seems obvious/natural / the intelligent decision /... to say that we should ...	

TOPIC

03

New sciences, better world?

Advances throughout the ages in physics, chemistry, medicine, engineering and many other branches of science have transformed our lives, very often for the better – you probably wouldn't want to have your teeth taken out without an anaesthetic! In this topic we look at two of the newest branches of science, cloning and genetic modification, both depending on the discovery of DNA, and at some of the practical and ethical issues that surround them.

Collect ideas

Describe the pictures above and point out which aspects of this topic they deal with.

1 In the future there will be dinosaurs (Extracts from a novel)

Crichton ['kraɪtn]

'In the future there will be dinosaurs' is the subtitle of the book *Jurassic Park* by the American novelist Michael Crichton, which was published in 1990. The book was turned into a film in 1993 by Steven Spielberg (followed later by some further sequels). You are going to read some extracts from the novel.

A Before you read

Talk in class. Have you seen any of the *Jurassic Park* movies? Describe what happens in them and whether or not you liked them, giving your reasons.

Extract 1: A first sight of the dinosaurs

John Hammond is the director of a bioengineering firm. After several years of experiments, one of his scientists has found a way of cloning dinosaurs and Hammond creates a zoo called Jurassic Park on an island off the coast of Costa Rica. The zoo is now ready to open and he invites two specialists in dinosaurs, Alan Grant and Ellie Sattler, and his firm's lawyer, Gennaro, to the island to inspect it. In this extract, the group is being shown around the island by Ed Regis, Hammond's director of publicity for the zoo.

A narrow path wound down the hill. The air was chilly and damp. As they moved lower, the mist around them thinned, and Grant could see the landscape better. It looked, he thought, rather like the Pacific Northwest, the Olympic Peninsula.

'That's right,' Regis said. 'Primary ecology is deciduous rain forest. Rather different from the vegetation on the mainland, which is more classical rainforest. But this is a microclimate that only occurs at elevation, on the slopes of the northern hills. The majority of the island is tropical.'

Down below, they could see the white roofs of large buildings, nestled among the planting. Grant was surprised: the construction was elaborate. They moved lower, out of the mist, and now he could see the full extent of the island, stretching away to the south. As Regis had said, it was mostly covered in tropical forest.

To the south, rising above the palm trees, Grant saw a single trunk with no leaves at all, just a big curving stump. Then the stump moved, and twisted round to face the new arrivals. Grant realized he was not looking at a tree at all.

He was looking at the graceful, curving neck of an enormous creature, rising fifty feet into the air.

He was looking at a dinosaur.

'My God,' Ellie said softly. They were all staring at the animal above the trees. 'My *God*.'

2 *mist:* Nebel
5 *primary:* main, most important
deciduous: with plants that lose their leaves each year
7 *elevation:* ground that is higher than its surrounding area
slope: Abhang
9 *nestled:* located in a sheltered position, partly hidden
10 *elaborate:* complicated
13 *trunk:* thick stem of a tree from which branches grow

22 *dumpy:* short and fat
24 *lumbering:* moving in a slow, heavy way
dull: not bright or shiny
peer: look carefully
alert: quick and intelligent
26 *foliage:* leaves and branches together
32 *overwrought:* excited and nervous
sales pitch: speech to encourage people to purchase things

Her first thought was that the dinosaur was extraordinarily beautiful. Books portrayed them as oversize, dumpy creatures, but this long-necked animal had a gracefulness, almost a dignity, about its movements. And it was quick – there was nothing lumbering or dull about its behaviour. The sauropod peered alertly at them, and made a loud trumpeting sound, rather like an elephant. A moment later, a second head rose above the foliage, and then a third, and a fourth.

'My God,' Ellie said again.

Gennaro was speechless. He had known all along what to expect – he had known about it for years – but he had somehow never believed it would happen, and now, he was shocked into silence. The awesome power of the new genetic technology, which he had formerly considered to be just so many words in an overwrought sales pitch – the power suddenly became clear to him. These animals were so big! They were enormous! Big as a house! And so many of them! Actual damned dinosaurs! Just as real as you could want.

Gennaro thought: We are going to make a fortune on this place. A *fortune*.

He hoped to God the island was safe.

B Understanding the text

1. Outline the central event in the extract and briefly explain the background to it.
2. Compare the reactions of Ellie and Gennaro to the dinosaurs. What do they tell you about a possible conflict that might arise in the novel?

C Analysing the text

▶ Glossary 2.2.1

1. Identify and explain the point of view used by the writer.
2. Look at the **SPOTLIGHT** below. Identify Crichton's narrative technique. Give examples.

SPOTLIGHT ON 'Showing' and 'telling' as narrative techniques

Novels and stories are all about things happening and about the feelings and thoughts of the characters. The writer can 'tell' us about these (e.g. 'she was amazed', 'the evening was beautiful' etc.). Or, he may 'show us' by allowing us to experience things indirectly through the characters' actions, words, thoughts and feelings. This usually makes reading more interesting, especially at dramatic moments, and it forces the reader to construct their own picture of what is happening. For example, in the extract above the scenery is not described, but we experience it mostly through Grant's eyes. So we feel we are there with Grant and imagine we are walking with his group. Compare also:

Showing: She walked up and down the train platform, checking her watch every now and then. Time had barely passed, yet it seemed she had been there for hours. She stopped and tapped her foot on the ground. Her mouth went tight and her forehead wrinkled into a frown. She sighed, loudly. 'Where the hell is he?' she muttered to herself.

Telling: She had been waiting for her boyfriend for twenty minutes and she was getting really cross and impatient.

✕ **Spotlight task** Rewrite ll. 19–27 using telling. Start like this: 'Ellie was amazed.'

The dinosaur had a long neck and moved quickly. Ellie thought it was …
There was more than one dinosaur in the forest. The group saw them when …
The dinosaur looked at them. Its expression seemed quite …

Extract 2: Creating dinosaurs

After their first sight of the dinosaurs, the group goes to the laboratory where the dinosaurs are bred. Here we meet Dr. Wu, one of Hammond's scientists, Dr. Malcolm, a famous mathematician who visits the zoo, and Tim, Hammond's grandson.

The sign on the door said EXTRACTIONS and, like all the doors in the laboratory building, it opened with a security card.

Inside [...] Regis introduced Henry Wu, a slender man in his thirties. 'Dr. Wu is our chief geneticist. I'll let him explain what we do here.'

Henry Wu smiled. 'At least I'll try,' he said. 'Genetics is a bit complicated. But you're probably wondering where our dinosaur DNA comes from.'

'It crossed my mind,' Grant said.

'As a matter of fact,' Wu said, 'there are two possible sources. Using the Loy antibody extraction technique, we can sometimes get DNA directly from dinosaur bones.'

'What kind of a yield?' Grant asked.

'Well, most soluble DNA is leached out during fossilization, but twenty percent of the proteins are still recoverable by grinding up the bones and using Loy's procedure.'

'And you've adapted that technique here?' Grant asked.

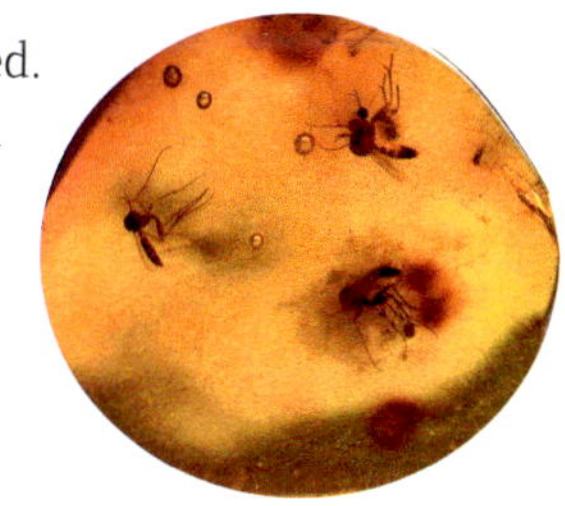
Insects preserved in amber

'Only as a backup,' Wu said. 'As you can imagine, a twenty percent yield is insufficient for our work. We need the entire dinosaur DNA strand in order to clone. And we get it here.' He held up one of the yellow stones. 'From amber – the fossilized resin of prehistoric tree sap.'

Grant looked at Ellie and then at Malcolm.

'That's really quite clever,' Malcolm said, nodding.

'I still don't understand,' Grant admitted.

'Tree sap,' Wu explained, 'often flows over insects and traps them. The insects are then perfectly preserved within the fossil. One finds all sorts of insects in amber – including biting insects that have sucked blood from larger animals.'

'Sucked the blood,' Grant repeated. His mouth fell open. 'You mean sucked the blood of dinosaurs ...'

'Hopefully, yes.'

'And then the insects are preserved in amber ...' Grant shook his head. 'I'll be damned – that might just work.'

(Wu takes the group to the next room and explains how the DNA is injected into eggs and how these are then hatched. Tim, Hammond's grandson, has joined the group.)

'Any other questions? No? Then we'll go to the nursery, where the newborns are.'

It was a circular room, all white. There were some incubators of the kind in hospital nurseries, but they were empty at the moment. Rags and toys were scattered across the floor. A young woman in a white coat was seated on the floor, her back to them.

'What've you got here today, Kathy?' Dr. Wu asked.

1 *extraction:* (here) process of removing an important substance from sth.
7 *cross so.'s mind:* come into so.'s thoughts
11 *yield of sth.:* total amount of sth. produced
12 *soluble:* löslich
leech sth. from sth.: suck sth. out of sth.
13 *grind sth. up:* break sth. into tiny pieces
20 *amber:* Bernstein
resin: Gießharz
21 *tree sap:* Pflanzensaft
34 *incubator:* Brutschrank
35 *rag:* torn piece of cloth

A computer-generated image of a velociraptor

'Not much,' she said. 'Just a baby raptor.' [...]

The animal on the floor was about a foot and a half long, the size of a small monkey. It was dark yellow with brown strips, like a tiger. It had a lizard's head and long snout, but it stood upright on strong hind legs, balanced by a thick straight tail. Its smaller front legs waved in the air. It cocked its head to one side and peered at the visitors staring down at it.

'Velociraptor,' Alan Grant said, in a low voice.

'Velociraptor mongoliensis,' Wu said, nodding. 'A predator. This one's only six weeks old.'

'I just excavated a raptor,' Grant said, as he bent down for a closer look. Immediately the little lizard sprang up, leaping over Grant's head into Tim's arms.

'Hey!'

'They can jump,' Wu said. 'The babies can jump. So can the adults, as a matter of fact.'

Tim caught the velociraptor and held on to him. [...] 'Will he hurt me?'

'No. She's friendly.'

'Are you sure about that?' asked Gennaro, with a look of concern.

'Oh, quite sure,' Wu said. 'At least until she grows a little older. But, in any case, the babies don't have any teeth, even egg teeth. [...] Most dinosaurs are born with egg teeth – little horns on the tip of the nose, like rhino horns, to help them break out of the eggs. But raptors aren't. They poke a hole in the eggs with their pointed snouts, and then the nursery staff has to help them out.'

'You have to help them out,' Grant said, shaking his head. 'What happens in the wild?'

'In the wild?'

'When they breed in the wild,' Grant said. 'When they make a nest.'

'Oh, they can't do that,' Wu said. 'None of our animals is capable of breeding. That's why we have the nursery. It's the only way to replace stock in Jurassic Park.'

'Why can't the animals breed?'

'Well, as you can imagine, it's important that they not be able to breed,' Wu said. 'And whenever we faced a critical matter like this, we designed redundant systems. That is, we always arranged at least two control procedures. In this case, there are two independent reasons why the animals can't breed. First of all, they're sterile, because we irradiate them with X-rays.'

39 *raptor = velociraptor:* a meat eating dinosaur species
41 *strip:* stripe
lizard: Eidechse
43 *cock sth.:* raise sth. (a body part) at an angle
46 *predator:* animal that kills and eats other animals
48 *excavate sth.:* dig sth. up from the ground
58 *rhino:* Nashorn
60 *snout:* long nose of some types of animals
66 *replace stock:* (here) bring in new animals when old ones have died
67 *breed:* make babies
69 *redundant system:* doppelt gesichertes System

'And the second reason?'

'All the animals in Jurassic Park are female,' Wu said, with a pleasant smile.

Malcolm said, 'I should like some clarification about this. Because it seems to me that irradiation is fraught with uncertainty. The radiation dose may be wrong, or aimed at the wrong anatomical area of the animal –'

'All true,' Wu said. 'But we're quite confident we have destroyed gonadal tissue.'

'And as for them all being female,' Malcolm said, 'is that checked? Does anyone go out and, ah, lift up the dinosaurs' skirts to have a look? I mean, how does one determine the sex of a dinosaur, anyway?'

'Sex organs vary with the species. It's easy to tell on some, subtle on others. But, to answer your question, the reason we know all the animals are female is that we literally make them that way: we control their chromosomes. [...] We all start life as females. It takes some kind of added effect – such as a hormone at the right moment during development – to transform the growing embryo into a male. But left to its own devices, the embryo will naturally become female. We tend to refer to some of them as male – such as the Tyrannosaurus rex; we call it a 'him' – but in fact, they're all female. And, believe me, they can't breed.'

76 *irradiate sth./sb.*: jdn./etwas bestrahlen
fraught with sth.: (here) full of sth.
78 *gonadal tissue*: Keimdrüsengewebe
87 *left to your own devices*: sich selbst überlassen

D Understanding the text

Describe briefly how dinosaurs are created in Jurassic Park and what special characteristics they have (and why).

E Analysing the text

1. Characterise Dr Wu, Grant and Dr Malcolm as presented in this extract. Think in particular about their attitudes towards the creation of the dinosaurs.
2. The writer needs to explain at this point how dinosaurs are created in Jurassic Park. Explain how he does this, referring to the distinction between showing and telling.
3. At this point in the novel, the author is beginning to shape the plot. He has done his exposition (we know about the island and have met all the characters). We are now in the 'rising action' phase, i.e. a conflict is beginning to develop. Looking at this extract, what piece of information do you think may be significant later for the development of the story? Speculate about what kind of problem or conflict will arise soon and what role the different characters will play in it.

▶ Glossary 2.2.1

▶ Glossary 2.1

The author draws particular attention to the fact that ... by ...			
The idea that ... seems essential/strange/relevant/meaningful for me because ...			
Dr Wu's / Grant's / Dr Malcom's	reaction / statement / approach / ...		implies that ...
Trouble/action / interesting developments in the story	is/are	predictable/doubtful/likely/uncertain	because ...
Because of what we have already learned about his character, I think Dr Wu / Grant / Dr Malcom is likely to ...			
I guess/reckon/predict/doubt/think/presume that ... because ...			

Extract 3

In Jurassic Park, visitors tour the island in electric cars which run on a fixed track. They are given a commentary about what they are seeing. The group is now touring the park in two cars.

'Looks like rain,' Ed Regis said, glancing up at the sky.

The Land Cruisers had stopped again, near the sauropod swamp. A large herd of *apatosaurs* was grazing at the edge of the lagoon, eating the leaves of the upper branches of the palm trees. In the same area were several duckbilled hadrosaurs, which in comparison looked much smaller. [...]

'The big animals you see are commonly called *Brontosaurus*,' the recording said, 'but they are actually *Apatosaurus*. They weigh more than thirty tons. That means a single animal is as big as a whole herd of modern elephants. And you may notice that their preferred area, alongside the lagoon, is not swampy. [...] They prefer dry land. [...] The dinosaurs of Jurassic Park don't breed,' the recording said. 'The young animals you see were introduced a few months ago, already hatched. But the adults nurture them anyway.'

There was the rolling growl of thunder. The sky was darker, lower, and menacing.

'Yeah, it looks like rain, all right,' Ed Regis said.

The car started forward, and Tim looked back at the hadrosaurs. Suddenly, off to one side, he saw a pale yellow animal moving quickly. There were brownish stripes on its back. He recognised it instantly. 'Hey!' he shouted. 'Stop the car!'

'What is it?' Ed Regis said.

'Quick! Stop the car!'

'We move on now to see the last of our great prehistoric animals, the stegosaurs,' the recorded voice said.

'What's the matter, Tim?'

'I saw one! I saw one out in the field there!'

'Saw what?'

'A *raptor*! In that field!'

'The stegosaurs are a mid-Jurassic animal, evolving about a hundred and

2 *sauropod:* large dinosaur with a long neck and tail
swamp: area covered with water in which plants grow
4 *duckbilled:* dinosaurs with heads similar to modern ducks
12 *nurture sth.:* take care of sth., look after sth.
13 *menacing:* scary

seventy million years ago,' the recording said. 'Several of these remarkable herbivores live here at Jurassic Park.'

'Oh, I don't think so, Tim,' Ed Regis said. 'Not a raptor.'

'I did! *Stop the car*!'

There was a babble on the intercom, as the news was relayed to Grant and Malcolm. 'Tim says he saw a raptor.'

'Where?'

'Back at the field.'

'Let's go back and look.'

'We can't go back,' Ed Regis said. 'We can only go forward. The cars are programmed.'

'We can't go back?' Grant said.

'No,' Regis said. 'Sorry. You see, it's kind of a ride –'

'Tim, this is Professor Malcolm,' said a voice cutting in on the intercom. 'I just have one question for you about this raptor. How old would you say it was?'

'Older than the baby we saw today,' Tim said. 'And younger than the big adults in the pen. The adults were six feet tall. This was about half that size.'

'That's fine,' Malcolm said.

'I only saw it for a second,' Tim said.

'I'm sure it wasn't a raptor,' Ed Regis said. 'It couldn't possibly be a raptor. Must have been one of the othys. They're always jumping their fences. We have hell of a time with them.'

'I know I saw a raptor,' Tim said.

(The group moves on in the car. They see a sick animal in a field being treated by Dr Harding, the park's vet, and they stop. Dr. Grant wanders off to look around. He finds something and calls the others over …)

'It's not very impressive,' Gennaro said. He held the white fragment, no larger than a postage stamp, up on his fingertip in the fading light. 'You sure about this, Alan?'

'Absolutely sure,' Grant said. 'What gives it away is the patterning on the interior surface, the interior curve. Turn it over and you will notice a faint pattern of raised lines, making roughly triangular shapes.'

'Yes, I see them.'

'Well, I've dug out two eggs with patterns like that at my site in Montana.'

'You're saying this is piece of dinosaur eggshell?'

'Absolutely,' Grant said.

Harding shook his head. 'These dinosaurs can't breed.'

'Evidently they can,' Gennaro said.

'That must be a bird egg,' Harding said. 'We have literally dozens of species on the island.'

Grant shook his head. 'Look at the curvature. The shell is almost flat. That's from a very big egg. And notice the thickness of the shell. Unless you have ostriches on this island, it's a dinosaur's egg.'

27 *herbivore:* animal that only eats plants
31 *babble:* talking that cannot be easily understood
intercom: (here) radio communication system
39 *ride:* moving machine that one rides on for fun
43 *pen:* cage, area surrounded by a fence
53 *give sth. away:* show sth. is true
patterning: Musterung
54 *interior:* inside
64 *evidently:* obviously
68 *ostrich:* Strauß

70 *insist:* say firmly that sth. is true

'But they can't possibly breed,' Harding insisted. 'All the animals are female.'
'All I know,' Grant said, 'is that this is a dinosaur egg.'
Malcolm said, 'Can you tell the species?'
'Yes,' Grant said. 'It's a velociraptor egg.'

[From: *Jurassic park* by Michael Crichton, 1991]

F Understanding the text

Outline the main events in the text, explaining their overall significance in the plot.

G Analysing the text

▶ Glossary 2.1

1. When we read this extract we sense that something dramatic is about to happen. Examine how Crichton manages to create suspense.
2. One of the themes of the book is the reliability of technology. Analyse Crichton's attitude to technology as it is expressed in *Jurassic Park*. Examine how he builds up this idea in the extracts.

H Reacting to all the extracts

Imagine that it is now a month or so after the events on the island. You are a journalist and you have heard that something terrible has happened in the meantime. You interview Dr Grant and Ellie. Imagine what may have happened (you may even know from the book or film), then write your article. You can write either:
- a factual 'hard news' story about the events or
- a leading article, in which you express your personal views about the significance of the events.

▶ Glossary 1.2

Decide before you begin whether you are writing for a popular or a quality newspaper and adapt your article (language, length etc.) accordingly.
It does not matter if you are not a hundred percent sure of what happens in the book or the film: make up any details you need yourself.

KEY FACTS The real Jurassic Park: cloning animals

Dolly the sheep

The first successfully cloned animal was Dolly, a female sheep. Dolly was created in 1996 at the Roslin Institute (part of the University of Edinburgh, Scotland) by a team of scientists led by Dr Ian Wilmut.
The process used was called nuclear transfer. You can see how this works in the diagram on the next page.
Dolly died at the relatively young age of 7 – Ian Wilmut did not think this was because she had been cloned, but there is still debate about this.

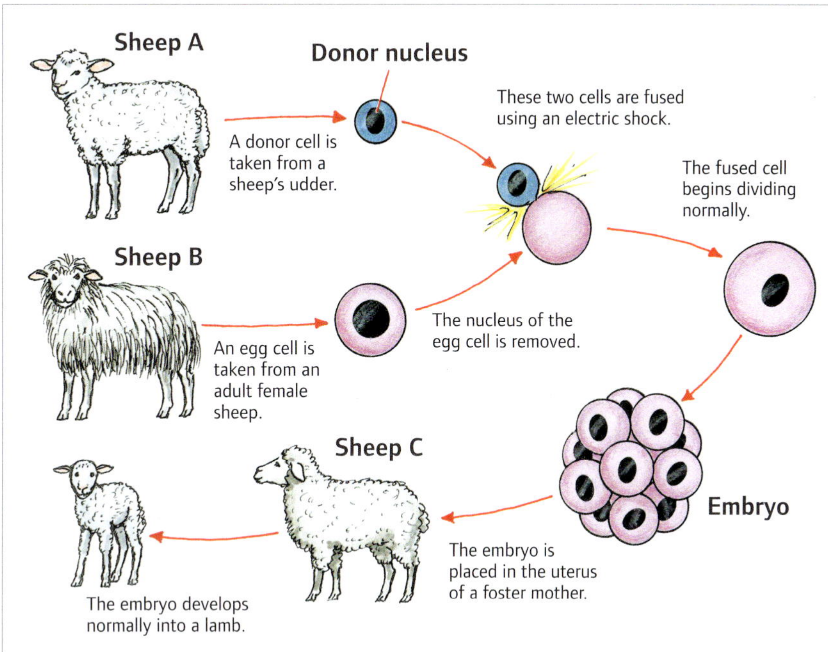

Cloning since Dolly

Cloning animals is still a developing science and it is enormously complicated. There were 277 attempts at cloning Dolly before it was successful, but since then, many animals have been cloned. In the USA cloned pigs and cattle are considered safe for consumers. The situation is the same in the EU, provided that products are carefully tested and clearly labelled. Critics of the process point out, however, that cloned animals often develop defects and suffer during their short lives.

Jurassic Park

So what about the possibility of a real Jurassic Park and the cloning of an extinct species? As in the book and the film, the problem remains finding 'good' DNA that can be cloned and the prospects of that are still slim. Another possibility that scientists are looking at, however, is of using cloning to help preserve endangered species. DNA could be taken from a species of which there are only a few animals left and stored. The DNA could be used later to bring the animal back and increase numbers as soon as their habitat has been restored. Many are sceptical about this, however, not only because preserving the animals' natural habitat is a much better way to save them.

22 *prospects:* the chances of being successful
26 *habitat:* place where a particular type of animal is normally found

▶ Activity chest 4

Activity

Make a 'cheat sheet' to sum up the text orally.

2 Feeding the world (An article from an online encyclopaedia)

With the world population forecast to grow from 7 billion now to around 10 billion by the end of the 21st century and global warming affecting the climate, producing enough food to feed everyone is a major challenge. So, does GM (genetic modification) hold the answer? You are going to explore this issue with a role play activity.

KEY FACTS Genetic modification

Genetic modification means that genes are artificially added to, or taken away from, the DNA of an organism before it is grown. New genes are usually taken from the DNA of another species and inserted into the cell nucleus of the 'host' species. This can occur in nature as well but by using artificial gene transfer scientists can choose exactly which genes they want to add to a species.

3 *species* [spi:ʃi:z]: biologische Art

A Preparing for the role play

1. Divide the class into two halves. One group is a large international company which produces genetically engineered seeds to grow GM crops. The other group is an environmental organisation which is opposed to GM. Find a good name for your company or organisation.
2. Your task in your groups now has two steps:

   Step 1: Produce some written material to persuade people about your point of view about GM foods. For the company, this could be a series of advertisements for your products or maybe a full-page advertisement for a newspaper which explains what you do and why GM is a good thing. For the environmentalists, your material could also be a full-page ad, a brochure, a series of campaign posters, or a web text. Both groups can use the information on pp. 261–264 for their material, but you can, of course, go online for more information and ideas if you want.

   ▶ Activity chest 10

   Step 2: A television company has invited people from the company and the environmental organisation for a televised panel discussion about the issues in front of a live audience. Hold the discussion.

What are some of the advantages of GM foods?

- **Pest resistance** Crop losses from insect pests can be staggering, resulting in devastating financial loss for farmers and starvation in developing countries. Farmers typically use many tons of chemical pesticides annually. Consumers do not wish to eat food that has been treated with pesticides because of potential health hazards, and run-off of agricultural wastes from excessive use of pesticides and fertilizers can poison the water supply and cause harm to the environment. Growing GM foods such as B.t. corn can help eliminate the application of chemical pesticides and reduce the cost of bringing a crop to market.
- **Herbicide tolerance** For some crops, it is not cost-effective to remove weeds by physical means such as tilling, so farmers will often spray large quantities of different herbicides (weed-killer) to destroy weeds, a time-consuming and expensive process that requires care so that the herbicide doesn't harm the crop plant or the environment. Crop plants genetically-engineered to be resistant to one very powerful herbicide could help prevent environmental damage by reducing the amount of herbicides needed. For example, Monsanto has created a strain of soybeans genetically modified to be not affected by their herbicide product Roundup®. A farmer grows these soybeans which then only require one application of weed-killer instead of multiple applications, reducing production cost and limiting the dangers of agricultural waste run-off.
- **Disease resistance** There are many viruses, fungi and bacteria that cause plant diseases. Plant biologists are working to create plants with genetically-engineered resistance to these diseases.
- **Cold tolerance** Unexpected frost can destroy sensitive seedlings. An antifreeze gene from cold water fish has been introduced into plants such as tobacco and potato. With this antifreeze gene, these plants are able to tolerate cold temperatures that normally would kill unmodified seedlings. […]
- **Drought tolerance / salinity tolerance** As the world population grows and more land is utilized for housing instead of food production, farmers will need to grow crops in locations previously unsuited for plant cultivation. Creating plants that can withstand long periods of drought or high salt content in soil and groundwater will help people to grow crops in formerly inhospitable places.
- **Nutrition** Malnutrition is common in third world countries where impoverished peoples rely on a single crop such as rice for the main staple of their diet. However, rice does not contain adequate amounts of all necessary nutrients to prevent malnutrition. If rice could be genetically engineered to contain additional vitamins and minerals, nutrient deficiencies could be alleviated. For example, blindness due to vitamin A deficiency is a common problem in third world countries. Researchers at the Swiss Federal Institute of Technology Institute for Plant Sciences have created a

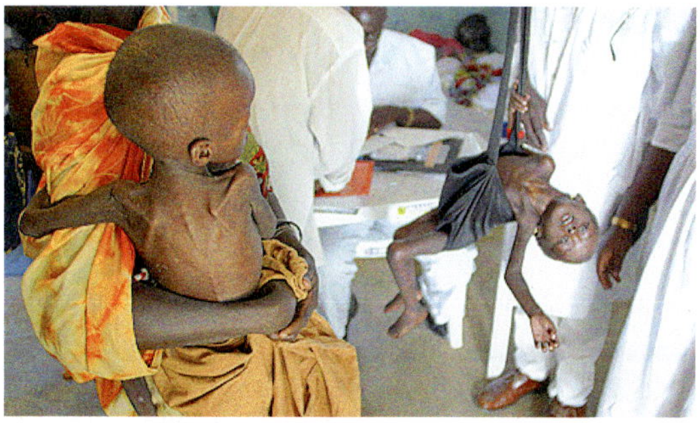

1 *pest resistance:* Widerstandsfähigkeit gegen Schädlinge
crop: plant grown in large quantities for food
staggering: shocking, surprising
2 *starvation:* Verhungern
5 *hazard:* danger
run-off: liquids that runs off land into rivers
waste: rubbish, things that are thrown away
7 *B.t. corn:* corn that has been genetically modified
9 *herbicide:* Pflanzenschutzmittel
weed: Unkraut
10 *tilling:* preparation of land to be used to grow crops
15 *Monsanto:* American company that creates genetically modified crops
20 *fungus:* Pilz
23 *seedling:* young plant grown from a seed (= Samen)
27 *drought* [draʊt]: long period of time without rain
salinity tolerance: (here) ability to survive in areas with high salt contents
30 *soil:* top layer of the earth in which plants grow
32 *malnutrition:* poor health caused by lack of food
impoverished: very poor
35 *staple:* basic type of food which is eaten a lot
38 *nutrient:* substance needed to keep living things alive
43 *alleviate sth.:* make sth. less hard

strain of 'golden' rice containing an unusually high content of beta-carotene (vitamin A). Since this rice was funded by the Rockefeller Foundation, a non-profit organization, the Institute hopes to offer the golden rice seed free to any third world country that requests it. Plans were underway to develop golden rice that also has increased iron content. However, the grant that funded the creation of these two rice strains was not renewed, perhaps because of the vigorous anti-GM food protesting in Europe, and so this nutritionally-enhanced rice may not come to market at all.

- Pharmaceuticals Medicines and vaccines often are costly to produce and sometimes require special storage conditions not readily available in third world countries. Researchers are working to develop edible vaccines in tomatoes and potatoes. These vaccines will be much easier to ship, store and administer than traditional injectable vaccines.

What are some of the criticisms against GM foods?

ENVIRONMENTAL HAZARDS

- **Unintended harm to other organisms** Last year a laboratory study was published in *Nature* showing that pollen from B.t. corn caused high mortality rates in monarch butterfly caterpillars. Monarch caterpillars consume milkweed plants, not corn, but the fear is that if pollen from B.t. corn is blown by the wind onto milkweed plants in neighboring fields, the caterpillars could eat the pollen and perish. Although the *Nature* study was not conducted under natural field conditions, the results seemed to support this viewpoint. Unfortunately, B.t. toxins kill many species of insect larvae indiscriminately; it is not possible to design a B.t. toxin that would only kill crop-damaging pests and remain harmless to all other insects. This study is being reexamined by the USDA, the U.S. Environmental Protection Agency (EPA) and other non-government research groups, and preliminary data from new studies suggests that the original study may have been flawed. This topic is the subject of acrimonious debate, and both sides of the argument are defending their data vigorously. Currently, there is no agreement about the results of these studies, and the potential risk of harm to non-target organisms will need to be evaluated further.

A monarch butterfly

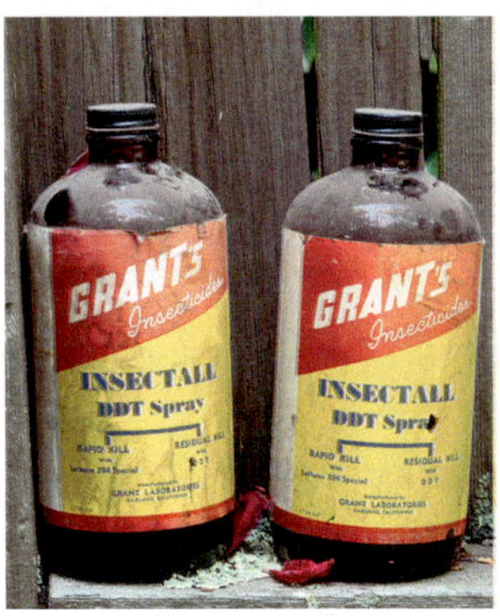

- **Reduced effectiveness of pesticides** Just as some populations of mosquitoes developed resistance to the now-banned pesticide DDT, many people are concerned that insects will become resistant to B.t. or other crops that have been genetically-modified to produce their own pesticides.

50 *iron content:* Eisengehalt
54 *vaccine:* Impfstoff
55 *storage condition:* environment in which a material must be kept
56 *edible:* safe to eat
57 *administer sth.:* provide sth.
61 *Nature:* world's most quoted scientific magazine
mortality: death
62 *caterpillar:* Raupe
68 *perish:* die
71 *toxin:* poison
larva: insect that has just come out of an egg
indiscriminately: randomly
74 *USDA:* US Department of Agriculture
76 *flawed:* not perfect, with mistakes
77 *acrimonious:* angry

- **Gene transfer to non-target species** Another concern is that crop plants engineered for herbicide tolerance and weeds will cross-breed, resulting in the transfer of the herbicide resistance genes from the crops into the weeds. These 'superweeds' would then be herbicide tolerant as well. Other introduced genes may cross over into non-modified crops planted next to GM crops. The possibility of interbreeding is shown by the defense of farmers against lawsuits filed by Monsanto. The company has filed patent infringement lawsuits against farmers who may have harvested GM crops. Monsanto claims that the farmers obtained Monsanto-licensed GM seeds from an unknown source and did not pay royalties to Monsanto. The farmers claim that their unmodified crops were cross-pollinated from someone else's GM crops planted a field or two away. More investigation is needed to resolve this issue.

There are several possible solutions to the three problems mentioned above. Genes are exchanged between plants via pollen. Two ways to ensure that non-target species will not receive introduced genes from GM plants are to create GM plants that are male sterile (do not produce pollen) or to modify the GM plant so that the pollen does not contain the introduced gene. Cross-pollination would not occur, and if harmless insects such as monarch caterpillars were to eat pollen from GM plants, the caterpillars would survive.

Another possible solution is to create buffer zones around fields of GM crops. For example, non-GM corn would be planted to surround a field of B.t. GM corn, and the non-GM corn would not be harvested. Beneficial or harmless insects would have a refuge in the non-GM corn, and insect pests could be allowed to destroy the non-GM corn and would not develop resistance to B.t. pesticides. Gene transfer to weeds and other crops would not occur because the wind-blown pollen would not travel beyond the buffer zone. Estimates of the necessary width of buffer zones range from 6 meters to 30 meters or more. This planting method may not be feasible if too much acreage is required for the buffer zones.

HUMAN HEALTH RISKS

- **Allergenicity** Many children in the US and Europe have developed life-threatening allergies to peanuts and other foods. There is a possibility that introducing a gene into a plant may create a new allergen or cause an allergic reaction in susceptible individuals. A proposal to incorporate a gene from Brazil nuts into soybeans was abandoned because of the fear of causing unexpected allergic reactions. Extensive testing of GM foods may be required to avoid the possibility of harm to consumers with food allergies. Labeling of GM foods and food products will acquire new importance [...].
- **Unknown effects on human health** There is a growing concern that introducing foreign genes into food plants may have an unexpected and negative impact on human health. A recent article published in *Lancet* examined the effects of GM potatoes on the digestive tract in rats. This study claimed that there were appreciable differences in the intestines of rats fed GM potatoes and rats fed

94 *lawsuit:* Rechtsprozess
95 *patent infringement:* Patentverletzung
97 *royalties:* Honorare
98 *cross-pollinated:* von einem fremden Organismus bestäubt
103 *target:* Ziel
species [spiːʃiːz]: Spezies
108 *cross-breed:* Kreuzung
112 *buffer zone:* Pufferzone
120 *feasible:* possible
acreage: land on which plants are grown
125 *susceptible:* (here) likely to be harmed
incorporate sth.: include sth.
132 *the Lancet:* British medical magazine
133 *digestive tract:* Verdauungstrakt
134 *appreciable:* large enough to be noticed
intestines: Gedärme

unmodified potatoes. Yet critics say that this paper, like the monarch butterfly data, is flawed and does not hold up to scientific scrutiny. Moreover, the gene introduced into the potatoes was a snowdrop flower lectin, a substance known to be toxic to mammals. The scientists who created this variety of potato chose to use the lectin gene simply to test the methodology, and these potatoes were never intended for human or animal consumption.

On the whole, with the exception of possible allergenicity, scientists believe that GM foods do not present a risk to human health.

ECONOMIC CONCERNS

Bringing a GM food to market is a lengthy and costly process, and of course agribiotech companies wish to ensure a profitable return on their investment. Many new plant genetic engineering technologies and GM plants have been patented, and patent infringement is a big concern of agribusiness. Yet consumer advocates are worried that patenting these new plant varieties will raise the price of seeds so high that small farmers and third world countries will not be able to afford seeds for GM crops, thus widening the gap between the wealthy and the poor. It is hoped that in a humanitarian gesture, more companies and non-profits will follow the lead of the Rockefeller Foundation and offer their products at reduced cost to impoverished nations. Patent enforcement may also be difficult, as the contention of the farmers that they involuntarily grew Monsanto-engineered strains when their crops were cross-pollinated shows. One way to combat possible patent infringement is to introduce a 'suicide gene' into GM plants. These plants would be viable for only one growing season and would produce sterile seeds that do not germinate. Farmers would need to buy a fresh supply of seeds each year. However, this would be financially disastrous for farmers in third world countries who cannot afford to buy seed each year and traditionally set aside a portion of their harvest to plant in the next growing season. In an open letter to the public, Monsanto has pledged to abandon all research using this suicide gene technology.

[From: www.csa.com]

136 *scrutiny:* (here) careful examination
137 *lectin:* protein which can be used to attach two cells together
138 *mammal:* Säugetier
145 *return (n):* amount of profit
157 *viable:* possible
158 *germinate:* auskeimen
162 *pledge (n):* make a strong promise

✕ **Extra** You are a blogger who posts in German. You read the internet article above and find some new insights there about genetic modification. In German, write your post. Remember – keep your readers' attention and remember that they may be interested that you are writing from a German perspective (in some countries, people may have different ideas about GM).

TOPIC 04

Sci-fi!

In this topic you are going to look at the literary genre science fiction.

Collect ideas

1. In groups, brainstorm the sci-fi films you have seen or the sci-fi books (magazines, cartoons etc.) you have read. Collect titles in class and talk about the books, films etc. saying what happened and why you liked (or didn't like) them.
2. In groups again, think in more detail about the stories you know and complete the mindmap below. When you have finished, do the following tasks and report to the class:
   - give examples of stories in which the action was most important;
   - give examples of stories that deal with an important idea and say how the story explores this idea;
   - thinking of your answers above, try to define science fiction as a genre.

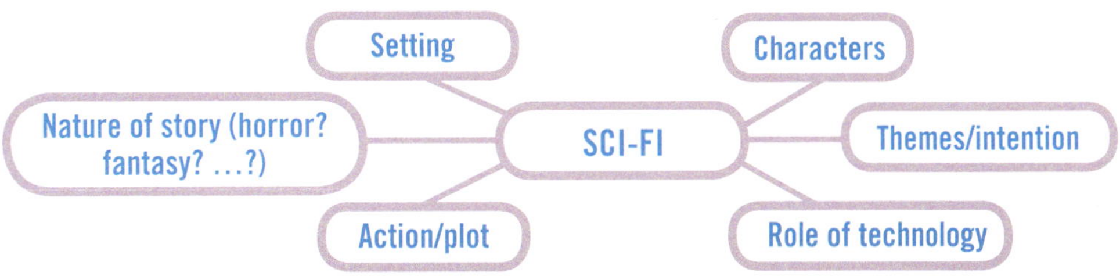

▶ Activity chest 9

3. Look at the picture above. Using your imagination, outline a sci-fi story you could write based on it (don't write it completely, just sum up the idea, setting etc.). Organise a 'Gallery walk' to show it to other students.

1 Choosing a memory keeper (Extracts from a short story)

You are going to read extracts from the short story *Chocco*, published in 1994 by the American writer Ernest Callenbach. In these extracts, you will read the narrator talking about certain events to a group of listeners.

Extract 1: The ceremony begins

I, the thirty-first Memory Keeper of our people, had served for forty-seven years. I learned the history of the Sun People through a long apprenticeship from my predecessor, who taught me all the knowledge and legends that have come down to us. Now the time had come to give over to my successor. We would gather in the largest and finest of our kivas for the choice between two young candidates, Jon and Mikal – my students for many years. One of them would now be chosen Memory Keeper, and I would become only his adviser. To him would come the role of teaching the people their past, and he would be honoured among us, along with our other leaders, men and women – our Water Chief, our Poetry Chief, our Planting and Harvesting Chief, our Healing Counselor, and our Mediation Chief.

Our people are curious and thoughtful and prize knowledge. They demand that their Memory Keeper serve them well. We would pass tonight the great divide and go from winter toward spring. The choosing of a new Memory Keeper is also a fateful divide. For without reliable memories a people cannot find its way into the future.

I took a last deep breath of the cool air and went down the ladder into the kiva. Only a little fading light came through the center opening. Young people were lighting a fire in the raised stone hearth and preparing the incense bundles. On the stone bench that ran around the windowless wall of the kiva the elder councillors were already sitting, silently waiting. Some of these women were so old that nobody really knew their ages – they were older than my great-grandmother. Others were younger and still vigorous. All, I knew, had active, challenging minds. Some had their eyes closed, meditating. Perhaps a few were napping while they waited. Some stared ahead, but what they saw I could not guess. As is the custom of most peoples who have managed to survive on this continent, these women choose our leaders and determine our destiny. They had the respect of us all.

A young woman now moved around the kiva circle, spreading incense smoke on intricate diagonals, guided by the wall niches that held our most powerful prayer sticks. A young man, her helper, provided each person with a graceful pottery bowl containing pine nuts, which would sustain us through the long night ahead. Then all sat quietly for a period, as we do before beginning any important event.

Finally I put the sacred feather wand into its ceremonial bowl and placed them in the holy alcove to indicate that the session had begun. Then I moved into the light flaring up from the fire and addressed the elder women. For this occasion I somehow found myself speaking more slowly and heavily than usual – as if it was not just my own voice speaking, but that of my whole lineage.

'Let us begin,' I said. 'Our procedures here have been proven through many generations. Both candidates to become our new Memory Keeper are fine young men. They have become wise in the history of our people, the evolution of our language, our astronomical and biological science. But for the particular topic to be dealt with in this session, I have chosen – the Machine People.'

2 *apprenticeship:* Lehre
3 *predecessor:* person who did a job before sb. else
10 *harvesting:* act of cutting and gathering crops
mediation: attempt to end an argument between two people
12 *divide:* Kluft
18 *hearth:* (here) fireplace
incense bundle: Bund Weihrauch
23 *nap (v):* sleep for a short time
28 *intricate:* complicated, with a lot of small details
30 *sustain sb.:* (here) give sb. enough energy
32 *wand* [wɒnd]: Zauberstab
33 *alcove:* Mauernische
36 *lineage:* family history

I confess to a certain harshness in this choice, for I knew it would put my young students to the severest interpretive tests they could face. Our memories of the Machine People are a key to our culture. If these are not kept straight and true, we could become fearfully lost, as the Machine People had.

'Jon and Mikal,' I continued, 'I must now set more precisely the questions we will deal with, and to begin I have chosen these: what do we know of the Machine People, and what lessons do we learn from them, or more precisely from the ruins of their culture – since that is all that remains to us? […]

I rolled one of the dice we use in our probability games to determine who would begin. It fell to Jon. I turned, bowed, and addressed him.

'Speak to us first of general things, for our history is vast and complex, and our relation to the Machine People is dark and deceptive. Then Mikal will also have his chance to speak generally, before we address more particular questions.'

42 *harshness:* cruel quality
50 *dice:* Würtel
53 *deceptive:* likely to make people believe untrue things

A Understanding the text

1. Summarise what you learn about the speaker, the society in which he lives and its customs. Find adjectives to characterise the society. Describe the parallels that may exist to other real societies past or present.
2. Outline the ceremony that is about to begin, its participants and its function.
3. From what you have learned so far, speculate about where the story is set and who the 'Machine People' are.
4. The narrator makes various remarks about the importance of what is happening. Find examples. Explain what they tell you about the society of *Chocco.*

▶ Glossary 2.1

Extract 2: Jon

I passed Jon the speaking stick. He straightened his body, closed his eyes momentarily, and took in slow breaths. Then he began, in his usual bright and lively way.

'It is a daunting task to try and understand a people who lived almost a thousand years ago. But one thing we must keep uppermost in our minds: the Machine People were no less intelligent than we are. After all, they had the same brains we have, the same physiology exactly. If their lives are opaque to us in many ways, it is because we cannot yet decipher from the fragmentary remains left to us what it was they occupied those large brains with, and why. But we have pieced out a clear enough picture of their world to recognize their amazing achievements. The terrible collapse that followed might tempt us to suspect them of limited mental capacity, but it must have been cultural disorders and misadaptations that brought their world to its end.

'We are reasonably sure of what they did not know. They may have had some knowledge of astronomy but it was never embodied in lasting stoneworks. They were ignorant of biology – all our excavations and analyses have revealed no knowledge of the sacred plants and their powers, and we can detect no signs that they understood the cyclic interconnections that constitute Gaia, the living earth-world. Judging from remnant patches of their crop plants that have been found, they bred only a few crops, and solely for quantity of output, and not, as we do, for disease resistance, taste, or variety – let alone genetic diversity.

4 *daunting:* frightening, intimidating
7 *opaque:* (here) unclear
8 *decipher sth.:* succeed in finding the meaning of sth.
10 *achievement:* thing that has been done successfully
12 *misadaptation:* not adjusting appropriately to an environment or situation
17 *sacred:* holy, connected to a religion
18 *cyclic:* regularly repeated
interconnection: Querverbindung
constitute Gaia: make up the Earth
19 *remnant patch:* area that still exists

'The ignorance of the Machine People in these crucial areas must have somehow been related to the fact that they occupied such large amounts of their time in producing and contemplating physical artifacts, which they created in astounding variety and complexity. Compared to our houses, theirs must have been full of clutter – we find their ruins littered with the remains of complicated devices, most of them with unknown purposes. Even more mysterious are the huge collections of almost identical artifacts unearthed in some large structures – things like dishes and pots. These structures were not inhabited, for no kitchens or household refuse have been found in them. They were once surrounded by flat, paved surfaces, as large as many cornfields. So perhaps these collections were used in some kind of group meditation ceremonies.

'The Machine People were very numerous, so they had no reserve land to wander and hunt in, and to allow to lie fallow for future gardens. We can calculate easily that, because of their primitive farming methods, and because they paved over such large amounts of good soil, their farms could not have produced enough food to support their numbers. So they must have brought food in from long distances, perhaps after stealing it. Some believe, including myself, that this was one of the purposes of the large, winged metal craft of which we have found the wreckage – they must have had the ability to fly through the air, carrying goods as well as living humans.

'They were obviously a powerful people in some ways, but childlike. We find no evidence of poetry among them, though it may have been kept on perishable materials. Their remaining inscriptions are mostly names of persons, presumably rulers, though of course they also left names if many dead carved on stones or bronze plaques in their burying grounds, apparently as a way of aiding weak memories of their ancestors. Their lives were probably very restricted emotionally, with little spiritual development and only primitive ceremonies. They evidently had small interest in personal ornamentation – their graves reveal no jewelry of any artistic quality. Nothing is known of their music and dances, unfortunately. Perhaps they had none, though it is hard for us to imagine people existing without them.

'Their sense of place must have been vastly different from ours. We know they lived in separated buildings, and all but their oldest towns lacked central gathering places, perhaps because they were suspicious or hostile toward one another.

'That could also explain why they moved around incessantly. We have found almost everywhere, even in the driest desert, great broad paved tracks they built, showing astonishing skill in geometry as well as unbelievable determination to push rocks and earth out of their way. Apparently they traveled upon these tracks with wheeled metal vehicles. Although no complete ones have ever been discovered, and rust damage to the remains is severe, we believe these were powered by some flammable fluid. Perhaps the constant moving about of the Machine People had some spiritual aim. But it may also have been mere restlessness due to the impoverished nature of their lives.'

24 *contemplate sth.:* think about sth.
artefact: (here) object
26 *clutter:* lot of things in an untidy state
littered with sth.: messily full of sth.
30 *paved:* covered in neat, flat stones
34 *reserve land:* (here) spare area on which nothing is built
35 *lie fallow:* not be used for growing crops so that the quality of the land will improve
43 *craft:* (here) vehicle
44 *wreckage:* Wrackteile
49 *perishable:* likely to decay
inscription: (here) words cut into stone
51 *carved:* cut
59 *gathering place:* place at which people meet
61 *incessantly:* without stopping
67 *flammable fluid:* liquid that can catch fire
69 *impoverished:* (here) without any good qualities

B Understanding the extract

1. Work in groups to complete a chart like the one below, then report to the class. Orally, sum up the kind of place Chocco seems to be.

HOW THE MACHINE PEOPLE LIVED	HOW JON INTERPRETS THIS	WHAT THIS TELLS US ABOUT CHOCCO
- no astronomy in lasting stoneworks - no sacred plants - …	- MP had only little knowledge of astronomy. - MP did not know about plants. - …	- Astronomy is important in C & there are stoneworks. - C has lots of knowledge about plants.

2. Talk in class. What new information do we learn in this extract about when and why the Machine People's civilisation came to an end? What aspect of life today do you think the author is referring to?

Extract 3: Mikal

Here Jon sat down, looking fairly content. I knew that he could have talked on for hours. He evidently preferred to let the night's drama complicate itself early on – leaving more strategic possibilities, depending on what approach Mikal took. He had done well. A good Memory Keeper must not only possess a vast and accurate memory, he must be eloquent and convincing in what he says. Jon showed remarkable empathetic powers, even concerning the Machine People. Moreover, in the regular rhythms and careful organization of his delivery, he made it clear that he had been paying careful attention to my own deliberate manner.

Nonetheless, no history (or story) is entirely objective. Each teller subtly inflects the tale. There is no innocence in history. Jon, although he had been extraordinarily faithful in giving a rounded summary of our long discussions and analyses, had omitted certain things we know – about language among the Machine People, for instance. We have recovered enough decipherable fragments to have a fair grasp of the language the Machine People in this region spoke, which is a distant progenitor of our own speech. Jon had also put his individual interpretation on other bits of knowledge – for instance, I had to admire his idea that the Machine People engraved tombstones as a way of aiding weak memories. The idea was hypothetical, of course, but he had duly acknowledged that, and it bore his usual mark of friendly ingenuity.

When the talking stick came to him, Mikal began his first turn with a much fiercer tone than Jon had adopted.

'What is most important for us to remember about the Machine People? That they do not deserve honor. Indeed, we must learn from them what must be avoided, not what must be done.

'It's true that puzzles abound concerning the Machine People. We may never know for sure why they died off exactly when they did. But we can explain quite surely why their culture could not have endured – why it became vulnerable. They were arrogant, and their survival instincts had atrophied. They were rich in possessions, which convinced them they were virtuous and wise, whereas they were merely temporarily lucky. We know that many of their machines, not just the wheeled ones, ran by the burning of fuels – including the black rock we call coal.

2 *evidently:* obviously
4 *approach to sth.:* way of dealing with sth.
6 *empathetic power:* great ability to understand and share the feelings of others
11 *inflect sth.:* change the meaning of sth. by expressing it in a certain way
innocence: state of being without guilt
15 *grasp:* (here) understanding
16 *progenitor:* Vorläufer
19 *bear a mark:* show a sign
20 *ingenuity:* ability to think of clever new things
22 *fierce:* angry and aggressive
26 *abound:* exist in large numbers
28 *endure:* survive
29 *atrophy:* become weak
30 *virtuous:* good

They tried another form of fuel also, mysterious in its operations, known in old legends as Hot Rods. This fuel caused explosions that polluted wide areas and caused much disease and also deformity in children. It is even probable that the deformities and stillbirths that we still experience are the result of the Machine People's adoption of this fuel, for legends say that among the First People such troubles were rare.

'Yet in time all these fuels ran out, and so dependent on mechanical devices had the Machine People become that they were no longer competent to insure their own biological survival. But what we should pay attention to is not just that they failed to maintain their underlying resources, as Jon explained. More seriously, it appears that their leaders served only their own interests, and so allowed the forests, soils, and rivers to be overexploited and become barren. They even tolerated the poisoning of the air, so that in time their crop plants failed. They became helpless against diseases and pests that had developed resistance to their poisons. Their crops failed, and they starved everywhere on the planet, fighting one another over the remaining scraps of food.

'Only in a few remote places, such as our blessed home Chocco, were people saved from this great madness. Our real ancestors, those who left the ways of the Machine People and prepared this place for us, were protected by the holiness of Chocco, which drew them here. They were fit to reoccupy the structures left by the First People, those who came long before the Machine People, because they respected the spiritual qualities of these structures – grace and modesty and fitting into the landscape. They promised to cherish them, along with the drawings the First People had incised on canyon walls. And so they prospered.

'The Great Warming happened to have lucky effects here, increasing the rain-fall a little but not adding too much heat. So our ancestors were able to raise corn and beans and squash, and find pine nuts, and dig roots and pick berries. In the greener forests, deer and bear and rabbits were again abundant for the hunters. Our ancestors learned to plant cotton and tend sheep. They knew how to weave cloth from cotton and wool, and also from yucca fibers.

'And so our ancestors survived, and left us their tested commandments for survival: restrain our numbers, limit our consumption, remember that the spiritual is the measure and meaning of all things. We have faithfully followed these commandments, and so we have continued to live here, thirty generations since the Die-Off, while the Machine People managed only ten generations before their collapse. To me, this speaks strongly to the superiority of our ways.

[From: *'Chocco'* by Ernest Callenbach, 1994]

35 *deformity:* condition in which a part of the body is not the normal shape
36 *stillbirth:* birth in which a baby is born dead
44 *soil:* top layer of the earth in which plants grow
barren: unfruchtbar
45 *crop:* plant grown in large quantities for food

C Understanding the extract

Talk in class. With all the information you now have, sum up who the Machine People were, how their civilisation ended, how Chocco was founded, why it succeeded, and what relationship there is between the two societies. Speculate also about who the 'First People' might have been.

D Analysing all the extracts

1. On the basis of what you have learned from Mika, compare the society of Chocco with that of the Machine People.
2. Examine the message of the story and analyse how the author puts his ideas across.
3. Do some research on the definition of science fiction and compare it to your own definition. Examine to what extent this short story can be called an example of science fiction.

E Reacting to all the extracts

1. Talk in class. How effective did you find Callenbach's story based on what you know from these extracts? Would you be interested to read more? Why or why not?
2. Do you think that science fiction is generally a good way to explore ideas such as global warming, technology etc.? Say why.

▶ Activity chest 15

3. Write the following quotations about the future on a sheet of paper, then discuss them in a 'Walk-talk-write'.

'As for the future, your task is not to foresee it, but to enable it.'

Antoine de Saint-Exupéry

'With the past, I have nothing to do; nor with the future. I live now.'

Ralph Waldo Emerson

'The future is an opaque mirror. Anyone who tries to look into it sees nothing but the dim outlines of an old and worried face.'

Jim Bishop

'The world is full of people whose notion of a satisfactory future is, in fact, a return to the idealised past.'

Robertson Davies

'He who controls the present, controls the past. He who controls the past, controls the future.'

George Orwell

✕ **Extra** Write your own science fiction short story – or the beginning of one. You could develop your ideas from p. 265 or choose any one of the topics that have been dealt with in this sequence and put across your ideas about it in a story.

REFERENCE SECTION

Activity chest

ACTIVITY CHEST

▶ 1 Appointments

Appointments Calendar

Time	Partner
10.00 h	
12.00 h	
14.00 h	

Purpose: finding a partner to work with

- Make an appointments calendar and fill in a partner's name for each time.
- Keep the calendar in your file so you can use it each time for this activity.
- The teacher gives you a task and the time to use: for example, 12 o'clock. Your regular partner for 12 o'clock is the student you work with for the task.

▶ 2 Brainstorming

Purpose: collecting ideas

- You can do this alone, but more usually in a group.
- Use a large sheet of paper.
- Write down (in a group you can have a 'secretary' for this) *any* ideas that come into your mind. At this stage, it is not important to think how 'good' or 'bad' they are. Be creative!
- Then look through and cross out ideas that are not relevant or helpful.
- Agree on and list your final ideas. It often helps to put the 'best' ideas at the top of your list.

ACTIVITY CHEST

▶ 3 Bus stop

Purpose: finding a partner to work with

- Decide on two or three places in the classroom which are 'bus stops'.
- Work alone on your task. When you have finished, go to one of the bus stops.
- Your partner is a student who is already at, or comes to your bus stop.

ACTIVITY CHEST

▶ 4 Cheat sheets (Spickzettel)

Purpose: summarising a text for a short talk

- Go through the text underlining or noting down key words and phrases.
- List the words and phrases on a small piece of paper. Cross out *all* words that are not absolutely necessary. Ideally, you should have only one key word for each part of the text.
- Use the 'cheat sheet' to give your summary. Use the key words to remind yourself of what you need to say, but otherwise use your own words as far as possible. Do not simply repeat the original text.

ACTIVITY CHEST

▶ 5 Double circles

Purpose: comparing your ideas with those of other students

- Arrange your classroom so that students can sit opposite each other in pairs: put chairs in 'double circles' in the centre of the room, or on both sides of rows of tables in a horseshoe.
- Begin the activity. Work with the student opposite you. Then when your teacher tells you to, students on the outside move clockwise around the circle / horseshoe. Continue until you have spoken to 3-6 other students.

ACTIVITY CHEST

▶ 6 Expert groups

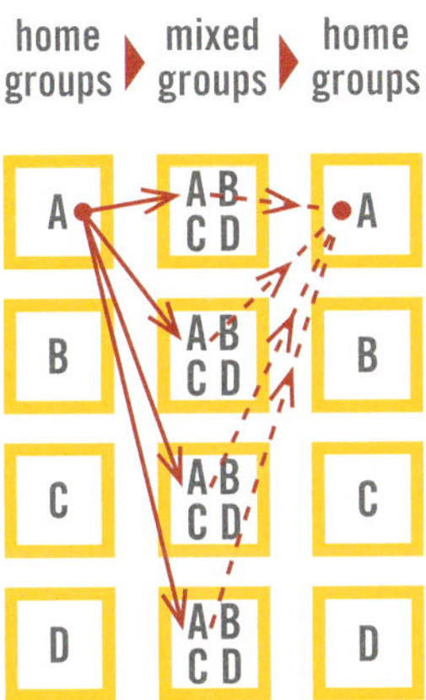

Purpose: studying several texts (or a longer text in sections)

- Divide the class into groups of 3-4. Give each group a letter name (A, B, C, ...), one letter for each of the texts / sections you are going to study. For four texts, you will need groups named A, B, C, D. These A, B, C, D groups are called your 'home groups'.
- In your home group, study 'your' text: you have to become 'the experts' on it and prepare a short talk so that you can explain it to others who do not know it.
- Form new groups. Each new group should have in it students from an A group, a B group, a C group and a D group. Give your talk to your mixed group. The others in the group listen, take notes, and if necessary ask you questions.
- Return to your home group and, in turns, report back what you learned about the other texts, comparing your ideas and correcting any points if necessary. Produce a summary together of all the texts / sections.

ACTIVITY CHEST

▶ 7 Fish-bowl

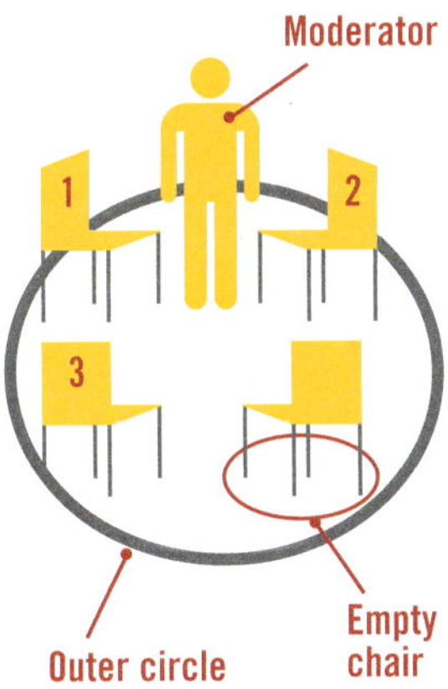

Purpose: discussing a topic as a class

- Work in groups to collect and make notes of your ideas for the task you have been given.
- When you have done this, you are ready to begin the discussion. The teacher can lead the discussion (be the 'moderator') or you can choose a student.
- Choose a person from your group to sit on one of the chairs in the middle of your classroom – in the 'fish-bowl'. In the diagram there are three chairs, but you can have more (or choose more than one person from your group to sit in the fish-bowl).
- All the other students now sit round the fish-bowl in the outer circle.
- Your group representatives put forward your group's ideas, but any student can at any time join the discussion by going into the fish-bowl and sitting on the empty chair. This can be to add a point to what your representative has said – or to disagree if necessary.
- At the end of the discussion everyone goes to sit in the outer circle. Now you can talk as a whole class about what you have heard.

ACTIVITY CHEST

▶ 8 Freeze-frames (freeze-frame tableaux)

Purpose: 'bringing alive' a situation, theme, etc. that you have read about

- Your teacher gives you a theme for your tableau, or asks you to choose one (e.g. from a story or poem) to illustrate with a tableau.
- Work in groups. Your task is to show the situation or theme by standing, sitting, etc. as a group in a such a way that people looking can see and understand what is

happening and the ideas, feelings and so on behind the situation. You can only stand, sit, etc. – you must not move!
- It often helps to choose one person in your group to be a 'director' – to help everyone build the tableau.
- In groups, one at a time, show your tableau to the class. Allow plenty of time for the other students to look at it and discuss it.
- You can also add to your tableau the idea of a 'reporter'. This can be a student from your group who can use an (imagined) microphone to interview one of the characters in the tableau, or students from the class can come and interview a character.
- Explain your tableau to the class, then the class should comment on it.

ACTIVITY CHEST

► 9 Gallery walk

Purpose: presenting and explaining to the class a poster made in your group
- Divide the class into groups of 4–5 students. These are your 'home' groups.
- In your home group, work on the task you have been given and make a poster which shows your ideas, etc. Every person in your group must be able to explain the poster.
- Put up the posters of all the groups on the classroom walls – as far apart as possible.
- Make new groups of 4–5. Each new group must have in it one student from each of the old (home) groups.
- When the teacher tells you, each group goes to one of the posters. The person in the group who is the expert on the poster (the person from the home group which made it), explains the poster to the others. Experts should also be ready to answer questions.
- Move round in your groups until you have seen all the posters.
- Discuss in class all the posters you saw – which did you like best? Why?

ACTIVITY CHEST

► 10 Panel discussions

Purpose: to discuss the pros and cons of an argument
- Divide the class first into two groups. One group is going to put forward arguments 'for' something, the other group the arguments 'against'. The important thing is to argue your case in front of the class as well as you can – even if you do not necessarily agree with it. Be convincing!
- Each group talks about their topic and finds 3-4 important points that they want to make. One student can be the 'secretary' and list these on a large piece of paper.
- Then each group divides into smaller groups – one group for each of the key aspects – and works to develop ideas about it. After a given time, choose a group speaker.
- Put chairs for the speakers at the front of the classroom. They can sit in a row facing the class, or the 'for' and 'against' speakers can sit opposite each other in two groups.
- The discussion now proceeds as follows. A speaker from a 'for' group presents his / her ideas (no longer than two minutes). Then a speaker from an 'against' group presents his/her ideas (two minutes again). Now these two speakers have one minute to react to what each has just said – so if the 'for' speaker hears an 'against' argument that he/she wants to reply to immediately, this can be done in the minute. Continue like this until all group speakers have spoken and reacted.
- Now, in your original groups again, collect and list all the points you heard in the discussion both 'for' and 'against'. Who do you think won the discussion and why? Each group in turn tells the class its final opinion (with the reasons). You can also organise a vote.

ACTIVITY CHEST

▶ 11 Peer review (Peer conferences)

Purpose: correcting and improving a text you have written

- The teacher gives you a writing task. When everyone in the class has a finished text, form groups of 3-4.
- In the groups, pass round everyone's text, so that you all read all the texts. When you read, your aim is to look for language mistakes, how well the text is structured (its 'logic'), how clear the ideas are, etc., so that the writer can afterwards correct and improve the text.
- You can write your comments directly on to the text, or as a group you can develop a 'checklist', like the one below.
- Discuss your comments with the writer of the text. For example, ask what something means if it is not clear, and point out errors.
- Be sure to give positive as well as negative feedback! Say what you think is good as well as what is bad.

	TEXT 1	TEXT 2	TEXT 3
Language mistakes?			
Good title?			
Logical and clear?			
...?			

ACTIVITY CHEST

▶ 12 Placemats

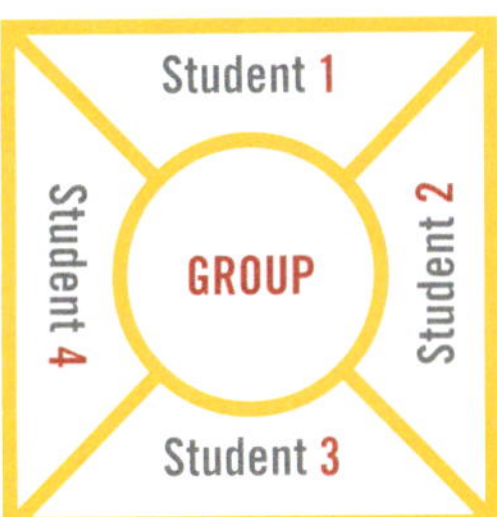

Purpose: collecting and agreeing on ideas in a group

- Work in groups of 3–4 (the diagram shows four students).
- Place a large sheet of paper in the middle of your group table. Mark out the paper as shown in the diagram with sections around the outside for students and a circle (or square) in the centre for the group as a whole.
- Each student begins by writing his / her own ideas in their place on the placemat.
- After a given time, look at what everyone has written, and by discussing together, agree on those ideas which represent what everyone in the group thinks.
- Write these into the centre of the placemat. You can now use the group's ideas to make a group report.

ACTIVITY CHEST

▶ 13 Think-Pair-Share (T-P-S)

Purpose: comparing your ideas with a partner's

- Think about your task and make notes – it may be a list of ideas, key words, etc. Your teacher may give you a time limit for this.
- Find a partner. First one student, then the second, presents his / her ideas to the other. Don't show your ideas to your partner, say them out loud. When you listen to your partner, be ready to interrupt with questions and comments.
- You can now tell the class your ideas: one student can speak for both of you, or you can report separately.

ACTIVITY CHEST

▶ 14 Silent discussions

Purpose: discussing a topic in a group – but in writing, not with spoken words

- Place a large sheet of paper on the table in the middle of your group. In the centre, write the topic, theme, question, etc. that you are going to discuss.
- Write your ideas onto the sheet. It is easier to understand if each student writes in a different place on the sheet and uses a different colour.
- When everyone has written their first ideas, begin to read what others have written on the sheet and add your comments to them – just as you would reply in a conversation.
- When all the group has finished writing, you can look through all the ideas and begin to organise/summarise them.

ACTIVITY CHEST

▶ 15 Walk-Talk-Write

Purpose: collecting ideas as a class

- Put up large sheets of paper around the classroom (as far apart as possible). On each sheet there is a question or topic you have to think about – an 'impulse'.
- Divide into groups. There should be as many groups as there are pieces of paper.
- In your groups, collect ideas about all the impulses.
- When your teacher tells you, each group goes to one of the pieces of paper and writes up its ideas.
- Now, in groups, move round clockwise to the next piece of paper. Read and discuss the ideas that are written on it and add your own. You can go round all the pieces of paper more than once, adding new ideas and comments each time.
- At the end, talk as a class about the ideas that were collected.

Glossary

Alphabetical list of key words in the glossary. They are printed in **bold** in the glossary. The numbers refer to the sections in the glossary.

A

act *2.3.1*
action *2.1*
  external ~ *2.1*
  falling ~ *2.1*
  internal ~ *2.1*
  rising ~ *2.1*
actor *2.3.1*
ad / advert / advertisement *1.2*
alliteration *3.1*
allusion *3.1*
alternate rhyme *2.4.1*
anaphora *3.1*
antagonist *2.1*
antithesis *3.1*
argumentative text type *1.1*
article
  leading ~ *1.2*
  magazine ~ *1.2*
  news ~ *1.2*
  newspaper ~ *1.2*
assonance *3.1*
atmosphere *2.1*
autobiography *2.2.2*

B

biography *2.2.2*
blog *1.2*
bridge *2.4.2*

C

case study *1.2*
character *2.1*
  flat ~ *2.1*
  round ~ *2.1*
characterisation *2.1*
  direct / explicit ~ *2.1*
  indirect / implicit ~ *2.1*
chorus *2.4.2*
cliché *3.1*
climax *2.1*
comedy *2.3.2*
contrast *3.1*
couplet *2.4.1*

D

denouement *2.1*
device: stylistic / rhetorical ~ *3.1*
direct characterisation *2.1*
drama *2.3*

E

editorial: *1.2*
ending: open ~ *2.1*
enumeration *3.1*
epiphora *3.1*
euphemism *3.1*
exaggeration *3.1*
exposition *2.1*
external action *2.1*

F

falling action *2.1*
feature article *1.2*
fictional text *2*
first person narrator *2.2.1*
first-hand-account *1.2*
flashback *2.2.1*
flat character *2.1*
foreshadowing *2.2.1*
formal letter *1.2*
formal style *3.2*

H

hyperbole *3.1*

I

imagery *3.1*
indirect characterisation *2.1*
informal style *3.2*
informative text type *1.1*
instructive text type *1.1*
internal action *2.1*
intro *2.4.2*
irony *3.1*

L

language *3.1*
leader *1.2*
leading article *1.2*
letter to the editor *1.2*
letter *1.2*
  formal ~ *1.2*
  ~ to the editor *1.2*
  ~ of application *1.2*
limited point of view *2.2.1*
line *2.4.1*
litotes *3.1*

M

magazine article *1.2*
metaphor *3.1*
mode of presentation *2.2.1*

N

narrative text *2.2*
narrator *2.2.1*
  first person ~ *2.2.1*
  third person ~ *2.2.1*
neutral style *3.2*
news article *1.2*
newspaper article *1.2*
non-fictional text *1.1*
novel *2.2.2*

O

omniscient narrator *2.2.1*
onomatopoeia *3.1*
open ending *2.1*
outro *2.4.2*

P

panoramic presentation *2.2.1*
personification *3.1*
persuasive text type *1.1*
play *2.3*
plot *2.1*
poem *2.4.1*
poet *2.4.1*
point of view *2.2.1*
  limited ~ *2.2.1*
  unlimited ~ *2.2.1*
presentation *2.2.1*
  mode of ~ *2.2.1*
  panoramic ~ *2.2.1*
  scenic ~ *2.2.1*
protagonist *2.1*
pun *3.1*

Q

quatrain *2.4.1*

R

register *3.2*
repetition *3.1*
report *1.2*
rhetorical device *3.1*
rhetorical question *3.1*
rhyme *2.4.1*
  alternate ~ *2.4.1*
  rhyming couplet *2.4.1*
  scheme ~ *2.4.1*
rhythm *2.4.1*
rising action *2.1*
round character *2.1*

S

speaker of a poem *2.4.1*
satire *3.1*
scene *2.3.1*
scenic presentation *2.2.1*
setting *2.1*
short story *2.2.2*
showing *2.2.1*
simile *3.1*
slang *3.2*
soliloquy *2.3.1*
song *2.4.2*
sonnet *2.4.1*
speech *1.2*
stage directions *2.3.1*
stanza *2.4.1*
style *3.2*
  formal ~ *3.2*
  informal ~ *3.2*
  neutral ~ *3.2*
stylistic device *3.2*
suspense *2.1*
symbol *3.1*

T

telling *2.2.1*
text
  fictional ~ *2*
  non-fictional ~ *1*
  narrative ~ *2.2*
third person narrator *2.2.1*
tone *3.2*
tragedy *2.3.2*
turning point *2.1*

U

understatement *3.1*
unlimited point of view *2.2.1*

V

verse *2.4.2*

W

weblog *1.2*
wordplay *3.1*

GLOSSARY
► 1 Non-fictional texts

GLOSSARY
► 1.1 Important features of non-fictional text types

Non-fictional texts can be divided into different **text types.** These categories depend on the main aim of the text.

► SPOTLIGHT ON
Argumentative texts, p. 55

Category 1: Informative	These give information: their aim is to inform the reader. Informative texts are sometimes further divided into three groups: - purely factual (just facts: a railway timetable, for example), - descriptive (describe a person, place, event, etc.), - expository (give facts, but also explain them and often add comments and opinions).
Category 2: Argumentative	These express an opinion by discussing a topic with the reader – usually showing the arguments for and against something.
Category 3: Persuasive	These try to persuade or influence the reader. A typical example is an advertisement.
Category 4: Instructive	These tell the reader how to do something. An example is the instructions which come with a new mobile phone. (This is probably the type you meet least in your exam.)

NOTE: Most texts do not belong in just one category. A persuasive advertisement, can also inform the reader; an argumentative text also tries to persuade the reader that a particular opinion is the right one. It is, therefore, better in most cases to talk of a dominant text type: the most important basic category.

GLOSSARY
► 1.2 Examples of non-fictional text types

a **Advertisement (ad** or **advert)**
Dominant text type: persuasive.
Important features:
- The advertisement tries to influence the reader through text (advertising blurb), pictures and design (colours, size of the text);
- Advertisements in Europe and many other parts of the world are strictly controlled: they must be 'legal, decent, honest and truthful'. However, advertisers sometimes use hidden ways to influence consumers. One example is 'greenwashing'.

b **Blog (weblog)**
Dominant text type: all categories.
Important features:
- Whatever the text type, most blogs are personal – written by one person or a particular group of people about their personal experiences;
- Blogs are an electronic (online) medium and typically use links to organise information. They can also be multi-media, with sound, video and pictures as well as text.

c **Case study**
Dominant text type: informative.
Important features:
- The aim of a case study is to use a specific example of something to make clear a

general situation. An example would be one person's individual story about a problem they have had online to help readers to understand the general problems that everyone can have when they use the internet;
- When you read a case study look for (a) the specific details of what it tells you, then (b) how these facts, etc. can relate to a bigger picture. How could other people find themselves in a similar situation? How could their experiences be the same or different? How typical is the example in the case study? What could readers learn from the case study? (Perhaps to have the same success as the person in the study, or to avoid the mistakes this person made.)

d **First-hand account** *(= Augenzeugenbericht)*
Dominant text type: informative.
Important features:
- A text that is written or spoken by a person who is present at a certain incident or who experiences something directly.

e **Formal letter**
Dominant text type: argumentative.
Important features:
- The layout of formal letters is fixed (addresses at the top, signature at the bottom, etc). The beginning *(Dear)* and ending *(Yours sincerely)* are also fixed, and there is always a subject line *(Application for a work placement)*;
- Formal letters have a particular **style** (► Glossary 3.2). The language is formal (polite) and many phrases are standard *(I would like to apply for … / As you will see from my enclosed CV / I look forward to hearing from you soon)*.

f **Letter to the editor** *(= Leserbrief)*
Dominant text type: informative.
Important features:
- It is a letter written by a reader to a newspaper. It is often a reaction to an article in that newspaper, but may also comment on a topic of general interest;
- It may support or criticise an opinion expressed in another article or express the reader's opinion on a certain topic.

g **Newspaper news article**
Dominant text type: informative (expository).
Important features:
- The aim of a news article is to inform readers of things that have happened – events. Journalists often call these facts hard news. To help the reader understand the events, the journalist sometimes gives background information and adds explanations where necessary;
- To write the story, the journalist almost always interviews people involved in the events, and their words are given in the article as quotes;
- When we look through a newspaper as readers, we often choose the particular articles we want to read because they look interesting, and news stories always, therefore, begin with a headline which sums up the story. There is often also a photo which catches our eye. In addition, news stories also usually have a particular structure: they are clearly divided into paragraphs (often one sentence long), and the most important paragraphs are put at the beginning of the story so that we read them first;

- Good news stories (for example, in quality newspapers) give facts only. The journalist does not try to influence or persuade the reader about what to think. However, some articles (usually in tabloid newspapers) do contain a hidden opinion and do try to influence the reader. This kind of article is called biased (opposite: unbiased / objective).

h **Newspaper leading article**

Dominant text type: argumentative.
Important features:
- A leading article (also called a **leader** or **editorial**) is the place where the newspaper expresses its opinion about an event in the news, usually on a special page inside the paper. The key features are: the article has a clear structure, with the topic at the beginning, arguments for and against in the middle, and a conclusion at the end; the language can sometimes be complex (good leaders are aimed at educated readers); the article may use the pronoun 'we' (= the newspaper), but more usually expresses opinions indirectly (for example, with the passive).

i **Newspaper (or magazine) feature article**

Dominant text type: informative.
Important features:
- Feature articles are generally about topics of general interest. Often longer than news stories, they aim to both inform and entertain the reader at the same time with interesting facts about a topic;
- The structure of the article can vary, but it generally introduces the topic at the beginning, gives information about it in the middle, and makes a comment or draws a conclusion at the end.

j **Report**

Dominant text type: informative.
Important features:
- Reports are generally written about a situation, event, etc. in order to give the reader clear information. This often happens in business, but there can also, for example, be a report by an au pair about his/her experiences;
- The essential aspect of a report is that the information must be easy to understand, so there is a standard structure (introduction, facts paragraph by paragraph, conclusion, name of the writer).

k **Speech**

Dominant text type: persuasive.
Important features:
- Although a speech is spoken, you often have to look at it as a text;
- Speeches are given by many people (by politicians, for example) in order to put across a very clear opinion and to persuade the audience. Speech makers, therefore, are careful to address the audience – talk directly to the people listening – and speak in a highly personal way;
- One of the key aspects of a speech is also the **language** used (► Glossary 3). It is often dramatic and emotional, and may contain a lot of **rhetorical devices** (► Glossary 3.1).

GLOSSARY ► 2 Fictional texts

GLOSSARY ► 2.1 Fictional text types

► SPOTLIGHT ON
Fictional genres, p. 184

Fictional texts are divided into:

Narrative texts	short stories, novels that tell a story (► Glossary 2.2)
Drama	plays (► Glossary 2.3)
Poems and **songs**	'lyrical' texts (► Glossary 2.4)

NOTE: we do not normally classify fictional texts as 'informative', 'persuasive', etc.

Important features:
- the **setting:** where and when the story takes place and the **atmosphere**, the feeling or mood created in a text by its author;
- the **characters:** the people in the story. The main character is usually called the **protagonist** [prəʊ'tæɡənɪst]; the character who opposes him or her is called the **antagonist** [- '- - -]. There are two types of characters: **flat characters** (they more or less represent a single personality trait and they do not develop) and **round characters** (they are more lifelike, with more than one personality trait, and usually change in the course of a story);
- **characterisation:** the way in which characters are presented by the author. There are two kinds of characterisation: **direct/explicit characterisation** (the reader is told what kind of person a character is by the narrator, the character himself or another character) or **indirect/implicit characterisation** (the reader finds out about a character's personality by analysing his behaviour, his choice of words or the opinions he expresses);
- **action** *(= Handlung)* is everything that happens in a fictional text. It can be either **internal** (things that go on in a character's mind, his thoughts or feelings) or **external** (events that take place and things that characters do);
- **language:** the language of fictional texts is usually characterised by such things as **images** (► Glossary 3.1) and the **style** (► Glossary 3.2) of the writer;
- **plot** *(= Handlung)*: the structure of events in a fictional text. Stories are structured in particular ways to get and hold the reader's attention, and to tell the story so that it is interesting to read. One way the writer often does this is with **suspense:**
  introducing a mystery to which the reader wants to know the answer. A plot usually develops in different stages:

the **exposition**	The characters, setting etc. are introduced.
the **rising action**	A conflict is developed.
the **climax / turning point**	The conflict reaches its highest point.
the **falling action**	There is a change in the conflict or suspense.
the **denouement** [ˌdeɪ'nuːmɒ̃] / the solution (which may also be an **open ending**)	The suspense is reduced. In an open ending, the conflict is not fully resolved; the reader is left wondering what might happen next.

GLOSSARY
▶ 2.2 Narrative texts

GLOSSARY
▶ 2.2.1 Important features of narrative texts

▶ SPOTLIGHT ON
Analysing narrative texts, p. 102

▶ SPOTLIGHT ON
Point of view, p. 26

- The **point of view** *(= Erzählperspektive)* is the perspective from which a story is told. The point of view can be **limited** (e.g. when a story is told from the perspective of a character who cannot know everything that occurs and may interpret what is happening in a very subjective way). So a **first person narrator** *(= Ich-Erzähler)* always has a limited point of view. A **third person narrator** *(= personaler Erzähler)* can have either a **limited point of view** (if he observes the events from the perspective of one of the characters) or an **unlimited point of view** (if he moves freely in place and time and may enter the minds of other characters). He is then called an **omniscient** [ɒm'nɪsiənt] narrator *(= auktorialer Erzähler)*, a narrator who 'knows everything'. This third person narrator is *not* the author but simply someone outside the story who is an **observer**;
- **Mode of presentation** *(= Darstellungsart)*: the way a narrator tells his story. There are two modes of presentation and in most narrative texts both are combined: **showing** (also called **scenic presentation**: the author shows in detail what is happening, takes his time to describe the characters' emotions or thoughts) and **telling** (also called **panoramic presentation**: the author sums up the events of a longer period of time in a few sentences);

▶ SPOTLIGHT ON
'Showing' and 'telling', p. 252

- Writers do not always stick to the chronological order of events. Instead they may use **flashbacks** *(= Rückblende)* (they go back to an event in the past that is important to the present) or **foreshadowing** *(= Vorausdeutung)* (they hint at events that will happen in the future).

GLOSSARY
▶ 2.2.2 Types of narrative texts

- A **novel** *(= Roman)* is a long and complex narrative. Its structure and storyline are usually more complicated than those of shorter narrative texts (such as short stories), so there is more room for a detailed development of the plot, characters and settings. Novels are often subdivided into chapters;
- A **short story** *(= Kurzgeschichte)* is a short piece of narrative prose that can usually be read in one sitting. Short stories concentrate on one character, dilemma or problem. In contrast to novels, they focus on one single aspect that undergoes development in the course of the story, so the characters and the situation are not fully developed;
- An **autobiography/biography** is a book about a person's life – either written by the person themselves (autobiography) or by somebody else (biography).

GLOSSARY
▶ 2.3 Drama/Play

GLOSSARY
▶ 2.3.1 Important features of drama *(= Schauspiel, Drama)*

- **Dramas** (or **plays**) are not written to be read but to be performed by **actors** *(= Schauspieler)* on **stage** in a theatre and watched by an audience;
- A play is usually divided into several **acts** *(= Akte)* and the acts may be subdivided into **scenes** *(= Szenen)*. In classical drama, there were usually five acts, but modern plays normally consist of three and sometimes only of one act;
- The essential element of all plays is the **characters**, the people in the play. Good

plays show us a lot about their feelings and emotions in the situations in which they find themselves. Characters also usually change during the play – they develop;
- Drama means 'tension' – often conflict between characters;
- Spoken language: we find out what is happening in plays by what the characters say, and we often have to read between the lines in order to understand a situation. Plays also use spoken language which can, for example, include slang and other informal ways of speaking;
- A **soliloquy** [sə'lɪləkwiː] *(= Monolog)* is a speech made by a character in a play in which his or her thoughts, emotions or motives are revealed;
- **Stage directions** *(= Bühnenanweisungen)* are the written form of a drama often contains a description of its setting, movements or actions of the characters, the sound or lighting etc. This helps the actors perform a play.

GLOSSARY ▶ 2.3.2 Types of drama

- A **tragedy** *(= Tragödie)* is a type of drama in which the protagonist goes through a series of misfortunes that finally lead to his or her downfall. This downfall is usually brought about by the protagonists themselves, e.g. through pride or weakness;
- A **comedy** *(= Komödie)* is a type of drama which deals with a topic in an amusing way. It always has a happy ending.

GLOSSARY ▶ 2.4 Poems and songs

GLOSSARY ▶ 2.4.1 Important features of a poem

▶ SPOTLIGHT ON
Elements of poetry, p. 91

- A **poem** *(= Gedicht)* is a piece of creative writing that is structured by **lines** *(= Verse)* and **rhythm**. The lines of a poem are often arranged into groups called **stanzas** *(= Strophen)*. It can express personal thoughts and feelings (**lyrical poem**) or it can tell a story (**narrative poem**);
- The **speaker of a poem** *(= lyrisches Ich)* is the fictional person who speaks the text of a poem. In theory, the speaker is not identical to the writer;
- Some poems make use of **rhyme** *(= Reim)*. How the lines of a poem rhyme is called its **rhyme scheme** [raɪm skiːm] and it is described with letters. A rhyme scheme a-b-a-b means that the first line rhymes with the third and the second with the fourth; it is called an **alternate rhyme** *(= Kreuzreim)*. The rhyme scheme a-a-b-b is called **rhyming couplets** *(= Paarreim)*;
- **Poetic language:** poems are generally short compared to stories and plays, but the writer (the **poet)** wants to say a lot in a few lines. To do this, he or she often uses language in a very special way so that the words have a strong effect on the reader. There are usually lots of **rhetorical devices** (▶ Glossary 3.1), and **images** (▶ Glossary 3.1) are particularly important in poems.
- A **sonnet** is a form of poem that consists of 14 lines. There are various forms of sonnets: for example, Shakespeare's sonnets consist of three **quatrains** (a stanza with four lines) and a **couplet** (two lines which rhyme).

GLOSSARY

▶ 3.2 Style

▶ SPOTLIGHT ON
Style, p. 85

Style means the way in which a text is written. If you are asked to analyse the style of a text, you should examine aspects such as the register and the tone of the text:

- **tone** *(= Ton):* shows a writer's attitude to his or her topic; it can be serious, humorous, ironic, playful, formal, angry, etc.;
- **register** *(= Sprachebene):* is the level of language that a writer uses in a particular text. It can be either **formal**, **neutral** or **informal**.

Formal style	Involves a complex sentence structure and many sophisticated words (often of Latin origin). It is used for serious purposes, for example essays, academic publications, or in official situations.
Neutral style	Falls between formal and informal style. It is used in feature articles or reports and it is the style usually employed by educated people.
Informal style	Is characterised by simple sentences, short forms (e.g. 'can't', 'we'll'), phrasal verbs and colloquial words. It is used between friends or in relaxed, unofficial situations. Informal style also includes **slang**, i.e. very informal language that is mainly used in dialogue between people of the same age or from a similar background.

Skills

1 Working with written texts
1.1 Understanding a text
1.2 Analysing a text
1.2.1 Communicating with texts
1.2.2 Reading and analysing non-fictional texts
1.2.3 Reading and analysing narrative prose
1.2.4 Reading and analysing poetry
1.2.5 Reading/watching and analysing drama

2 Working with visuals
2.1 Working with pictures
2.2 Working with cartoons

3 Working with statistics

4 Working with film and video
4.1 Camera angles
4.2 Camera distances
4.3 Two shots
4.4 Camera movements
4.5 Other video and film techniques

5 Writing
5.1 Writing skills: general
5.2 Writing skills: special text formats

6 Listening
6.1 Listening for gist
6.2 Listening for detail: taking notes

7 Speaking
7.1 Classroom discussions
7.2 Debating
7.3 Making a report
7.4 Making a formal presentation
7.5 Explaining your ideas to other students

8 Working on projects
8.1 Organising a project
8.2 Doing research
8.3 Quoting

9 Working on your language skills
9.1 Working with a grammar book
9.2 Working with a monolingual dictionary
9.3 Working with a bilingual dictionary
9.4 Learning new words
9.5 Dealing with unknown words
9.6 Paraphrasing
9.7 Mediating
9.8 Translating

SKILLS

▶ 1 Working with written texts

In class tests and exams, you can generally speaking expect three basic tasks on a written text:

Understanding the text (comprehension): showing you understand **what** is said.
Analysing the text (analysis): showing you understand **why** and **how** a text is written in a particular way.
Reacting to the text: showing you can **express an opinion** about the text, or use it as a basis for **creative writing** (an email, story, newspaper article, etc. that you write yourself).

SKILLS

▶ 1.1 Understanding a text

Step 1: Take stock

Texts can be read in three different ways:

Skimming	This means reading for a quick, general understanding – often called **reading for gist**. Read through as quickly as you can, concentrating simply on building up a picture of the text in your mind. Do not worry about unknown words.

Scanning	This means reading to find specific information. You do this when you look at a railway timetable or a holiday brochure. Make sure you have a clear idea before you read of the information you need, and let your eyes move over the text until you find the place where you think it is. Then look closely at that part.
Reading for detail	This is what you do most often when you study a text in order to answer detailed questions on it. The key steps are very important. Essentially, you must begin by understanding the text generally (skimming). Look at headlines and pictures that give you an idea about what the text is about. Find the overall structure of the text as this helps a great deal in understanding what the writer says. **NOTE:** Do not, at this stage, worry about unknown words. Read again. Still do not look up words in a dictionary. Try to work out (deduce) as far as you can what unknown words mean from the context – the sentence as a whole and the words around the unknown word. Think of other words that are like the unknown word (for example, another word in the same word family). There may be words in other languages that can help you, too. Finally, if you are still not sure, then you can use your dictionary.

Marking up a text will be useful when you study a text in detail, especially if you later work on a task based on that text. It means highlighting certain passages or adding comments in the margins (= *Rand*) of the text. Of course you should only do this with photocopies or books that you own!
If you want to mark passages of your text, there are many possibilities: you can circle, underline or highlight them. Use each form of marking for a different purpose. But be careful not to mark the whole text! You may also want to add symbols such as arrows (= Pfeile) or exclamation marks, or to write keywords in the margins.

Step 2: Present your findings

a **Make a summary**

Many tasks ask you to sum up / summarise the text or outline the main points of the text. This means that you have to write a summary of the text as a whole. These are the important aspects of writing a summary:

- A summary contains all the important information in the original text, but is shorter: normally a summary should never be longer than 1/2 of the original.
- The most common tense to use in a summary is the simple present.
- Use your own words. Do not copy from the text!
- Do not use direct speech. Report any important words spoken in indirect speech.

'NO COPYING!' rule: Never copy directly from a text in summaries or when answering questions!

b **Sum up a specific element of a text**

The task on a text can also be to find and point out particular parts. In an argumentative text, this could, for example, be the writer's arguments 'for' something (arguments 'against' are not relevant), or you may be asked to sum up a particular part of a story. Write your summary as described above, but be very careful to answer the question. Any other information you include is irrelevant and makes your answer confusing and inaccurate.

SKILLS ▶ 1.2 Analysing a text

SKILLS ▶ 1.2.1 Communicating with texts

▶ SPOTLIGHT ON
Fictional genres, p. 184

Analysing texts (**text analysis**) is an important skill and it is helpful to begin by understanding how we communicate generally, and then look specifically at how we communicate with texts. These are illustrated by the diagram on the left.

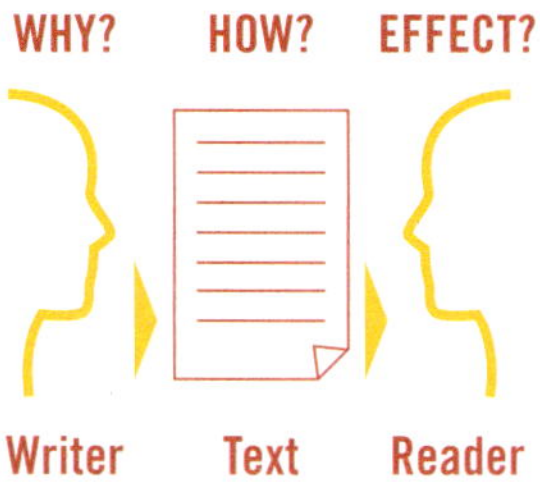

- We can think of all communication as 'sending a message'. Person A sends a message to person B.
- The message can be of many kinds – spoken or written. When we communicate with texts, the message takes the form of a written text.
- When we analyse a text, we look at it to answer the questions: Why does the writer write the text? How does he / she write it? What is the effect on the reader?

a **Why?**

What is the writer's intention (goal) when writing the text? (to inform? persuade? move emotionally?)

b **How?**

How does the writer write the text so as to achieve his/her goal? For example:
- the **text type** (▶ Glossary 1, 2) the writer chooses (fictional, non-fictional, informative, …);
- the **structure** of the text (parts, paragraphs, headlines, …);
- the **language** and **style** (▶ Glossary 3) the writer uses (formal, informal, poetic, …) and special devices (ways of using language) like **images** (▶ Glossary 3.1) in the text or repeating certain words.

▶ SPOTLIGHT ON
Style, p. 85;
Rhetorical devices, p. 217

c **Effect?**

Every technique a writer uses has an effect on the reader, and it is an important part of analysing a text to explain what the effect is. For example:
- The **text type** the writer chooses may be familiar to the reader, so that he or she has an idea before reading of roughly what to expect;
- The **structure** of the text may make it easier for the reader, to follow the writer's thoughts;
- The **language** the writer uses may make a certain impression on the reader. For example, detailed or scientific language in an encyclopedia makes the reader feel the information is accurate and that he/she can trust the writer;
- Special devices, especially in fictional texts, can have a very strong emotional effect on the reader, making the text seem amusing, dramatic, shocking, …

SKILLS ▶ 1.2.2 Reading and analysing non-fictional texts

▶ SPOTLIGHT ON
Argumentative texts, p. 55

Step 1: Skim

Gain a quick, general understanding of the text by **skimming** (▶ Skills 1.1) it.

Step 2: Structure

Examine the structure of the text: identify the subtopics dealt with in each paragraph (= *Absatz*).

Step 3: Summarise

If you are asked to do a summary, or if you need to remember the content of the text, collect and structure the important information, then write a summary (▶ Skills 1.1, Step 2).

Step 4: Analyse
Analyse the **language** (▶ Glossary 3.1) and **style** (▶ Glossary 3.2) of the text . Examine who the text was written for and assess whether the text is convincing.

Step 5: React
Form your opinion about the topic. Analyse whether reading the text has changed or confirmed it.

SKILLS

▶ SPOTLIGHT ON
Analysing narrative texts, p. 102

▶ SPOTLIGHT ON
Point of view, p. 26

▶ 1.2.3 Reading and analysing narrative prose

Step 1: Take stock
Find out about the following aspects of the text and make notes:
- its **narrator** and **point of view** (▶ Glossary 2.2.1): it is important to know who tells the story (a **first** or **third person** or **omniscient narrator**, ▶ Glossary 2.2.1) and to understand why the author has chosen this **point of view** (▶ Glossary 2.2.1);
- the **action** and **plot** (▶ Glossary 2.1): analyse whether the author puts the events in chronological order or if there are **flashbacks** (▶ Glossary 2.2.1). The author may also tell two connected stories within one story. Examine which events are important for the development of the story. Analyse the **climax** and/or **turning point** (▶ Glossary 2.1) of the story. Examine the ending (Is it an **open ending** or a **denouement/ solution**, ▶ Glossary 2.1) and its effect on the reader;
- the **characters**: are they **round** or **flat** (▶ Glossary 2.1)? Does the author characterise them through **explicit** or **implicit characterisation** (▶ Glossary 2.1)?
- the **mode of presentation** (▶ Glossary 2.2.1): does the writer present characters, settings or events by telling or by showing them (▶ Glossary 2.2.1)?

▶ SPOTLIGHT ON
'Showing' and 'telling', p. 252

Step 2: Present your findings (▶ Skills 5)
- When you write your findings down, make it clear that you are talking about the text, not about real life. Use expressions like:
  In her story the author deals with the topic of …
  The short story is about …
  Characters are presented in a way that …;
- When you identify the point of view or stylistic devices, don't just mention them, but explain what effect they may have on the reader. Use expressions like:
  The author chose the perspective of … in order to …
  The reader identifies with the first person narrator because …
  The text is full of images/metaphors/personification. This helps the reader …;
- When you present your findings, always prove them with examples from the text (▶ Skills 8.3): *The writer uses many similes (e.g. 'My love is like a rose', l. XX).*

SKILLS

▶ SPOTLIGHT ON
Elements of poetry, p. 91

▶ 1.2.4 Reading and analysing poetry

Step 1: Take stock
- Get a general understanding of the **poem** (▶ Glossary 2.4.1) by reading it several times. It is often helpful to read it out loud. Then examine and make notes on the following aspects:
  - the theme or topic of the poem;
  - the type of poem: is it lyrical or narrative?;
  - the **speaker** (if there is one) (▶ Glossary 2.4.1) and who the speaker is addressing;
  - the intention of the poem.

- Find out how the poem is composed by analysing:
  - how many **stanzas** (► Glossary 2.4.1) the poem has;
  - if it is a special type of poem (e.g. a **sonnet**) (► Glossary 2.4.1);
  - the **rhyme scheme** (if there is one) (► Glossary 2.4.1) and its effect;
  - if there are changes e.g. in rhyme that stress a certain line or passage.
- Have a close look at the language and analyse:
  - whether it is simple or more elevated;
  - whether there are any **images** (► Glossary 3.1) and what effect they have.

Step 2: Present your findings (► Skills 5)

Structure your findings, then present them in a three-step-approach:

- Write an introduction which contains the title of the poem, the name of its author and its main topic, e.g.
  The poem '(title)' by '(author)' was written in … and deals with …
  In his/her poem (author's name) describes / thinks about …;
- Write the main body of your interpretation. Here you present your findings on the poem's structure, form and language. Remember: Do not just list your findings but explain their effects:
  The poem is made up / composed of …, which follow the rhyme scheme … This creates an impression of monotony/regularity.
  The language is simple/elevated, which underlines the feeling of …
  The imagery suggests/conveys …
  The poem contains a great deal of imagery / figures of speech (e.g. …). These are used to …;
- Write a conclusion. Here you say whether you think the poem is effective:
  In general / All in all, the poem's rhyme scheme / imagery contribute to …
  The poem succeeds in showing/conveying/expressing …

SKILLS

► 1.2.5 Reading/watching and analysing drama

When reading and analysing a **drama/play** (► Glossary 2.3), always bear in mind that plays are meant to be performed on stage: try to imagine how the stage and the **characters** (► Glossary 2.1) look and how the characters speak, move and interact.

Step 1: Take stock

- Examine and make notes on the following aspects:
  - the division of the play into **acts** and **scenes** (► Glossary 2.3.1). With the beginning of a new scene there often also is a change in **action**, **plot** (► Glossary 2.1), time and/or place ;
  - language and dialogue: the language used by the characters usually tells you something about their social status. Finally consider what function the dialogue has: it may be used to move the action forward, to describe the setting or to give information about the characters;
  - the **characters** (► Glossary 2.1): Look closely at how they interact: does one of them dominate the conversation, what kind of arguments do they put forward, etc. Do not only consider what they say, but also what the **stage directions** (► Glossary 2.3.1) or other characters say about them;

- the **stage directions** (► Glossary 2.3.1): read them to get a good idea of how the stage and the characters look. They may include lighting or sound, which can influence the atmosphere created on stage;
- the audience or reader: does the writer involve the audience (e.g. by a character addressing them)? Does he/she leave anything to the audience's imagination? Does the audience at some stage know more than a character in the play? His/her words may then have a different meaning for the audience than for the character.

Step 2: Present your findings (► Skills 5)

- When you write your findings down, make it clear that you are talking about the play, not about real life. Use expressions like:
  In the play … the author deals with the topic / issue of …
  The play is divided into … acts/scenes, which corresponds to …;
- Do not only say what the play is about, but describe the author's intentions:
  A conflict develops between … and … They represent / stand for …
  The play has an open ending. This demonstrates that the playwright does not want to present a solution to the topic of … / problems/conflicts.

SKILLS ► 2 Working with visuals

The following words and phrases may be helpful:

In the centre/background/foreground …
In the top/bottom left/right hand corner …
On the left/right hand side …
At the top/bottom …
There is/are … / You can see …

SKILLS ► 2.1 Working with pictures

You are often asked to describe a picture and say what effect it has on the viewer. These are the important aspects to consider:

a **Who? What? Where?**
- Describe the people and where they are (the setting);
- Use the present continuous to describe what is happening;
- Say where in the picture you can see certain things: in the foreground, in the background, at the top (of the picture), at the bottom (of the picture), on the left/right, in the centre (of the picture);
- Some parts of the picture may be in (sharp) focus, others out of focus (blurred).

b **The message?**
- What image / idea / feeling does the picture convey? What is its 'message'?
- How does it convey this message? For example: which is the most important element in the picture? how do the setting / colours, etc. emphasise certain ideas? is the picture dark / bright / colourful / frightening / dramatic / full of action / quiet and calm?

SKILLS

▶ SPOTLIGHT ON
Cartoons, p. 144

▶ 2.2 Working with cartoons

Working with cartoons is similar to working with pictures (▶ Skills 2.1) to some extent, but since their intention is often to express an opinion or to make people aware of something, it is important to bear that aspect in mind. Consider the following aspects when working with a cartoon:

a **What? Where? When?**
- Find out where and when the cartoon was published (and, if possible, who the cartoonist is). This may help you to understand the message of the cartoon. For example, a conservative newspaper will be more critical of a socialist politician than a liberal paper;
- Define what it is about, which topic it deals with;
- Say how many frames *(= Bilder)* it consists of;
- Describe the important details in the cartoon. Make sure that you only describe details that contribute to the message of the cartoon;
- Read the caption *(= Bildunterschrift)*, speech or thought bubbles *(= Sprech-/ Gedankenblase)* and all other language items you may find in the picture. Make sure you understand them.

b **The message?**
Here, you will often have to resort to your background knowledge to find out in what context the cartoon is set.
- Describe whether the figures are presented in a positive or negative light and say how this is achieved;
- Analyse whether the cartoonist uses **irony** (▶ Glossary 3.1) and whether he/she tries to evoke associations;
- If the cartoon contains **symbols** (▶ Glossary 3.1), explain what they stand for and why they are used;
- Explain the point the cartoonist is trying to make by examining the source, the language items and the picture together.

SKILLS ▶ 3 Working with statistics

▶ SPOTLIGHT ON
Interpreting statistics, p. 34

a Forms of presentation

Statistics or numbers can be presented in different ways:

- **Tables** are used to list numbers in an ordered way. They are useful to present raw data, but not for quick and easy orientation;
- **Line graphs** show the development of something over a period of time. They show tendencies or trends and they are often used to compare two or more different developments;
- **Bar charts** are used to compare the amounts, quantities, sizes, etc. of two or more different things. They can also be used to show change between two points in time;
- **Pie charts** consist of a circle which is divided into different sectors/segments. These represent parts of a whole, usually in the form of percentages.

Table

year	number of people
1970	14,070
1980	18,490
1990	16,905
2000	16,890
2010	18,690

Line graph

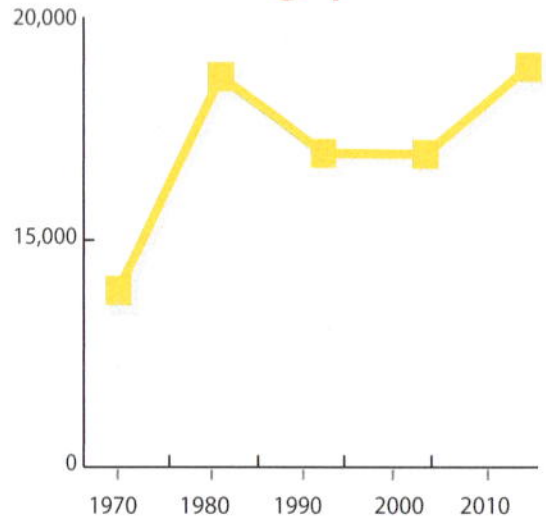

Bar chart

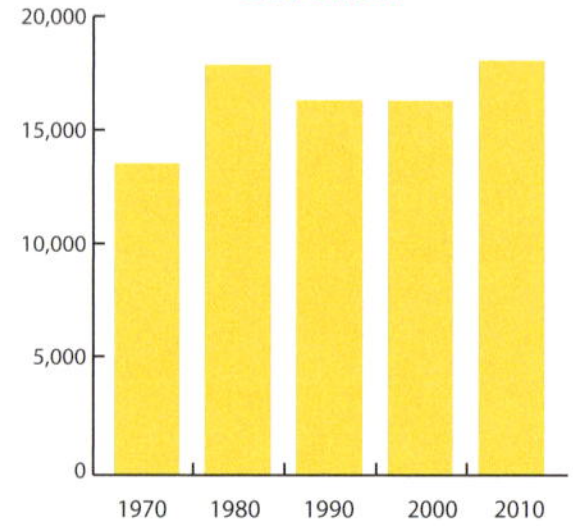

Pie charts

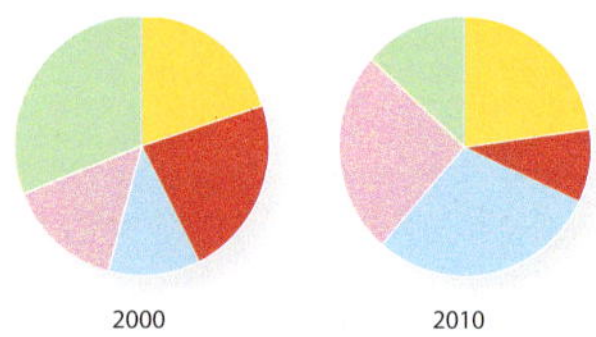

b Analysing tables and graphs

- Always consider the source of a diagram, i.e. where, when and by whom it was published. Check if the numbers are up-to-date and whether the source is reliable;
- Read all the information about a chart carefully. Are the numbers **absolute numbers** (e.g. 14.070) or are they **percentages** (e.g. 15%)? The title or the **key** (i.e. the information next to the graph = *Legende*) will tell you this;
- When you look at visual presentations of numbers, check whether the numbers themselves have been given and prove that they have been visualised accurately: are the **amounts** and **time periods** all the same size or do they differ so that they are no longer trustworthy? Are **proportions** *(= Zahlenverhältnisse)* represented accurately? Have the numbers been rounded up or down so that they are meaningless?
- If conclusions are drawn from statistics, think carefully: Is the given conclusion really what the numbers suggest? Are there other possible interpretations?

c Presenting statistics

- Choose the appropriate form to present your statistics: Should your audience have access to exact figures? Then a table might be best. Or should they get a quick overview? Then choose some form of graph or chart;
- Explain briefly what the diagram shows: topic, time covered, source, whether absolute numbers or percentages are used;
- Describe the relevant parts of your diagram;
- State which conclusions you draw from your numbers.

SKILLS ▶ 4 Working with film and video

When you watch a film, you need to use your listening skills (▶ Skills 6). However, the essential characteristic of video and film is that it is a medium which uses moving images to tell the story. This means learning to 'read' how these images work. The main tool used by video and film makers to tell their story is the **camera**. In addition, they can also use **sound** (**music** or **'voiceovers'**, for example) to add certain effects. On the following pages, you can see the different **shots** *(= Einstellungen)*, **angles** *(= Kamerawinkel)* and **camera movements** *(= Bewegungen)* that **directors** *(= Regisseure)* regularly use – and why – and some other important elements of film and video making techniques.

SKILLS ▶ 4.1 Camera angles

SHOT	EXAMPLE	WHAT THE SHOT DOES
aerial shot *(= Vogelperspektive, extreme Aufsicht)*		Also sometimes called a **bird's eye shot**, this shows a scene from high in the air (in some cases even from above the Earth itself). Its main function is to show the viewer where the events in the film are happening. This is often called an **establishing shot**.
high angle shot *(= Aufsicht)*		Films are mostly about people (the characters): what they do and what happens to them. In the real world, we see things like this at eye level (at the level of our eyes). In a movie, the eye level shot is also the normal way to show the story.
eye level shot *(= Normalsicht)*		The camera can, however, be above (or below) characters and events, and this creates a particular effect. Filming from above often gives the impression that the person in the scene is somehow 'small': less important than other characters or, as in this example, afraid and worried.
low angle shot *(= Untersicht, Froschperspektive)*		This shot has the opposite effect to a high angle shot. Seen from below, a character can seem 'large': more important than others, and as in this example dangerous and threatening. 'Brave' characters are also often filmed with a low angle shot to make us admire them.

SKILLS

▶ 4.2 Camera distances

SHOT	EXAMPLE	WHAT THE SHOT DOES
extreme long shot *(= Panorama, Super-totale)*		Extreme long shots are almost always outside and show the place where the scene is happening. They are another kind of establishing shot. In this shot we can also just see the main character in the scene – an empty street in a cowboy town in the Wild West.
long shot *(= Totale)*		Long shots (also called **full shots** or **wide shots**) show a whole person (or people). They show the character(s) and the scene they are part of.
medium shot *(= Halbtotale, Halbnah)*		A medium shot (or **mid shot)** shows more of the character: the upper part of the character's body from roughly the knees or hips up. Shots like these are good at showing what the character is doing and some of his or her body language.
close-up *(= Großaufnahme)*		Close-ups are one of the most important shots in films and videos. Longer shots show us where the character is, but close-ups almost always show us the character's face and his or her facial expressions: what the character is feeling and thinking at that moment.
extreme close-up *(= Detailaufnahme)*		As the German word 'Detailaufnahme' tells you, an extreme close-up shows a small detail – here the character's eyes. These shots are extremely dramatic and the viewer feels very close to the character.

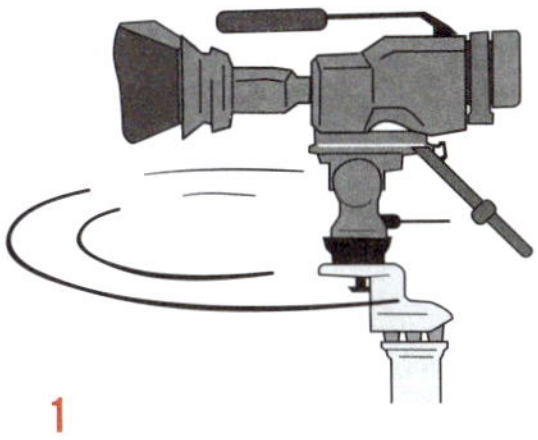

1

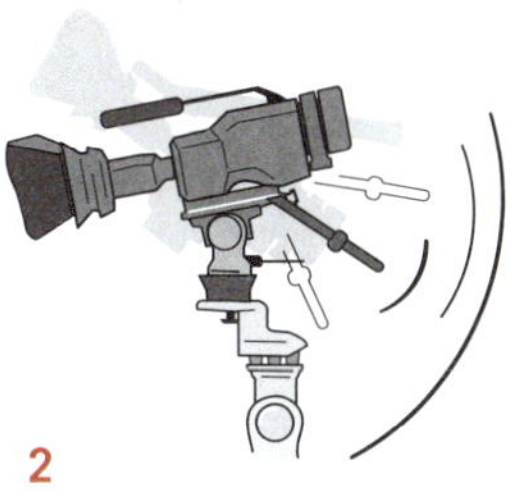

2

3

SKILLS ▶ 4.3 Two shots

SHOT	EXAMPLE	WHAT THE SHOT DOES
two shot *(= Einstellung mit zwei Personen)*		A two shot is any shot in which there are two characters (there are also three shots, four shots, etc.). Usually medium shots, two shots very often show a conversation. We can see both characters from the front or, as here, both characters from the side.
over the shoulder shot *(= Über-die-Schulter-Einstellung)*		Very often when the scene in a film is a conversation, we see the face of one character (A) over the shoulder of the second (B). This allows the viewer to see clearly what A is thinking and feeling during the conversation.
reaction shot *(= Gegeneinstellung)*		In a reaction shot, the camera now goes round to the other side of the conversation and we see how character B reacts.

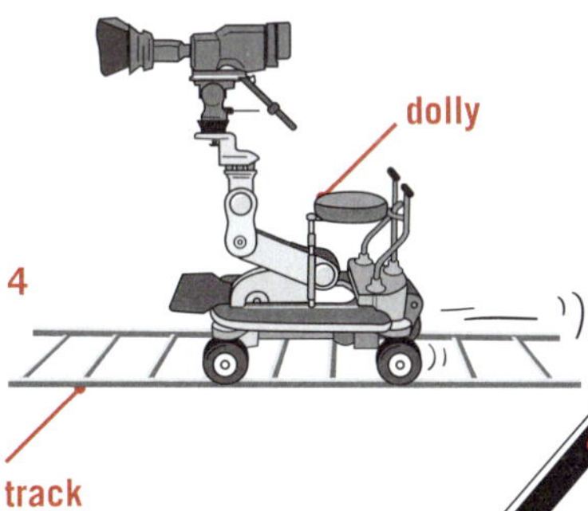

4

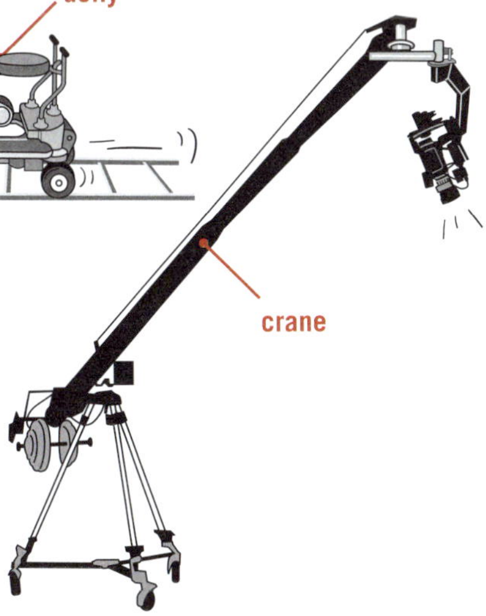

5

SKILLS ▶ 4.4 Camera movements

In most scenes in a movie, the director does not move the camera to shoot a scene – the camera is static and the shots are static shots. From time to time, though, and for certain effects, the camera can move.

1 **pan / panning shot** *(= Schwenk)*. The camera moves from side to side – e.g. to show a large scene.

2 **tilt** *(= vertikaler Schwenk)*. The camera moves up and down.

3 **zoom in** *(= Ranfahrt)* **/ zoom out** *(= Wegfahrt)*. A character, scene, etc. seems to get closer or farther away.

4 **tracking shot** *(= Mitschwenk / Fahrt)*. The camera on the **dolly** moves with a character (often on a **track**).

5 **crane shot.** A crane can show a scene from above – and move with a character, car, etc.

SKILLS
▶ 4.5 Other video and film techniques

Film and video makers use other techniques, too. Below are a few important ways in which they tell their story in films, documentaries, etc.

a **Sound**

Sound techniques include:
- **background music:** usually to create an atmosphere in a scene, or to connect different scenes;
- **voiceover** ('Stimme aus dem Off'): we hear a voice, but do not see the speaker. In video documentaries and news programmes the voice often gives a commentary on what we are watching;
- **off-screen questions:** sometimes in news and documentary videos, an interviewer that we do not see on screen asks questions. This allows us to concentrate on the interviewee.

b **Visual details**

Film and video makers tell their story through moving images. This means that they often give the viewer information with visual details. There are many different kinds, for example:
- We see a plane flying over very low, and know we must be near an airport;
- A quick shot (**cutaway shot** = *Zwischenschnitt*) shows us an object, detail, etc. that helps us to understand the action;
- We see an American flag on a flagpole near a house. This tells us we are in the USA (and maybe that Americans are patriotic people).

c **Lighting**

How light or dark a scene is adds a lot to the atmosphere of the film. Think of all those horror movies in which terrible things happen in a dark, old house!

SKILLS
▶ 5 Writing

SKILLS
▶ 5.1 Writing skills: general

Step 1: Plan
- It is almost impossible to write a good text if you are trying to do two things at the same time: (1) work out your ideas and (2) write a text in English. Before you begin writing, therefore, you should plan – know what you want to say;
- One way is to **make notes.** Make these in English. Making notes in German and then translating them afterwards into English does not work. Be brief. Your aim is not to write a text but rather to collect key words and ideas. The only person who has to understand your notes is *you* – you can turn them later into full sentences;
- Another good way to plan is with a **mindmap**;

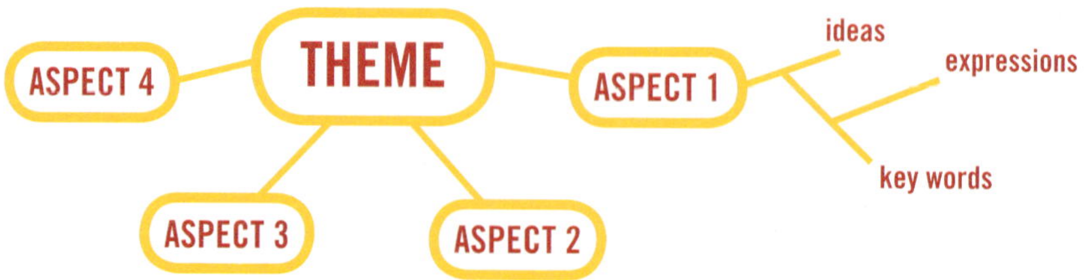

MINDMAPPING
- Mindmaps help you to collect and plan ideas ready for a writing (or speaking) task. You can make them alone or in a group. - Draw a flat circle in the middle of a piece of paper and write into it the central theme of your mindmap (ADOLESCENCE, WORLD PROBLEMS, NEWS, …). - Around this, in smaller circles, arrange the main aspects of the theme. For ADOLESCENCE that could be: family life, careers, relationships, problems, etc. - Thinking then of each aspect at a time, add ideas, key words and expressions connected to each.

- To plan your text, you can also write an **outline**: this is a formal way of structuring your notes and helps you write a coherent text. An outline is set up as a kind of hierarchy (cf. the example on the right);
- Once you've decided on a structure for your text, you can organise your material/information to follow your structure.

1. Introduction
2. Main idea 1
   2.1 Important fact 1
   2.2 Important fact 2
   …
3. Main idea 2
   3.1 Important fact 1
   3.2 Important fact 2
   …
4. Conclusion

Step 2: Make a first draft

Once you have a plan and you have organised your material, you can start the actual writing process. Follow your outline or mindmap and write a first, very rough draft. Don't waste a lot of time on getting everything right; just try to jot down your flow of ideas. If you don't know an English word, note the German equivalent. Leave lots of room to add or correct things later.

Step 3: Revise your text

Read what you have written and make improvements:
- If you have a dictionary, look up the words you wrote in German. If you don't, paraphrase (► Skills 9.6);
- Don't use the same sentence structures every time – use relative pronouns, connectors and other grammatical devices to produce **interesting sentences**;
- Don't repeat the same words over and over again – try to **vary how you express things**;
- Build up a **bank of useful expressions** and phrases that you can use to give your sentences a structure;
- Divide the text into **paragraphs** so that the ideas are **clear** and connect them **logically**;
- Remember your reader. Help him or her to follow your thoughts with 'signals' in the text, for example: *I would like to begin by discussing … / I would now like to go on to examine … / This point is the most important of all: … / We can illustrate this with the following example: … / In conclusion, therefore, we can say that …*;
- Check that you have used enough connectors to link your ideas and sentences. **Connectors** (or **linking words / linkers**) are words that help you express a logical relation:

Organisation	Firstly, … Secondly, / Then …, Finally …
Reason	Due to / because of / as a result of … Therefore / So, …
Addition	In addition / Moreover … / In addition to … / Besides …

Contrast	Although ... / In spite of ... / Whereas ... / However, / But nevertheless ... On the one hand ..., on the other hand ...
Example	For example, / for instance, ... / ... e.g. ... / ... such as ...
Result and consequence	As a consequence / All in all, / Consequently ... / To sum up / To conclude ...

- Add interesting introductory sentences and/or a final sentence to your text;
- Set your work aside for some time and do something else. You should have a fresh perspective on what you have written when you return to it.

Step 4: Check (then check again)

- Read critically – look hard for mistakes. (Tell yourself: 'There are some!');
- Look particularly at language where you have made mistakes before. Most people make the same mistakes many times;
- When you correct your text, make sure the correction is clear and that your reader knows what the final version is;
- Check the content, style, grammar, spelling and punctuation. Consider whether the sentence structure is clear;
- Check whether the ideas in your text develop from paragraph to paragraph;
- If you can, give your text to a friend and ask him/her to check your text again.

Step 5: Rewrite

- Make a clean copy of your work.

SKILLS

► 5.2 Writing skills: special text formats

a Writing a comment

A typical task is often to comment on a text you have read – for example, on a website. Often the comment is a reply to the writer:

- Say what you are commenting on: *I am writing about your post on your blog about / I was interested in what you said in your last post about ... and would like to tell you some of my ideas;*
- Give your personal opinions using 'I';
- Give your personal opinion using 'I' and back up (justify) your answer saying exactly where and why you agree or disagree with the writer. Make sure your arguments are clear and logical:
  I quite agree with what you said about X because ...
  I can't agree with you (I'm afraid) because ...
  As I see it, ... My reasons are as follows ...

b Writing a letter to the editor

Readers can react to **newspaper** and **magazine** (or e-zine) **articles** (► Glossary 1.2) by writing a **letter to the editor** (► Glossary 1.2):

- These letters are much like a comment (see above) – they begin by saying what you are writing about *(your article about ... in your newspaper on* [date] ...), and agree/disagree with the article and express your personal viewpoint. Be polite and formal in your letter;
- Begin with *Dear Sir;*
- Sign your letter with your name and the town/country where you live.

c Writing a review

When you react to a fictional text – a short story, for example – you may be asked to write a review (e.g. for a school magazine):
- Begin with a quick summary of the story – say (in the simple present) what happens in it;
- Give your opinion. Say what was good and so why you liked the text – or what was not so good and so why you did not like it. Include plenty of examples from the story to illustrate your viewpoint;
- At the end, you can give the text a rating (often done with 'stars'), and either recommend it to your readers *(You should definitely read this story)* or not recommend it *(Do not waste your time with this story!).*

► SPOTLIGHT ON
Creative writing, p. 134

d Creative writing

After reading a text you may be asked to react to it with a piece of creative writing. Some typical examples could be:
- re-telling a story from the point of view of one of the characters in it (► Glossary 2.2.1);
- writing a poem (► Glossary 2.4.1);
- writing a newspaper article (► Glossary 1.2) about an event in the text you read;
- writing a diary or report (► Glossary 1.2) in which you imagine an experience you have had.

The following steps can help you with your creative writing:
- Think about the type of text you have to write – a diary, a story, etc. Use the style and features that are typical of this kind of writing. There is usually some model that you can follow when you have to do a task like this – often the text you have just read and are reacting to.
- Think about your readers (young or older? people you know or do not know?). This shapes the text you write.
- In a free writing task (one where you can invent the details, characters etc.), it often helps to brainstorm ideas, especially in a group.
- As always, check your writing afterwards for mistakes and ways to improve its logic and structure (► Skills 5.1: Step 4).

e Writing a covering letter

If you apply for a work placement or a job, you normally write a **covering letter** and a **CV** (**curriculum vitae** = *Lebenslauf*; (► Skills 5.2).
- A covering letter is a formal letter in which you introduce yourself to a possible employer and try to convince him/her that you are the best candidate;
- It shouldn't be longer than one page;
- It consists of the following elements:

ELEMENT OF A COVERING LETTER	TIPS
Your street address, telephone number and e-mail address	Put them on the top right hand side. Do not write your name here.
Addressee's name and address	Put them on the left hand side.
Date	Goes on the right hand side, under your address.
Address	'Dear Mr. X' or, if you don't know the addressee's name, 'Dear Sir or Madam'.

Main part This part should consist of four parts:	
the opening:	Name the job you are applying for or say where you got the company's name from. Careful: As a covering letter is a formal letter, don't use the word *job*, but rather *post* or *vacancy*. Likewise, don't use contracted forms such as 'can't/don't': *I read your advertisement for a/an … with (great) interest in the (name of a newspaper) of (date).* *I am therefore writing to apply for the post of …;* *After …, I am now looking for a position in …*
your suitability:	Briefly describe your qualifications, skills and experience: *As you can see from the enclosed CV …;* *I have two years' experience as …;* *I am currently attending X school and I will be completing my A-levels in …*
your motivation:	Say why you are applying to this particular company and what you hope to achieve in the post: *I hope to be able to use my knowledge of … in this position;* *I am highly interested in your post because it would enable me to …*
the ending:	Say when you are available for an interview and add that you would appreciate a positive reply: *I am available for interview …;* *I look forward to hearing from you.*
Greeting	*Yours sincerely* (addressee's name is known) / *Yours faithfully* (addressee's name is unknown)
Your handwritten signature	
Your name typed	
Enclosures *(= Anlagen)*	You will usually write 'Enc. CV', meaning that you enclose a CV.

f **Writing a CV *(curriculum vitae, = Lebenslauf)***

A **CV**, which in American English is called a **résumé**, presents relevant information about yourself in a structured way. To apply for a job, you send a CV together with a **covering letter** (► Skills 5.2 e). When writing a CV, stick to the following guidelines:

- Start the CV with the heading 'Curriculum Vitae', then write your name, address, telephone number and e-mail address;
- Don't give your date of birth or details about your family in an English CV;
- At the beginning, you may write a profile that sums up your personal strengths, e.g. 'I am a highly-motivated and enthusiastic graduate with previous experience in office work'.
- Stress the positive aspects about yourself;
- Structure the CV in a suitable way; categories might be 'personal details', 'education', 'skills', 'work experience', 'hobbies and interests';
- When you list e.g. the schools you have attended, put them in reverse chronological order; this means that you start with the school you attended last;
- Don't sign an English CV;
- Don't send a photo of yourself.

SKILLS ▶ 6 Listening

SKILLS ▶ 6.1 Listening for gist

The first task with a listening text is to get a general understanding of the text – to listen for gist.

- Listen right through without worrying about understanding every word. Get a general picture of what is being said and of the overall structure of the listening text: a conversation, interview, podcast, scene with several people, voice telling a story, …
- Listen to how the voices are speaking and any background or context. What feelings and emotions are behind the words? What is happening while people are speaking?
- Usually, you want to note down or sum up what you have heard, and it is best to do this after you have listened. First write down just key words or phrases, then develop your notes in more detail, or organise them into a short text.

SKILLS ▶ 6.2 Listening for detail: taking notes

The practical problem when you listen for detail in a text is often that you have to listen and at the same time take notes:

- Don't write whole sentences. Note down key words and phrases only. The important thing is that *you* can understand your notes afterwards;
- Use abbreviations and numbers, for example:

and	+	is	=
and so / therefore	⟶ or >	is not	≠
very	v.	about / roughly	≈
and so on	etc.	twenty-five years	25 yrs.
for example	e.g.	half / three quarters	½ ¾

- With many listening tasks you can develop a listening grid (after you have listened for gist and before you listen for detail). You can write notes into this as you listen:

WHO?	*interviewer = Peter Smith / interviewee = Karen*
WHY?	*K went round world by train + ship*
WHEN?	*last yr / Jan-Oct*
HIGHLIGHTS?	*China / S. America / Australia – all v. interesting*
PROBLEMS?	*ill in Tibet / lost money in France*
LEARNED?	*be independent / slow down!*
PLANS?	*work camp next yr in Chile*

SKILLS ▶ 7 Speaking

SKILLS ▶ 7.1 Classroom discussions

In classroom work you are often asked to discuss a text you have read.

- Don't be afraid to try! 'With hands and feet' is also a way of getting ideas across;
- Use the phrases on the inside cover of your book. They give your sentences a structure;
- Learn how to agree and disagree with other students politely. This is very important

for native speakers of English. You will seem 'German' if, in real conversations later, you are too direct and abrupt.

SKILLS

▶ 7.2 Debating

▶ SPOTLIGHT ON
A formal debate, p. 151

A debate is a formal discussion of a **'motion'** or **'proposal'** (i.e. a controversial topic) that ends in a vote. To hold a successful debate, you have to collect and organise good arguments and present them as convincingly as possible.

Step 1: Organising the debate

- Collect a motion and phrase it in the following way: 'This house would ...' or 'This house believes ...';
- The class divides into two groups, one for and one against the motion. Research and collect as many arguments for your side as you can. Your personal opinion is irrelevant – you must argue for your team. Prepare good examples to support your points. Think of arguments for the opposing view and of ways to answer them;
- Rank the arguments in order of importance;
- Decide on the amount of time (e.g. 3–6 minutes) each speaker will have;
- Choose two speakers for each side, a chairman and a timekeeper. The rest of the class is the audience, called **'floor'**.

Step 2: Holding the debate

A debate runs along the following lines:

- Speaker 1 **proposes** the motion (= argues in favour of the motion);
- Speaker 2 **opposes** the motion (= argues against the motion);
- Speaker 3 adds new arguments in favour of the motion;
- Speaker 4 adds new arguments against the motion;
- The debate is then opened to the floor: the audience questions the teams;
- There may be a break of 5–10 minutes so that both teams can prepare their **rebuttal speech** *(= Widerlegung)*;
- One speaker from each team (normally the first speaker) delivers the rebuttal speech. He/She answers the questions posed by the opposition and the floor and summarises the team's main points;
- During the debate, the **chairperson** thanks each speaker and introduces the next. He/She does not comment on what has been said;
- The **timekeeper** ensures that the speakers know how much time they have. One minute before the time is up the timekeeper announces: 'Last minute', and when the time is up he/she announces: 'Time is up'.

Step 3: After the debate

- The house (i.e. everyone except for the chairperson) **votes on the motion**. This means they decide which group was better: which of them presented the best arguments and spoke most convincingly. The vote has got nothing to do with their personal opinion on the motion!
- When the votes have been counted, the chairperson announces: *'For the motion: (number of votes); against the motion: (number of votes). I declare the motion carried/ defeated by ... votes.'*
- As a sign of respect, the speakers of the opposing sides shake hands.

SKILLS

▶ 7.3 Making a report

You are often asked to report your group's ideas to the class after doing a task:
- Every member of the group should be able to make the report. Don't leave it always to the same students. If possible, arrange it so that more than one student gives your group report – each one reporting on a different aspect of your ideas;
- Don't write a text and read it aloud. Make notes and use these to help you to speak spontaneously;
- Think of your listeners: put forward your ideas logically; explain difficult words you have used; sum up at the end to emphasise the main points again;
- Ask for questions and be ready to answer them.

SKILLS

▶ 7.4 Making a formal presentation

In most cases, at the end of a project, you have to present it to the class – you have to make a formal presentation. These are the basic rules for a good presentation.

RULES FOR A SUCCESSFUL PRESENTATION

- If you have worked in a group, decide exactly who gives your presentation. Presentations usually work best if more than one person speaks.
- Use 'visuals'. It is a fact that we receive 80 per cent of information through our eyes and only 20 per cent through our ears. Help your listeners with an overhead projector or a large piece of paper on which you list main points and show diagrams or pictures to help them to take in what you say.
- Don't write a text and simply read it aloud. Speak from notes and sound spontaneous.
- Speak slowly and loudly. Talk to the students at the back of the class.
- Look at your listeners. Eye contact is important.
- Structure your talk clearly. People in business who frequently make presentations always say that you should:
  - 'Tell the audience what you are going to say': *I (we) would like to speak today about ... / I will begin by ... then I will go on to look at ... / Finally, I will ....*
  - 'Say it': give the main part of your presentation. Again, help the audience as much as possible to follow your ideas with phrases such as: *OK, I have spoken about .... I would now like to go on to ... / The next main point I want to make is ... / I would like to turn now to ...*
  - 'Tell the audience what you have said': sum up your main points with phrases such as *That brings me to the end of my talk, and I would like just to sum up the main points / To sum up, then, ...*
- Most presentations normally end with a chance for the listeners to ask questions. You can invite them to do this with a phrase such as: *Thanks for listening. Now, are there any questions?*

SKILLS

▶ 7.5 Explaining your ideas to other students

In some classroom activities, you have to explain ideas to a student from another group, or to students in your own group.
- Do this by talking, not by showing your notes. The aim of the task is to practise speaking;
- Allow the person / people listening plenty of time to take notes and answer any questions they have about things which are not clear;
- At the end, ask your listener(s) to repeat back to you what they understood. There may be things that are not quite right.

SKILLS ▶ 8 Working on projects

SKILLS ▶ 8.1 Organising a project

Project work is normally done in small groups. The project may be to find information and present it to the class, or to make a poster, leaflet, etc.

- Work first as a group and brainstorm ideas (▶ Activity chest 2). Get a clear plan of how you are going to organise your project;
- Divide up the work so that each member of the group has her / his own clear task;
- Set times when each task should be ready – the project will not work if one member of the group is not finished on time. It is a good idea to choose one student who keeps an eye on how the project is going;
- If you are asked to present your findings to the class, check here for further tips: **Making a report** (▶ Skills 7.3), **Making a formal presentation** (▶ Skills 7.4), **Explaining your ideas to other students** (▶ Skills 7.5).

SKILLS ▶ 8.2 Doing research

Part of your project work (but often also of your writing tasks) will mean that you look for information about a certain topic yourself – you *research* a topic.

a **Doing research: general**

Step 1: Be clear

Before starting your research, make sure that you know exactly what your topic is. Write it down in one sentence, then list a number of **key words** that you will need to research.

Step 2: Use general works of reference

- To get a first overview, start with encyclopaedias, e.g. Wikipedia;
- If possible, use only sources in English. This will give you a lot of useful words and phrases and you needn't translate your findings into English;
- Never trust your sources: in order to find out how reliable your source is, examine its point of view, find out more about the writer and always double-check with another source.

Step 3: Find the information you need

Use **skimming** (▶ Skills 1.1) and **scanning** (▶ Skills 1.1) to find out whether your material is relevant for your topic or where the information needed is.

Step 4: Make notes

- Copy relevant parts of the text. Always add the exact source (e.g. a website, a book title with page number) so that you remember later where you got your information or the quote from (▶ Skills 8.3);
- Index cards are useful for making notes: You can note information or quotes and their sources on them. Later, when you start structuring your material, it is easier to bring them into a suitable order (▶ Skills 5.1).

b **Doing research on the internet**

With internet sources there are two main difficulties: firstly, there is a huge amount of information on offer and it may be difficult for you to find exactly what you are looking for. Secondly, there is the problem of reliability: since anyone can publish on

the internet, you never know if the information given is correct and balanced.
If you use a search engine, here are some tips to help you limit your hits and to find exactly what you want:

- Set the 'Language' settings on your search engine to 'English'. This way you will only get webpages written in English;
- Use concrete headwords and combine them to narrow down your search. For example, if you look for information on globalisation and sustainable development in India and you enter 'globalisation', you will get more than 8 million hits. If you enter 'globalisation+sustainable development+India', you get only half as many hits;
- If you want to search for an exact phrase, e.g. 'sustainable solutions', put the words in quotation marks ('xx').

SKILLS ▶ 8.3 Quoting

Quoting is used when you want to support your own statements by pointing to evidence from the text you are working with. Basically, there are two ways of fitting an author's words into your text: you can either **paraphrase** the text (or parts of it) (▶ Skills 9.6) or you can **quote** it **word for word**. If you quote, you must copy the text 1:1! In both cases you have to make sure that you indicate precisely from which source the material is taken (website, title of book or article, page and/or line number).
The tricky thing about quoting is that you have to integrate the quotations into your own sentences as smoothly as possible. The following tips may help you:

- Use quotation marks ('xx') to indicate beginning and end of the quote:
  The writer of the article considers London to be 'the coolest city on earth' (p. 53, ll. 11–12);
- Use different introductory phrases with your quotations:
  According to the writer, …
  The article goes on to say that …
  The writer regrets that …
- Quotes must be given exactly as they appeared in the original. If it is necessary to shorten or to expand them, then this must clearly be shown (usually with the help of square brackets [ ]): *'It [London] became the place for European companies to borrow money […]', the journalist points out (Level Crossing, p. 53, ll. 45–46);*
- If you quote from a poem, you indicate the lines by using the dash /: *James Berry's poem begins with the lines 'I walk-in a Brixtan Markit / believin I a respectable man.' (ll. 1–2).)*

SKILLS ▶ 9 Working on your language skills

SKILLS ▶ 9.1 Working with a grammar book

The most difficult thing about using a grammar book is to find the correct entry. Therefore you should:

- get to know your grammar book. Look at the most important parts (e.g. table of contents, list of grammar terms and, above all, the index (= Register) at the back of the book) and find out how they are organised;
- read the tips on how to use the grammar book. These will tell you what features your grammar book has, e.g. what the symbols mean, what the different colours are used

for, how **bold** and *italic* print are used;
- learn the correct grammatical terms;
- always read the rules together with the examples given. Watch for hints about frequent mistakes.

SKILLS ▶ 9.2 Working with a monolingual dictionary

You probably think a monolingual (i.e. English-English) dictionary only helps you to find out the meaning of words you don't know. But if you know how to use it, a monolingual dictionary can also help you to find a word you don't know or show you how to use a word.
Look for an overview of the symbols and abbreviations used in the dictionary that you use. Study them carefully. Have a look at any keyword you like and work out what the symbols and abbreviations tell you about this specific word. Here is an example from the *Oxford Advanced Learner's Dictionary*.

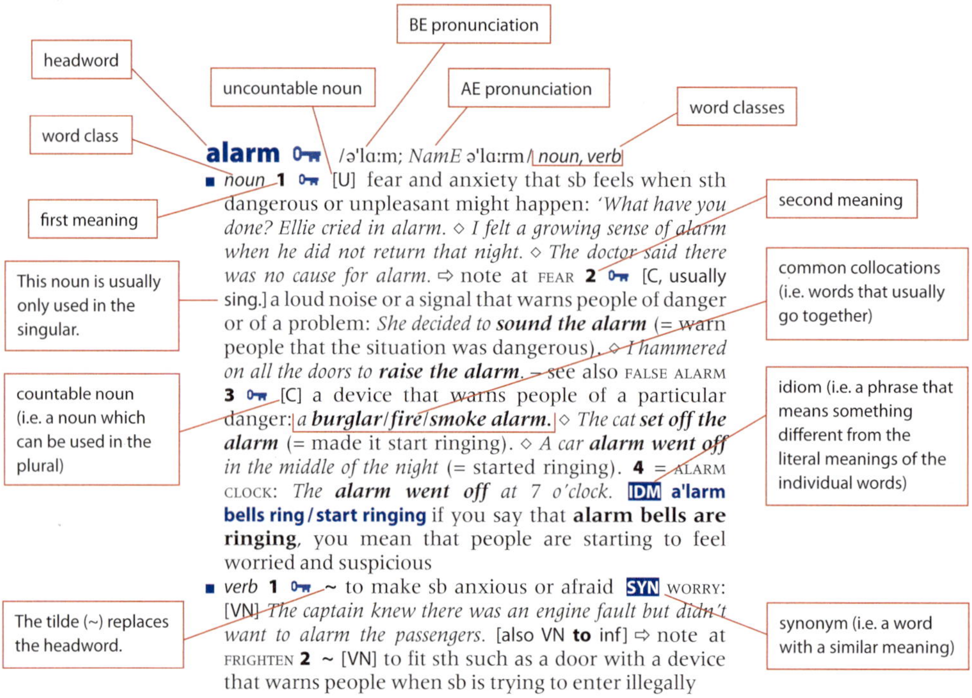

SKILLS ▶ 9.3 Working with a bilingual dictionary

It may seem very straightforward, but in fact, looking for the right word in a bilingual dictionary can be very tricky and cause many mistakes in your writing.
- For example, a German word may have more than one meaning. You will then have to decide which English word is the correct translation. For example:
  Absatz (= part of a shoe): heel
  (= number of items you have sold): sales
  (= part of a text): paragraph
  groß: a big problem – a large family – a great success
- A German word may have a completely different grammar from the English equivalent.

jemanden diskriminieren = discriminate against sb.
Ich habe einige wichtige Informationen für Sie. (plural noun) = I've got some important information for you. (singlar noun)

Be aware of these pitfalls and try to avoid them by:
- looking closely at the information your dictionary offers you beyond the translation (e.g. grammatical information, example phrases etc.);
- double-checking with your monolingual dictionary (► Skills 9.2) if you are unsure what the meaning of the English word is.

SKILLS ► 9.4 Learning new words

There are many different ways of learning new words. How well different techniques work depends on the individual learner. So try out some of the tips given below and find out which of them are helpful for you:
- Collect old and new words that belong to a topic and structure them (e.g. in a mind-map or list);
- Use cards with a German word on one side and the English word on the other; then learn them;
- Write new words on Post-its and stick them around your bedroom. You will then see them again and again;
- Write sentences or phrases and leave out the words you want to learn. Then try to fill them in.

There are three rules, however, which probably apply to everybody:
- Don't learn too many words at the same time, 7–10 should be enough;
- Set aside a short period of time every day for your vocab work – this is better than spending half a day revising on the day before your exam;
- Repeat, repeat, repeat!

SKILLS ► 9.5 Dealing with unknown words

When you read English texts, there will always be words you don't understand. Don't worry – and don't look up every word! You don't have to know every single word to understand a text! Here are some techniques that will help you understand more without using a dictionary:
- Look at the surroundings of the word: these may include headlines, pictures, charts;
- Think of words that look or sound similar, either in English or in German. For example, if you know the word muscle, it will be quite easy for you to guess what *muscular* means. Or *reduce* may remind you of *reduzieren*;
- Prefixes *(= Vorsilben)* and suffixes *(= Nachsilben)* can help you: if you know that *pre-* often means *before*, then *pre-war, (to) preheat, (to) prejudge sb*. won't pose any problems for you.

SKILLS ► 9.6 Paraphrasing

Paraphrasing is a helpful strategy if you don't know a particular word: you can communicate the meaning without using the word itself. There are various ways of paraphrasing a word:
- You can use phrases like 'a type of … / a kind of …':

It is a type of bird with extremely long and colourful tail feathers: a peacock;
It is a kind of material. It comes from sheep and you make pullovers out of it: wool;

- You can use synonyms or antonyms:
  It's the opposite of peace: war;
  It's the same as / a synonym of clever: smart;
- You can use a word with a general meaning (e.g. 'somebody / a person', 'something') and add a clause that defines it:
  It's a person who does operations on people: a surgeon;
  It's a tool that you use to make holes in walls: a drill.

Paraphrasing is also used when you put a passage or a complete text in your own words (e.g. to avoid a direct quotation ► Skills 8.3).

SKILLS ► 9.7 Mediating

Mediating is a technique used to make communication possible between people who do not share a common language. More specifically, it means summarising (orally or in writing) a spoken or written text in another language (► Skills 1.1: Step 2).

Step 1
Make sure you know what information the person you are mediating for needs. If you are given a specific assignment, make sure you know what situation you are supposed to imagine and what kind of text you are supposed to produce (it may be an article for a magazine, for example).

Step 2
Read through your material and try to get the gist of it. When mediating, you are supposed to pass it on without giving your opinion on it.

Step 3
Decide what information your reader/addressee needs to know by asking yourself *who? what? when? where? why?* questions. You may have to arrange this information in an order that differs from the text.

Step 4
Write your text:

- adapt your language, **style** and **register** (► Glossary 3.2) to your addressee – you may for example be writing a **formal** article or a letter to a friend;
- if you don't know an English word, try to **paraphrase** it (► Skills 9.6).

SKILLS ► 9.8 Translating

When you translate, you transfer a written text from one language to another. The aim is to be as close as possible to the original text as regards sentence structure, **tone**, **style**, **register** etc (► Glossary 3.2).

Step 1
First read the whole text to find out what it's about.

Step 2
Translate the text sentence by sentence. Try to keep close to the original, but you may have to:

- break a sentence in two or combine two sentences to one;
- use a different tense or structure:
  She wanted me to look after her pets. – Sie wollte, dass ich auf ihre Tiere aufpasse.

I've never been to Thailand. – Ich war noch nie in Thailand.
He wasn't given enough time. – Man hat ihm nicht genug Zeit gelassen.
We used to go by bike. – Wir sind immer mit dem Fahrrad gefahren.

Step 3

Read your text again and make sure that it's consistent. It ought to sound as if it had been written in the target language, not as if it had been translated.

Exam Practice

EXAM PRACTICE

▶ 1 How to prepare for the exam

▶ 1.1 Preparation with earlier test papers

DON'T throw your earlier test papers away and pretend they're history.

If you want to be successful in your exam, it is vital to know where your weaknesses lie and to improve in those areas. Have a look at your old test papers and find out about your 'favourite' mistakes:

1. highlight the different types of mistakes (e.g. *gr = grammar, sp = spelling, voc = vocabulary, …*);
2. see which category needs most attention;
3. correct the mistakes in writing.

Also, have a look at your teacher's comments at the bottom of the test paper and identify the areas you should concentrate on, e.g. doing precisely what the assignment says, structuring a text, etc. Then get helpful training materials (books, worksheets, websites, etc.) and work on your weak spots. For all the areas that are not language-related, this exam practice will help you prepare for the exam.

EXAM PRACTICE

▶ 1.2 Clever planning and time-management

When preparing for or sitting an exam, time is precious, so make careful use of it!

a **Before the exam**

Practice

1 With the help of your earlier test papers, list the areas you want to work on. These may include:
A) getting to know your dictionary;
B) learning facts about relevant topics and structuring your knowledge (e.g. with file cards, mindmaps);
C) learning vocabulary (on topics such as the American Dream, or for special tasks such as describing a character, making a point, contradicting etc.);
D) revising your grammar;
E) structuring your text and linking your sentences;
F) getting a feeling for the language by reading and listening to English texts;
G) studying and practising opening or closing sentences.

DON'T enjoy life until the last minute and then set aside the last 24 hours before the exam for non-stop learning.

2 Rank those areas according to importance. For example, if you feel that you know your grammar quite well, then plan to do other things first and come back to grammar topics if you still have time.

3 See how many weeks there are left, then make a timetable that tells you when to do what:

WEEK	A	B	C	D	E	F	G	...
1		Empire	environment	tenses		X		...
2		India	characterisation		X		X	...
3		American Dream	linking words	adverbs		X		...
...	...	...	...	...	...	...	...	...

b **During the exam**

In the exam, don't just start writing in the hope that you will finish on time – plan your work! If your exam is e.g. from 8–12.30, the following may be a useful plan:

DON'T start writing your answer to task 1 right away because others are doing that too and it gives you the feeling you're doing something. Look at all the tasks, prepare your writing and plan your work.

Start	*To do*
8.00	Read the texts and the tasks. Make sure you know what you're expected to do.
8.20	Prepare task 1: Mark up the text, make notes, write (► Skills 1.1: Step 1).
9.35	Have a break
9.40	Prepare task 2: Mark up the text, make notes, write (► Skills 1.1: Step 1).
10.55	Have a break
11.00	Prepare task 3: Mark up the text, make notes, write (► Skills 1.1: Step 1).
12.15	Revise and proofread your text (► Skills 5.1: Steps 3–5)
12.30	Hand in your paper

EXAM PRACTICE

► 2 How to deal with the tasks

► 2.1 How to choose the best texts and tasks

In many exam situations you will be given the choice between two or more texts. In order to make the right decision, you should:

DON'T make your choice within one minute just because you have read key-words that sound familiar.

1. read the titles of the texts, their subheadings, the sources;
2. read all the tasks and make sure you understand them. If necessary, use your dictionary;
3. skim the texts and quickly try to identify the keywords. Then scan them for information that may help you to work on the tasks (► Skills 1: Skimming; ► Skills 1: Scanning; ► Exam Practice 2.2);
4. decide if the tasks will be difficult or easy for you. Consider the following questions:
   - do I know enough about the topic?
   - do I understand the tasks? (► Words for tasks, p. 343)
   - have I found enough material in the text to work on the tasks?
   - do I know sufficient vocabulary to write about them?
5. compare what you have found about the texts and tasks, then make your decision.

EXAM PRACTICE

► 2.2 How to understand a text

There are two possibilities: You can skim and scan a text or you can try out the'SQ3R'-method.

a **First skimming, then scanning a text** (► Skills 1.1: Step 1)
By skimming a text, you find out its main point or topic: focus on the title, sub-headlines, repeated key-words, first and last sentences of paragraphs.
By scanning a text, you can find out if and where the text covers specific topics or points; you scan the text quickly in search for one or more specific ideas.

b **Using the 'SQ3R'-method**

1. Survey: try to identify the main point of the text and remember as much as you can about the topic.
2. Questions: form questions that you would like to be answered by the text. This will increase your own interest and filter out important elements. Usually these questions are the classic 'w'-questions (who? what? why? where?).
3. Read: go through the text and its individual parts closely now. Remember your survey and try to find answers to your questions on the way. Highlight important passages (► Skills 1.1: Step 1).
4. Recall: try to answer your questions now (but use your own words!). If the text doesn't answer your questions, don't worry, go back to step 2 and start again from there.
5. Review: look at your results again and work out how the parts of the text are connected. Did you identify the main point correctly in the first place?

EXAM PRACTICE

► 2.3 How to connect the text to your knowledge

A text is good if it makes you interested in its topic, but it is even better if it evokes topics you are familiar with or you have dealt with. So if you read a text, take some time to connect the text with what you know. For example, a text about the rising popularity of flexible mobile phones could activate your knowledge about apps or future technology. Or, a text about secret racial discrimination in the USA could activate your knowledge about the Civil Rights Movement, Martin Luther King or President Obama's career.

EXAM PRACTICE

► 2.4 How to use visual aids

Visual aids such as mindmaps or tables (► Skills 5.1: Step 1) help our minds to structure and remember things better. In the months before your exam, experiment with them and find out which visual method works best for you. Practise it as much as you can.

DON'T stick to the motto 'drawing things is for babies' and start spontaneously writing down what comes to mind.

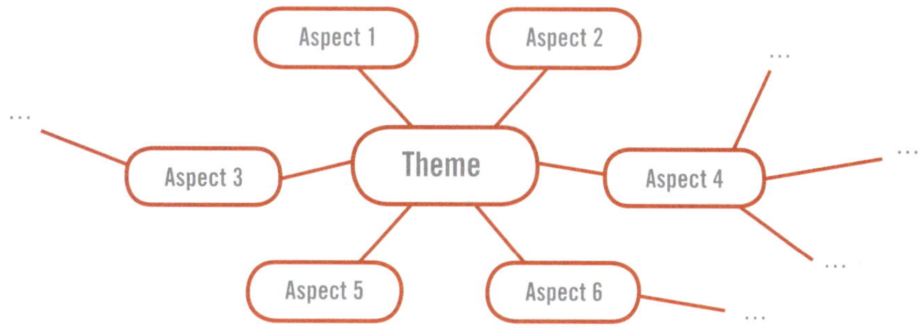

Practice

Silver-spoon voluntourism

Picking up trash and pulling weeds may not sound terribly posh, but at a growing number of high-end resorts, where rooms often cost $400 or $500 a night, these activities are becoming yet another hotel amenity. One morning you can sleep in and order room service, and the next you can serve breakfast at a soup kitchen.

The trend is part of a larger movement toward voluntourism, i.e., trips with a heavy focus on volunteering. But unlike programs like Habitat for Humanity that pair weeklong projects with unglamorous accommodations, hotel-organized excursions generally take up no more than a day, and participants can cap off the experience back at the ranch with $15 cocktails and a night on high-thread-count sheets.

Many of these short-term voluntourism projects involve hard work. The Mandarin Oriental in Miami, for instance, offers a two-night package in which guests spend a morning removing invasive plants and assisting with recycling programs in Everglades National Park. The Fairmont Mission Inn and Spa in Sonoma, Calif., recently invited guests to help fix up a hiking trail.

But perhaps no luxury-hotel brand has ventured as far into voluntourism as Ritz-Carlton. […] Sue Stephenson, vice president of the Company's Community Footprints initiative, says the half-day programs range from assisting local food banks to participating in music therapy for disabled kids.

The excursions are designed to connect tourists with the communities they visit. 'When done correctly, these programs can also help maintain the natural environments that are the draw for particular regions of the world,' says Kara Hurst, a top executive at Business for Social Responsibility, a non-profit that develops corporate-social-responsibility initiatives.

Silver-spoon voluntourism has its critics, of course. Christopher Elliott, a syndicated travel columnist and blogger in Orlando, Fla., thinks these efforts are aimed at wealthy guests 'who want to soothe their guilty conscience by doing something that's billed as "giving back." '

Still, it's hard to find fault with hotels that link local charities to potential donors. And do guests get discounts for being do-gooders? On the contrary, some hotels charge participants an extra $40 or more to cover transportation and other costs associated with their manual labor.

[From: *TIME magazine*, 16 November 2009]

1 *pull weeds:* pull plants out of the ground that you don't want to grow there
3 *amenity:* luxury, pleasant service
11 *high-thread-count sheets:* luxury bed sheets
23 *draw* (n): thing that attracts people
24 *executive* [-'---]: manager
31 *donor:* person who gives something, e.g. money, for a good cause

For possible solutions: **Webcode:** LC323180-314

1 Skim the text and say what it's about.
2 Scan the text for information on the following:
  - the kind of work that is done by volunteers;
  - the number of hotels that participate in the programme;
  - reactions to the programme.
3 Use the SQ3R-method to understand the text. Make notes.
4 In what areas does this text relate to your knowledge or experiences? Make notes.
5 Make a mindmap to present the most important aspects of voluntourism in a structured way.

EXAM PRACTICE

► 3 How to score content points

► 3.1 Comprehending and summarising texts

In task 1 of most exam papers you are asked to show that you have understood the contents of the text ('*What* is expressed?'). 'Text' here can mean different kinds of material, it may be a fictional or a non-fictional text or a visual.

DON'T copy complete phrases from the original text and integrate them into your summary just because they are so well expressed. Use your own words!

a You may be asked to summarise the text in your own words, or you may find instructions such as 'describe' or 'point out' (► Words for tasks, p. 344).
Take your time to fully understand the text and to prepare your answer.
This will be a basis for the following tasks, too. Make use of the skimming/scanning-technique or the SQ3R-method (► Exam Practice 5.1).

b You may also find formats such as multiple choice or true/false. See Exam Practice 5.1 for tips on how to handle them.

EXAM PRACTICE

► 3.2 Analysing texts

Here you are asked to 'analyse' a text, i.e. to describe what means it uses and to what effect ('*How* is it expressed? For what *purpose*?'). You may also find verbs such as 'examine' or 'characterise' (► Words for tasks, p. 344). Make sure that you don't simply list the means an author uses, but that you also describe the effect they have.

DON'T squeeze certain aspects into your analysis because you forgot to mention them in your summary. Summary and analysis **MUST** be kept separate.

Possible findings with regard to non-fictional texts:
- use of facts and figures, statistics → creates reliability;
- use of quotations from experts → creates reliability;
- direct address of the reader → includes the reader, involves them in the situation;
- use of examples and illustrations → increases comprehensibility;
- use of rhetorical questions → makes the reader think, makes them interested;
- use of irony → makes the reader smile and follow the criticism.

Possible findings with regard to fictional texts:
- use of metaphors and imagery → creates a picture in the reader's mind;
- use of inner monologue → allows the reader to follow a character's thoughts;
- use of exclamations or unfinished sentences → illustrates e.g. tension or lack of concentration;
- use of a certain type of narrator → creates distance or closeness/identification between character and reader (► Glossary 2.2.1).

EXAM PRACTICE

► 3.3 Interpretation/Comment / Creative writing

The third task in your exam is usually to go beyond the text. You may be asked to 'assess' or 'interpret', to 'discuss' or 'comment on' something. A second type of task implies creative writing – this could be a letter to the editor reacting to the article you have just analysed or the inner monologue of a character in the story you have worked on.

Possible instructions for interpretations:
- 'Evaluate whether or not the writer succeeded in producing a convincing piece of writing.'
- 'Interpret the cartoon. Include aspects of Britain's role in the world in the past and present.'

Possible instructions for comments:
- 'Comment on the mother's attitude concerning racial relations and relate it to the problem of identity many African Americans are confronted with.'
- 'Discuss whether nurture or nature plays a more important role in an individual's life.'

Possible instructions of creative writing:
- 'Imagine Willy Loman writes a letter to his boss. Compose this letter.'
- 'Write a speech to a group of young businessmen on the topic "Gene food –curse or blessing for our world?"'

EXAM PRACTICE

▶ 3.4 Check your contents

Your summary of a text has got:
- the present tense;
- no direct speech;
- no statistics or examples (non-fictional texts);
- no metaphors or poetic language (fictional texts);
- no quotations;
- 30–40% of the number of words in the original text;
- a clear paragraph structure;
- no interpretation, personal opinion, or text-analysis.

Your analysis of a text has got:
- 2–5 examples from the text that support your results, marked as quotations and with line-numbers;
- no elements of a summary;
- a conclusion that states what effects the author wants to reach with the means he/she uses.

Your interpretation:
- begins with an introductory sentence repeating the given task and showing its relevance;
- contains a condensed analysis of the points that the (non-fictional) text tries to make and the effect it has (maybe also without wanting to);
- describes and/or compares characters (in a fictional text) and describes the context of the given excerpt within the complete literary work.

Your comment:
- begins with an introductory sentence repeating the given task and showing its relevance;
- discusses pros and cons of an issue and comes to a conclusion;
- has a meaningful structure, for example past – present – future;
- wants to make one or more specific points clear to an addressee;
- contains your personal opinion supported by arguments.

Your creative text:
- uses only the kind of language and style appropriate for the character from whose perspective you are writing;
- is plausible considering your knowledge of a text, its characters, the situation.

Practice

Sherman McCoy, 38, is a successful bond market trader on Wall Street. He works as chief salesman for the investment company Pierce&Pierce. With his wife Judy, an interior designer, and their daughter Campbell he lives in an expensive flat near Central Park, Manhattan.

How these sons of the great universities, [...] now flocked to Wall Street and to the bond trading room of Pierce & Pierce! How the stories circulated on every campus! If you weren't making $250,000 a year within five years, then you were either grossly stupid or grossly lazy. That was the word. By age thirty, $500,000 – and that sum had the taint of the mediocre. By age forty you were either making a million a year or you were timid and incompetent. *Make it now!* [...]

Masters of the Universe! The roar filled Sherman's soul with hope, confidence [...] and righteousness. Yes, righteousness! Judy understood none of this, did she? None of it. Oh, he noticed her eyes glazing over when he talked about it. Moving the lever that moves the world was what he was doing – and all she wanted to know was why he never made it home for dinner.

When he did make it home for dinner, what did she want to talk about? Her precious interior-decorating business and how she had gotten their apartment into Architectural Digest, which, frankly, to a true Wall Streeter was a fucking embarrassment. Did she commend him for the hundreds of thousands of dollars that made her decorating and her lunches and whatever the hell else she did possible? No, she did not. She took it for granted. [...]

He picked up the telephone and was ready to resume work on the greatest coup of his young career, [...] when he spotted something out of the corner of his eye. He *detected* it – righteously! – [...] *Arguello was reading a newspaper.*

Ferdinand Arguello was a junior bond salesman, twenty-five or -six years old, from Argentina. He was leaning back in his chair nonchalantly reading a newspaper, and even from here Sherman could see what it was: *The Racing Form. The Racing Form!* The young man looked like a caricature of a South American polo player. He was slender and handsome; he had thick wavy black hair, combed straight back. He was wearing a pair of red silk moiré suspenders. *Silk moiré.* The bond department of Pierce & Pierce was like an Air Force fighter squadron. Sherman knew it even if this young South American didn't. As the number one bond salesman, Sherman had no official rank. Nevertheless, he occupied a moral eminence. You were either capable of doing the job and willing to devote 100 percent to the job, or you got out. The eighty members of the department received a base salary, a safety net, of $ 120,000 a year each. This was regarded as a laughably small sum. The rest of their income came from commissions and profit-sharing. [...]

The day didn't start with small talk and coffee [...] You were expected to get on the telephone and start making money.

[From: Tom Wolfe, *The Bonfire of the Vanities*, 1988]

2 *bond trading:* Handel mit Rentenanleihen
5 *taint of the mediocre:* impression of a poor performance
8 *roar:* loud noise (here: of shouting orders and telephoning)
9 *righteousness:* firm belief or feeling that what you do is right
10 *glaze over:* begin to look bored
11 *lever:* Hebel
28 *silk moiré suspenders:* elastic strings to hold your trousers instead of a belt made of silk and with an exquisite pattern
30 *squadron:* group of military aircraft
32 *eminence:* status in which people respect you and accept you as a model

For possible solutions:
Webcode: LC323180-318

1 Summarise Sherman McCoy's emotions and principles as shown in this extract.
2 Analyse the style the author uses to give us an insight into the protagonist's state of mind.
3 a McCoy's self-image as a 'Master of the Universe' will ultimately lead to his downfall and he will find himself in an extreme situation. Compare McCoy with other characters from literature that have to cope with extreme situations.
b Write a dialogue between McCoy and Arguello. Keep in mind that Sherman is angry on the one hand, but a 'moral eminence' on the other.
c 'Job-satisfaction, money-making, good personal relationships: in today's world it is impossible to combine all three factors.' Discuss.

EXAM PRACTICE

▶ 4 How to score style points and structure your text

▶ 4.1 How to structure your text

Comments or interpretations, which you usually write as the third part of your exam, consist of three parts:

I. Introduction
II. Main part: main idea 1, main idea 2, …
III. Conclusion

But what should you write in each part? Here are some suggestions:

a **Introduction: start off with e.g.:**
- a reference to a highly topical event *(There has been a heated controversy on …);*
- quote a well-known person *('I am living testament that change is possible,' Obama said …);*
- bring up the topic with sentences like *It is a well-known fact that …, It would hardly be an exaggeration to say that …, So the question arises whether ….*

DON'T let your text look like a massive block of lines.

Write like this:

Rather than this:

b **Main part: Structure your arguments and present them clearly:**
- start with: *First of all, To begin with I would like to …, In my opinion …, To my mind …);*
- link your ideas and arguments *(In addition, …; moreover, …; besides; furthermore, …);*
- make comparisons (*In comparison with, …, compared with, …, as … as, more … than …);*
- show contrasts *(On the one hand, … on the other hand …; however, …; It is true that …, but …);*
- give examples (This serves to illustrate …; for example; for instance; e.g.; such as …);
- agree or disagree (X is quite right when …; I completely agree with …; I have a few reservations about …; It is completely/absolutely wrong to believe that …);
- finish with your strongest argument (The main argument for …; The logical conclusion from all this is …).

c **Conclusion:**
- clearly indicate that you have reached the conclusion (To conclude; In conclusion …; To sum up, …; Weighing the pros and cons, …);
- refer to the introduction (All in all I reject the view that …);
- answer the question (Taking all arguments into consideration, people should not …);
- give an outlook (Science will solve the next global crises …).

Make sure that you also indicate through the layout of your text when a part of your text ends: begin a new line or even leave one line empty.

Practice

1 You are meant to write an essay on the topic 'We're living in an age of too much information'. Collect ideas and structure them.
2 Write your first sentence and your conclusion.

EXAM PRACTICE

▶ 4.2 How to use connectors

Make sure to link your ideas and establish their logical connections with the help of connectors (▶ Skills 5.1: Step 3).

For possible solutions: **Webcode:** LC323180-319

Practice

Note down which of the connectors in the box goes with which number. Sometimes more than one connector is possible.

clearly – for example – for that reason – furthermore – however – in my opinion – on the one hand – on the other hand – that is why – to sum up – yet

Our trouble-shaken world already faces many enormous problems, but in time we could be confronted with one more: a huge food crisis, which could even hit industrialized countries. (1) we should focus our attention on the causes for such a crisis and its possible solutions. (2), population growth is a main factor for a possible food crisis. Population numbers have been rising exponentially and don't look like they'll slow down any time soon. (3), I don't think there is an obvious political solution to this issue: population growth is a natural process that should not be dealt with by clever policies or strict laws. One area where I think solutions do exist concerns environmental pollution, which destroys food crops. Increasing CO_2 emissions are damaging the environment. (4), politicians worldwide have been discussing measures and projects which could address this issue. The Kyoto Protocol, (5), unites political leaders in the decision to cut CO_2 outputs levels within a time limit. We usually see science as a potential answer to all the world's troubles. (6), a surprising problem has recently arisen in the world of scientific development. In the search for ways to meet the present and future energy needs, experts have come up with a method of extracting oil from crops. (7) this is fantastic – it could mean less CO_2 emissions. (8) the consequences could be disastrous – millions are starving in underdeveloped countries, and using crops for oil instead of food could actually kick off a food crisis. (9) I would suggest feeding starving people first and making oil of whatever crops are left over. (10), we can see that population growth and environmental problems seem to be the main factors responsible for an impending world food crisis, which could only be a decade away. (11), solutions will have to be introduced quickly if they are to have any effect at all.

EXAM PRACTICE

▶ 4.3 How to form good sentences

Score style points by using well-formed sentences and by varying your sentence-structure:
- start sentences with an adverb that comments on your whole sentence: 'Not surprisingly, electric cars are still much more expensive than normal cars';
- put your subordinate clauses first from time to time: 'Although Arthur Miller wrote his play in 1949, its themes remain topical today';
- avoid overly long sentences: don't add thought after thought connected by *and*, but begin a new sentence from time to time;
- use conjunctions such as *but, when, while, although* etc. to link main clauses and subclauses;
- try to use passives as well as active sentences: 'The drama expresses ...' (active) vs. 'In the drama, a criticism of ... is expressed' (passive);
- dare to use participle constructions: 'Blaming the old government for an increase in taxes, voters gave their votes to the opposition';
- avoid repetitions and don't start every second sentence with 'there is'.

EXAM PRACTICE

▶ 4.4 How to add precision to your text

Avoid unspecific words such as *nice, say, good* but use more meaningful words.

For possible solutions:
Webcode: LC323180-320

Practice

Match the meaningful words in the box to their rather meaningless counterparts:

say – ask – think – want – big – small – good – bad.

absurd – be of the opinion – believe – claim – considerable – demand – desire – doubt – effective – enquire – essential – excellent – express – hardly noticeable – imagine – inadequate – inappropriate – inconvenient – insignificant – minor – need – object – outstanding – problematic – query – question – require – respectable – show – significant – sizeable – slight – state – striking – suitable – unfortunate – yearn for – wonder

EXAM PRACTICE

▶ 4.5 How to use the correct register

In most of the texts you write in an exam, you will be required to use quite a formal level of English, so you must avoid all examples of informal English (e.g. *well, wanna, 'cause, something like that, you know, I mean, can't/don't/won't*). The only exception is creative texts, where you may have to use informal English e.g. if you are writing dialogue.

For possible solutions:
Webcode: LC323180-321

Practice

Improve the style in the following text. The comments in blue will help you.

Online shopping has been good. *[unspecific word]* *[add a conjunction]* It can be problematic. Deliveries of your ordered goods can take too long. *[add a connecting word]* They may arrive at a bad time. Drive-thru supermarkets *[add a connector]* can be a good solution for the shoppers. Customers can bring their shopping list to the supermarket, where someone *[unspecific word]* will be waiting for them and will do their shopping while they can relax or use the internet facilities or take their kids *[register]* to the playground, which the supermarket provides for free, and don't *[register]* have to do everything themselves. *[overly long sentence]*

EXAM PRACTICE

▶ 5 How to handle special exam formats

▶ 5.1 Mediation

A mediation task is a combination of a summary and a translation – and in addition there is usually a situation or addressee given.
Here are some essentials on mediation:
- read the text carefully (at least twice);
- use the accustomed methods to filter out the relevant information (▶ Exam Practice 2.2);
- always consider the imaginary situation in which you are supposed to be mediating: check carefully what information from the text is essential;
- (re-)arrange the main ideas of the original text if necessary; your new text may have a different structure from the original;
- keep in mind who you are writing for (your boss at work, your friends in another country, etc.); your style must be adequate for your addressee. Do not copy the style of the original!
- the mediation text should be shorter than the original; concentrate on important things, leave out details or metaphors and avoid repetitions.

DON'T cling to the text and translate word for word.

▶ 5.2 Reading and listening comprehension

In your exams, you may encounter formats such as multiple choice or true/false/not given. Here are some tips on how to handle them:
- read or listen to the text first to get an overall idea of its topic;
- read the statements given carefully so that you know what information you must watch out for. Make sure you understand whether only one option is correct or more than one;
- if you are not sure about the correct answer, don't panic: use your common sense to rule out unlikely options. If you are still not sure, at least take a clever guess.

Even if you don't know the correct answer, **DON'T** close your eyes and rely on luck.

Practice

But while Facebook's meteoric growth may indeed be slowing, including in Canada, experts say it's far too soon to secure a burial plot beside social networking pioneer Friendster. "I don't think they're dead or falling flat on their face just yet," said Timothy Hickernell, an analyst with Info-Tech Research Group, who tracks the social networking phenomenon in North America.

In the U.K., for example, Facebook still boasts about 8.5 million users. That translates into about one out of every six people in the country. Globally, Facebook claims to have a user base of 67 million.

Canada, meanwhile, boasts the third-largest number of Facebook users in the world behind the U.K. and the United States, where Facebook originated. Analysts here estimate one of every four Canadians have Facebook accounts.

Kaan Yigit, an analyst at Solutions Research Group, said his own data shows that Facebook's growth rate has slowed considerably in Canada over the past few months – a finding he attributes to the suspicion that most Canadians between 12 and 34 are already on Facebook.

"The thing about Facebook fatigue is that it's primarily an older phenomenon," Yigit said. He said people over the age of 40 are more likely to find Facebook time-consuming and rife with potential work-life conflicts. "I don't see any fatigue in the younger, 12 to 34 age group, because with those people, it's really not an option not to have Facebook. Otherwise, you're not in the loop."

[From: *The Toronto Star*, 7 March 2008]

For possible solutions: **Webcode:** LC323180-322

Tick the correct option. Only one option is correct.

1 Facebook's popularity …
- a) … seems to be growing fast;
- b) … seems to be growing more slowly than before;
- c) … seems to be sinking;
- d) … has disappeared completely.

2
- a) Canada has got more Facebook users than the UK.
- b) Canada has got a higher countrywide percentage of Facebook users than the UK.
- c) The USA has got almost 70 million Facebook users;
- d) Around 16% of all people worldwide are Facebook users.

3 An expert believes that …
- a) … people between 12 and 34 are not so interested in Facebook because of possible work-life conflicts;
- b) … people over 40 are interested in Facebook because it helps them to solve work-life conflicts;
- c) … people between 12 and 34 are not so interested in Facebook because they are tired of using it;
- d) … people over 40 are not so interested in Facebook because in their eyes it is a time-killer and not helpful.

EXAM PRACTICE

▶ 5.3 Oral exam and communication practice

Your exam can be the classical oral exam where you first present your findings on a text and then have an interview with your examiner/teacher.
Or it can be a communication practice with 2 or 3 students involved. This normally consists of:
- a short monologue in which you and your fellow student present the results of a task one after another;
- a dialogue in which you and your fellow student discuss an issue and reach an agreement.

Here are some tips:
1. practise speaking loudly at home, talking to your parents or to the mirror;
2. write down key words only in your preparation time; don't write down and then read full sentences;
3. in the exam, have the courage to correct yourself or look for words, but stay fluent in your talk. Use fillers such as: *well, basically, I see, you know*;
4. use the right register; i.e. don't be too formal or too informal;
5. present a clear point and make yourself understood (coherence);
6. react politely and adequately in a conversation to make your position clear; some phrases may be: *I share your opinion, but I'd like to add …, I can agree with you on that point to a certain extent, but we should not forget …; by and large I am of the same opinion, however, …; I can see your point, but don't you think there is also …, You are certainly right here, but …; Frankly, I don't quite share your opinion here …;*
7. don't hesitate to ask your partner to repeat or specify what he or she said if you haven't understood.

For possible solutions: **Webcode:** LC323180-323

Practice

Discussing gender roles

You and your partner are preparing a presentation about the topic of gender roles and how they define an individual's identity. Each of you has found a picture which shows a certain interpretation of gender roles. As your presentation is fairly long already you can only use one picture. You are now discussing which picture to choose.

1 Describe the photo.
2 Explain and justify why you believe that your photo is the best.
3 Try to come to an agreement about which photo to use.

Business English and Everyday English

BUSINESS ENGLISH ▶ 1

Placing an order

Chasers Mode GmbH
Neckarstraße 37
47226 Duisburg
Tel +49 (0) 203-874523-0 | Fax +49 (0) 203-874523-11
Mail info@chasers.de | Website www.chasersdulsburg.de

Router T Shirt Design Limited
83 Court Lane
London
SE21 7BD
England

10 September 2011

Trial order

Dear Mr Crawley

Many thanks for your offer of 28 August. We would like to place an order for the items listed below at the prices you quoted:

1	3 (three) boxes: blue graphic T shirt, TSBG	€ 49 / box	€ 147
2	8 (eight) boxes: french graphic T shirt, TSFG	€ 49 / box	€ 392
3	7 (seven) boxes: smile graphic T shirt, TSSG	€ 49 / box	€ 343
4	1 (one) box: green/red baseball cap, BCGR	€ 49 / box	€ 49

We note that all prices are 15% below trade price. We also note that you will allow us a further cash discount for payment in full received within 14 working days of delivery.

Thank you for dealing with our enquiries so quickly. We look forward to receiving our order soon.

Yours sincerely
Chasers Mode GmbH

Emma Linkmann

For possible solutions:
Webcode: LC323180-325

1. Find synonyms for the following:
   - a further cut in price;
   - days from Monday to Friday;
   - give (a price for sth.);
   - an order you make to test a product;
   - the price at which goods are sold to shops:
   - act of bringing sth. to sb.

BUSINESS ENGLISH

▶ 2 Acknowledging an order

Here, Ben Crawley acknowledges receipt of the trial order from Chasers Mode by fax. He does not need to report all the details.

To	Chasers Mode	**Date**	12 September 2011
Fax	+49 (0) 203-874523-11	**About**	acknowledgment of order
For	Anna Linkmann	**Pages**	1

CM

FAX MESSAGE

Router T Shirt Design Limited
83 Court Lane | London | SE21 7BD
Tel +44 (0) 208-299-3333 | Fax +44 (0) 208-299-3334
www.routerdesigns.co.uk | e-mail info@routerdesigns.co.uk

Dear Ms Linkmann

We acknowledge receipt of your trial order of 10 September on the terms quoted in our offer of 28 August.

Many thanks for your order. We hope you will be completely satisfied with our products. If you have any questions in the meantime, please don't hesitate to get in touch.

Yours sincerely

Ben Crawley

cc Leo Morgan

For possible solutions:
Webcode: LC323180-326-1

1. Replace the underlined words with words from the box.

allow – dealing with – delivery – information – items – offer – payment – place – promptly – receive – repeat – satisfied – trial

   a We are pleased with the suggested price.
   b We would like to make an order for the following articles.
   c Routers Designs always propose a cash discount for prompt settlement.
   d Thank you for handling our enquiry so quickly.
   e Please leave 12 working days for the shipment of your order.

2. Find the English translations for the following German words:
   - *Bestellung*
   - *Angebot*
   - *Konditionen*
   - *Empfang*
   - *Auftragsbestätigung*

BUSINESS ENGLISH

▶ 3 Telephoning

For possible solutions:
Webcode: LC323180-326-2

1. Complete the dialogue with suitable phrases from the box.

how can I help you? – may I ask who's calling? – could you put me through – hold the line – I'm afraid – may I speak to – call again later – a message – speaking – a meeting

Oliver Stevenson would like to speak to Ms Jones. Emma Martell is a telephone assistant at Jones & Co., where Ms Jones works. Sophie Burt is Ms Jones' assistant.

Emma Good afternoon. Jones & Co. …?
Oliver Oh yes, good afternoon. … to Ms Jones' office, please?
Emma Certainly. …, please?
Oliver My name's Oliver Stevenson.
Emma …, please, Mr Stevenson.

Sophie Good afternoon. Ms Jones' office. Sophie Burt … .
Oliver Hello, its Oliver Stevenson here. … Ms Jones, please?
Sophie … Ms Jones is in … at the moment.
Oliver Oh. I suppose I can … . Do you know when she'll be finished?
Sophie I can't really say. Although I could give her … for you.
Oliver Thanks, but I'd prefer to talk to her myself. Could you ask her to call me when she's free?
Sophie Of course, Mr Stevenson.

2. Match the headings below with the sentences on the next page.

Asking for information – Saying somebody is not available – Putting a caller through – Phoning somebody – Getting out of trouble – Answering the phone – Offering help – Saying goodbye

A Good morning. Primatech Limited. Can I help you?
B I'll ask Ms Jones to call you back as soon as possible.
C I'm afraid Mr Stevenson is at lunch at present.
D Could I speak to somebody in Human Resources, please?
E May I have your e-mail address, please?
F Good afternoon. Sophie Burt speaking.
G I'm afraid Ms Roseberry is in a meeting at the moment.
H Just one moment, please. I'll see if Ms Martell is free.
I Could you speak a little more slowly, please?
J I'll put you through to somebody who can speak English.
K What was the name again, please?
L My name is Hugo Flynn. Can I speak to Ms Bucks, please?
M Could you give me his phone number, please?
N I'm sorry, but Ms Harper is speaking on another line at present.
O May I ask who's calling, please?
P Can I put you through to her secretary?
Q Thank you for your call. Goodbye.
R May I speak to whoever is in charge of marketing, please?
S Would you like to call back, or should Mr Webb call you?
T Could you hold the line, please? I'll put you through to PR.
U I'm sorry, but Ms Jones is out of the office today.
V Can you spell that for me, please?
W Goodbye and thanks a lot for your help.
X I'm sorry, I didn't understand that. Could you say it again, please?
Y Can I give Ms Jones a message?
Z I'm sorry, but Ms Michaelson is not available at the moment.

BUSINESS ENGLISH

► 4 Communicating by mail, SMS and chat

Imagine that you are planning to attend a 'Young Leaders' course at a school in London to improve your English, your debating skills and your knowledge of important current issues. The school's website offers the chance to chat with a school employee during certain hours, or to send them an email.

For possible solutions: **Webcode:** LC323180-327

1. During the four weeks you plan to be in England, you would like to spend the first two weeks at the school in London, then stay with your uncle, who lives in Brighton, for a week, and then go to back to London to do the last week of classes. The website only gives a price for a full month course. You would like to know whether it is possible to do what you are planning, and what the price would be. Write an e-mail to the school to find out. You should
   - use a clear subject line (one word only is not helpful)
   - start and finish your email as you would in a business letter
   - be as concise as possible
   - include a signature with your name and address.
2. You still have some questions about the course and so you decide to chat with a school employee online. Look at the following chat transcript between a student and an employee.

GlobalYouthLeadership:	Welcome to GYL, my name is Jason. How can I help you?
Guest:	Hi, I'm Sascha Limski. I've got a few Qs about the course.
GlobalYouthLeadership:	that's wot I'm here 4! go right ahead
Guest:	Ok. The website says all meals are included. I'm a vegetarian. Will that be ok?
GlobalYouthLeadership:	no prob – ther R even sum vegans on the course this year!
Guest:	gr8! My other Q is: will I have to share a room?
GlobalYouthLeadership:	yes. don't worry tho. it's a way to make friends :o) + if there's a prob, you can always swap
Guest:	Ok.
GlobalYouthLeadership:	anything else?
Guest:	Thats all thx
GlobalYouthLeadership:	ur welcome! cu in july
Guest:	cu :D

For possible solutions: **Webcode:** LC323180-328

a Find abbreviations and smilies in the transcript and write down what they mean in normal English. If you don't know, try and guess what they stand for. Add other English chat abbreviations that you know.

b Describe and comment on the conventions Jason uses regarding punctuation, spelling and grammar.

TIPS FOR 'TEXTSPEAK'

- To shorten a lot of words, you can just delete the vowels: *weekend = wknd; football = ftbll; help = hlp.*
- 'Lol' can mean 'laughing out loud' (to show something is funny) or 'lots of love' (at the end of a text).
- Only use textspeak with other young people. Older people might not understand it or even think that it's rude.
- Don't forget about punctuation completely. Full stops, and even commas, can still help make your text clearer.
- Read your text quickly before you send it. If your message isn't perfectly clear, you'll have to add some correct grammar and spelling

EVERYDAY ENGLISH

▶ 1 Eating out

Lukas and Hannah, two teenagers from Cologne, are in Banbury, visiting their English friends from an exchange trip they did two years ago. On their first day, Leo and Harriet, their old exchange partners, take them out to a pizza restaurant for lunch.

Leo:	This is it! Luigi's. It serves the best pizzas in Banbury.
Harriet:	This is our favourite restaurant. We come here all the time.
Hannah:	It doesn't look like much from the outside.
Leo:	That's the point! You can eat delicious pizza here, and you don't have to fight for a table, or stand in a queue with a bunch of tourists!
Lukas:	*(laughing)* Hey! What's wrong with tourists!
Harriet:	He's only joking. Come on, let's go inside.

Harriet: A table for four please.
Waitress: By the window or in the corner over there? Your choice.
Lukas: I say we sit by the window.
Leo: One table by the window, coming right up!
Waitress: Here are your menus. Today's specials are written on the board on the wall. Would you like to order some drinks?
Harriet: I'll have a diet coke, please.
Hannah: The same for me, please.
Lukas: What beers do you serve?
Waitress: Organic beer from Sam Smiths, but I'll have to see your ID to serve you that, sir.
Lukas: *(confused)* What?
Leo: *(whispers)* You have to be eighteen to order alcohol in the UK. Even in a restaurant. If you're sixteen or seventeen you can only drink if you're with an adult.
Lukas: Oh, ok. I'll take a lemonade then.
Leo: Me too, please.

Waitress: Here are your drinks. Are you ready to order yet?
Harriet: Just a couple more minutes, thanks. I think we need a bit longer to look at the menu.
Lukas: But we can order some starters to share. Some garlic bread and some dough balls, please.
Waitress: No problem.
Hannah: I'm really not sure what I'll have as a main course. What can you recommend?
Harriet: Well, do you want something vegetarian or a pizza with meat?
Hannah: Ummm. No meat. But I do like fish.
Leo: Then you have to get the 'Romana'. Mozzarella, anchovies, spinach and caramelised onion. It's delicious.
Hannah: Sounds good! Can we share a salad as a side dish, too?
Harriet: Good idea … What about you Lukas? Do you need any help with the menu?
Lukas: No thanks. I'm having a 'Bavarian'. Oregano, mozzarella and German sausage! The taste of home!
Hannah: *(sarcastic)* How adventurous!

Hannah: That was delicious … But I'm so full. I don't think I'll be able to move!
Harriet: We warned you it was good!
Waitress: All finished? I'll just take your plates then, thank you. Would you like to see the dessert menu? Or some tea or coffee for you?
Leo: No thanks, just the bill, please.

Waitress: Here you go.
Lukas: Oh, can we have separate bills please?
Waitress: *(annoyed)* What?
Harriet: *(whispers)* We don't really do that in England. (to waitress) Don't worry, we'll split the bill ourselves.
Hannah: Who's going to work out how much everyone has to pay?

Leo: Well, I've got a calculator on my mobile. So that's five pounds fifty for you Hannah, plus one eighty for the diet coke. Then there's the garlic bread plus the dough balls plus the salad. So, if I divide that by four ... Hmmm, this is tricky. Wait a second, I'll start again.

Hannah: How unpractical!

For possible solutions: **Webcode:** LC323180-330

1. Make a list of useful vocabulary for ordering in a restaurant.
2. Find the English translations for this restaurant vocabulary: *Hauptspeise, Nachspeise, Vorspeise, Gericht, Speisekarte, Beilage, Tagesgericht, Rechnung*.
3. Work in a group of three or four. One of you is the waiter/waitress, the others are guests going out for dinner at a restaurant. Act out a roleplay, starting the moment the guests come into the restaurant. Take it in turns to be the waiter/waitress. Incorporate a different situation into your roleplay each time:
   - *a guest that wants something that's not on the menu*
   - *a rude waiter/waitress*
   - *a guest under eighteen who wants to order an alcoholic drink*
   - *a waiter/waitress who keeps bringing the wrong meals*
   - *a guest that needs some help to understand the menu*

EVERYDAY ENGLISH

▶ 2 Shopping

Tom, a teenager from Wiesbaden, is in Glasgow visiting Laura, his English friend. On his second day in the city, Laura takes him out shopping.

Tom: What do you think of these blue sport shoes? They're cool, right?

Laura: I wouldn't call them sport shoes. And for that price I don't think you'd want to get them dirty playing football. But yes, that is a nice pair of trainers.

Tom: Where's the assistant. I'll ask whether they have them in my size.

Laura: He's over there. Hello, excuse me ...

Assistant: Hi. Can I help you?

Tom: Yes please. I'd like to know whether you have these trainers in my size.

Assistant: No problem. What size would that be?

Tom: Umm. Forty-three.

Assistant: That's a nine in UK sizes. Hmmm. I don't think we've got any size nines in that colour in stock. But if you'll just wait a second I can check in the store cupboard for you.

Tom: Thanks.

Laura: If they don't have blue ones, these red ones are similar. Do you like them?

Tom: I've already got a pair of red ones like that at home in Germany.

Laura: Or these white ones?

Tom: They're almost the same as the ones I'm wearing now!

Laura: Haha, Tom. Maybe it wouldn't be so bad if they don't have your size after all. I think you've already got enough pairs of trainers.

Assistant: You're in luck! This is our last pair in blue. Would you like to try them on?

Tom: Thanks. Yes, I will try them on.

Laura: Oh, they look great, Tom. They suit you, and they go with your jeans. Now walk around a bit so you can see whether they're comfortable or not.
Tom: (laughing) Good idea, mum! … Hmmm. This isn't quite right. These are a bit tight.
Laura: Maybe they're too small … Look, it says forty-four in here in your own pair of trainers. You need a bigger size.
Assistant: Forty-four is a UK size ten. We've got plenty of size tens in stock. I'll just fetch you a pair right now.

Tom: Yes, these size ten trainers are perfect. Cool and comfortable. I'll buy them, thank you.
Assistant: OK, if you just give them to me I'll put them back in the box for you. I'll keep them behind the counter so you can have a look around and pay when you're ready.
Tom: Thanks. Here you go. Yes I think I will have a quick look around the shop again before I pay.
Laura: Oh, come on Tom. You don't need another pair of shoes.

For possible solutions: **Webcode:** LC323180-331

1. Read the dialogue, then translate the following words: *etwas anprobieren, zu etwas passen, jemandem stehen, an der Kasse, am Lager.*
2. Make a list of useful vocabulary for clothes shopping in England.
3. Work with a partner. One of you is a shop assistant, the other a customer. As the customer, think of a suitable item you want to buy (colour, size, style, etc.) before you start your dialogue. Change roles when you have finished. Incorporate a different situation into your roleplay each time:
   - a *a shopper that doesn't know what size they need*
   - b *an item that is only available in a different colour*
   - c *an item that is damaged*
   - d *a shopper that wants to try on a lot of different sizes/styles*
   - e a *shop assistant that tries to convince a shopper to buy unsuitable clothes.*

EVERYDAY ENGLISH

▶ 3 Going to the doctor

If you are in an English-speaking country and you become ill or injured, you will need to pay a visit to the doctor. What would you say if the doctor asked you the following questions?
- What can I do for you today?
- Can you describe the pain?
- What are your symptoms?

And then you have to listen to the doctor's diagnosis, prognosis and suggested cure … That's a lot to take in. Read the following dialogue.

Dr Rogers: Hello, I'm Dr Rogers.
Tim: Hi, I'm Tim. Tim Reinhardt.
Dr Rogers: Ok, Tim. What can I do for you today?
Tim: I've got a pain in my left ear. It's gone red and I can't hear very well.
Dr Rogers: Earache, I see. And how long have you had this pain?
Tim: Three days I think. But it was only very bad yesterday and today.

Dr Rogers:	Ok. And can you describe it. Is it a throbbing pain?
Tim:	Throbbing?
Dr Rogers:	Does it get stronger and weaker?
Tim:	Oh, *pulsierend*. Yes, it is.
Dr Rogers:	And does it improve or get worse when you do different things?
Tim:	What kind of things?
Dr Rogers:	Oh, maybe when you lie down, or when you take a deep breath?
Tim:	No, not really.
Dr Rogers:	Ok, I'm just going to shine a light in your ear and have a look ... Hmmm. Yes, that's very red and sore. You have an ear infection. But it's nothing to worry about. Just some swelling. But I'm going to prescribe you some antibiotics just to be on the safe side, seeing as the infection has already lasted a few days.
Tim:	And can I take something for the pain?
Dr Rogers:	Of course, you can just buy some ordinary Paracetamol at the chemist's. That should do the trick ... Ok, so take this prescription to the chemist's, and then take the antibiotics once a day for a week, even if the infection goes away before that.
Tim:	Thanks a lot.
Dr Rogers:	No problem. And take a rest today. That'll speed up your recovery. Don't go dashing around too much outside.
Tim:	I'll do that! Thanks for your help. Goodbye.

For possible solutions:
Webcode: LC323180-332-1

1. Write down the doctor's diagnosis, prognosis, method of examination and suggested cure for Lukas's problem.
2. Make a mindmap or list words and phrases from the dialogue that cover common complaints, then add to it with other words that you know.
3. Work with a partner. One of you is a patient, the other a doctor. As the patient, think of a common complaint that you might have whilst in an English-speaking country. Change roles when you have finished and base your roleplay on a different complaint each time.

EVERYDAY ENGLISH

▶ 4 Finding a place to live

If you are abroad for a longer period of time – e.g. for a work placement – you will need to rent accommodation, i.e. a place to live. In England, this will mean looking at flat share listings, either on the internet or in the back pages of a local newspaper. To be successful you will have to know
- how to read them
- how to interpret what is written
- how to go about getting the flat or room you want.

For possible solutions:
Webcode: LC323180-332-2

1. Especially in the pages of a newspaper, listings are meant to take up very little space and are therefore full of abbreviations. Look at the examples from a London newspaper. See how many abbreviations you can turn into complete words, then 'translate' one advert into 'normal' English. If you have problems understanding the abbreviations, do task 2 first.

Dalston
Sgl room in cosy flat share. To share with one prof man (41) and alsatian. MUST like dogs. n/s. Nearest tube is Dalston Junction. £90 p.w. –
0721 278 6657

Hackney
Dble room in converted church, sharing w / artist couple. Creative applicants only. Easy-going, sociable environment. Hackney Central tube and rail stations only 7 minute walk.
£110 p.w. – 0736 359 0870

Islington
Dble room in spacious flat. Share w / 2 women, 1 man, 26–31. Very close to buses, Angel tube station (10 minutes to Kings X station) and pubs, bars and restaurants around City Rd. £150 p.w. –
0798 111 8374

Camden sgl room in well-appointed pad, close to Chalk Farm tube. All mod cons. Share w / prof couple.
£600 pcm – 0759 298 9867

2. Match the following abbreviations and words to their explanations or complete words:

dble	nice, well equipped
cosy	per calendar month
gdn	be good for sb.
mod cons	flat
n/s	modern conveniences, i.e. bathroom and kitchen with
pad (infml)	garden, i.e. ground floor
pcm	per week
p.w.	London underground system
prof	non-smoking
sgl	professional person, i.e. a person with a job
suit sb.	single
tube	with
well appointed	small, comfortable
w /	double

3. Which room would interest you most if you were:

a a sculpture student who smokes and likes to have parties?
b a young vegetarian teacher on a small budget?
c a journalism intern who needs good travel connections to get to work?
Explain your choices.

Wordfields

▶ **Sequence 1:** Britain: past, present and future

- accent; *speak with an ~*
- anglophone (adj); *~ country/person*
- class; *upper/middle/working ~*
- colony; colonial; colonisation
- cosmopolitan; *~ city/attitude*
- cuisine [kwɪ'zi:n]; *Asia/British/fusion ~*
- culture
- economy; *a strong/weak ~*
- the British Empire
- etiquette; *cultural/old-fashioned ~*
- financial; *~ centre/crisis*
- history / historical / historian
- humour; *good/bad sense of ~*
- immigrate / immigrant / immigration
- innovative ['ɪnəveɪtɪv]
- international; *~ business/relations*
- majority / minority; *ethnic ~*
- manners; *good/bad/table ~*
- monarchy / monarch; *constitutional ~*
- multicultural / multiculturalism
- nation; *a rich/poor ~*
- national identity
- nostalgia / nostalgic
- political party
- political spectrum; *left/right wing ~*
- politics / political / politician
- posh *(infml)*
- common *(infml)*
- power; *a world ~ / balance of ~*
- Prime Minister
- racist (n; adj) / racism
- renowned / famous
- rule (n); *British ~*
- rule/govern sb./sth.
- secular; *a ~ society/government*
- snobbish; *~ attitude/behaviour*
- society; *British/equal/classless ~*
- the Commonwealth
- the House of Commons
- the House of Lords
- the Houses of Parliament
- wealth [welθ]; *~ distribution / national ~*

▶ **Sequence 2:** North American dreams

- abolish sth. / abolition; *~ of slavery*
- administration; *the Obama A~*
- African American
- aspiration / aspire to sth.
- Bill of Rights
- capitalism / capitalist (n; adj)
- colonist / colony; colonial
- commerce / commercial
- Congress
- constitution
- Declaration of Independence
- democracy / democratic
- equality; *racial ~; social ~*
- explorer / exploration / explore sth.
- federal; *~ government; ~ state*
- founder / found sth.
- freedom / liberty
- heritage; *cultural ~; African ~*
- immigrant / emigrant
- independence / self-rule
- melting pot; *~ culture*
- migration; *voluntary ~*
- mosaic; *cultural ~*
- multiculturalism; *~ policy*
- native; *~ people; N~ American*
- patriot / patriotism
- pilgrim
- pioneer
- power; *world ~; economic ~; military ~*
- president
- racism / racial discrimination
- resource; *food ~ / natural ~*
- rebel against sth. / rebellion
- revolution / revolt against sth.
- right; *human ~s / natural ~s / civil ~s*
- rural / urban / suburban
- senator; *state ~*
- settler; settle a country
- slavery
- state; *~ capital*
- territory
- trade; *international ~*

Sequence 3: Going global

- Americanisation
- brain drain *(infml)*
- communication / communicate
- competition / competitor / compete with sb.
- consumer; *~ pressure / ~ product*
- culture; *popular ~*
- currency
- democratisation
- developing country
- exchange; *~ of information / ~ of goods and capital*
- exploitation / exploit sb./sth.
- export; *an ~ economy*
- financial; *~ dominance/incentive/difficulty*
- freedom; *~ of trade/movement/speech*
- GDP (Gross Domestic Product)
- global; *~ village/power/politics*
- immigration / immigrant
- import (n) / import sth.
- industry (n) / industrial (adj)
- inequality; *financial ~*
- integration; *social/racial/economic ~*
- international; *~ trade / ~ market*
- investment / invest in sth.
- manufacturer / producer
- military; *~ intervention / ~ threat*
- multiculturalism / multicultural
- outsource sth. ['aʊtsɔːs]
- political; *~ development*
- population; *~ growth / ~ control*
- refugee [refju'dʒiː] / seek refuge from sth.
- restriction; trade ~
- society; *an international/democratic ~*
- sweatshop
- technology
- the European Union
- the International Monetary Fund
- the United Nations
- tourism
- transnational/multinational; *a ~ company*
- transportation; *~ of goods/people*
- wealth distribution; *unfair/equal ~*
- worldwide

▶ **Sequence 4:** India rising

- Bollywood
- boom (n, v); *economic ~ / population ~*
- caste [kɑːst]
- class; *~ system / ~ pyramid*
- civilisation; *ancient ~*
- corruption; *political ~*
- democracy [- '- - -] / democratic [,- -' - -]
- development
- discrimination; *caste ~*
- disparity; *wealth ~*
- displacement
- dowry / ~ death
- economy
- empire; *the British E~*
- entrepreneurism
- globalisation
- Hinduism / Hindu
- independence
- industry; *film ~ / technology ~*
- infrastructure
- Islam / Muslim
- melodrama
- modernisation
- myth / legend
- oursource sth. / outsourcing; *labour ~*
- partition
- poverty; *live in ~*
- Raj
- rural; *~ population*
- sectarian; *~ violence*
- slum; *~ dweller*
- suppression
- tradition
- unification
- untouchability
- urban; *~ area*

▶ **Sequence 5:** Shakespeare and his world

- act out sth. / actor
- adaptation; *modern ~*
- audience / spectator
- box office
- character / role
- comedy
- conflict / feud
- dramatic; *~ tension / ~ device*
- genre
- Golden Age
- groundling
- history / a historical play
- household / family
- murder
- patron; *~ of the arts*
- perform sth. / performer
- playwright
- plot / storyline
- poetry
- production; *~ of a play*
- prologue / introduction / opening
- put on a play
- reign; *Elizabeth I's ~*
- Renaissance
- rhetorical; *~ device*
- romance
- rythm
- scene; *set the ~ / balcony ~*
- sonnet
- speech; make/give a ~
- stage; *put sth. on ~*
- suicide; *commit ~*
- suitor / love interest
- theatre
- tragedy
- verse
- villain
- workshop; *drama ~*

▶ **Sequence 6:** Future worlds

- affluent / affluence
- afterlife
- all-powerful / totalitarian
- capitalism
- class / *belong to a ~*
- community / group / tribe
- control sth. / dominate sth. / govern sth.
- desire sth. / want sth.
- dystopia / dystopian; *a ~ society*
- egalitarialism / equality
- enlightenment / insight
- environment; *protect the ~*
- future / destiny / fate
- green; *~ movement/politics*
- happiness / bliss
- harmony; *live in ~ with …*
- heaven / paradise
- idyllic / perfect
- imaginary / fictitious [fɪkˈtɪʃəs]
- literature / writings / essay
- living standard
- pacifist / nonviolent / peaceful
- politics
- primitive; *~ culture/society*
- realistic
- respect
- ruler / leader
- science-fiction; *~ author/film*
- socialism
- spiritual / religious
- suffer (v)
- surveillance / observation
- sustainable; *~energy/living*
- technology
- tolerance / benevolence / kindness
- unite / join sth.
- utopia / utopian; *a ~ society*
- wealth / wealthy

Acknowledgements

Photos / Illustrations

Cover: © Jeremy Woodhouse / Digital Vision / Getty Images

Sequence 01: **p. 10:** A: © Simon James / Alamy, B: © Grant Terry / Shutterstock images; **p. 11:** C: © Michael Kemp / Alamy, D: © intoit / Shutterstock images, E: © Kamira / Shutterstock images, F: © Glyn Kirk / Action Plus Sports Images / Alamy, G: © Janine Wiedel Photolibrary / Alamy; **p. 12:** © Caro Fotoagentur / Frank Sorge; **p. 13:** A: © North Wind Picture Archives / Alamy, B: © The Art Archive / Alamy, C: © The National Archives of the UK, ref. CO956/426; **p. 14:** left: © Walker Historical Picture Archive / Alamy, right: © Hilary Morgan / Alamy; **p. 16:** © Hulton Archive / Getty Images; **p. 17:** left: © Sean Sexton / Hulton Archive / Getty Images, right: From: J. N. Gupta's LIFE AND WORKS OF ROMESH CHUNDER DUTT, 1911; **p. 19:** left: © http://www.britishempire.co.uk, right: © ullstein bild / adoc-photos; **p. 21:** © Eliot Elisofon / Time & Life Pictures / Getty Images; **p. 22:** © Reproduced by permission of University of Cambridge Museum of Archaeology & Anthropology (N.71822.GIJ); **p. 23:** © Reproduced by permission of University of Cambridge Museum of Archaeology & Anthropology (N.71526.GIJ); **p. 27:** © Sam Toren / Alamy; **p. 28:** left: © Chris Radburn / picture alliance / empics, middle: © Justin Kase zsixz / Alamy, right: © Richard Baker / Alamy; **p. 29:** left: © Richard Bryant / Arcaid / picture alliance, right: © Schapowalow / Robert Harding; **p. 30:** © Pictor International / ImageState / Alamy; **p. 31:** left: © Lebrecht Music and Arts Photo Library / Alamy, middle: © Richard Baker / Alamy, right: © Rupert Rivett / Alamy; **p. 32:** A: © dpa-Fotoreport / picture alliance / dpa / epa, B–D: © Crown Copyright; **p. 33:** charts: © Carlos Borell, Berlin; **p. 34:** charts: © Yvonne Thron, Berlin; **p. 35:** © ITN Source; **p. 36:** © Grant Triplow / Daily Mail; **p. 37:** © Homer W. Sykes / Alamy; **p. 38:** © studiomode / Alamy; **p. 39:** © Adrian Sherratt / Alamy; **p. 40:** chart: © Yvonne Thron, Berlin (source: Neighbourhood Statistics, 2007), map: © Ruth Lupton / Anne Power / CASE (Centre for Analysis of Social Exclusion); **p. 41:** © David Burrows / Shutterstock images; **p. 42:** © Effigie / Leemage / Writer Pictures; **p. 44:** © Rana Miah und Vidya Thirunarayan / BBC Video Nation; **p. 45:** © Used by permission of Random House Group Archive & Library; **p. 46:** © Angelo Giampiccolo / Shutterstock images; **p. 47:** © Wojciech Kozlowski / Shutterstock images; **p. 51:** cartoon: © Alan Cavanagh / www.caricatures-ireland.com, map: © Victor Soares / Shutterstock images; **p. 52:** left: © ullstein bild / SIPA, right: © Volkhard Binder, Berlin; **p. 53:** © Caro Fotoagentur / Rupert Oberhaeuser; **p. 56:** © ullstein bild / Schirner X; **p. 57:** © Rachelle Burnside / Shutterstock images; **p. 58:** chart: © Yvonne Thron, Berlin; **p. 60:** © Oleg Zabielin / Shutterstock images.

Sequence 02: **p. 62:** © 2009 fotofriends / Shutterstock images; **S. 63:** 2: © Sergei Bachlakov / Shutterstock images, 3: © Bettmann / Corbis, 4: © Duncan Walker / iStockphoto.com, Statue of Liberty: © Vlad Ghiea / Shutterstock images; **p. 64:** © Archive Images / Alamy; **p. 66:** © David Spindel / SuperStock / Corbis; **p. 67:** © North Wind Picture Archives / Alamy; **p. 69:** © North Wind Picture Archives / Alamy; **p. 70** and **p. 72:** © Vintage Images / Alamy; **p. 73:** left: © Archive Pics / Alamy, right: © Marmaduke St. John / Alamy; **p. 74:** © Peter Foley / epa / dpa-Report / picture alliance; **p. 75:** © alle 12 / iStockphoto.com; **p. 76:** © pixelbully / Alamy; **p. 77:** © Ian Shive / Aurora Photos / Alamy; **p. 78:** © Times-Picayune / Landov; **p. 79:** top left: © Frank Marc Frei / LOOK Die Bildagentur der Fotografen GmbH / Alamy, bottom right: © Henrik Bolin / Shutterstock images; **p. 80:** © John Lund / Blend Images / Alamy; **p. 82:** top left: © Enigma / Alamy, bottom right: © David Young-Wolff / Alamy; **p. 83:** © Songquan Deng / Shutterstock images; **p. 86:** © Frank Tozier / Alamy; **p. 87:** © North Wind Picture Archives / Alamy; **p. 88:** top: © imagestate / HIP / Ann Ronan / Picture Library / picture alliance, bottom: © Walter G. Acre / Shutterstock images; **p. 89:** © Christopher Felver / Corbis; **p. 92:** © Landov Lykson / dpa / picture alliance; **p. 93:** © Caitlin Mirra / Shutterstock images; **p. 96:** stop sign: © Mark Peterson / Corbis, family: © Ron Tech 2000 / iStockphoto.com, canoe: © Schapowalow / Robert Harding, totem poles: © Gunter Marx Photography / Corbis, shop: © Ron Tech 2000 / iStockphoto.com, Calgary: © Jeff Whyte / iStockphoto.com, group of people: © momentimages / Tetra Images / Corbis, Rocky Mountains: © Robert McGouey / Alamy, inuit: © Ocean / Corbis, Cree Indian child: © Tim Graham / Sygma / Corbis; **p. 97:** © Illustrious / iStockphoto.com; **p. 98:** © The Protected Art Archive / Alamy; **p. 100:** © Corbis; **p. 105:** © Megapress / Alamy; **p. 106:** © Aerial Archives / Alamy; **p. 107:** bottom left: © Bob Betenia / Alamy, top right: © Chris Wattie / Reuters / Corbis; **p. 109:** © Carlos Osorio / GetStock.com.

Sequence 03: **p. 112:** A: © hfng / Shutterstock images, B: © Megapress / Alamy; **p. 113:** C: © Stephen Mulcahey / Alamy, D: © EdBockStock / Shutterstock images, E: © photobank.kiev.ua / Shutterstock images, F: © UN Photo / Albert Gonzalez Farran, G: © africa924 / Shutterstock images, H: © JetKat / Shutterstock images; **p. 114:** © Zhernov Vadim / ITAR-TASS Photo / Corbis; **p. 116:** © Korotayev Artyom / ITAR-TASS Photo / Corbis; **p. 117:** © Allan Symon Gerry / Alamy; **p. 119:** © Jean-Paul Nerrière; **p. 121:** © EDHAR / Shutterstock images; **p. 122:** © Worldspec / NASA / Alamy; **p. 123:** top: Volkhard Binder, Berlin (source: NSSO's: National Sample Survey Organisation's), bottom: © 2006 SASI Group (University of Sheffield) and Mark Newman (University of Michigan) / www.worldmapper.org; **p. 124:** © World Vision Australia; **p. 125**: top: © Frank Piasecki Poulsen / Koncern TV / Gebrüder Beetz-Filmproduktion, bottom: © Purepix / Alamy; **p. 126:** top: © Peter J. Wilson / Shutterstock images, bottom: © Jan Martin Will / Shutterstock images; **p. 128:** © Ariel Skelley / Blend Images / Alamy; **p. 129:** © Michelle Gilders / Alamy; **p. 130:** top left: © Matt Shonfeld / Aurora Photos / Alamy, middle right: © UN Photo / Marie Frechon, bottom left: © Mike Greenslade / Alamy; **p. 131:** backdrop: © byllwill / iStockphoto.com, map: © Volina / Shutterstock images, bottom: © RichardBakerSudan / Alamy; **p. 132:** top: © Michael Hanson / Aurora Photos / Alamy, bottom: © Alain Evrard / Imagestate Media Partners Limited – Impact Photos / Alamy; **p. 133:** © Roger Arnold / Alamy; **p. 135:** © UN Photo / Albert Gonzalez Farran; **pp. 136–137:** charts: © Yvonne Thron, Berlin (source: UNHCR); **p. 138:** top: © sepavo / Shutterstock images, bottom: © Jenny Matthews / Alamy; **p. 139:** © Jeremy Sutton-Hibbert / Alamy; **p. 140:** © picture alliance / Photoshot; **p. 142:** © Colin McPherson / Corbis; **p. 143:** A: © Polyp (Paul Fitzgerald) / www.cartoonstock.com, B: © John Bogenschutz / Tone Deaf Comics / http://www.tonedeafcomics.com, C: © 2004 Patrick Chappatté ('Oursourcing', *The International Harald Tribune*, 9/21/2004) / Cagle Cartoons, D: © 2007 Patrick Chappatté ('World Economic Forum', *Le Temps*, Switzerland, 1/26/2007) / Cagle Cartoons; **p. 144:** E: © 2005 Milt Priggee ('Globalization', *Puget Sound Business Journal*, 6/27/2005) / Cagle Cartoons, F: © 2005 Andy Singer ('Globalization Invading Markets', PoliticalCartoons.com, 11/15/2005) / Cagle Cartoons; **p. 145:** left: © Ronald Weir / Albaimages / Alamy, right: © REUTERS / Jerry Lampen (China); **p. 147:** © Saeed Khan / AFP / Getty Images; **p. 148:** © Owen Price / iStockphoto.com; **p. 149:** © Frank Waldecker / LOOK Die Bildagentur der Fotografen GmbH / Alamy; **p. 150:** grapes: © Manuel Velasco / iStockphoto.com, plane: © JetKat / Shutterstock images; **p. 151:** © Dmitriy Shironosov / Alamy.

Sequence 04: p. 152: left: © Walter Bibikow / Jon Arnold Images Ltd / Alamy, right: © Tibor Bognar / Alamy; **p. 153:** © Walter Bibikow / Jon Arnold Images Ltd / Alamy; **p. 153:** pyramid: © Published with permission from Infosys Limited, George V in Delhi: © The Print Collector / Alamy, woman with headscarf: © Brandon Bourdages / Shutterstock images, farmers: © AJP / Shutterstock images; **p. 154:** A: © Travel India / Alamy, B: © Jeremy Richards / Shutterstock images, C: © Rafal Cichawa / Shutterstock images, D: © thefinalmiracle / Shutterstock images, map: Volkhard Binder, Berlin; **p. 155:** left: © Simon Podgorsek / iStockphoto.com, right: © ajaykampani / iStockphoto.com; **p. 156:** left: © Jamo Gonzalez Zarraonandia / Shutterstock images, right: © Hulton-Deutsch Collection / Corbis; **p. 157:** © Bettmann / Corbis; **p. 158:** Nehru: © Hulton-Deutsch Collection / Corbis, Jinnah: © INTERFOTO / Alamy, Mountbatten: © Bettmann / Corbis; **p. 159:** © Bettmann / Corbis; **p. 161:** © Keystone Pictures USA / Alamy; **p. 162:** women sorting rubbish: © Jeremy Richards / Shutterstock images, scooter: © David R. Frazier / Photolibrary, Inc. / Alamy, call center: © Nevada Wier / Corbis, fields: © Tom Bible / Alamy; **p. 163:** © Video supplied by BBC Motion Gallery; **p. 164:** © Peter Horree / Alamy; **p. 166:** left: © Marcel Clemens / Shutterstock images, right: © LiteChoices / Shutterstock images; **p. 168:** Volkhard Binder, Berlin (source: www.downtoearth.org); **p. 169:** © Richard Smith / Alamy; **p. 170:** © Lionel Derimais / Alamy; **p. 172:** left: © Dinodia Photos / Alamy, middle: © MediaStorm LLC, Brooklyn, NY, right: © Orange Line Media / Shutterstock images; **p. 173:** left: © Simon Jarratt / Corbis, right: © Amanda Koster / Corbis; **p. 174:** © Ajay Bhaskar / Shutterstock images; **p. 175:** © Ocean / Corbis; **p. 177:** © MediaStorm LLC, Brooklyn, NY; **p. 179:** © Mark Gillow / iStockphoto.com; **p. 180:** © Mark Yuill / Shutterstock images; **p. 181:** © Jorge Royan / Alamy; **p. 183**: left: © CELADOR FILMS / Kobal Collection, right: © Dinodia Photos / Alamy; **p. 184:** © Allstar Picture Library / Alamy; **p. 185:** © Sophie Bassouls / Corbis; **p. 186:** © FILM 4 / CELADOR FILMS / PATHÉ INTERNATIONAL / Kobal Collection; **p. 188:** © FILM 4 / CELADOR FILMS / PATHÉ INTERNATIONAL / Kobal Collection; **p. 190:** top left: © FILM 4 / CELADOR FILMS / PATHÉ INTERNATIONAL / Kobal Collection, bottom right: © CELADOR FILMS / Kobal Collection; **p. 191:** © CELADOR FILMS / Kobal Collection; **p. 192:** © Catherine Karnow / Corbis.

Sequence 05: p. 194: © Hulton Archive / iStockphoto.com; **p. 195:** Macbeth: © Geraint Lewis / Alamy, Shakespeare in Love: © AF archive / Alamy; Globe Theatre Neuss: © Karl F. Schöfmann / imagebroker / Alamy, Globe Theatre London: © Gregory Wrona / Alamy, students on stage: © Hill Street Studios / Blend Images / Corbis; **p. 196:** © c. / Shutterstock images; **p. 197:** © ullstein bild / TopFoto; **p. 198:** left: © Georgios Kollidas / iStockphoto.com, top right: © Corbis, bottom right: © ullstein bild / Granger Collection; **p. 199:** © Robert Stainforth / Alamy; **p. 201:** © John Robertson / Alamy; **p. 202:** top left: © Inga Ivanova / Shutterstock images, top right: © wtamas / Shutterstock images, bottom: Deborah Feingold / Corbis; **p. 204:** © Andrei Nekrassov / Shutterstock images; **p. 206:** © Classic Image / Alamy; **p. 207:** © Anna Jurkovska / Shutterstock images; **p. 208:** © Robbie Jack / Corbis; **p. 209:** © Vanni

Archives / Corbis; **p. 210:** Ellie Kurttz © Royal Shakespeare Company; **p. 211:** © Chris Ballentine / Paul Thompson Images / Alamy; **p. 212:** © ullstein bild / Lebrecht Music & Arts Photo Library; **p. 214:** © Robbie Jack / Corbis; **p. 215:** Ellie Kurttz © Royal Shakespeare Company; **p. 218:** left: © Moviestore Collection Ltd / Alamy, middle: © Moviestore Collection Ltd / Alamy, right: © ullstein bild – Lieberenz; **p. 219:** © INTERFOTO / Alamy; **p. 221:** Ellie Kurttz © Royal Shakespeare Company; **pp. 226–227:** Extract from Macbeth, Act 2 Scene 2, by William Shakespeare. Edited with a modern English translation and illustrated by Simon Greaves. Copyright © 2003 by Simon Greaves. Reproduced by permission of Timber Frame Publications Ltd, www.shakespearecomics.com.

Sequence 06: p. 228: A: © Fraser Hall / Robert Harding World Imagery / Corbis, B: © Martin Allinger / Shutterstock images; **p. 229:** C: © Marcio Eugenio / Shutterstock images, D: © Deco Images II / Alamy, E: © Dmitry Pichugin / Shutterstock images, F: © Andrey Kekyalyaynen / Shutterstock images, G: © AF archive / Alamy; **p. 230:** © Edwin Levick / National Geographic Society / Corbis; **p. 231:** © INTERFOTO / Alamy; **p. 233:** © ullstein bild / Granger Collection; **p. 234:** © ullstein bild – Granger Collection; **p. 236:** © ullstein bild – CINETEXT; **p. 237:** © StormStudio / Alamy; **p. 238:** map: © Volkhard Binder, Berlin, guest house, Auroville: © Urba Images; **p. 239:** chart: © Yvonne Thron, Berlin (source: www.auroville.org); **p. 240:** © The Print Collector / Alamy; **p. 241:** top left: © Juice Images / Alamy, bottom left: © Stefan Witas / iStockphoto.com, middle: © incamerastock / Alamy, top right: © gmutlu / iStockphoto.com, bottom right: © Linden Research, Inc.; **p. 242:** top: © Newspix / Richard Hatherly, bottom: DVD: © Henry Leib / iStockphoto.com, TV: © Aaron Amat / Shutterstock images, telephone: © bluehand / Shutterstock images, mp3 player: © Ayaaz Rattansi / iStockphoto.com, radio: © Serggod / Shutterstock images, laptop: © addan / iStockphoto.com; **p. 243:** bottom left: © Joe Fox / Alamy, top right: © Ju-Lee / iStockphoto.com; **p. 245:** © Paul Kingsley / Alamy; **p. 247:** top: © royalcaribbeanoasis, bottom: © Linden Research, Inc.; **p. 248:** © Image Source / Alamy; **p. 249:** © franckreporter / iStockphoto.com; **p. 250:** dentist: © Mary Evans Picture Library / Alamy, Frankenstein: © Photos 12 / Alamy, cartoon: © INKCINCT Cartoons / www.inkcinct.com.au, sheep: © Spiderstock / iStockphoto.com, DNA: © pagadesign / iStockphoto.com; **p. 251:** © Ryan Brocklehurst / iStockphoto.com; **p. 253:** © Paul McKeown / iStockphoto.com; **p. 254:** © Doug Steley A / Alamy; **p. 256:** © Murray Close / Sygma / Corbis; **p. 257:** © Murray Close / Sygma / Corbis; **p. 258:** © Jeremy Sutton-Hibbert / Alamy; **p. 259:** © Gabi Heinisch, Berlin; **p. 260:** © melhi / iStockphoto.com; **p. 261:** Ton Koene / Visuals Unlimited / Corbis; **p. 262:** bottom left: © Galen Rowell / Corbis, top right: © Phil Degginger / Alamy; **p. 263:** © Olli Foolish / Shutterstock images; **p. 265:** © pptbackgrounds.0fees.net; **p. 266:** © Tim Hall / Robert Harding Picture Library Ltd / Alamy; **p. 268:** © Terry Smith Images / Alamy; **p. 270:** left: © Ken Welsh / Design Pics Inc. / Alamy, right: © J. M. Labat / Visual & Written SL / Alamy.

Reference Section: p. 294: charts: © Yvonne Thron, Berlin; **pp. 295–297:** © Soo Lee, Köln; **p. 323:** bottom left: © Rachel Donahue / iStockphoto.com, top right: © Miroslav Georgijevic / iStockphoto.com.

Texts

Sequence 01: pp. 21–25: © Chinua Achebe / Heinemann Education Publishers 1996; **pp. 29–30:** © Crown copyright 2007; **p. 33:** (statistics): © Populuslimited.com; **p. 36:** © Rachel Porter / Daily Mail; **pp. 37–38:** © 2009 Danny King; **p. 42:** © James Berry 1995; **pp. 45–49:** Copyright © 2001 by Bali Rai; **pp. 53–54:** © James Harding / *Times online*; **pp. 57–58:** © Charles Grant 2008; **pp. 60–61:** Jürgen Krönig: 'A new phase in Britain's postwar history has begun' / © Jürgen Krönig 2010.

Sequence 02: pp. 74–76: Copyright © 1999 by Frank McCourt; pp. 78–81: Copyright © 2009 by Dave Eggers; **pp. 82–84:** Copyright © 2004 by Tamar Jacoby; **p. 87:** © 1966 by Robert Hayden; **p. 89:** © 1992 Simon Ortiz; **pp. 92–93:** Kelly Knaur: 'Hurricane Katrina – The Storm That Changed America' / © Time Inc., Home Entertainment, 2005; **pp. 98–101:** Copyright © Lawrence Hill 2007; **pp. 105– 106:** John Ibbitson: 'Let sleeping dogs lie', from: 'Uneasy partners. Multiculturalism and Rights in Canada' by Janice Gross Stein et al. © 2007 John Ibbitson; **pp. 107–108:** from 'One nation or many?' / © The Economist 2006; **pp. 109–110:** Nicholas Keung and Lesley Ciarula Tayor: 'New Canadians flock to better life in suburbs' / © *Toronto Star* 2009; **p. 111:** Jörg Michel: 'Die Reise zu sich selbst' / © Jörg Michel, 2011.

Sequence 03: p. 114: © Paul Boelcke / Nestlé; **pp. 117–118:** Steve Schifferes: 'Shanghai: Creating a Gobal City' / © BBC / Steve Schifferes, 2007; **p. 122:** © 1997-2011 Family Care Foundation; **pp. 126–127:** Thomas C. Schelling: 'The Economics of Global Warming' / © 2011 Thomas C. Schelling / The Newsweek/Daily Beast Company LLC; **pp. 128–129:** Published by Sandy and Thomas Peters TOPICS Online Magazine – © 1997–008 topics.mag@gmail.com; **pp. 133–134:** Copyright © Hajar Ali 2008; **pp. 135–141:** © UNO; **pp. 145–146:** Ambrose Evans Prichard: 'HSBC sees China and America leading global mega-boom' / © Ambrose Evans-Prichard, 2011 / *Daily Telegraph*; **pp. 146–147:** Robyn

Meredith and Suzanne Hoppough: 'Why Globalization is Good' / Copyright © 2011 Forbes.com LLC TM. All Rights Reserved; **p. 148:** Cody Hodge: 'The environment impact of globalisation' / © 2002–2011 Helium, Inc. All Rights Reserved; **pp. 149–150:** from: 'Briefing: The World for Sale – An Introduction to Corporate Globalisation' / www.foe.co.uk / © Friends of the Earth (FOE), London, 2003.

Sequence 04: pp. 157–159: Kallie Szczepanski: ‚What was the Partition of India?' http://asianhistory.about.com/od/india/f/partitionofindiafaq.htm. © 2011 About.com. All rights reserved; **pp. 164–165:** Randeep Ramesh: 'The best and worst of times: Indian families from across the social divides describe how their lives have changed' © Guardian News & Media Ltd 2011; **p. 167:** from: 'Poverty in India' / © Stanley St Labs. All Rights Reserved; **pp. 170–171:** Randeep Ramesh: 'I've witnessed the arrival of a golden age' / © Guardian News & Media Ltd 2011; **pp. 175–176:** © Vidyut; **pp. 178–182:** © by Salman Rushdie, 1994; **pp. 185–187:** © by Vikas Swarup, 2005; **pp. 188–191:** © by Simon Beaufoy, 2008; **pp. 192–193:** © 2010 Bollywood World Entertainment. All Rights Reserved.

Sequence 05: pp. 196–197: © Royal Shakespeare Company; **pp. 199–200:** © Bill Bryson 2007, reprinted by permission of Harper Perennial, an imprint of HarperCollins Publishers; **pp. 219–220:** © terasof.de; **pp. 221–222:** Susan Bassnett: 'Shakespeare's in danger. We have to act now to avoid a great tragedy' / © Susan Bassnett / The Independent, 2011; **pp. 223–224:** © Spark Notes LLC, All Rights Reserved.

Sequence 06: pp. 233–237: © The Estate of Eric Blair, 1949; **pp. 238–239**: © 2008–2011, Auroville.com; **pp. 243–246:** © Susan Maushart 2010, 2011; **pp. 248–249:** Sophie Goodchild: 'Britian becoming a Big Brother Society' / © Sophie Goodchild / *The Independent*, 2007; **pp. 251–258:** © Michael Crichton 1991 / reprinted by permission of The Random House Group Ltd.; **pp. 261–264:** Deborah B. Whitman: 'Genetically Modified Foods: Harmful or Helpful?', released April 2000 / © 2011 ProQuest. All Rights Reserved; **pp. 266–270:** © 1994 by Ernest Callenbach. Reprinted by permission of the author; Reference Section: **p. 308:** © Oxford University Press; **p. 314:** Matt Villano: 'Room Service and a Shovel: The Rise of Voluntourism' / © 2011 Time Inc. All rights reserved; **p. 317:** © 1987 by Tom Wolfe; **p. 322:** Chris Sorensen: 'Facebook status update: Is it over already?' / © Copyright *Toronto Star* 1996–2011.

Words for tasks ('Operatoren')

WORD	USED FOR ...	EXAMPLE
analyse *(analysieren)*	Analysing texts	*Analyse how the writer uses rhetorical devices to convey his ideas.*
assess *(beurteilen)*	Reacting to texts	*Assess the importance of sustainable development.*
characterise *(charakterisieren)*	Analysing texts	*Characterise the main person in the story. Characterise the writer's intentions when he wrote this article.*
comment (on) *(kommentieren)*	Reacting to texts	*Comment on the article's point of view.*
compare *(vergleichen)*	Analysing texts	*Compare the feelings of the children in the story with those of their parents.*
contrast *(kontrastieren)*	Analysing texts	*Contrast the two different views on homelessness expressed in the text.*
delineate *(beschreiben, darstellen)*	Understanding texts	*Delineate the concept of multiculturalism.*
describe *(beschreiben)*	Understanding texts	*Describe the plans the government has to deal with the problem.*
discuss *(diskutieren)*	Reacting to texts	*Discuss the most important issues raised by the writer of this blog.*
evaluate *(einschätzen, bewerten)*	Reacting to texts	*Evaluate the impact of the speech on people's awareness of global warming.*
examine *(untersuchen, prüfen)*	Analysing texts	*Examine the language used by the writer in the song lyrics.*
explain *(erklären)*	Analysing texts	*Explain how the writer of this article presents her/his point of view to the reader.*
illustrate *(erläutern, veranschaulichen)*	Analysing texts	*Illustrate with examples how the video uses technical devices to report a story.*
interpret *(interpretieren)*	Reacting to texts	*Interpret the poem's message.*
juxtapose *(gegenüberstellen)*	Analysing and reacting to texts	*Juxtapose the writer's concept of freedom with concepts you have discussed in class.*
justify *(begründen)*	Reacting to texts	*Say whether the song could appeal to teenagers and justify your opinion.*
outline *(umreißen, skizzieren)*	Understanding texts	*Outline what the writer says in this article about online dangers for teenagers.*
point out *(benennen, darlegen)*	Understanding texts	*Point out the main event the writer of the article writes about.*
present *(darstellen)*	Understanding texts	*Present the situation of the characters.*
put into the context of *(in Zusammenhang bringen mit)*	Analysing texts	*Put this speech into the context of the post-colonial experience in India.*
relate *(in Beziehung setzen zu)*	Analysing and reacting to texts	*Relate the writer's ideas to Jacoby's concept.*
show *(zeigen)*	Analysing texts	*Show the character's arrogance.*
state *(darlegen)*	Understanding texts	*State in your own words the theme of the film.*
summarise / write a summary of *(zusammenfassen)*	Understanding texts	*Summarise / Write a summary of the main points of the text.*
write + *(text type)*	Writing texts	*Write a letter to the editor / a speech.*